SECOND EDITION

COUNSELING THE CULTURALLY DIFFERENT

Theory and Practice

Derald Wing Sue, Ph.D.

California State University—Hayward

David Sue

Western Washington State University

A Wiley-Interscience Publication

John Wiley & Sons

New York • Chichester • Brisbane • Toronto • Singapore

This publication is designed to provide accurate and
authoritative information in regard to the subject
matter covered. It is sold with the understanding that
the publisher is not engaged in rendering legal, accounting,
or other professional service. If legal advice or other
expert assistance is required, the services of a competent
professional person should be sought. *From a Declaration
of Principles jointly adopted by a Committee of the
American Bar Association and a Committee of Publishers.*

Library of Congress Cataloging-in-Publication Data

Sue, Derald Wing.
   Counseling the culturally different: theory and practice / by
Derald Wing Sue and David Sue. — 2nd ed.
     p. cm.
   Includes bibliographical references.
   ISBN 0-471-84269-9
    1. Cross-cultural counseling. I. Sue, David. II. Title.
BF637.C6S85   1990
158' .3—dc20   89–78080

This book is dedicated to . . .

*my wife Paulina Wee Sue, son Derald Paul Sue,
and daughter Marissa Catherine Sue*
—DWS

*my wife Diane M. Sue, son Joe, and
daughters Jenni and Christi*
—DS

Preface

Since publication of the first edition of *Counseling the Culturally Different: Theory and Practice*, we have been most gratified at its wide acceptance and success in the field. Indeed, a recent study (Ponterotto & Sabnani, 1989) concluded that it was the most influential and most frequently cited book published on multicultural counseling, and that it could be considered a "classic." As stated in the preface to the first edition, we were motivated to write such a text because of our belief that traditional counseling theory and practice have done great harm to the culturally different. Our intent was to challenge the counseling and mental health professions to address this charge, and to begin the needed process of developing new methods, concepts, and services more appropriate to the life experiences of culturally diverse groups.

Since those criticisms were made, we have seen a substantive increase in the amount of published materials (empirical, theoretical, and practice-oriented) on multicultural counseling or minority mental health. For example, many more texts on the topic are now available, and almost all professional organizations have devoted special issues of their journals to it. In addition, some exciting new areas, with major implications for multi-cultural counseling, are now being explored. One of these, racial/cultural identity development theories, along with White identity development theories, promises to add a new and important dimension to our work and knowledge. We are pleased to see an increase in the sophistication of conceptual models and empirical research in cross-cultural counseling.

While these changes have been a most welcome development, the field continues to lack integration. With very few exceptions, there have been infrequent attempts to (a) present a theory or conceptual framework by which to add meaning to the mental health literature and counseling issues of all minority groups, (b) identify similarities and differences among the various ethnic groups as they relate to mental health notions and practices, and (c) provide a wider focus on how the sociopolitical system affects minorities and counseling.

The second edition of *Counseling the Culturally Different: Theory and Practice* is an attempt to rectify these issues. It is intended to serve as a major text in counselor education programs that address issues of the culturally different, and to provide a basic text for use as an adjunct to courses in school counseling, social change, foundations of counseling, counseling theories, and the like. While originally intended for use in counseling courses, the book has also found widespread acceptance in schools of nursing, social work, and public health. We believe the text's strength is that it presents a discussion of issues relevant to the culturally different in the United States, a discussion that cuts across all ethnic and racial minorities. It provides a conceptual framework by which to understand the minority experience in the United States, the role counseling has played with respect to larger societal forces, and the practice of cross-cultural counseling in public schools, mental health agencies, industries, correctional settings, and the like. In addition, specific minority groups are given individual treatment to contrast similarities and differences.

ORGANIZATION OF THIS EDITION

Counseling the Culturally Different: Theory and Practice has been completely revised, updated, and reorganized. Those of you acquainted with the first edition will note some similarities with the current one. We have retained the original division of the text into three parts: Part I, "Issues and Concepts in Cross-Cultural Counseling"; Part II, "Counseling Specific Populations"; and Part III, "Critical Incidents in Cross-Cultural Counseling." However, there are major changes in this edition that are the result of current changes in the field and our rethinking of earlier models in cross-cultural counseling. Approximately 80% of the text is new or substantially revised.

Part I, "Issues and Concepts in Cross-Cultural Counseling," deals with the broad conceptual and theoretical foundations of cross-cultural counseling. The main purpose of this part is to discuss issues, to critically analyze data, and to propose concepts of cross-cultural counseling common to most culturally different groups in the United States. Chapter 1, "The Politics of Counseling," traces and discusses the historical and contemporary role of counseling as it relates to the culturally different. Because of its historical content, this chapter remains essentially intact. Counseling and its relationship to the culturally different are seen within the political framework of the larger society. The racist and damaging effects that current mental health practices and standards are having on minorities are revealed. These effects permeate the mental health literature, the standards used to judge normality and abnormality, and our graduate training programs.

Chapter 2, "Barriers to Effective Cross-Cultural Counseling," extends this thesis to the actual process of counseling. The values and life experiences of minorities are compared and contrasted to certain generic characteristics of counseling. Culture-bound values, class-bound values, and language factors are systematically presented. The fact that most counselors and mental health practitioners adhere to these values and unwittingly impose them on the culturally different is a source of serious concern. These values oftentimes act as barriers to effective cross-cultural counseling.

Chapter 3, "Cross-Cultural Communication/Counseling Styles," is completely new. It provides a conceptual rationale for the need to develop culture-specific intervention strategies when working with American Indians, Asian Americans, Blacks, and Hispanics. The chapter is organized along three dimensions: (1) culture-bound values associated with communication styles, especially nonverbal ones (proxemics, kinesics, paralanguage, and high-low context factors); (2) nonverbal communication as a source of reflections and triggers to racial biases; and (3) counseling as representative of "temporary cultures." Counseling styles are seen as forms of communication that may prove inappropriate to the communication styles of various racial groups.

Chapter 4, "Sociopolitical Considerations of Mistrust in Cross-Cultural Counseling," discusses how a history of oppression, discrimination, and racism has affected the way minorities perceive the mental health professional. Rather than being pathological, mistrust actually represents a healthy survival mechanism developed by culturally different groups to survive in our society. However, its manifestation in counseling and therapy can cause great difficulties for even the most enlightened and well-meaning counselor. To aid the reader, social influence theory is used to (1) identify the important factors that make a counselor influential, (2) discuss how these may be differentially operative for culturally different clients, and (3) address the question of whether a counselor who is culturally different can work effectively with a client.

Chapter 5, "Racial/Cultural Identity Development," is a new chapter integrating and discussing racial identity development and its relationship to counseling. The erroneous belief that all Asians are the same, all Blacks are the same, all Hispanics are the same, and so forth, is clearly inaccurate. This chapter proposes a model that defines five stages of development experienced by oppressed people as they struggle to understand themselves in terms of their own culture, the dominant culture, and the oppressive relationship between the two cultures. For each level of identity, corresponding beliefs, attitudes, and behaviors that may help counselors understand their clients better are discussed. In addition, we briefly discuss White Identity Development as a similar model that White people appear to move through in developing a nonracist White identity.

Chapter 6, "Cross-Cultural Family Counseling," is also new. This chapter clearly outlines and explains how definitions of the family differ from one group to another. Western concepts of the family are usually bound to the "nuclear family" or those related by blood. Yet almost all the minority groups discussed in this text have an extended family definition that may encompass aunts, uncles, godparents, friends, neighbors, and even a larger unit like the tribe. How do these differences interfere with our ability to do family counseling? This chapter proposes a conceptual model that may help the counselor work more effectively with minority families.

Chapter 7, "Dimensions of World Views," has been updated to incorporate new work in the field, but it remains essentially intact. Recent work in the field continues to reveal that the very act of counseling may become a form of cultural oppression when the counselor and client do not hold the same world view. We propose a general working theory of how race and culture-specific factors interact to produce people with differing world views. It is suggested that one of these world views, internal locus of control and responsibility, is characteristic of Western counseling approaches and assumptions.

Chapter 8, "The Culturally Skilled Counselor," ends this part of the text by discussing and presenting characteristics that contribute to the culturally effective counselor. In addition, it proposes a model that will help us analyze relevant processes and goals in cross-cultural counseling.

While Part I deals primarily with concepts common to most racial/ ethnic minorities, Part II, "Counseling Specific Populations," recognizes the uniqueness of culturally diverse populations. Thus, separate chapters, each discussing the counseling of one of four different groups, follow: Chapter 9, "Counseling American Indians"; Chapter 10, "Counseling Asian Americans"; Chapter 11, "Counseling Black Americans"; and Chapter 12, "Counseling Hispanic Americans." These chapters have been completely rewritten by the authors. Originally these chapters were written by individuals representing their own ethnic groups. We have chosen not to repeat this process for several reasons. First, while the original chapters were on the whole well received, their wide variations in writing styles and content focus caused some problems for readers who found it difficult to integrate Part I concepts and theory with the individual chapters. Second, Rene (Art) Ruiz, a close friend and respected colleague and the author of Chapter 8 in the first edition, unexpectedly passed away. We would like to take this opportunity to thank Edwin Richardson and Elsie J. Smith for their individual chapter contributions to the successful first edition. Being sensitive to the fact that errors in perspective may result when one attempts to write about groups other than one's own, we have constantly asked colleagues to review our works and to provide suggestions for improvement. We have also relied heavily on published materials by multicultural specialists in the various racial/ethnic groups.

Part III, "Critical Incidents in Cross-Cultural Counseling" (Chapter 13), has been completely revised. The many new cases are intended to portray cross-cultural counseling issues/dilemmas. These cases may be used for teaching/training and are all related to the first two sections. They are intended to help students and professionals (1) identify cultural points of view and responses, (2) show how two cultural dictates may lead to misunderstandings, (3) increase awareness of sociopolitical ramifications of cross-cultural counseling, (4) reveal how traditional counseling approaches may clash with cultural values, and (5) suggest alternative ways of dealing with the critical incident.

We hope that this text will be as well received as the first edition. Cross-cultural counseling is an exciting and challenging field, and we must all take the initiative in reaching out to learn, advance, and grow. Cultural diversity is a fact of life, and how we deal with it will have major implications for the quality of life in the United States.

ACKNOWLEDGMENTS

In closing, we would like to thank a few individuals who have had significant impact on our personal and professional lives. In many respects, these are the people who have not only influenced our thoughts, but also given us much personal support. First and foremost are our families: for D.W. Sue, my wife Paulina, son Derald Paul, and daughter Marissa; for D. Sue, my wife Diane, son Joe, and daughters Jenni and Christi. The years we spent conceptualizing and revising this book would not have been possible without their love and understanding. Second, thanks to our parents, who taught us to be proud of who and what we are—Chinese Americans. Third, thanks to colleagues and tutors—Donald Atkinson, Malachi Andrews, Manuel Casas, Robert Carter, Ursula Delworth, Leo Goldman, Janet Helms, Allen Ivey, Judy Katz, George Morten, Thomas Parham, Paul Pedersen, Joe Ponterotto, Edwin Richardson, Dan Romero, Rene Ruiz, Elsie Smith, Joseph Trimble, and Steve Weinrach. Fourth, thanks to our many culturally diverse students, who challenged us and taught us to understand their many world views. Last but not least, special thanks to our brother, Stanley, for his help and encouragement with this book. Part of this text was developed from National Institutes of Mental Health Grant No. ROI MH44331.

Derald Wing Sue

David Sue

Contents

PART I   ISSUES AND CONCEPTS IN CROSS-CULTURAL COUNSELING, *1*

Chapter 1   The Politics of Counseling, *3*
Chapter 2   Barriers to Effective Cross-Cultural Counseling, *27*
Chapter 3   Cross-Cultural Communication/Counseling Styles, *49*
Chapter 4   Sociopolitical Considerations of Mistrust in Cross-Cultural Counseling, *75*
Chapter 5   Racial/Cultural Identity Development, *93*
Chapter 6   Cross-Cultural Family Counseling, *118*
Chapter 7   Dimensions of World Views, *137*
Chapter 8   The Culturally Skilled Counselor, *159*

PART II   COUNSELING SPECIFIC POPULATIONS, *173*

   Chapter   9   Counseling American Indians, *175*
   Chapter 10   Counseling Asian Americans, *189*
   Chapter 11   Counseling Black Americans, *209*
   Chapter 12   Counseling Hispanic Americans, *227*

PART III   CRITICAL INCIDENTS IN CROSS-CULTURAL COUNSELING, *243*

   Chapter 13   Critical Incident Cases, *245*

   References, *290*

   Indexes, *317*

PART I

ISSUES AND CONCEPTS IN CROSS-CULTURAL COUNSELING

What is cross-cultural/multicultural counseling? Is it any different from other forms of counseling? Are American Indians, Asian Americans, Black Americans, and Hispanic Americans so different from Whites that a different counseling/therapy style is called for? Why aren't theories of counseling and psychotherapy equally applicable to all groups? If I need to change my counseling approach with culturally different individuals, do I need to do the same if I work with a minority family? Why are culturally different clients so distrustful of counseling? After all, aren't we there to help them? Can a person of another race/culture counsel a client effectively? What are some barriers to effective cross-cultural counseling? How can they be overcome? What are some characteristics of the culturally skilled and effective counselor?

These are just a few of the important questions Part I attempts to address. More than anything else, Chapters 1 through 8 make it clear that cross-cultural counseling cannot be separated from the broader sociopolitical environment. How counseling is rooted in and reflects the dominant values, beliefs, and biases of the larger society, how the minority experience in the United States has influenced their world view, how traditional counseling and psychotherapy may represent cultural oppression for the minority client, and how counselors must take steps to view the minority client in a different way are the themes presented throughout.

CHAPTER 1

The Politics of Counseling

On June 19, 1982, Vincent Chin, a Chinese American, was beaten to death with a baseball bat by two White male auto workers. According to witnesses, the two men mistook Chin for a Japanese and blamed him for the loss of jobs in the U.S. auto industry. Prior to the fatal beating, the men were heard to make angry racial slurs at Chin. The two men were convicted of manslaughter but were sentenced to only three years' probation and a fine of $3,750 each. The incident and sentence drew a storm of protest from the Asian community and prompted some to say "An Asian's life is worth only $3,750 in this country."

In August 1989, Yusef Hawkins, a Black teenager, was killed by a gang of White youths in Brooklyn's mostly White Bensonhurst section. Hawkins and three other companions were answering an advertisement for a used car when the fateful incident occurred. They were set upon by neighborhood Whites carrying baseball bats, two-by-fours, and golf clubs. The White youths were apparently angered by a local White woman's dating of a Black youth and believed he was about to attend her birthday party. Shouting racial epithets, they stalked Hawkins until one of the White youths pulled a gun and shot him to death. The killing was reminiscent of the 1986 Howard Beach incident where another Black man was chased by a group of Whites who shouted "Niggers, out of the neighborhood." They chased the Black man who was subsequently hit by a car and killed.

Another incident occurred in 1987 on ABC's highly touted late-night news program "Nightline." In an effort to acknowledge the historic breaking of the color barrier in baseball, the interviewer asked Al Campanis, a Dodger executive at the time, why there were not more Black executive managers and coaches in baseball. His answer was that Blacks lack the "right stuff" to become front-office executives. His interview, carried on national television, drew a howl of protests from minorities throughout the United States as evidence of racism in the power structures of baseball.

In the Superior Court of the State of California in and for the County of Santa Clara Juvenile Division, a judge made highly racist and derogatory comments to a Hispanic family. He accused a young Hispanic juvenile of being lower than an animal, of having no moral upbringing, and his pregnant sister (unmarried) as probably doomed to a life of three or four marriages and half a dozen children before she turned 18. The judge, in a highly charged tone, accused the Mexican people of being "miserable, lousy, and rotten people," of having no right to live among human beings, and that perhaps Hitler was right in advocating genocide. While the judge was censured for these comments and forced to retract them publicly, he was reelected the following term.

A White female elementary school teacher in Oklahoma had planned an ethnic minority appreciation day for her sixth-grade class. As there was a large number of American Indian students in her class, part of the day was devoted to a unit on Native American heritage. One of the American Indian students had designed a bonnet and dress of her tribe. While her fellow students expressed appreciation and admiration for her costume and tribal dance demonstration, the teacher was reported to have remained silent. Several days later the female student received a low grade for her participation in the activities. According to the student, the teacher had praised her dance technique and beautiful costume, but had stated that (a) the costume was not typical of her tribe, (b) her dance was not traditional, and (c) the assignment was graded on "authenticity, not fantasy." When the parents heard about the remarks, they demanded a meeting with the teacher and principal. During the meeting, the father expressed anger at "White folks always telling Indians who we are." The teacher's only response was to show the parents an anthropology book with what she claimed to be the typical head gear and costume of the family's tribe.

These and countless examples indicate that racism is alive, well, and thriving in the United States. Indeed, the 1980s have seen a historic rise in the incidents of overt racism throughout the country. The incidents have ranged from murder and mayhem to physical attacks, threats, and racial epithets. These reports are even more disturbing in light of the apparent erosion of the nation's oldest civil rights law. For example in 1989 alone, the U.S. Supreme Court, with a conservative majority, has ruled that (a) cities may not set aside a fixed percentage of public contracts for minorities, (b) civil rights plaintiffs may not use statistics on job segregation to prove illegal discrimination, (c) White males may file reverse discrimination challenges against court-approved affirmative action programs, and (d) minorities or women may not challenge an unfair seniority policy after it has been in force for 300 days.

University and college campuses, supposed bastions of enlightenment and democracy, have also reported an alarming rise of racism (*Black Issues in Higher Education*, 1989). Ugly racial incidents, such as the burning of a cross in a Black student's dormitory room, the taunting of a Black female as "dark meat" by Dartmouth football players, the spray painting of racial slurs on the walls of a minority cultural center at Smith College, and the victimizing of Hispanic students with racial epithets and attacks by a fraternity group in Berkeley, have been well documented.

It may seem surprising and unusual for us to open a book on *Counseling the Culturally Different* with these examples. Aren't these incidents only tangentially related to the topic of cross-cultural counseling? Why should we give it such broad prominence? After all, as mental health practitioners, we are here to help people, not oppress them. While these last statements may be correct in philosophy, they fail to recognize several important facets of counseling and psychotherapy with minority clients.

First, the world view of the culturally different is ultimately linked to the historical and current experiences of racism and oppression in the United States. A culturally different client is likely to approach counseling with a great deal of healthy suspicion as to the counselor's conscious and unconscious motives in a cross-cultural context. That a counselor is "supposed to help" or that definitions of counseling encompass certain philosophical assumptions such as (a) a concern and respect for the uniqueness of clients, (b) an emphasis on the inherent worth and dignity of all people regardless of race, creed, color, or sex, (c) a high priority placed on helping others attain their own self-determined goals, (d) valuing freedom and the opportunity to explore one's own characteristics and potentials; and (e) a future-oriented promise of a better life is not enough to foster trust (Aubrey, 1977; Atkinson, Morten, & Sue, 1989; Brammer, 1977; Hansen, Stevic, & Warner, 1982; Katz, 1985; Pedersen, 1987, 1988). Many of these goals had their roots in the educational guidance movement of the early 1900s and reflected democratic ideals such as "equal access to opportunity," "pursuit of happiness," "liberty and justice for all," and "fulfillment of personal destiny." While these lofty ideals may seem highly commendable and appropriate for the counseling profession, they have oftentimes been translated in such a manner as to justify support for the status quo (Adams, 1973; Jones, 1985; Jones & Seagull, 1977; Katz, 1985).

That counseling has failed to fulfill its promises to the culturally different has been a frequent theme voiced by minority group authors since the mid-1960s. In reviewing the minority group literature on counseling, Pine (1972) found the following views on counseling to be representative of those held by many minority individuals:

> . . . that it is a waste of time; that counselors are deliberately shunting minority students into dead end nonacademic programs regardless of student potential, preferences, or ambitions; that counselors discourage students from applying to college; that counselors are insensitive to the needs of students and the community; that counselors do not give the same amount of energy and time in working with minority as they do with White-middle-class students; that counselors do not accept, respect, and understand cultural differences; that counselors are arrogant and contemptuous; and that counselors don't know how to deal with their own hangups. (p. 35)

Pine's cogent summary of minority group perceptions of the counseling profession continues to be as valid today and indicates a gap existing between the ideals of counseling and its actual operation with respect to the culturally different. While counseling enshrines the concepts of freedom, rational thought, tolerance of new ideas, and equality and justice for all, it can be used as an oppressive instrument by those in power to maintain the status quo. In this respect, counseling becomes a form of oppression in which there is an unjust and cruel exercise of power to subjugate or mistreat large groups of people. When used to restrict rather than enhance the well-being and development of the culturally different, it may entail overt and covert forms of prejudice and discrimination. Thus, the world view of the culturally different client who comes to counseling boils down to one important question: "What makes you, a counselor/therapist, any different from all the others out there who have oppressed and discriminated against me?"

This question brings us to a more personal level. Just as the two auto workers, the White youngsters, the sports team executive, the judge, and the teacher could be racist in thought, beliefs, and deeds, so also can counselors and therapists be subject to inheriting and repeating the biases of the society. Racism runs deep and dies hard! Scratch the surface and you'll find beliefs that are all evidence of the sociopolitical climate in which we are raised—for example, beliefs that Asians are the cause of U.S. economic woes, that Blacks lack the intellectual "essentials" to advance in our society, that there is nothing worse than the intermingling of races, that Hispanic culture/people are lower than animals and should be destroyed, and that American Indians must fit White preconceived definitions. To say that we have somehow escaped our racist upbringing, that we are not perpetuators of racism, or that the racial climate is improving is to deny reality. As mental health professionals, we have a personal and professional responsibility to (a) confront, become aware of, and take actions in dealing with our biases, stereotypes, values, and assumptions about human behavior, (b) become aware of the culturally different client's world view, values, biases, and assumptions about human behavior, and (c) develop appropriate help-giving practices, intervention strategies, and structures that take into account the historical, cultural, and environmental experiences/influences of the culturally different client.

This book is about counseling the culturally different. Its main thesis is that counseling and psychotherapy do not take place in a vacuum isolated from the larger social-political influences of our society. Cross-cultural counseling oftentimes mirrors the state of interracial relationships in the wider society. It serves as a microcosm reflecting Black-White, Asian-White, Hispanic-White, American Indian-White, and minority-majority race relations.

This first chapter attempts to explore the many ways in which counseling and psychotherapy have failed with respect to the culturally different. This failure can be seen in three primary areas: (a) counselor education and training programs, (b) counseling and mental health literature, and (c) counseling process and practice. We deal with only the first two areas in this chapter. Counseling process and practice is discussed in the next chapter.

COUNSELOR EDUCATION AND TRAINING PROGRAMS

While national interest in the mental health needs of ethnic minorities has increased in the past decade, the human service professions, especially clinical and counseling psychology, have failed to meet the particular mental health needs of this population (Bernal & Padilla, 1982; Casas, 1982; Casas, Ponterotto, & Gutierrez, 1986; Ibrahim & Arrendondo, 1986; Ponterotto & Casas, 1987; President's Commission on Mental Health, 1978; Smith, 1982; D. W. Sue et al., 1982). Ethnic minority groups (particularly American Indians, Asian Americans, Blacks, and Hispanics) represent roughly 20% of the total U.S. population. Evidence reveals that the minority population, in addition to the common stresses experienced by everyone else, is more likely to encounter problems such as immigrant status, poverty, cultural racism, prejudice, and discrimination. Yet studies continue to reveal that American Indians, Asian Americans, Blacks, and Hispanics tend to underutilize traditional mental health services (S. Sue, Allen, & Conaway, 1975; S. Sue & McKinney, 1974; S. Sue, McKinney, Allen, & Hall, 1974). What is even more puzzling and disturbing were findings that minority clients tended to terminate counseling/therapy at a rate of > 50% after only one contact with the therapist. This was in marked contrast to the less than 30% termination rate among White clients.

How are we to explain these startling statistics? One explanation may be that minorities are mentally healthier than their White counterparts, have less need for services, and require fewer sessions to effect a "cure." We give this reason with "tongue in cheek," because it is not unusual for researchers to use data to support a point of view that may be quite inaccurate. It is ironic that the mental health literature, as we shall shortly see, has historically portrayed minorities as mentally unhealthy and pathological.

It is our contention that the reasons why minority-group individuals underutilize and prematurely terminate counseling/therapy lie in the biased nature of the services themselves. The services offered are frequently antagonistic or inappropriate to the life experiences of the culturally different client; they lack sensitivity and understanding, and they are oppressive and discriminating toward minority clients.

One of the major reasons for therapeutic ineffectiveness in cross-cultural counseling lies in the training of mental health professionals (Casas, 1984; D. W. Sue, 1982; S. Sue, Akutsu, & Higashi, 1985). The training of mental health professionals has often resulted in therapists' inheriting the racial and cultural bias of their forebears (Katz, 1985; D. W. Sue & D. Sue, 1977; Wrenn, 1985).

Most graduate programs give inadequate treatment to mental health issues of ethnic minorities. Cultural influences affecting personality formation, career choice, educational development, and the manifestation of behavior disorders are infrequently part of mental health training (Arbona, 1990; Arrendondo-Dowd & Gonzales, 1980; Bryson & Bardo, 1975). When minority-group experiences are discussed, they are generally seen and analyzed from the "White middle-class perspective." In programs where minority experiences have been discussed, the focus tends to be on their pathological lifestyles and/or a maintenance of false stereotypes. The result is twofold: (1) professionals who deal with mental health problems of ethnic minorities lack understanding and knowledge about ethnic values and their consequent interaction with a racist society, and (2) counseling practitioners are graduated from our programs believing minorities are inherently pathological and that counseling involves a simple modification of traditional White models.

This ethnocentric bias has been highly destructive to the natural help-giving networks of minority communities. Oftentimes mental health professionals operate under the assumption that racial and ethnic minorities never had such a thing as "counseling and psychotherapy" until it was "invented" and institutionalized in Western cultures (White & Parham, 1990). For the benefit of "those" people, the mental health movement has delegitimized natural help-giving networks that have operated for thousands of years by labeling them as unscientific, supernatural, mystical, and not consistent with "professional standards of practice." Then mental health professionals are surprised to find that there is a high incidence of psychological distress in the minority community, that their treatment techniques do not work, and that the culturally different do not utilize their services.

Contrary to this ethnocentric orientation, we need to expand our perception of what constitutes mental health practices. Equally legitimate methods of treatment are nonformal or natural support systems (Brammer, 1985; J. C. Pearson, 1985) so powerful in many minority groups (family, friends, community self-help programs, and occupational networks), folk-healing methods (Padilla & DeSynder, 1985), and indigenous formal systems of therapy (Draguns, 1981). Instead of attempting to destroy them, we should be actively trying to find out why they may work better than Western forms of counseling and therapy.

Definitions of Mental Health

A number of individuals have pointed out how counseling and psychotherapy tend to often assume universal (*etic*) applications of their concepts and goals to the exclusion of culture-specific (*emic*) views (Draguns, 1981; D. W. Sue, 1977; Trimble, 1990; Wrenn, 1962, 1985). Likewise, counselor education programs have often been accused of fostering *cultural encapsulation,* a term first coined by Wrenn (1962). The term refers specifically to (a) the substitution of model stereotypes for the real world, (b) the disregarding of cultural variations in a dogmatic adherence to some universal notion of truth, and (c) the use of a technique-oriented definition of the counseling process. The results are that counselor roles are rigidly defined, implanting an implicit belief in a universal concept of "healthy" and "normal."

If we look at criteria used by the mental health profession to judge normality and abnormality, this deficiency becomes glaring. Several fundamental approaches that have particular relevance to our discussion have been identified (Buss, 1966; D. Sue, D. W. Sue, & S. Sue, 1990): (a) normality as a statistical concept, (b) normality as ideal mental health, and (c) abnormality as the presence of certain behaviors (research criteria).

First, statistical criteria equate normality with those behaviors that occur most frequently in the population. Then abnormality is defined in terms of those behaviors that occur least frequently. For example, data collected on IQs may be accumulated and an average calculated. IQ scores near the average are considered normal, and relatively large deviations from the norm (in either direction) are considered abnormal. In spite of the word *statistical,* however, these criteria need not be quantitative in nature: Individuals who talk to themselves, disrobe in public, or laugh uncontrollably for no apparent reason are considered abnormal according to these criteria simply because most people do not behave in that way. Statistical criteria undergirds our notion of a normal probability curve so often used in IQ tests, achievement tests, and personality inventories.

Statistical criteria may seem adequate in specific instances, but they are fraught with hazards and problems. For one thing, they fail to take into account differences in time, community standards, and cultural values. If deviations from the majority are considered abnormal, then many ethnic and racial minorities that exhibit strong subcultural differences from the majority have to be so classified. When we resort to a statistical definition, the dominant or most powerful group generally determines what constitutes normality and abnormality. For example, if a group of Blacks were to be administered a personality test and it was found that they were more suspicious than their White counterparts, what would this mean?

Some psychologists and educators have used such findings to label Blacks as paranoid. Statements by Blacks that "The Man" is out to get them may be perceived as supporting a paranoid delusion. This interpretation, however, has been challenged by many Black psychologists as being inaccurate (Grier & Cobbs, 1968; Jones, 1985; Jones & Seagull, 1977; Mays, 1985). In response to their slave heritage and a history of White discrimination against them, Blacks have adopted various behaviors (in particular, behaviors toward Whites) that have proven important for survival in a racist society. "Playing it cool" has been identified as one means by which Blacks, as well as members of other minority groups, may conceal their true thoughts and feelings. A Black person who is experiencing conflict, anger, or even rage may be skillful at appearing serene and composed. This tactic is a survival mechanism aimed at reducing one's vulnerability to harm and exploitation in a hostile environment (White & Parham, 1990).

The personality test that reveals Blacks as being suspicious, mistrustful, and "paranoid" needs to be understood from a larger social-political perspective. Minority groups who have consistently been victims of discrimination and oppression in a culture that is full of racism have good reason to be suspicious and mistrustful of White society. In their book *Black Rage*, Grier and Cobbs (1968) point out how Blacks, in order to survive in a White racist society, have developed a highly functional survival mechanism to protect them against possible physical and psychological harm. The authors perceive this "cultural paranoia" as adaptive and healthy rather than dysfunctional and pathological. Indeed, some Third World psychologists have indicated that the absence of a "paranorm" among minorities may be more indicative of pathology than its presence. The absence of a paranorm may indicate either poor reality testing (denial of oppression-racism in our society) and/or naiveté in understanding the operation of racism.

Second, the concept of ideal mental health has been proposed as one of the criteria of normality by psychologists Carl Rogers and Abraham Maslow. Such criteria stress the importance of attaining some positive goal. For example, consciousness-balance of psychic forces (Freud, 1960; Jung, 1960), self-actualization/creativity (Maslow, 1968; Rogers, 1961), competence, autonomy, and resistance to stress (Allport, 1961; White, 1963), or self-disclosure (Jourard, 1964) have all been proposed. The discriminatory nature of such approaches is grounded in the belief of a universal application (all populations in all situations) and reveals a failure to recognize the value base from which the criteria are derived. The particular goal or ideal used is intimately linked with the theoretical frame of reference and values held by the practitioner. For example, the psychoanalytic emphasis on "insight" as a determinant of mental health is a value in itself (London, 1989; Lowe, 1969). Many writers (Atkinson, Maruyama, & Matsui, 1978; Berman, 1979; Bryson & Bardo, 1975; Dauphinais, Dauphinais, & Rowe, 1981; D. W. Sue et al., 1982; D. W. Sue & D. Sue, 1977) have pointed out that certain socioeconomic groups and ethnic minorities do not particularly value "insight."

Furthermore, the use of self-disclosure as a measure of mental health tends to neglect the earlier discussion presented on the "paranorm." One characteristic often linked to the healthy personality is the ability to talk about the deepest and most intimate aspects of one's life; to self-disclose. This orientation is very characteristic of our counseling and therapy process in which clients are expected to talk about themselves in a very personal manner. The fact that many minorities are reluctant to initially self-disclose can place them in a situation where they are judged to be mentally unhealthy and, in this case, "paranoid."

Definitions of mental health such as competence, autonomy, and resistance to stress are related to White middle-class notions of individual maturity. Ivey (1981) and Banks (1977) discuss how the counseling profession originated from the ideological milieu of individualism. Individuals make their lot in life. Those who succeed in society do so on the basis of their *own* efforts and abilities. Successful people are seen as mature, independent, and possessing great ego strength. Apart from the potential bias in defining what constitutes competence, autonomy, and resistance to stress, the use of such a person-focused definition of maturity places the blame on the individual. When a person fails in life, it is because of his/her own lack of ability, interest, maturity, or some inherent weakness of the ego. If we see minorities as being subjected to higher stress factors in society (Deloria, 1969; Ruiz & Padilla, 1977; Smith, 1985; D. W. Sue, 1975) and placed in a one-down position by virtue of racism, then it becomes quite clear that the definition will tend to portray the lifestyle of minorities as inferior, underdeveloped, and deficient. Ryan (1971) and others (Avis & Stewart, 1976; Banks & Marten, 1973; Caplan & Nelson, 1973; Ivey & Authier, 1978; Katz, 1985) have referred to this process as "blaming the victim." Yet a broader system analysis would show that the economic, social, and psychological conditions of minorities are related to their oppressed status in America.

Thus, the use of ideal mental health as the sole criterion tends to present multiple problems. Which goal or ideal should be used? The answer depends largely on the particular theoretical frame of reference or values embraced by those posing the criteria. Their unbridled imposition without regard to social-cultural influences would lead us to conclude that almost all minorities in the United States are unhealthy.

Third, an alternative to the previous two definitions of abnormality is a research one. For example, in determining rates of mental illness in different ethnic groups, "psychiatric diagnosis," "presence in mental hospitals," and scores on "objective psychological inventories" are frequently used. Diagnosis and hospitalization present a circular problem. The definition of normality-abnormality depends on what mental health practitioners say it is! In this case, the race or ethnicity of mental health professionals is likely to be different from that of minority clients. Bias on the part of the practitioner with respect to diagnosis and treatment is likely to occur (Snowden & Cheung, 1990). Yamamoto, James, and Palley (1968) found that minority clients tended to be diagnosed differently and to receive less preferred modes of treatment.

Furthermore, the political and societal implications of psychiatric diagnosis and hospitalization were forcefully pointed out over 20 years ago by Laing (1967, 1969) and Szasz (1970, 1971). Laing believes that individual madness is but a reflection of the madness of society. He describes schizophrenic breakdowns as desperate strategies by people to liberate themselves from a "false self" used to maintain behavioral normality in our society. Attempts to adjust the person back to the original normality (sick society) are unethical.

Szasz states this opinion even more strongly:

> In my opinion, mental illness is a myth. People we label "mentally ill" are not sick, and involuntary mental hospitalization is not treatment. It is punishment ... The fact that mental illness designates a deviation from an ethnical rule of conduct, and that such rules vary widely, explains why upper-middle-class psychiatrists can so easily find evidence of "mental illness" in lower-class individuals; and why so many prominent persons in the past fifty years or so have been diagnosed by their enemies as suffering from some types of insanity. Barry Goldwater was called a paranoid schizophrenic ... Woodrow Wilson, a neurotic ... Jesus Christ, according to two psychiatrists ... was a born degenerate with a fixed delusion system. (Szasz, 1970, pp. 167–168)

Szasz sees the mental health professional as an inquisitor, an agent of society exerting social control on those individuals who deviate in thought and behavior from the accepted norms of society. Psychiatric hospitalization is believed to be a form of social control for persons who annoy or disturb us. The label "mental illness" may be seen as a political ploy used to control those who are different, and counseling is used to control, brainwash, or reorient the identified victims to fit into society. It is exactly this concept that many minorities find frightening. For example, many Asian Americans, American Indians, Blacks, and Hispanics, are increasingly challenging the concepts of normality and abnormality. They feel that their values and lifestyles are often seen by society as pathological and thus are unfairly discriminated against by the mental health professions.

In addition, the use of "objective" psychological inventories as indicators of maladjustment may also place minorities at a disadvantage. One example concerning the "paranorm" has already been given. Most minorities are aware that the test instruments used on them have been constructed and standardized according to White middle-class norms. The lack of culturally unbiased instruments makes many feel that the results obtained are invalid. Indeed, in a landmark decision in the State of California (*Larry P. v. California*, 1986), Judge Peckham ruled in favor of the Association of Black Psychologists' claim that individual intelligence tests such as the WISC-R, WAIS-R, and Stanford Binet could not be used in the public schools on Black students. The improper use of such instruments can lead to an exclusion of minorities in jobs and promotion, to discriminatory educational decisions, and to biased determination of what constitutes pathology and cure in counseling/therapy (Halleck, 1971; London, 1988; Lonner & Sundberg, 1985; Pavkov, Lewis & Lyons, 1989).

D. Sue, D. W. Sue, and S. Sue (1990) have noted some primary objections to testing and the consequent classification that oftentimes results. When a diagnosis becomes a label, it can have serious consequences. First, a label can cause people to interpret all activities of the affected individual as pathological. No matter what a Black person may do or say that breaks a stereotype, his or her behavior will seem to reflect the fact that he or she is less intelligent than others around him or her. Second, the label may cause others to treat an individual differently even when he or she is perfectly normal. Third, a label may cause those who are labeled to believe that they do indeed possess such characteristics.

An old study by Rosenthal and Jacobson (1968) has shown how a label can cause differential treatment. They randomly assigned school children to either of two groups. Teachers were told that tests of one group indicated they were intellectual "bloomers" (gaining in competence and maturity); the other group was not given this label. After a one-year interval, children from both groups were retested (they had also been tested the year before). The experimenters found that the group identified as "bloomers" showed dramatic gains in IQ.

How did this occur? Many have speculated that the label led teachers to have higher intellectual expectations for the "bloomers" and thus to treat them differently. Even though there was no significant difference in IQ between the two groups to begin with, differences were present by the end of the year. It is not difficult to speculate that stereotypes of various racial and ethnic minorities will result in differential treatment based upon preconceived notions. In addition, the Rosenthal and Jacobson study suggests not only that teachers behave differently, but also that labels may affect the children. It is possible that when people are constantly told by others that they are stupid or smart, they may come to believe such labels (self-fulfilling prophecy). If people ascribe certain stereotypical traits to a racial minority or an ethnic group, then it is reasonable to believe that they will behave differently toward the group and cause cognitive and behavioral changes among members of the group.

These factors lend support to the belief that counseling is an egocentric part of the Establishment that interprets behavior exclusively from its reference point and attempts to fit minorities into the "White experience."

These universal definitions of "healthy" and "normal" that are accepted unquestioningly in most graduate programs also guide the delivery of mental health services. Thus the culturally encapsulated counselor may become a tool of his/her own dominant political, social, or economic values. Ethnocentric notions of adjustment tend to ignore inherent cultural-class values, allowing the encapsulated person to be blind to his/her own cultural baggage. The net result has been that mental health services have demanded a type of racial and cultural conformity in client behavior that has been demeaning and that has denied different ethnic minorities the right to their cultural heritage.

Curriculum and Training Deficiencies

It appears that much of the universal definitions of mental health that have pervaded the counseling and psychology profession has been primarily due to severe deficiencies in training programs. Various specialists (Arrendondo, 1985; Ponterotto & Casas, 1987; Smith, 1982; D. W. Sue et al., 1982) have asserted that the major reason for ineffectiveness in working with culturally different populations is the lack of culturally sensitive material taught in the curricula. It has been ethnocentrically assumed that the material taught in traditional mental health programs is equally applicable to all groups. Even now, when there is high recognition of the need for a cross-cultural curricula, little work and movement in this direction has occurred. McFadden and Wilson (1977) relate that less than 1% of the respondents in a survey of counselor education programs reported instructional requirements for the study of non-White cultures. More recently, Parham and Moreland (1981) surveyed 33 doctoral programs in counseling psychology and found that potential minority applicants did not apply because course offerings appeared to lack a non-White perspective and that the academic environment was nonsupportive of minority concerns, needs, and issues. Other more recent surveys (Arrendondo-Dowd & Gonzales, 1980; Wyatt & Parham, 1985) conclude that there was minimal inclusion of culturally sensitive training materials at American Psychological Association approved Ph.D. training programs. Many cross-cultural specialists (Carney & Kahn, 1984; Casas et al., 1986; Corvin & Wiggins, 1989; Ponterotto & Casas, 1987; D. W. Sue & Pedersen, 1977), in examining mental health programs, concluded that the collection and dissemination of information on cross-cultural counseling and the training of culturally skilled counselors have been hindered by several problems in addition to the obvious pervasive bias and racism inherent in such programs.

First, while there has been much talk about what is wrong with things and what needs to be done, little action has taken place. Much of the problem resides in a lack of direction and the tedious process of developing new programs and practices. Our failure to advance quickly can be traced to the haphazard manner in which we have approached the task and the low priority given to this area. For example, Ponterotto & Casas (1987) indicate that cross-cultural programs tend to be developed at institutions only because of a strong commitment by a minority faculty member who was interested in the field. This bodes poorly for programs throughout the United States because of the paucity of minority psychologists entering the field.

Second, cross-cultural counseling programs are noticeably deficient in relating race and culture-specific incidents and counseling skills that the culturally competent counselor must possess. Effective interracial or cross-cultural counseling has suffered because a systematic approach to teaching counseling skills relevant to the culturally different has not occurred. While consciousness raising, cognitive understanding, and affective dimensions are important, there is a strong need to relate these components to specific skills in working with the culturally different. The gap between awareness, understanding, and behavior has led to failure in training programs (D. W. Sue et al., 1982).

Third, and related to the previous point, the use of media-based training packages is beginning to play a broad and important role in the training of school counselors and mental health practitioners. Especially noteworthy are those by Ivey (Ivey, 1986; Ivey & Authier, 1978; Ivey & Gluckstern, 1976) Egan (1982), Carkhuff (1986), and Kagan (1986). These media-based packages present systems for teaching basic helping skills. They have pulled the veil of mystery from professional helpers to reveal the principal components of the therapeutic act. These helping skills and attitudes can be taught to the uninitiated, as well as to prospective professionals.

While such systems are available for the general teaching of counseling skills to school counselors and mental health professionals, they (excluding Ivey's) are not designed for training in cross-cultural counseling or therapy. They are heavily based on a Western framework and lack validation regarding their appropriateness for cross-cultural counseling/ therapy modes. Furthermore, while the specific skills they identify seem to constitute the basic helping ones for any mental health professional, the differential use of these skills and the particular combinations most appropriate to the culturally different have not been researched. The result is the lack of any comparable cross-cultural training system of the caliber and specificity to the ones mentioned previously.

Last, cross-cultural training often assumes that the mere acquisition of cultural knowledge and the academic teaching of appropriate counseling skills are enough to train an effective cross-cultural counselor. While cognitive understanding and counseling-skill training are important, what is missing for the trainee is self-exploration of one's own racism (Corwin & Wiggins, 1989; Sabnani, Ponterotto & Borodovsky, in press). Without a strong antiracism training component, trainees (especially Whites) will continue to deny responsibility for the racist system that oppresses their minority clients. Thus, White trainees may continue to view racism from an intellectual perspective that allows them to distance themselves from the true meaning of cross-cultural work. As a result, several cross-cultural specialists have begun to develop White identity development models that have implications for specific training goals and tasks needed to advance trainees through the antiracism stages (Corwin & Wiggins, 1989; Helms, 1984; Ponterotto, 1988; Sabnani, Ponterotto & Borodovsky, in press).

It is this very issue of cultural encapsulation and its detrimental effects on minorities that has generated training recommendations from the Vail Conference (Korman, 1974), Austin Conference (1975), and Dulles Conference (1978). More recently, the Division of Counseling Psychology of the APA (D. W. Sue et al., 1982) endorsed cross-cultural training competencies. The 1987 National Psychology Conference sponsored by Division 17 also addressed this issue. All conferences noted the serious lack and inadequacy of psychology training programs in dealing with religions, racial, ethnic, sexual, and economic groups. Selected recommendations included advocating (a) that professional psychology training programs at all levels provide information on the political nature of the practice of psychology, (b) that professionals need to "own" their value positions, (c) that client populations ought to be involved in helping determine what is "done to them", (d) that evaluation of training programs include not only the content, but also an evaluation of the graduates, and (e) that continuing professional development occur beyond the receipt of any advanced degree.

Perhaps the most important recommendation to arise from these conferences was the importance of identifying and assessing competencies of psychologists as they relate to the culturally different. In addition, the importance of providing educational experiences that generate sensitivity and appreciation of the history, current needs, strengths, and resources of minority communities was stressed. Students and professionals should be helped to understand the development and behavior of the group being studied, thus enabling them to (a) use their knowledge to develop skills in working with minority groups, and (b) develop strategies to modify the effects of political, social, and economic forces on minority groups. The curriculum must focus on immediate social problems and needs. It must stimulate an awareness of minority issues caused by economic, social, and educational deprivation. The curriculum must also be designed to stimulate this awareness not solely at a cognitive level. It must enable students to understand feelings of helplessness and powerlessness, low self-esteem, poor self-concept, and how they contribute to low motivation, frustration, hate, ambivalence, and apathy. Each course should contain (a) a *consciousness-raising* component, (b) an *affective* component, (c) a *knowledge* component, and (d) a *skills* component.

COUNSELING AND MENTAL HEALTH LITERATURE

Many writers have noted how the social science literature, and specifically research, has failed to create a realistic understanding of various ethnic groups in America (Jones & Korchin, 1982; Mays, 1985; D. W. Sue & S. Sue, 1972; S. Sue, Ito, & Bradshaw, 1982; Sumada, 1975; Thomas & Sillen, 1972). In fact, certain practices are felt to have done great harm to minorities by ignoring them, maintaining false stereotypes, and/or distorting their lifestyles. As mentioned previously, mental health definitions may be viewed as encompassing the use of social power (Tedeschi & O'Donovan, 1971) and functioning as a "handmaiden of the status quo" (Halleck, 1971, p. 30). It is clear that organized social science is part of the Establishment from which its researchers are usually drawn; moreover, organized social science often is dependent on the Establishment for financial support. Ethnic minorities frequently see counseling in a similar way—as a discipline concerned with maintaining the status and power of the Establishment. As a result, the person collecting and reporting data is often perceived as possessing the social bias of his/her society.

D. W. Sue (1975) and S. Sue and Morishima (1982) note that social sciences have generally ignored the study of Asians in America. This deficit has contributed to the perpetuation of false stereotypes that has angered many of the younger Asians concerned with raising consciousness and group esteem. When studies have been conducted on minorities, research has been appallingly unbalanced. In an early hard-hitting article, Billingsley (1970) points out how "White social science" has tended to reinforce a negative view of Blacks among the public by concentrating on unstable Black families instead of on the many stable ones. Such unfair treatment has also been the case in studies on Hispanics that have focused on the psychopathological problems encountered by Mexican Americans (Laval, Gomez, & Ruiz, 1983; Ruiz, 1981). Other ethnic groups such as the Native Americans (Atkinson, Morten, & Sue, 1989; Everett, Proctor, & Cortmell, 1983; Richardson, 1981) and Puerto Ricans (Christensen, 1974) have fared no better. Even more disturbing is the assumption that the problems encountered by minorities are due to intrinsic factors (racial inferiority, incompatible value systems, etc.) rather than to the failure of society (D. W. Sue & S. Sue, 1972; Katz, 1985).

S. Sue and Kitano (1973) in their analysis of the literature portrayal of the Chinese and Japanese in the United States conclude that there is a strong correlation between stereotypes and the conditions of society. When economic conditions were poor, Asians were portrayed as nonassimilable, sexually aggressive, and treacherous. However, when economic conditions dictated a cheap labor supply, stereotypes became more favorable. While there are many aspects of how minorities are portrayed in social science literature, two of them seem crucial for us to explore: (a) minorities and pathology, and (b) the relevance of research.

Minorities and Pathology

When we seriously study the "scientific" literature of the past relating to the culturally different, we are immediately impressed with how an implicit equation of minorities and pathology is a common theme. The historical use of science in the investigation of racial differences seems to be linked with White supremacist notions. Thomas and Sillen (1972) refer to this as "scientific racism" and cite several historical examples to support their contention: (a) 1840 census figures (fabricated) were used to support the notion that Blacks living under unnatural conditions of freedom were prone to anxiety, (b) mental health for Blacks was contentment with subservience, (c) psychologically normal Blacks were faithful and happy-go-lucky, (d) influential medical journals presented fantasies as facts supporting the belief that the anatomical, neurological, or endocrinological aspects of Blacks were always inferior to those of Whites, (e) the Black person's brain is smaller and less developed, (f) Blacks were less prone to mental illness because their minds were so simple, and (g) the dreams of Blacks are juvenile in character and not as complex as Whites.

Furthermore, the belief that various human groups exist at different stages of biological evolution was accepted by G. Stanley Hall (1904). He stated explicitly that Africans, Indians, and Chinese were members of adolescent races and in a stage of incomplete development. In most cases, the evidence used to support these conclusions was fabricated, extremely flimsy, or distorted to fit the belief in non-White inferiority (Thomas & Sillen, 1972). For example, Gossett (1963) reports how, when one particular study in 1895 revealed that the sensory perception of Native Americans was superior to that of Blacks and that of Blacks to Whites, the results were used to support a belief in the mental superiority of Whites. "Their reactions were slower because they belonged to a more deliberate and reflective race than did the members of the other two groups" (p. 364). The belief that Blacks were "born athletes" as opposed to scientists or statesmen derives from this tradition. The 1987 statement by then Dodger executive Al Campanis that Blacks are not mentally capable of being front-office executives or managers indicates such stereotypes still operate. The fact that Hall was a well-respected psychologist often referred to as "the father of child study" and first president of the American Psychological Association did not prevent him from inheriting the racial biases of the times.

The Genetically Deficient Model. The portrayal of the culturally different in literature has generally taken the form of stereotyping them as "deficient" in certain "desirable" attributes. For example, de Gobineau's (1915) *Essay on the Inequality of the Human Races* and Darwin's (1859) *The Origin of Species by Means of Natural Selection* were used to support the genetic intellectual superiority of Whites and the genetic inferiority of the "lower races." Galton (1869) wrote explicitly that African "Negroes" were "half-witted men" who made "childish, stupid and simpleton like mistakes," while Jews were inferior physically and mentally and only designed for a parasitical existence on other nations of people. Terman (1916) using the Binet scales in testing Black, Mexican American, and Spanish Indian families concluded that they were uneducable.

That the genetic deficient model still exists can be seen in the writing of Shuey (1966), Jensen (1969), Herrnstein (1971), and Shockley (1972). As recently as 1989, Professor Rushton of the University of Western Ontario presented a much-criticized study at the American Association for the Advancement of Science convention. He claimed that human intelligence and behavior were largely determined by race, that Whites have bigger brains than Blacks, and that Blacks are more aggressive. These "scientists" have adopted the position that genes play a predominant role in determination of intelligence. Shockley (1972) has expressed fears that the accumulation of weak or low intelligence genes in the Black population will seriously affect overall intelligence. Thus, he advocates that people with low IQs should not be allowed to bear children; they should be sterilized. This train of thought may have been expressed by Andy Rooney, a well-known commentator on "60 Minutes," when he said, "Blacks have watered down their genes because the less intelligent ones are the ones that have the most children. They drop out of schools early, do drugs, and get pregnant." In all fairness to Rooney, it must be said that he denies making such comments, although CBS took disciplinary action.

Even more disturbing have been allegations that the late Cyril Burt, eminent British psychologist, fabricated data to support his contention that intelligence is inherited and that Blacks have inherited inferior brains. Such an accusation is immensely important when one considers that Burt is a major influence in American and British psychology, is considered by many to be the father of educational psychology, was the first psychologist to be knighted, was awarded the APA's Thorndike Prize, and that his research findings form the foundation for the belief that intelligence is inherited. The charges, leveled by several people (Dorfman, 1978; Gillie, 1977; Kamin, 1974) can be categorized into four assertions: (a) that Burt guessed at the intelligence of parents he interviewed and later treated his guesses as scientific facts, (b) that two of Burt's collaborators never existed and Burt wrote the articles himself while using their names, (c) that Burt produced identical figures to three decimal points from different sets of data (a statistical impossibility), and (d) that Burt fabricated data to fit his theories. In a thorough review of one of Burt's most influential publications, Dorfman (1978) concludes:

> Cyril Burt presented data in his classic paper "Intelligence and Social Class" that were in perfect agreement with a genetic theory of IQ and social class. A detailed analysis of these data reveals, beyond reasonable doubt, that they were fabricated from a theoretical normal curve, from a genetic regressions equation, and from figures published more than 30 years before Burt completed his surveys. (p. 1177)

The Cyril Burt fiasco may represent another instance of scientific racism.

The questions about whether there are differences in intelligence between races is both a complex and emotional one. The difficulty in clarifying this question is compounded by many factors. Besides the difficulty in defining "race," there exist questionable assumptions regarding whether research on the intelligence of Whites can be generalized to other groups, whether middle-class and lower-class ethnic minorities grow up in similar environments to middle- and lower-class Whites, and whether test instruments are valid for both minority and White subjects. More important, we should recognize that the "average values" of different populations tells us nothing about any one individual. Heritability is a function of the population, *not* a trait. Ethnic groups all have individuals in the full range of intelligence, and to think of any racial group in terms of a single stereotype goes against all we know about the mechanics of heredity. Yet much of social science literature continues to portray ethnic minorities as being genetically deficient in one sense or another.

The Culturally Deficient Model. Well-meaning social scientists who challenged the genetic deficit model by placing heavy reliance on environmental factors, nevertheless, tended to perpetuate a view that saw minorities as culturally "disadvantaged," "deficient," or "deprived" (Katz, 1985; Mays, 1985). Instead of a biological condition that caused differences, the blame now shifted to the lifestyles or values of various ethnic groups (Baratz & Baratz, 1970; Smith, 1977; D. W. Sue et al., 1982; Sumada, 1975). The term "cultural deprivation" was first popularized by Riessman's widely read book, *The Culturally Deprived Child* (1962). It was used to indicate that many groups perform poorly on tests or exhibit deviant characteristics because they lack many of the advantages of middle-class culture (education, books, toys, formal language, etc.). In essence, these groups were culturally impoverished! Sumada (1975) summarizes studies which take the position that a host of factors place many minority persons in such a position as to hinder their success in school and society at large: (a) nutritional factors—malnutrition contributes to physical and mental impairment, (b) environmental factors—crowded and broken homes, dilapidated and unaesthetic areas (lack of books, toys, pictures, etc.), (c) psychological factors—lower self-concepts, poor motivation, absence of successful male models, lack of parental encouragement and interest in education, and fear of competing with Whites, (d) sociocultural factors—exposure to a culture with slum and ghetto values, and (e) linguistic factors.

While Riessman meant such a concept to add balance to working with minorities and ultimately to improve their condition in America, some educators of the time (Clark, 1963; Clark & Plotkin, 1972; Mackler & Giddings, 1965) strenuously objected to the term. First, the term *culturally deprived* means to lack a cultural background (slaves arrived in America culturally naked), which is contradictory because everyone inherits a culture. Second, such terms cause conceptual and theoretical confusions that may adversely affect social planning, educational policy, and research. For example, the Moynihan Report (Moynihan, 1965) asserts that "at the heart of deterioration of the Negro society is the deterioration of the Black family. It is the fundamental source of the weakness in the Negro community" (p. 5). Action thus was directed toward infusing "White" concepts of the family into the Black ones. Third, Baratz and Baratz (1970) point out that cultural deprivation is used synonymously with the deviation from and superiority of White middle-class values. Fourth, these deviations in values become equated with pathology in which a group's cultural values, families, or lifestyles transmit the pathology. Thus it provides a convenient rationalization and alibi for the perpetuation of racism and the inequities of the socioeconomic system.

The Culturally Diverse or Different Model. There are many who now maintain that the culturally deficient model only serves to perpetuate the myth of minority inferiority. The focus tends to be a person-blame one, an emphasis on minority pathology, and a use of White middle-class definitions of desirable and undesirable behavior. D. W. Sue (1975) states that our use of a common standard assumption implies that to be different is to be deviant, pathological, or sick. Mercer (1981) claims that intelligence and personality scores for minority group children really measure how "Anglicized" a person has become. Baratz and Baratz (1970) suggest that minorities should no longer be viewed as deficient, but rather as "culturally different." The goal of society should be to recognize the legitimacy of alternative lifestyles, the advantages of being bicultural (capable of functioning in two different cultural environments), and the value of differences.

Since publication of the first edition of this text, there has been increasing use of the term *culturally diverse.* It seems to imply that all racial/ethnic groups operate on a level playing field and that comparisons/descriptions are not made against just one standard (White ethnics).

RELEVANCE OF RESEARCH

So far, our discussion of minority portrayal in the professional literature has been a general one. We have made minimal reference to research as it relates to minorities in particular. Research findings are supposed to form the basis of any profession that purports to be a science. The data generated from research should be objective and free of bias. Yet what a researcher proposes to study and how he/she interprets such findings are intimately linked to a personal, professional, and societal value system (Jones & Korchin, 1982; S. Sue et al., 1982). Cheek (1987) goes so far as to assert that "social science is a vehicle of White supremacy".

We have already seen how personal and societal values may affect the interpretation of data as it relates to minorities. A very similar analogy can be drawn with respect to the counseling profession. For example, the profession's preoccupation with pathology tends to encourage the study of personality deficits and weaknesses rather than strengths or assets. Racist attitudes may intensify this narrow view, as minorities may be portrayed in professional journals as a neurotic, psychotic, psychopath, parolee, and so on, instead of as a well-rounded person.

It is not surprising that minority groups are often suspicious of the motives of the researcher. The researcher of ethnic matters may find his/her attitudes and values toward minority groups being challenged. No longer can the researcher claim that research is solely in the interest of science and morally neutral. Carl Rogers, a well-known humanistic psychologist, has stated, "If behavioral scientists are concerned solely with advancing their science, it seems most probable that they will serve the purpose of whatever group has the power" (as quoted in Brecher & Brecher, 1961, p. 20). C. W. Thomas (1970) has even voiced this thought in stronger form:

> White psychologists have raped Black communities all over the country. Yes raped. They have used Black people as the human equivalent of rats run through Ph.D. experiments and as helpless clients for programs that serve middle-class White administrators better than they do the poor. They have used research on Black people as green stamps to trade for research grants. They have been vultures. (p. 52)

Williams (1974) discusses two scientific research projects that illustrate this statement: the Tuskegee experiment and the Colville Indian Reservation Study.

The Tuskegee experiment was a 40-year federal experiment in which 600 Alabama Black men were used as guinea pigs in the study of what damage would occur to the body if syphilis were left untreated. Approximately 200 were allowed to go untreated even when medication was available for it. Records indicated that seven died as a result of syphilis, and an additional 154 died of heart disease that may have been caused by the untreated syphilis! Experiments of this type are ghastly and give rise to suspicions that minorities are being used as guinea pigs in other experiments of this sort.

That exploitation occurs in other ethnic communities is exemplified in the Colville Indian reservation disposition (Williams, 1974). An anthropologist, after gaining the trust and confidence of the Colville Indians in Washington, conducted a study of factionalism among the tribe. A subsequent study by another group of White researchers recommended that the best course of action for the Colville reservation was to liquidate its assets, including land, rather than consider economic development. Part of the justification for liquidation was based on the factionalism results obtained from the first study, and termination of the reservation was recommended. There were several primary issues about the actions that merit attention. First, the reservation was composed of 1.4 million acres of land that was rich in timber and minerals. There was strong pressure on the part of Whites to obtain the land. Second, the problems of factionalism were actually created by a society that attempted to "civilize" the Indians via Christianity and by White businesses that offered promises of riches. Third, many of the Indians confided in the White researcher and were led to believe that the information obtained would not be released.

It is this type of study, as well as the continual portrayal of ethnic communities and groups as deviants, that makes minorities extremely distrustful about the motives of the White researcher. Whereas social scientists in the past have been able to enter ethnic communities and conduct their studies with only minimal justification to those studied, researchers are now being received with suspicion and overt hostility. Minorities are actively raising questions and issues regarding the values system of researchers and the outcome of their research.

Concern with the ethics of research has led most educational institutions and government agencies to establish review boards whose purpose is to survey all research being conducted or proposed by investigators. The American Psychological Association adopted a set of guidelines, *Ethical Principles in the Conduct of Research with Human Participants,* part of which is intended to endorse and promote ethical principles in psychological research. The APA has also established a committee on scientific and professional ethics and conduct, which has the power to levy sanctions on members for violations of varying seriousness. The document put out by the APA raises questions such as the following: Under what conditions is it ethically acceptable to study residents of a ghetto, minority group members, the poor, prisoners, intellectually handicapped individuals, or college students? What are the motives of the researcher? Is research conducted for some definable good, or is it opportunistic, exploitative, and potentially damaging to the target populations?

Furthermore, many members of ethnic minorities find it difficult to see the relevance or applicability of much research conducted on them. This is especially true when they view the researcher as a laboratory specialist dealing with abstract, theoretical ideas rather than with the real human condition. Much hostility is directed toward the researcher who is perceived in this way. There is a growing feeling among ethnic minorities that research should go beyond the mere explaining of human behavior. Research should contribute to the concerns and betterment of the groups being studied. This concern is voiced not only by minorities, but also by many students, scholars, and the public. Ethnic minorities often view the researcher as a laboratory specialist interested in abstract theoretical ideas rather than as a person interested in the applicability of his/her findings. Baron (1971) points out that psychological researchers are often guilty of perpetuating this belief by failing to make clear and explicit the goals behind their pursuits. Indeed, many find this task distasteful. Much hostility, therefore, is directed at researchers of ethnic matters whom many minorities feel conduct narrow irrelevant studies that will not improve the human condition. There seems to be much justification for these charges.

First, graduate programs in the social sciences have traditionally been much more concerned with the training of academicians rather than practitioners. Several psychologists (Katz, 1985; Patterson, 1972), in their analysis of graduate education, point out that most programs use as the "root model" the experimental research scientist as the psychological paradigm. Patterson (1972) points out that this model has frequently hindered research dealing with social and psychological problems facing humankind. Since much exploratory work is needed in investigating complex social problems, the strong emphasis on rigorous methodology discourages much meaningful research dealing with problems of complex social issues. This discouragement is often seen in the status hierarchy of graduate programs. Experimental research is at the top of the ladder, with exploratory work at the bottom. Furthermore, manuscripts that may have meaningful implications in social contexts but that may not lend themselves to rigorous experimentation, are difficult to publish in the professional journals. Ethnic minorities who may desire to seek solutions to pressing social problems become alienated from such programs, which they feel are irrelevant and encapsulated from real social settings.

Second, many social researchers feel their responsibility is discharged with the publication of their results. Research data reported in the professional journals may be understandable to fellow professionals, but certainly not to many students and laypeople. All too often the publication of articles is written to impress colleagues and insure promotion and tenure (Goldman, 1977). The individuals and communities in such studies are often forgotten. Feedback in a form that is intelligible and usable by the particular communities is seriously lacking, and this contributes to feelings of exploitation. Researchers are increasingly being asked, "How will this study help us? Tell us in concrete terms, without your professional rationalizations and jargon, and we will decide whether you can have access to us or not."

A CALL TO THE PROFESSION

If counseling, as a profession, is to receive acceptance from the culturally different, it must demonstrate, in no uncertain terms, its good faith and ability to contribute to the betterment of a group's quality of life. This demonstration can take several directions.

First, the counseling profession must take initiative in confronting the potential political nature of counseling (Katz, 1985). For too long we have deceived ourselves into believing that the practice of counseling and the data base that underlie the profession are morally, ethically, and politically neutral. The results have been (a) subjugation of the culturally different, (b) perpetuation of the view that minorities are inherently pathological, (c) perpetuation of racist practices in counseling, and (d) provision of an excuse to the profession for not taking social action to rectify inequities in the system.

Second, the counseling profession must move quickly to challenge certain assumptions that permeate our training programs. We must critically reexamine our concepts of what constitutes normality and abnormality, begin mandatory training programs that deal with these issues, critically examine and reinterpret past and continuing literature dealing with the culturally different, and use research in such a manner as to improve the life conditions of the researched populations.

Ponterotto & Casas (1987) have made a forceful call for the inclusion of implementing cross-cultural competence in training programs. Their suggestions involve asking that the American Psychological Association (APA) and the American Association for Counseling and Development (AACD) develop an explicit definition of cross-cultural competence that would be infused in all accredited training programs. Accreditation boards such as APA's Division 17 and the Council for Accreditation of Counseling and related educational programs must incorporate this definition directly into guidelines. Arrendondo (1985) advocates developing licensing and credentialing procedures that create culturally competent counselors qualified to work with populations and the need to develop procedures for licensing counselors with cross-cultural competence.

What this boils down to is that educational programs can no longer present a predominantly White Anglo-Saxon Protestant (WASP) orientation. The study of minority group cultures must receive equal treatment and fair portrayal on all levels of education. Courses dealing with minority group experiences and internship practices must become a required part of the training programs. Training programs also need to reorganize the professional reward structure so that the practitioner receives equal status with the academician, and action or applied research should be encouraged even though it may not involve the epitome of rigorous experimental controls.

Third, research can be a powerful means of combating stereotypes and of correcting biased studies. The fact that previous studies have been used to perpetuate stereotypes (Billingsley, 1970) does not preclude the usefulness of research. If social scientists believe that research has been poorly conducted or misinterpreted to the detriment of minority groups, they should feel some moral commitment to investigate their beliefs. Unfortunately, this self-correcting process of ethnic research has been underdeveloped, since there is a shortage of minority social scientists contributing a minority-group point of view. The researcher cannot escape the moral and ethical implications of his/her research and must take responsibility for the outcome of his/her study. He/she should guard against misinterpretations and take into account cultural factors and the limitations of his/her instruments.

Fourth, there is a strong need for counseling to attract more ethnic minorities to the profession, complex as this issue is. Although many White professionals have great understanding and empathy for minorities, they can never fully appreciate the dilemmas faced by a minority member. Ethnic minorities can offer a dimension and a viewpoint that act as a counterbalance to the forces of misinterpretation. Furthermore, the cry for more minority professionals demonstrates the presence of a "credibility gap" between counseling and minority members (Ponterotto & Casas, 1987). With this addition of more minority counseling psychologists, trust among ethnic minorities may be enhanced.

Fifth, counselors must realize that many so-called pathological socio-emotional characteristics of ethnic minorities can be directly attributed to unfair practices in society. D. W. Sue et al. (1982), Herzog (1971), and Blau (1970) advocate a shift in research, from focusing on the poor and culturally diverse to focusing on the groups and institutions that have perpetuated racism and obstructed needed changes.

Another shift in focus can be to study the positive attributes and characteristics of ethnic minorities. Social scientists have had a tendency to look for pathology and problems among minorities. Too much research has concentrated on mental health problems and culture conflict of minorities, while little has been done to determine the advantages of being bicultural. Hopefully, such an orientation will do much to present a more balanced picture of different minority groups. It must be noted, however, that the researcher cannot selectively publish findings that perpetuate "good" characteristics of minority groups and that censure "bad" ones. This selectivity is not only unethical, but also serves to maintain misunderstandings in the long run.

Last, making research with minorities a community endeavor can do much to lower hostility and develop trust between researcher and subject. For example, a social scientist investigating minority groups in the community is often more effective if he/she discusses his/her ideas with community leaders and obtains their cooperation (Goering & Cummins, 1970; Klein, 1968; S. Sue et al., 1982). The inclusion of community members in different phases of research (interviewers, coordinators, etc.) can facilitate trust. This would require that social scientists clearly articulate their goals and methods to the community. Sanford (1970), in his discussion of student activism, notes that many students seldom know the implications or outcomes of the research conducted on them. He points out that research with student involvement can benefit its subjects by (a) helping them answer their questions and concerns, (b) helping them acquire understanding of themselves, and (c) helping them learn research skills. In this way, research will be educational for those being studied as well.

CHAPTER 2

Barriers to Effective Cross-Cultural Counseling

"Several years ago I was asked by a student services committee at a large public university to help identify factors that would make their services more relevant to the needs of minority students. Apparently, the office of student services, especially the Counseling Center, was under considerable pressures from minority groups to make changes amid charges of racism. The Counseling Center director and several staff members reported they had tried to encourage minority students to come for counseling, but their efforts had met with no success. A recent study by the university had revealed that while the student population was comprised of 16% Asian Americans, 17% Blacks, 3% Hispanics, and less than 1% American Indians, very few minorities used the center's services. The Counseling Center had a nationally known reputation as a fertile training program for interns doing work in socioemotional problems.

"My own investigation revealed that not only were the services heavily clinical (personal/emotional counseling) in nature, but they subscribed to the traditional one-to-one model. When counselors were asked the types of cases they preferred to work with, 85% of the counseling staff listed clinical while only 15% chose educational/vocational ones. Indeed, I quickly sensed a status hierarchy among the staff. At the top of the pecking order were those who primarily did clinical work and at the bottom were the educational/vocational counselors. In addition, the staff of 28 in the center had only three minority members."

The above example is one of several similar situations that the senior author has been involved in as an outside consultant. What possible barriers or impediments may be present that discourage minority students' participation? Is the institution discouraging certain culturally different clients from making use of its services? If so, what are these characteristics and why? Is the traditional counselor-client model effective in counseling minorities (nontraditional clients)? Let us use this case to illustrate the topic of this chapter.

The underrepresentation of minority clients in mental health services is not unusual. In a comprehensive series of studies mentioned earlier, S. Sue and associates (S. Sue, Allen, & Conaway, 1975; S. Sue et al., 1974; S. Sue & McKinney, 1975) found that American Indians, Asian Americans, Blacks, and Hispanics underutilized traditional mental health services and terminated therapy after only one contact at a rate of over 50% in comparison to a 30% rate for Anglo clients. Several primary reasons were identified at the Counseling Center for the low utilization rates.

First, it became obvious by a casual inspection of the Counseling Center staff that it was predominantly White. Of the minority group members present, one was a Black counselor, but the others were a Black clerical staff member and an Asian American vocational librarian.

The lack of minority professionals in the Counseling Center was a loud and clear message to certain culturally different students concerning the commitment of the institution and Center. The perception of many of the minority students was that the Counseling Center did not care about culturally different students, that it lacked understanding about their lifestyles and experiences, and that its efforts toward encouraging participation were not genuine and sincere. Rightly or wrongly, it was assumed by many of the students that the staff would not be able to relate to the minority-group experience of the students and, indeed, that the low minority representation resulted from racist policies and practices which discriminated against hiring minority staff. Thus, based on these perceptions, many of the students were actively discouraged from utilizing the services.

Second, how the services were offered to the university community was also crucial in its ability to relate to a culturally diverse student population. The above case makes it clear that the traditional services were one-to-one in nature in which the counselor received clients in his or her office. This type of approach, as Atkinson et al. (1989) point out, may actually be less appropriate than meeting the client in a different contextual environment. Rather than demanding that the client adapt to the counselor's culture, it may be better for the counselor to adjust to and work within the client's culture. In other words, alternative roles involve the counselor more actively in the client's life experiences than what we have traditionally been trained to do. Outreach roles, consultant roles, change-agent roles, or the use of the client's indigenous support systems may be more appropriate. Many minority group individuals find the one-to-one/in-office type of counseling very formal, removed, and alien. When counselors move out of their offices into the environments of their clients, it again indicates commitment and interest in the individual. According to this nontraditional view, counseling is not simply sitting down and talking with a client, but it may involve shooting basketball with the client in his or her home environment, playing billiards with the client, and working in situations where the minority individual is found (dormitories, the student union, etc.). Unfortunately, most training in counseling and clinical psychology does not give adequate experiences with these types of change-agent outreach programs. Indeed, counselors are often discouraged from meeting clients on their "home turf" because it is "unprofessional" and not a part of the counselor's role.

Third, the Counseling Center in this situation is defined as one that is very well known in terms of social-emotional counseling and emphasis. This again is not unusual in most counselor education training programs. Oftentimes counselor trainees are more intrigued with personal-emotional (psychiatric) issues rather than educational or vocational ones. Yet, it appears that many minority individuals are much more concerned with their vocational, educational, and career goals. For example, as we will see in Chapter 10, Asian Americans tend to be much more concerned with educational-vocational counseling and will come for these services at a high rate when offered. Much of this is due to cultural factors operating in the life of Asian Americans. When counseling staff tend to perceive educational-vocational counseling as less prestigious, then it is entirely possible that this is communicated to the student population. Additionally, many minority individuals may not trust talking about personal issues with White counselors and may be more amenable to dealing directly with vocational-educational career issues. This subject is discussed further in later chapters.

Last, the actual process of counseling and therapy may prove to be antagonistic or inappropriate to the life experiences of the minority client. A reading of this case does emphasize that it is characterized by a traditional one-to-one approach in which a client comes to an office, sits down, and talks about the most intimate aspects of his or her life. The primary medium of communication is verbal (talking—especially in standard English). Many minority individuals may find these broad characteristics quite discriminatory against them. For example, counseling and psychotherapy has frequently been referred to as "talk therapy" because one's ability to verbalize is the primary condition for counseling. A person who is relatively nonverbal, speaks with an accent, or uses nonstandard English may be placed at a disadvantage. The lack of bilingual counselors makes this fact even more glaring.

In the last chapter, we mentioned how the counseling profession had failed to contribute to the betterment of Third World groups in America. Counselor training programs and the portrayal of minorities in both the popular and scientific literature have oftentimes instilled within counselor trainees (a) monocultural assumptions of mental health, (b) negative stereotypes of pathology for minority lifestyles, and (c) ineffective, inappropriate, and antagonistic counseling approaches to the values held by minorities. As in the Counseling Center illustration, this damage is clearly seen in the actual practice of counseling and therapy.

COUNSELING CHARACTERISTICS

Counseling and psychotherapy may be viewed legitimately as a process of interpersonal interaction and communication. For effective counseling to occur, the counselor and client must be able to *appropriately* and *accurately send* and *receive* both *verbal* and *nonverbal* messages. While breakdowns in communication often happen between members who share the same culture, the problem becomes exacerbated between people of different racial or ethnic backgrounds. Many mental health professionals have noted that racial or ethnic factors may act as impediments to counseling (Bulhan, 1985; Carkhuff & Pierce, 1967; Ruiz & Padilla, 1977; Sue et al., 1982; Trimble, 1981; Vontress, 1981, 1971). Misunderstandings that arise from cultural variations in communication may lead to alienation and/or an inability to develop trust and rapport.

This chapter focuses on how the values of counseling and psychotherapy may be antagonistic to the values of Third World clients. How these values may distort communication and/or affect the counseling relationship between members of different backgrounds is explored. Implications for counseling are discussed. A conceptual scheme is presented that can be used to compare and contrast how language, culture, and class variables can be used to determine appropriate interventions. Such a comparative analysis is helpful in providing a means for examining the appropriateness of counseling approaches, not only for Third World clients but also for other special populations as well (women, the physically handicapped, and the elderly). What we cannot forget is that the basic issue remains the classic one of individual differences and their significance for counselors. For that reason, this analysis is also helpful in comparing the appropriateness of counseling for different individuals within a single culture.

Generic Characteristics of Counseling

We have repeatedly emphasized that counseling and psychotherapy are influenced by the social-cultural framework from which it arises. In the United States, White western European culture holds certain values that are reflected in this therapeutic process. All theories of counseling and psychotherapy are influenced by assumptions that theorists make regarding the goals for counseling, the methodology used to invoke change, and the definition of mental health and mental illness. Counseling and psychotherapy have traditionally been conceptualized in Western individualistic terms (Atkinson et al., 1989; Ivey, 1981, 1986). Whether the particular theory is psychodynamic, existential-humanistic, or behavioral in orientation, a number of individuals (Ivey, Ivey, & Simek-Downing, 1987; Katz, 1985) indicate that they share certain common components of White culture in their values and beliefs. Katz (1985) has described these components of White culture (see Table 7.2, Chapter 7). These values and beliefs have influenced the actual practice of counseling and psychotherapy as can be seen clearly in Tables 2.1 and 2.2.

TABLE 2.1
Generic Characteristics of Counseling

Culture	Middle Class	Language
Standard English	Standard English	Standard English
Verbal communication	Verbal communication	Verbal communication
Individual centered	Adherence to time schedules (50-minute sessions)	
Verbal/emotional/ behavioral expressiveness	Long-range goals	
Client-counselor communication	Ambiguity	
Openness and intimacy		
Cause-effect orientation		
Clear distinction between physical and mental well-being		
Nuclear family		

TABLE 2.2
Third World Group Variables

Culture	Lower Class	Language
	Asian Americans	
Asian language Family centered	Nonstandard English Action oriented	Bilingual background
Restraint of feelings	Different time perspective	
One-way communication from authority figure to person	Immediate, short-range goals	
Silence is respect		
Advice seeking		
Well-defined patterns of interaction (concrete structured)		
Private versus public display (shame/disgrace/pride)		
Physical and mental well-being defined differently		
Extended family		

TABLE 2.2 (cont.)
Third World Group Variables

Culture	Lower Class	Language
Blacks		
Black language	Nonstandard English	Black language
Sense of "people-hood"	Action oriented	
Action oriented	Different time perspective	
Paranorm due to oppression	Immediate, short-range goals	
Importance placed on nonverbal behavior	Concrete, tangible, structured approach	
Extended family		
Hispanics		
Spanish-speaking	Nonstandard English	Bilingual background
Group centered	Action oriented	
Temporal difference Family orientation	Different time perspective	
Different pattern of communication	Immediate short-range goals	
A religious distinction between mind/body	Concrete, tangible, structured approach	
Extended family		
American Indians		
Tribal dialects	Nonstandard English	Bilingual background
Cooperative, not competitive individualism	Action oriented Different time perspective	
Present-time orientation	Immediate, short-range goals	
Creative/experimental/intuitive/ nonverbal	Concrete, tangible, structured approach	
Satisfy present needs		
Use of Folk or supernatural explanations		
Extended family		

In the United States and in many countries, psychotherapy and counseling are used mainly with middle- and upper-class segments of the population. As a result, many of the values and characteristics seen in both the goals and process of counseling are not shared by Third World clients. Schofield (1964) has noted that therapists tend to prefer clients who exhibit the YAVIS syndrome: young, attractive, verbal, intelligent, and successful. This preference tends to discriminate against people from different minority groups or those from lower-socioeconomic classes. This has led Sundberg (1981) to sarcastically point out that therapy is not for QUOID people (quiet, ugly, old, indigent, and dissimilar culturally). D. W. Sue and S. Sue (1972) have identified three major characteristics of counseling that may act as a source of conflict for Third World groups.

First, counselors often expect their counselee to exhibit some degree of openness, psychological-mindedness, or sophistication. Most theories of counseling place a high premium on verbal, emotional, and behavioral expressiveness and the obtaining of insight. These are either the end goals of counseling or are the medium by which "cures" are effected. Second, counseling is traditionally a one-to-one activity that encourages clients to talk about or discuss the most intimate aspects of their lives. Individuals who fail in or resist self-disclosure may be seen as resistant, defensive, or superficial. Third, the counseling or therapy situation is often an ambiguous one. The client is encouraged to discuss problems while the counselor listens and responds. Relatively speaking, the counseling situation is unstructured and forces the client to be the primary active participant. Patterns of communication are generally from client to counselor.

Four other factors identified as generally characteristic of counseling are (a) monolingual orientation, (b) emphasis on long-range goals, (c) distinction between physical and mental well-being, and (d) emphasis on cause-effect relationships. With respect to the first, "good" standard English is the predominant vehicle by which communication occurs. To individuals who may not speak or use English well, the lack of bilingual counselors is a serious handicap to accurate communication. Furthermore, since counseling is generally isolated from the client's environment and contacts are brief (50 minutes, once a week), it is by nature aimed at seeking long-range goals and solutions.

Another important and often overlooked factor in counseling is the implicit assumption that a clear distinction can be made between mental and physical illness or health. Contrary to this Western view, many cultures may not make a clear distinction between the two. Such a separation may be confusing to Third World clients and cause problems in counseling.

Ornstein's work (1972) in which he identifies the dual hemispheric functioning of the brain also has intriguing implications for counseling. While the left hemisphere of the brain is involved with linear, rational, and cognitive processes, the right half tends to be intuitive, feeling, and experientially oriented. When both hemispheres are operating in a mutually interdependent fashion, they facilitate our functioning as human beings. Ornstein points out that the linear/logical/analytic/verbal mode of the left brain dominates Western thinking. The functioning of the right brain that is intuitive/holistic/creative/nonverbal has been neglected in Western culture and seen as a less legitimate mode of expression.

An analysis of the various American schools of counseling leads to the inevitable conclusion that Western counseling is left-brain oriented. Such an approach or world view may definitely clash with Eastern and American Indian philosophy. Thus, a left-brain orientation means a linear emphasis on cause-effect approaches and a linear concept of time. We deal with these concepts in greater detail in the next chapter.

In summary, the generic characteristics of counseling can be seen to fall into three major categories:

1. Culture-bound values—individual centered, verbal/emotional/ behavioral expressiveness, communication patterns from client to counselor, openness and intimacy, analytic/linear/verbal (cause-effect) approach, and clear distinctions between mental and physical well-being;

2. Class-bound values—strict adherence to time schedules (50-minute, once-or-twice-a-week meeting), ambiguous or unstructured approach to problems, and seeking long-range goals or solutions; and

3. Language variables—use of standard English and emphasis on verbal communication.

Tables 2.1 and 2.2 summarize these generic characteristics and compare their compatibility to those of four Third World groups.

SOURCES OF CONFLICT AND MISINTERPRETATION IN COUNSELING

While an attempt has been made to clearly delineate three major variables that influence effective counseling, these variables are often inseparable from one another. For example, use of standard English in counseling definitely places those individuals who are unable to use it fluently at a disadvantage. However, cultural and class values that govern conversation conventions can also operate via language to cause serious misunderstandings. Furthermore, the fact that many Blacks, Hispanics, and American Indians come from a predominantly lower-class background often compounds class and culture variables. Thus, it is often difficult to tell which are the sole impediments in counseling. Nevertheless, this distinction is valuable in conceptualizing barriers to effective cross-cultural counseling.

Culture-Bound Values

In simple terms, "culture" consists of all those things that people have learned to do, believe, value, and enjoy in their history. It is the totality of ideals, beliefs, skills, tools, customs, and institutions into which each member of society is born. While D. W. Sue and S. Sue (1972) have stressed the need for social scientists to focus on the positive aspects of being bicultural, such dual membership may cause problems for many minorities. The term "marginal" person was coined by Stonequist (1937) and refers to a person's inability to form dual ethnic identification because of bicultural membership. Third World people are placed under strong pressures to adopt the ways of the dominant culture. Third World people's own ethnicity or cultural heritage is seen as a handicap to be overcome, something to be ashamed of, and to be avoided. In essence, Third World people may be taught that to be different is to be deviant, pathological, or sick.

Many social scientists (Halleck, 1971; Katz, 1985; D. W. Sue et al., 1982) believe that psychology and therapy may be viewed as encompassing the use of social power and that therapy is a "handmaiden of the status quo." The counselor may be seen as an agent of society transmitting and functioning under Western values. An outspoken critic, Szasz (1970) believes that psychiatrists are like slave masters using therapy as a powerful political ploy against people whose ideas, beliefs, and behaviors differ from the dominant society. Several cultural characteristics of counseling may be responsible for these negative beliefs.

Individual Centered. Most forms of counseling and psychotherapy tend to be individual centered—that is, they emphasize the "I-thou" relationship. Pedersen (1987; 1988) notes that U.S. culture and society is based upon the concept of individualism and that competition between individuals for status, recognition, achievement, and so forth, forms the basis for Western tradition. He notes that not all cultures view individualism as a positive orientation; rather, it may be perceived in some cultures as a handicap to attaining enlightenment, one that may divert us from important spiritual goals. In many non-Western cultures, identity is not seen apart from the group orientation. The personal pronoun I in the Japanese language does not seem to exist. The notion of *atman* in India defines itself as participating in unity with all things and not limited by the temporal world.

Many societies do not define the psychosocial unit of operation as the individual. In many cultures and subgroups, the psychosocial unit of operation tends to be the family, group, or collective society. In traditional Asian American culture, according to S. Sue and Morishima (1982), one's identity is defined within the family constellation. The greatest punitive measure to be taken out on an individual by the family is to be disowned. What this means in essence is that the person no longer has an identity.

While being disowned by a family in Western European culture is equally negative and punitive, it does not have the same connotations as in traditional Asian society. Westerners, while they may be disowned by a family, are always informed and told that they have an individual identity as well. Likewise, many Hispanic individuals tend to see the unit of operation as residing within the family. Nobles (1976) and Mays (1985) also point to how the Black or African view of the world encompasses the concept of "groupness."

It is our contention that many Third World groups who use a different psychosocial unit of operation have different world views that may clash with the world views of White culture and society. This world view is reflected in all aspects of behavior. For example, many traditional Asian-American and Hispanic elders tend to greet one another with the question "How is your family today?" Contrast this with how most U.S. Americans tend to greet each other by asking, "How are you today?" One emphasizes the family perspective, while the other emphasizes the individual perspective.

Affective elements, oftentimes seen in counseling, can also be strongly influenced by the particular orientation one takes. In the United States, when individuals are accused of doing something wrong, they are most likely to experience feelings of *guilt*. However, in traditional societies that emphasize a group orientation, the most dominant affective element to follow a wrongful behavior is *shame*, not guilt. Guilt is an individual affect, while shame appears to be a group affect.

Counselors and therapists who fail to recognize the importance of defining this difference between individualism and group orientation will create difficulties in counseling. Oftentimes we are impressed by the number of individuals who describe traditional Asian clients as being dependent, unable to make decisions on their own, and lacking in maturity. Many of these analyses are based on the fact that many Asian clients do not see a decision-making process as an individual one. When an Asian client states to a counselor or therapist, "I can't make that decision on my own; I need to consult with my parents or family," he or she is seen as being quite immature. After all, therapy is aimed at helping individuals to "make decisions on their own" in a "mature" and "responsible" manner.

Verbal/Emotional/Behavioral Expressiveness. Many counselors and therapists tend to emphasize the fact that verbal/emotional/behavioral expressiveness is important in individuals. For example, we like our clients to be verbal, articulate, and to be able to express their thoughts and feelings clearly. Indeed, therapy is oftentimes referred to as "talk therapies" indicating the importance placed upon standard English as the medium of expression. Emotional expressiveness is also valued, as we like individuals to be in touch with their feelings and to be able to verbalize their emotional reactions. In some forms of counseling and psychotherapy, it is oftentimes stated that if a feeling is not verbalized and expressed by the client, it may not exist. We tend to value and believe that behavioral expressiveness is important as well. We like individuals to be assertive, to stand up for their own rights, and to engage in activities that indicate they are not passive beings.

All these characteristics of counseling can place culturally different clients at a disadvantage. For example, many cultural minorities tend not to value verbalizations in the same way that U.S. Americans do. In traditional Japanese culture, children have been taught not to speak until spoken to. Patterns of communication tend to be vertical, flowing from those of higher prestige and status to those of lower prestige and status. In a counseling situation, many Japanese clients, to show respect for a counselor who is older, "wiser," and who occupies a position of higher status, may respond with silence. Unfortunately, an unenlightened counselor or therapist may perceive this client as being "inarticulate" and less intelligent.

Emotional expressiveness in counseling and psychotherapy is frequently a goal and is highly desired. Yet, there are many cultural groups in which restraint of strong feelings is highly valued. For example, traditional Hispanic and Asian cultures emphasize that maturity and wisdom are associated with one's ability to control emotions and feelings. This applies not only to public expressions of anger and frustration, but also to public expressions of love and affection as well. Unfortunately, counselors unfamiliar with these cultural ramifications may perceive their clients in a very negative psychiatric light. Indeed, these clients are often described as inhibited, lacking in spontaneity, and/or repressed.

The senior author once did a research study at a well-known university in Southern California. The study involved identifying symptomology among Japanese American students using the counseling and psychiatric services. He was quite shocked and surprised when many of the psychiatric staff indicated they were very pleased to see research being done on the Japanese clients because, "Did you know they are one of the most repressed groups we have ever encountered?" We submit that this statement tends to overlook the fact that cultural forces may be operative in the Japanese-American clients' overall behavior in the counseling session. While the clients may be "repressed," the failure to consider cultural factors that dictate against public disclosures and feelings may prove a serious consequence.

During the last 10 years, it has become increasingly popular to emphasize expressiveness in a behavioral sense. For example, one need only note the proliferation of assertiveness training programs throughout the United States and the number of self-help books that are being published in the popular mental health literature. Many of these, such as *Stand Up for Your Own Rights* and *When I Say No, I Feel Guilty*, attest to the importance placed on assertiveness and standing up for one's own rights. This orientation fails to realize that there are cultural groups in which subtlety is a highly prized art. Yet, doing things indirectly can be perceived by the mental health professional as evidence of passivity and the need for this individual to learn assertiveness skills.

Counselors who value verbal, emotional, and behavioral expressiveness as goals in counseling, are transmitting their own cultural values. This generic characteristic of counseling is not only antagonistic to lower-class values, but also to different cultural ones. Wood and Mallinekrodt (1990) in their excellent review of assertiveness training, warn that therapists need to make certain that gaining such skills is a value shared by the minority client, and not imposed by the therapists. For example, statements by some mental health professionals that Asian Americans are the most repressed of all clients indicate they expect their counselees to exhibit openness, psychological-mindedness, and assertiveness. Such a statement may indicate a failure on the part of the counselor to understand the background and cultural upbringing of many Asian-American clients. Traditional Chinese and Japanese cultures may value restraint of strong feelings and subtleness in approaching problems.

Insight. Another generic characteristic of counseling is the use of insight in both counseling and psychotherapy. This characteristic assumes that it is mentally beneficial for individuals to obtain insight or understanding into their deep underlying dynamics and causes. Born from the tradition of psychoanalytic theory, many theorists tend to believe that clients who obtain insight into themselves will be better adjusted. While many of the behavioral schools of thought may not subscribe to this, most counselors in their individual practice use insight either as a process of counseling or as an end-product or goal.

We need to realize that insight is not highly valued by many culturally different clients. There are also major class differences as well. People from lower socioeconomic classes frequently do not perceive insight as appropriate to their life situations and circumstances. Their concern may revolve around questions such as "Where do I find a job?" "How do I feed my family?" "How can I afford to take my sick daughter to a doctor?" When survival on a day-to-day basis is important, it seems inappropriate for the counselor to use insightful processes. After all, insight assumes that one has time to sit back, to reflect and to contemplate about motivations and behavior. For the individual who is concerned about making it through each day, this orientation proves counterproductive.

Likewise, many cultural groups do not value insight. In traditional Chinese society, psychology is not well understood. It must be noted, however, that a client who does not seem to work well in an insight approach may not be lacking in insight or lacking in psychological-mindedness. A person who does not value insight is not necessarily one who is incapable of insight. Thus, there tend to be several major factors that affect insight.

First, many cultural groups themselves do not value this method of self-exploration. It is interesting to note that many Asian elders believe that thinking too much about something can cause problems. Lum (1982), in a study of the Chinese in San Francisco's Chinatown, found that many believe the road to mental health was to "avoid morbid thoughts." Advice from Asian elders to their children when they encountered feelings of frustration, anger, depression, or anxiety was simply "don't think about it." Indeed, it is often believed that the reason why one experiences anger or depression is precisely that one is thinking about it *too much!* The traditional Asian way of handling these affective elements is to "keep busy and don't think about it." Granted, it is more complex than this, because in traditional Asian families the reason why self-exploration is discouraged is precisely because it is an individual approach. "Think about the family and not about yourself" is advice given to many Asians as a way of dealing with negative affective elements. This is totally contradictory to Western notions of mental health—that it is best to get things out in the open in order to deal with them.

Second, many Third World psychologists have felt that insight is a value in itself. For example, it was generally thought that insight led to behavior change. This was the old psychoanalytic assumption that when people understood their conflicts and underlying dynamics, the symptoms or behavior would change or disappear. The behavioral schools of thought have since disproved this one-to-one connection. While insight does lead to behavior change in some situations, it does not always seem to do so. Indeed, behavioral therapies have shown that changing the behavior first may lead to insight (cognitive restructuring and understanding) instead of vice-versa. As an example, one of the authors once had considerable difficulties and apprehensions about asking members of the opposite sex out on social occasions. He would find it highly anxiety provoking to call a female friend on the phone and ask her out for a date. This bothered him so greatly that he sought counseling and was able to understand the basis of his anxieties. Briefly, it boiled down to the fact that he feared rejection and that the rejection, if it came, was always in some sense correlated with his own concept of masculinity. This insight made the author feel much better, but did not ever help him pick up the phone to ask a female friend out on a date! Of course, one can claim that the author did not achieve "true insight." We would then ask the question, "When does a person have insight?" We submit that the only answer, which is a highly value-based one, is that a client has insight when the therapist says that person has insight. This varies from therapist to therapist and from theory to theory.

Self-Disclosure (Openness and Intimacy). Most forms of counseling and psychotherapy tend to value one's ability to self-disclose and to talk about the most intimate aspects of one's life. Indeed, self-disclosure has often been discussed as a primary characteristic of the healthy personality.

The converse of this is that people who do not self-disclose readily in counseling and psychotherapy are seen as possessing negative traits such as being guarded, mistrustful, and/or paranoid. There are two difficulties in this orientation toward self-disclosure. One of these is cultural and the other is sociopolitical.

First, intimate revelations of personal or social problems may not be acceptable, since such difficulties reflect not only on the individual, but also on the whole family. Thus, the family may exert strong pressures on the Asian-American client not to reveal personal matters to "strangers" or "outsiders." Similar conflicts have been reported for Hispanics (Laval et al., 1983) and for American-Indian clients (Everett et al., 1983). A counselor who works with a client from a minority background may erroneously conclude that the person is repressed, inhibited, shy, or passive. Note that all these terms are seen as undesirable by Western standards.

Related to this example is the belief in the desirability of self-disclosure by many mental health practitioners. Self-disclosure refers to the client's willingness to tell the counselor what he/she feels, believes, or thinks. Journard (1964) suggests that mental health is related to one's openness in disclosing. While this may be true, the parameters need clarification. Chapter 1 used as an example the paranorm of Grier and Cobbs (1968). Vontress (1981) reports that people of African descent are especially reluctant to disclose to Caucasian counselors because of hardships they have experienced via racism. Few Blacks initially perceive a White counselor as a person of goodwill, but rather as an agent of society who may use the information against them. From the Black perspective, uncritical self-disclosure to others is not healthy.

The actual structure of the counseling situation may also work against intimate revelations. Among many American Indians and Hispanics, intimate aspects of life are shared only with close friends. Relative to White middle-class standards, deep friendships are developed only after prolonged contacts. Once friendships are formed, they tend to be lifelong in nature. In contrast, White Americans form relationships quickly, but the relationships do not necessarily persist over long periods of time. Counseling seems to also reflect these values. Clients talk about the most intimate aspects of their lives with a relative stranger once a week for a 50-minute session. To many culturally different people who stress friendship as a precondition to self-disclosure, the counseling process seems utterly inappropriate and absurd. After all, how is it possible to develop a friendship with brief contacts once a week?

Cause/Effect Orientation. Counseling and psychotherapy in Western culture and society has been described as being highly linear, analytic, and verbal. As indicated by Table 2.1, Western society tends to emphasize the so-called scientific method which involves objective rational linear thinking. Likewise, we oftentimes see descriptions of the therapist as being objective and neutral, rational and logical in thinking (Katz, 1985; Pedersen, 1988).

The therapist relies heavily on the use of linear problem solving as well as on quantitative evaluation that includes psychodiagnostic tests, intelligence tests, personality inventories, and so forth. This cause-effect orientation has been described by Ornstein (1974) as emphasizing left-brain functioning. That is, theories of counseling are distinctly analytical, rational, verbal, and strongly stress discovering cause-effect relationships.

The emphasis on symbolic logic is in marked contrast to the philosophy of many cultures. For example, American-Indian world views emphasize the harmonious aspects of the world, intuitive functioning, and a holistic approach—a world view characterized by right-brain activities (Ornstein, 1972), minimizing analytical, reductionistic inquiries. Thus, when American Indians undergo counseling, the analytic approach may violate their basic philosophy of life.

It appears that in U.S. society, the most dominant way of asking and answering questions about the human condition tends to be the scientific method. The epitome of this approach is the so-called experiment. In graduate schools we are oftentimes told that only in the experiment can we impute a cause-effect relationship. By identifying the independent and dependent variables and controlling for extraneous variables, we are able to test a cause-effect hypothesis. While correlational studies, historical research, and so forth, may be of benefit, we are told that the experiment represents the epitome of "our science." As indicated, other cultures may value different ways of asking and answering questions about the human condition.

Distinctions between Mental and Physical Functioning. Many American Indians, Asian Americans, Blacks, and Hispanics hold a different concept of what constitutes mental health, mental illness, and adjustment. Among the Chinese, the concept of mental health or psychological well-being is not understood in the same way as it is in the Western context. The Spanish-speaking surnamed do not make the same Western distinction between mental and physical health, argue Padilla, Ruiz, and Alvarez (1975). Thus, nonphysical health problems are most likely to be referred to a physician, priest, or minister. Third World persons operating under this orientation may enter counseling expecting counselors to treat them in the same manner that doctors or priests do. Immediate solutions and concrete tangible forms of treatment (advice, confession, consolation, and medication) are expected. For example, both authors, who are psychologists, remember the period in their lives when they entered the field of psychology. Their parents asked one question that drove home the differences in world view that various cultural groups have concerning this concept of psychology, psychological well-being, psychological adjustment, and mental health and mental illness: "How can you be called a doctor when you're not really a doctor?" This question indicates that for our parents, expectations were that doctors are medical doctors and not doctors of philosophy (Ph.D.). When our work with clients was explained as "sitting down and talking with individuals and helping them explore their thoughts and feelings," our father's response was, "Humph, they pay you for that?" Again, it was obvious that to them, this was not a legitimate form of work. After all, avoidance of morbid thoughts is the way to deal with psychological problems, not sitting down and talking about them.

Ambiguity. The ambiguous and unstructured aspect of the counseling situation may create discomfort in Third World clients. The culturally different may not be familiar with counseling and may perceive it as an unknown and mystifying process. Some groups, like Hispanics, may have been reared in an environment that actively structures social relationships and patterns of interaction. Anxiety and confusion may be the outcome in an unstructured counseling setting. The following example of a Hispanic undergoing vocational counseling illustrates this confusion:

> Maria W. was quite uncomfortable and anxious during the first interview dealing with vocational counseling. This anxiety seemed more related to ambiguity of the situation than anything else. She appeared confused about the direction of the counselor's comments and questions. At this point, the counselor felt an explanation of vocational counseling might facilitate the process.

COUNSELOR: Let me take some time to explain what we do in vocational counseling. Vocational counseling is an attempt to understand the whole person. Therefore, we are interested in your likes and dislikes, what you do well, your skills, and what they mean with respect to jobs and vocations. The first interview is usually an attempt to get to know you—especially your past experiences and reactions to different courses you've taken, jobs you've worked at, and so forth. Especially important are your goals and plans. If testing seems indicated, as in your case, you'll be asked to complete some tests. After testing we'll sit down and talk about what they mean. When we arrive at possible vocations, we'll use the vocational library and find out what these jobs require in terms of background, training, and so forth.

CLIENT: Oh! I see . . .

COUNSELOR: That's why we've been talking about your high school experiences. Sometimes the hopes and dreams can tell us much about your interests.

After this explanation, Maria participated much more in the interviews.

Patterns of Communication. The cultural upbringing of many minorities dictates different patterns of communication that may place them at a disadvantage in counseling. Counseling initially demands that communication move from client to counselor. The client is expected to take the major responsibility for initiating conversation in the session, while the counselor plays a less active role.

American Indians, Asian Americans, and Hispanics, however, function under different cultural imperatives that may make this difficult. These three groups may have been reared to respect elders and authority figures and "not to speak until spoken to." Clearly defined roles of dominance and deference are established in the traditional family. In the case of Asians, there is evidence to indicate that mental health is associated with exercising will power, avoiding unpleasant thoughts, and occupying one's mind with positive thoughts. Counseling is seen as an authoritative process in which a good counselor is more direct and active while portraying a father figure (Henkin, 1985; Mau & Jepson, 1988). A minority client who may be asked to initiate conversation may become uncomfortable and respond with only short phrases or statements. The counselor may be prone to interpret the behavior negatively, when in actuality it may be a sign of respect. We have much more to say about these communication style differences in the next chapter.

Class-Bound Values

As mentioned previously, class values are important to consider in counseling because Third World people are disproportionately represented in the lower socioeconomic classes. Traditional guidance practices that emphasize assisting the client in self-direction through the presentation of the results of assessment instruments and self-exploration via verbal interactions between client and counselor are seen as meaningful and productive. However, the values underlying these activities are permeated by middle-class ones that do not suffice for those living in poverty. We have already seen how this operates with respect to language. Bernstein (1964) has investigated the suitability of English for the lower-class poor in psychotherapy and has concluded that it works to the detriment of those individuals.

For the counselor who generally comes from a middle- to upper-class background, it is often difficult to relate to the circumstances and hardships affecting the client who lives in poverty. Lewis (1966) vividly described the phenomenon of poverty and its effects on individuals and institutions. For the individual, his/her life is characterized by low wages, unemployment, underemployment, little property ownership, no savings, and lack of food reserves. Meeting even the most basic needs of hunger and shelter is in constant day-to-day jeopardy. Pawning personal possessions and borrowing money at exorbitant interest rates only leads to greater debt. Feelings of helplessness, dependence, and inferiority are easily fostered under these circumstances. Counselors may unwittingly attribute attitudes that result from physical and environmental adversity to the cultural or individual traits of the person.

For example, note the clinical description of a 12-year-old child written by a school counselor.

> Jimmy Jones is a 12-year-old Black male student who was referred by Mrs. Peterson because of apathy, indifference, and inattentiveness to classroom activities. Other teachers have also reported that Jimmy does not pay attention, daydreams often, and frequently falls asleep during class. There is a strong possibility that Jimmy is harboring repressed rage that needs to be ventilated and dealt with. His inability to directly express his anger had led him to adopt passive aggressive means of expressing hostility, i.e., inattentiveness, daydreaming, falling asleep. It is recommended that Jimmy be seen for intensive counseling to discover the basis of the anger.

After six months of counseling, the counselor finally realized the basis of Jimmy's problems. He came from a home life of extreme poverty, where hunger, lack of sleep, and overcrowding served to severely diminish his energy level and motivation. The fatigue, passivity, and fatalism evidenced by Jimmy were more a result of poverty than some innate trait.

Likewise, Menacker (1971) points out that poverty may bring many parents to encourage children to seek employment at an early age. Delivering groceries, shining shoes, and hustling other sources of income may sap the energy of the schoolchild, leading to truancy and poor performance. Teachers and counselors may view such students as unmotivated and potential "juvenile delinquents."

Research documentation concerning the inferior and biased quality of treatment to lower-class clients is historically legend (Lerner, 1972; Lorion, 1973, 1974; Pavkav, Lewis & Lyons, 1989; Powell & Powell, 1983; Yamamoto, James, & Palley, 1968). In the area of diagnosis, it has been found that the attribution of mental illness was more likely to occur when the person's history suggested a lower-class rather than higher socioeconomic class origin. Many studies seem to demonstrate that clinicians given identical test protocols tend to make more negative prognostic statements and judgments of greater maladjustment when the individual was said to come from a lower- rather than a middle-class background.

In the area of treatment, Garfield, Weiss, and Pollack (1973) gave counselors identical descriptions (except for social class) of a 9-year-old boy who engaged in maladaptive classroom behavior. When the boy was assigned upper-class status, more counselors expressed a willingness to become ego-involved with the student than when lower-class status was assigned. Likewise, Habemann & Thiry (1970) found that doctoral-degree candidates in counseling and guidance more frequently programmed students from low socioeconomic backgrounds into a noncollege-bound track than a college-preparation one.

In an extensive research of services delivered to minorities and low socioeconomic clients, Lorion (1973) found that psychiatrists refer to therapy those persons who are most like themselves: White rather than non-White and those from upper Socioeconomic Status (SES). Lorion (1974) also points out that the expectations of lower-class clients are often different from those of psychotherapists. For example, lower-class clients who are concerned with "survival" or making it through on a day-to-day basis expect advice and suggestions from the counselor. Appointments made weeks in advance with short, weekly 50-minute contacts are not consistent with the need to seek immediate solutions. Additionally, many lower-class people, through multiple experiences with public agencies, operate under what is called "minority standard time" (Schindler-Rainman, 1967). This is the tendency of poor people to have a low regard for punctuality. Poor people have learned that endless waits are associated with medical clinics, police stations, and governmental agencies. One usually waits hours for a 10- to 15-minute appointment. Arriving promptly does little good and can be a waste of valuable time. Counselors, however, rarely understand this aspect of life and are prone to see this as a sign of indifference or hostility.

People from a lower SES may also view insight and attempts to discover underlying intraphysic problems as inappropriate. Many lower-class clients expect to receive advice or some form of concrete tangible treatment. When the counselor attempts to explore personality dynamics or to take a historical approach to the problem, the client often becomes confused, alienated, and frustrated. Abad, Ramos, and Boyce (1974) use the case of Puerto Ricans to illustrate this point. They feel the passive psychiatric approach that requires the client to talk about problems introspectively and to take initiative and responsibility for decision making is not what is expected by the Puerto-Rican client. Several writers (Menacker, 1971; Schindler-Rainman, 1967) have taken the position that poor people are best motivated by rewards that are immediate and concrete. A harsh environment, where the future is uncertain and immediate needs must be met, makes long-range planning of little value. Many lower SES clients are unable to relate to the future orientation of counseling. To be able to sit and talk about things is perceived to be a luxury of the middle and upper classes.

Because of the lower-class client's environment and past inexperience with counseling, the expectations of the minority individual may be quite different, or even negative. The client's unfamiliarity with the counseling role may hinder its success and cause the counselor to blame the failure on the client. Thus, the minority client may be perceived as hostile and resistant. The results of this interaction may be a premature termination of counseling. Ryan and Gaier (1968) conclude that students from upper socioeconomic backgrounds have significantly more exploratory interviews with their counselors. Winder and Hersko (1962) pointed out that middle-class patients tend to remain in treatment longer than lower-class patients. Furthermore, the now-classic study of Hollingstead and Redlich (1968) found that lower-class patients tend to have fewer ego-involving relationships and less intensive therapeutic relationships than members of higher socioeconomic classes.

Language Barriers

Western society is definitely a monolingual one. Use of standard English to communicate with one another may unfairly discriminate against those from a bilingual or lower-class background. Not only is this seen in our educational system, but also in the counseling relationship as well. The bilingual background of many Asian Americans (D. W. Sue & Kirk, 1972; D. W. Sue & Frank, 1973), Hispanics (Padilla et al., 1975), and American Indians (Attneave, 1972) may lead to much misunderstanding. This is true even if the Third World person cannot speak his/her own native tongue. Studies (Smith, 1957; Smith & Kasdon, 1961) indicate that simply coming from a background where one or both of the parents have spoken their native tongue can impair proper acquisition of English.

Even Blacks who come from a different cultural environment may use words and phrases (Black Language) not entirely understandable to the counselor. Smith (1973) points out that Black clients are expected to communicate their feelings and thoughts to counselors in standard English. For the ghetto student, this is a difficult task, since the use of nonstandard English is the norm. The lower-class language code involves a great deal of implicitness in communication—such as shorter sentences and less grammatical elaboration (but greater reliance on nonverbal cues). On the other hand, the language code of the middle and upper classes is much more elaborate, with less reliance on nonverbal cues, and entails greater knowledge of grammar and syntax.

Romero (1985) indicates that counseling psychologists are finding that they must interact with consumers who may have English as a second language, or who may not speak English at all. The lack of bilingual therapists and the requirement that the culturally different client communicate in English may limit the person's ability to progress in counseling and therapy. Marcos and Alpert (1976) report that if bilingual individuals do not use their native tongue in counseling, many aspects of their emotional experience may not be available for treatment. For example, because English may not be their primary language, they may have difficulties using the wide complexity of language to describe their particular thoughts, feelings, and unique situation. Clients who are limited in English tend to feel they are speaking as a child and choosing simple words to explain complex thoughts and feelings. If they were able to use their native tongue, they would easily explain themselves without the huge loss of emotional complexity and experience.

White (1984) believes that understanding Black communication styles and patterns is indispensable for counselors working in the Black community. Failure to understand imagery, analogies, and nuances of cultural sayings may render the counselor ineffective in establishing relationships and building credibility.

In counseling, heavy reliance is placed on verbal interaction to build rapport. The presupposition is that participants in a counseling dialogue are capable of understanding each other. Vontress (1971) points out how counselors oftentimes fail to understand a Black client's language and its nuances for rapport building. Furthermore, those who have not been given the same educational or economic opportunities may lack the prerequisite verbal skills to benefit from "talk therapy" (Calia, 1968).

A minority client's brief, different, or "poor" verbal responses may lead many counselors to impute inaccurate characteristics or motives to him/her. A counselee may be seen as uncooperative, sullen, negative, nonverbal, or repressed on the basis of language expression alone.

Since Western society places such a high premium on one's use of English, it is a short step to conclude that minorities are inferior, lack awareness, or lack conceptual thinking powers. Such misinterpretation can also be seen in the use and interpretation of psychological tests. So-called IQ and achievement tests are especially notorious for their language bias.

GENERALIZATIONS AND STEREOTYPES: SOME CAUTIONS

As can be seen in Table 7.1 (see Chapter 7), White cultural values are reflected in the generic characteristics of counseling (Table 2.1). These characteristics are summarized and can be compared with the values of four Third World groups: American Indians, Asian Americans, Blacks, and Hispanics (see Table 2.2). Although it is critical for counselors to have a basic understanding of counseling characteristics and Third World life values, there is the ever-present danger of overgeneralizing and stereotyping. For example, the listing of Third World group variables does not indicate that all persons coming from a minority group will share all or even some of these traits. Furthermore, emerging trends such as short-term and crisis counseling approaches and other less verbally oriented techniques differ from the generic traits listed. Yet it is highly improbable that any of us can enter a situation or encounter people without forming impressions consistent with our own experiences and values. Whether a client is dressed neatly in a suit or wears blue jeans, is a man or a woman, or of a different race will likely affect our assumptions about him/her. First impressions will be formed that fit our own interpretations and generalizations of human behavior. Generalizations are necessary for us to use; without them, we would become inefficient creatures. However, they are guidelines for our behaviors, to be tentatively applied in new situations, and they should be open to change and challenge.

It is exactly at this stage that generalizations remain generalizations or become stereotypes. *Stereotypes* may be defined as rigid preconceptions we hold about *all* people who are members of a particular group, whether it be defined along racial, religious, sexual, or other lines. The belief in a perceived characteristic of the group is applied to all members without regard for individual variations. The danger of stereotypes is that they are impervious to logic or experience. All incoming information is distorted to fit our preconceived notions. For example, people who are strongly anti-Semitic will accuse Jews of being stingy and miserly and then, in the same breath, accuse them of flaunting their wealth by conspicuous spending.

In using Tables 7.1, 2.1, and 2.2, the information should act as guidelines rather than absolutes. These generalizations should serve as the background from which the "figure" emerges. For example, belonging to a particular group may mean sharing common values and experiences. Individuals within a group, however, also differ. The background offers a contrast for us to see individual differences more clearly. It should not submerge but rather increase the visibility of the figure. This is the figure-ground relationship that should aid us in recognizing the uniqueness of people more readily.

CHAPTER 3

Cross-Cultural Communication/ Counseling Styles

Dr. Paul S, a Black professor in the counseling program, was addressing the entire graduate faculty about the need for a multicultural perspective in the department and the need to hire a Hispanic woman. Several of his White colleagues raised objections to the inclusion of more minority curriculum in the program because it would either (a) raise the number of units students would have to take to graduate, or (b) require the dropping of a course to keep units manageable. At one point, Dr. S rose from his seat, leaned forward, made eye contact with the most vocal objector, and, raising his voice, asked, "What would be wrong in doing that?" The question brought about the following exchange:

WHITE MALE PROFESSOR: *The question is not whether it's right or wrong. We need to look at your request from a broader perspective. For example, how will it affect our curriculum? Is your request educationally sound? What external constraints do we have in our ability to hire new faculty? Even if university funds are available, would it be fair to limit it to a Hispanic female? Shouldn't we be hiring the most qualified applicant rather than limiting it to a particular race or sex?*

DR. S: *[Raising his voice and pounding the table to punctuate his comments] I've heard those excuses for years and that's just what they are . . . a crock of you-know-what! This faculty doesn't sound very committed to cultural diversity at all!*

WHITE MALE PROFESSOR II: *Paul, calm down! Don't let your emotions carry you away. Let's address these issues in a rational manner.*

DR. S: *What do you mean? I'm not rational? That pisses me off! All I ever hear is we can't do this, or we can't do that! I want to know where you all are coming from. Are we going to do anything about cultural diversity? [Several faculty members on either side of Dr. S have shifted away from him. At this point, Dr. S turns to one of them and states:] Don't worry, I'm not going to hit you!*

WHITE MALE PROFESSOR: *I don't believe we should discuss this matter further, until we can control our feelings. I'm not going to sit here and be the object of anger and insults.*

DR. S: *Anger? What are you talking about? Just because I feel strongly about my convictions, you think I'm angry? All I'm asking for is how* you *stand on the issues.*

WHITE PROFESSOR: *I already have.*

DR. S: *No you haven't! You've just given me a bunch of intellectual bullshit. Where do you stand?*

WHITE PROFESSOR: *Mr. Chairman, I move we table this discussion.*

The preceding example of a Black/White interaction, witnessed by one of the authors, illustrates some very powerful and important features about cross-cultural communication styles. While we are concerned about the possibility of overgeneralization, this verbal/nonverbal exchange between a Black faculty member and several White colleagues has occurred in sufficient frequency to suggest that many Blacks and Whites have different styles of communication. Let us briefly analyze the example.

First, it is quite obvious from this exchange that the White professor perceived Dr. S to be "angry," "out of control," and "irrational." How did he arrive at that conclusion? No doubt part of it may have been the language used, but equally important were the nonverbals (raising of the voice, pounding on the table, prolonged eye contact, etc.). In a faculty meeting where White males predominate, the mode of acceptable communication is considered to be low-keyed, dispassionate, impersonal, and issue oriented. However, many Blacks not only define the issues differently, but also process them in a manner that is misunderstood by many Whites. Black styles tend to be high-keyed, animated, confrontational, and interpersonal. The differences in style of communication are not limited solely to an academic environment.

For example, in the political arena, noticeable differences can be observed between how Black and White politicians debate and communicate. When the Reverend Jesse Jackson gave the keynote address at the Democratic convention several years back, many of his supporters characterized his speech as "moving," "coming from the heart," and indicative of his "sincerity and honesty." Yet, many television commentators (mainly White newsmen) made observations that Jackson's address was like a "Baptist revival meeting," "pep rally," more "style than substance." They seemed to discredit his message because it was "too emotional."

These characterizations reveal a value judgment and possible misinterpretations occurring as a result of communication styles. Oftentimes, the presence of affect in a debate is equated with emotion (anger and hostility) and seen as counter to reason. Statements that Dr. S should calm down, not be irrational, and address the issues in an objective fashion are reflective of such an interpretation. Likewise, many Blacks may perceive White communication styles in a negative manner. Dr. S, in his attempt to find out where the White male professor was coming from, is disinclined to believe that his colleague does not have an opinion on the matter. Dealing with the issues on an intellectual level (even if the issues raised are legitimate) may be perceived as "fronting," a Black concept used to denote a person who is purposely concealing how he or she honestly feels or believes.

Second, it is very possible that differences in communication style may trigger off certain preconceived notions, stereotypes, or beliefs we may have about various minority groups. One of the most dominant White stereotypes is that of the "angry, hostile Black male who is prone to violence." Blacks are very aware of these stereotypes, as in the case of Dr. S's statement to one White colleague, "Don't worry, I'm not going to hit you!"

This example of a Black/White interaction and the misinterpretations is played out in countless everyday situations. They occur in sufficient frequency and consistency to raise the question, "Do Blacks and Whites differ not only in the content of a debate, but also in the style by which the disagreement is to be resolved?" Likewise, do different racial/ethnic groups differ in their communication styles? If they do, might not they create misunderstandings and misinterpretations of one another's behavior? What implications do communication styles have for "helping" or counseling styles? Do some counseling styles seem more appropriate and effective in working with certain racial/ethnic group members?

COMMUNICATION STYLES

In Chapter 2, we defined counseling as a process of interpersonal interaction and communication. For effective counseling to occur, both the counselor and client must be able to *send* and *receive* both *verbal* and *nonverbal* messages *accurately* and *appropriately*. In other words, counseling is a form of communication. It requires that the counselor not only *send* messages (make himself or herself understood), but also *receive* messages (attend to what is going on with the client). The definition for effective counseling also includes *verbal* (content of what is said) and *nonverbal* (how something is said) elements. Furthermore, most counselors seem more concerned with the *accuracy* of communication (let's get to the heart of the matter) rather than with whether the communication is *appropriate*. In traditional Asian culture, for example, subtlety is a highly prized art. The direct and confrontive techniques in counseling may be perceived by traditional Asian clients as "lacking in respect for the client," a "crude and rude form of communication," and "a reflection of insensitivity." In most cases, counselors have been trained to tune in to the content of what is said, rather than how something is said.

When we refer to communication style, we are addressing those factors that go beyond the content of what is said. Some communication specialists believe that only 30%–40% of what is communicated conversationally is verbal (Condon & Yousef, 1975; Ramsey & Birk, 1983). What people say and do is usually qualified by other things they say and do. A gesture, tone, inflection, posture, or eye contact may enhance or negate the content of a message. Communication styles have a tremendous impact upon our face-to-face encounters with others. Whether our conversation proceeds with fits or starts, whether we interrupt one another continually or proceed smoothly, the topics we prefer to discuss or avoid, the depth of our involvement, the forms of interaction (ritual, repartee, argumentative, persuasive, etc.) and the channel we use to communicate (verbal-nonverbal vs. nonverbal-verbal) are all aspects of communication style (Douglis, 1987; Wolfgang, 1985). Some refer to it as the "social rhythms" that underlie all our speech and actions. Communication styles are strongly correlated with race, culture, and ethnicity. Gender has also been found to be a powerful determinant of communication style (J. C. Pearson, 1985).

Reared in a White middle-class society, counselors may assume that certain behaviors or rules of speaking are universal and have the same meaning. This may create major problems for counselors and culturally different clients. Since differences in communication style are most strongly manifested in nonverbal communication, this chapter concentrates on those aspects of communication that transcend the written or spoken word. First, we explore how race/culture may influence several areas of nonverbal behavior: (a) proxemics, (b) kinesics, (c) paralanguage, and (d) high-low context communication. Second, we spend a brief time discussing the function and importance of nonverbal behavior as it relates to stereotypes and preconceived notions we may have of culturally different groups. Last, we propose a basic thesis that various racial minorities such as Asian Americans, American Indians, Blacks, and Hispanics possess a unique communication style that may have major implications for counseling. These implications suggest that certain counseling approaches (person centered, existential, rational, analytic, behavioral, etc.) may be more appropriate helping strategies for certain ethnic groups.

Nonverbal Communication

Although language, class, and cultural factors all interact to create problems in communication between the minority client and counselor, an oft-neglected area is nonverbal behavior (Harrison, 1983; Wolfgang, 1985). What a person says can either be enhanced or negated by his/her nonverbals. When a man raises his voice, tightens his facial muscles, pounds the table violently, and proclaims, "Goddamn it, I'm not angry!" he is clearly contradicting the content of the communication. If we all share the same cultural and social upbringing, we may all arrive at the same conclusion. Interpreting nonverbals, however, is made difficult for several reasons. First, the same nonverbal behavior on the part of an American Indian client may mean something quite different than if it was made by a White person. Second, nonverbals oftentimes occur outside our level of awareness. As a result, it is important that counselors begin the process of recognizing nonverbal communications and their possible cultural meanings. It is important to note that our discussion of nonverbal codes will not include all the possible nonverbal cues. Some of the areas excluded are time considerations, olfaction (taste and smell), tactile cues, and artifactual communication (clothing, hairstyle, display of material things, etc.) (Knapp, 1980; Ramsey & Birk, 1983; R. E. Pearson, 1985; Douglis, 1987).

Proxemics. The study of *proxemics* refers to perception and use of personal and interpersonal space. Clear norms exist concerning the use of physical distance in social interactions. Hall (1966) has identified four interpersonal distance zones characteristic of U.S. culture: intimate, from contact to 18 inches; personal, from 1½ feet to 4 feet; social, from 4 to 12 feet; and public (lectures and speeches), greater than 12 feet.

In this society, individuals seem to become more uncomfortable when others stand too close rather than too far away (Goldman, 1980). These feelings and reactions associated with a violation of personal space may range from flight, withdrawal, anger, and conflict (Baron & Needel, 1980; Pearson, 1985). On the other hand, we tend to allow this or move closer to people whom we like or feel interpersonal attraction for. Some evidence exists that personal space can be reframed in terms of dominance and status. Those with greater status, prestige, and power may occupy more space (larger homes, cars, or offices). However, different cultures dictate different distances in personal space. For Latin Americans, Africans, Black Americans, Indonesians, Arabs, South Americans, and French, conversing with a person dictates a much closer stance than normally comfortable for Anglos (Jensen, 1985). A Latin-American client may cause the counselor to back away because of the closeness taken. The client may interpret the counselor's behavior as indicative of aloofness, coldness, or a desire not to communicate. In some cross-cultural encounters, it may even be perceived as a sign of haughtiness and superiority. On the other hand, the counselor may misinterpret the client's behavior as an attempt to become inappropriately intimate, a sign of pushiness or aggressiveness. Both the counselor and the culturally different client may benefit from understanding that their reactions and behaviors are attempts to create the spatial dimension to which they are culturally conditioned.

Research on proxemics leads to the inevitable conclusion that conversational distances are a function of the racial and cultural background of the conversants (Susman & Rosenfeld, 1982; Wolfgang, 1985). The factor of personal space has major implications for how furniture is arranged, where the seats are located, where you seat the client, and how far you sit from him or her (Jensen, 1985; LaBarre, 1985). Latin Americans, for example, may not feel comfortable with a desk between them and the person they are speaking to. U.S. Americans, however, like to keep a desk between them and the other person. Some Eskimos may actually prefer to sit side by side rather than across from one another when talking about intimate aspects of their lives.

Kinesics. While proxemics refers to personal space, *kinesics* is the term used to refer to bodily movements. It includes such things as facial expression, posture, characteristics of movement, gestures, and eye contact. Again, kinesics appears to be culturally conditioned, with the meaning of body movements strongly linked to the culture.

Much of our counseling assessments is based upon expressions on people's faces (J. C. Pearson, 1985). We assume that facial cues express emotions and demonstrate the degree of responsiveness and/or involvement of the individual.

For example, smiling is a type of expression in our society which is believed to indicate liking or positive affect. People attribute greater positive characteristics to others who smile; they are intelligent, have a good personality, and are pleasant (Lau, 1982). However, when Japanese smile and laugh, it does not necessarily mean happiness but may convey other meanings (embarrassment, discomfort, shyness, etc.). Many Asians believe that smiling may suggest weakness.

For instance, among Asians such as the Japanese and Chinese, restraint of strong feelings (anger, irritation, sadness, and love or happiness) is considered to be a sign of maturity and wisdom. Children are taught that outward emotional expressions (facial expressions, body movements, and verbal content) are discouraged except for extreme situations (Yamamoto & Kubota, 1983). Counselors who are unenlightened may assume that their Asian-American client may be "lacking in feelings" or out of touch with them. More likely, the lack of facial expressions may be the basis of stereotypes such as the statement that Asians are "inscrutable," "sneaky," "deceptive," and "backstabbers."

A number of gestures and bodily movements have been found to have different meanings when the cultural context is considered (LaBarre, 1985). In the Sung Dynasty in China, sticking out the tongue is a gesture of mock terror and meant as ridicule; to the Ovimbundu of Africa, it means (when coupled with bending the head forward) "you're a fool"; a protruding tongue in the Mayan statues of the gods signifies wisdom; and in our own culture, the sticking out of the tongue is generally considered to be a juvenile quasi-obscene gesture of defiance, mockery, or contempt.

Head movements also have different meanings (Jensen, 1985; Eakins & Eakins, 1985). An educated Englishman may consider the lifting of the chin when conversing as a poised and polite gesture, but to U.S. Americans it may connote snobbery and arrogance ("turning up his nose"). While we shake our head from side to side to indicate "no," Mayan tribe members say "no" by jerking the head to the right.

Most Americans perceive squatting (often done by children) as improper and childish. In other parts of the world, people have learned to rest by taking a squatting position. On the other hand, when we put our feet up on a desk, it is believed to signify a relaxed and informal attitude. Yet, Latin Americans and Asians may perceive it as rudeness and arrogance, especially if the bottom of the feet is shown to them.

Shaking hands is another gesture that varies from culture to culture and may have strong cultural/historical significance. Latin Americans tend to shake hands more vigorously, frequently, and for a longer period of time. Interestingly, most cultures use the right hand when shaking. Since most of the population of the world is right-handed, this may not be surprising. However, some researchers believe that shaking with the right hand may be a symbolic act of peace, as in older times it was the right hand that generally held the weapons. In some Moslem and Asian countries, touching anyone with the left hand may be considered an obscenity (the left hand is an aid to the process of elimination or "unclean," while the right one is used for the intake of food or "clean"). Offering something with the left hand to a Moslem may be an insult of the most serious type.

Eye contact is, perhaps, the nonverbal behavior most likely to be addressed by mental health providers. It is not unusual for us to hear someone say, "notice that the husband avoided eye contact with the wife," or "notice how the client averted his/her eyes when . . ." Behind these observations is the belief that eye contact or lack of eye contact has diagnostic significance. We would agree with that premise, but in most cases, counselors attribute negative traits to the avoidance of eye contact: shy, unassertive, sneaky, or depressed.

This lack of understanding has been played out in many different situations when Black/White interactions have occurred. In many cases, it is not necessary for Blacks to look at one another in the eye at all times to communicate (Smith, 1981). A Black individual may be actively involved in doing other things when engaged in a conversation. Many White counselors may be prone to view the Black client as being sullen, resistant, or uncooperative. Smith (1981) provides an excellent example of such a clash in communication styles:

> For instance, one Black female student was sent to the office by her gymnasium teacher because the student was said to display insolent behavior. When the student was asked to give her version of the incident, she replied, "Mrs. X asked all of us to come over to the side of the pool so that she could show us how to do the backstroke. I went over with the rest of the girls. Then Mrs. X started yelling at me and said I wasn't paying attention to her because I wasn't looking directly at her. I told her I was paying attention to her (throughout the conversation, the student kept her head down, avoiding the principal's eyes), and then she said that she wanted me to face her and look her squarely in the eye like the rest of the girls

[who were all White]. So I did. The next thing I knew she was telling me to get out of the pool, that she didn't like the way I was looking at her. So that's why I'm here." (p. 155)

As this example illustrates, Black styles of communication may not only be different than their White counterparts, but may also lead to misinterpretations. Many Blacks do not nod their heads or say "uh huh" to indicate they are listening (Hall, 1976; Kochman, 1981; Smith, 1981). Going through the motions of looking at the person and nodding the head is not necessary for many Blacks to indicate that one is listening (Hall, 1976, 1974).

Statistics indicate that when White U.S. Americans listen to a speaker, they make eye contact with the speaker about 80% of the time. When speaking to others, however, they tend to look away (avoid eye contact) about 50% of the time. This is in marked contrast to many Black Americans who, when speaking, make greater eye contact and, when listening, make infrequent eye contact!

Paralanguage. The term *paralanguage* is used to refer to other vocal cues that individuals use to communicate. For example, loudness of voice, pauses, silences, hesitations, rate, inflections, and the like, all fall into this category. Paralanguage is very likely to be manifested forcefully in conversation conventions such as how we greet, address, and take turns in speaking. It can communicate a variety of different features about a person, such as age, gender, and emotional responses (Mehrabian, 1972; Mehrabian & Ferris, 1976) as well as the race and sex of the speaker (Lass, Mertz, & Kimmel, 1978).

There are complex rules regarding when to speak or yield to another person (Dublin, 1973; Jensen, 1985). For example. U.S. Americans frequently feel uncomfortable with a pause or silent stretch in the conversation, feeling obligated to fill it in with more talk. Silence is not always a sign for you, the listener, to take up the conversation. While it may be viewed negatively by many, other cultures interpret the use of silence differently. The English and Arabs use silence for privacy, while the Russians, French, and Spanish read it as agreement among the parties (Hall, 1966, 1976). In Asian culture (D.W. Sue & D. Sue, 1973), silence is traditionally a sign of respect for elders. Furthermore, silence by many Chinese and Japanese is not a floor-yielding signal inviting others to pick up the conversation. Rather, it may indicate a desire to continue speaking after making a particular point. Oftentimes silence is a sign of politeness and respect rather than a lack of desire to continue speaking.

The amount of verbal expressiveness in the United States, relative to other cultures, is quite high. Most U.S. Americans encourage their children to enter freely into conversations, and teachers encourage students to ask many questions and state their thoughts and opinions. This has led many foreigners to observe that U.S. youngsters are brash, immodest, rude, and disrespectful (Jensen, 1985). Likewise, teachers of minority children may see reticence in speaking out as a sign of ignorance, lack of motivation, or ineffective teaching when, in reality, the students may be showing proper respect (to ask questions is disrespectful because it implies that the teacher was unclear). American Indians, for example, have been taught that to speak out, ask questions, or even raise one's hand in class is an act of immodesty.

A counselor uncomfortable with silence or who misinterprets it may fill in the conversation and prevent the client from elaborating further. Even greater danger is to impute incorrect motives to the minority client's silence. One can readily see how counseling, which emphasizes talking, may place many minorities at a disadvantage.

Volume and intensity of speech in conversation are also influenced by cultural values. The overall loudness of speech displayed by many American visitors to foreign countries has earned them the reputation as being boisterous and shameless. In Asian countries, people tend to speak more softly and would interpret the loud volume of a U.S. visitor to be aggressiveness, loss of self-control, or anger. When compared to Arabs, however, people in the United States are soft-spoken. Many Arabs like to be bathed in sound, and the volume of their radios, phonographs, and televisions is quite loud. In some countries, where such entertainment units are not plentiful, it is considered a polite and thoughtful act to allow neighbors to hear by keeping the volume high. We in the United States would view such behavior as being thoughtless and an invasion of privacy.

A counselor working with culturally different clients would be well advised to be aware of possible misinterpretations as a function of speech volume. Speaking loudly may not indicate anger and hostility; and speaking in a soft voice may not be a sign of weakness, shyness, or depression.

Directness of a conversation or the degree of frankness also varies considerably among various cultural groups. Observing the English in their parliamentary debates will drive this point home. The long heritage of open, direct, and frank confrontation leads to heckling of public speakers and quite blunt and sharp exchanges. Britons believe and feel that these are acceptable styles and may take no offense at being the object of such exchanges. However, U.S. citizens feel that such exchanges are impolite, abrasive, and not rational. Relative to Asians U.S. Americans are seen as being too blunt and frank. Great care is taken by many Asians not to hurt the feelings of or embarrass the other person. As a result, use of euphemisms and ambiguity is the norm.

Since many minority groups may value indirectness, the U.S. emphasis on "getting to the point" and "not beating around the bush" may alienate others. Asian Americans, American Indians, and some Hispanics may see this behavior as immature, rude, and lacking in finesse. On the other hand, counselees from different cultures may be negatively labeled as evasive and "afraid to confront the problem."

High-Low Context Communication. Edward T. Hall, author of such classics as *The Silent Language* (1959) and *The Hidden Dimension* (1969), is a well-known anthropologist who has proposed the concept of high-low context cultures (Hall, 1976). A high-context (HC) communication or message is one that is anchored in the physical context (situation) or internalized in the person. Less reliance is placed on the explicit code or message content. A HC communication relies heavily on nonverbals and the group identification/understanding shared by those communicating. For example, a normal-stressed "no" by a U.S. American may be interpreted by an Arab as "yes." A real negation in Arab culture would be stressed much more emphatically. In Filipino culture, a mild, hesitant "yes" is interpreted as a polite refusal. In traditional Asian society, to extend an invitation only once for dinner would be considered an affront, because it implies you are not sincere. One must extend an invitation several times encouraging the invitee to accept. Arabs may refuse an offer of food several times before giving in. However, most of us believe that a host's offer can be politely refused with just a "no, thank you."

If we pay attention to just the explicit coded part of the message, we are likely to misunderstand the communication. According to Hall (1976) low-context (LC) cultures place a greater reliance on the verbal part of the message. In addition, LC cultures have been associated with being more opportunistic, more individual rather than group oriented, and as emphasizing rules of law and procedure (Smith, 1981).

It appears that the United States is a LC culture (although it is still higher than the Swiss, Germans, and Scandinavians in the amount of contexting required). China, perhaps, represents the other end of the continuum where its complex culture relies heavily on context. Asian Americans, Blacks, Hispanics, American Indians, and other minority groups in the United States also emphasize HC cues.

HC communication, in contrast to LC, is faster, as well as more economical, efficient, and satisfying. Because it is so bound to the culture, it is slow to change and tends to be cohesive and unifying. LC communication does not unify but changes rapidly and easily.

Hall (1976) gives the example of how twins who have grown up together can and do communicate more economically (HC) than two lawyers during a trial (LC). Bernstein's (1964) work in language analysis refers to restricted codes (HC) and elaborated codes (LC). Restricted codes are observed in families where words and sentences collapse and are shortened without loss of meaning. However, elaborated codes, where many words are used to communicate the same content, are seen in classrooms, diplomacy, and law.

Black culture has been described as HC. For example, it is clear that many Blacks require fewer words than their White counterparts to communicate the same content (Jenkins, 1982; Stanback & Pearce, 1985; Weber, 1985). A Black male who enters a room and spots an attractive, "fine-looking lady" may stoop slightly in her direction, smile, and may tap the table twice while vocalizing a long drawn out "uh huh." What he has communicated would require many words from his White brother to convey the same message! The fact that Blacks may communicate more by HC cues has led many to characterize them as nonverbal, inarticulate, unintelligent, and so forth.

Another example of how HC and LC orientations may lead to misunderstandings was a recent situation that occurred during a cross-cultural communications conference. Social scientists from Asia, the Pacific, and the mainland United States were invited to attend a conference in Hawaii. It was run very much like most typical sessions. All invitees were to present an original piece of research (45 minutes) on cross-cultural communications, and then a respondent would react to it (10 minutes.) Contrasting communication styles became immediately apparent. If the presenters were Asian, they would go through an elaborate ritual of expressing gratitude for being invited, derogating the self, praising those in the audience, and so forth. With slight variations, this behavior occurred consistently whether the Asian person was a presenter or respondent. If the latter, the person would apologize for his/her naiveté, praise the paper, and spend only a short time critiquing it. When the presenter or respondent was someone from the U.S. mainland, the White researcher would attend directly to the task. Critiques were direct and to the point.

During mealtimes, many of the participants from the mainland would indicate that their Asian counterparts did not seem to realize the weaknesses in some of their colleagues' research papers. On the other hand, many of the Asian participants expressed reluctance to continue because the "Americans" were too blunt in their remarks. As a result, they could be shamed in public and "lose face." They did not want to continue with the conference if the respondent to their paper was from the U.S. mainland. Such reactions were due in large part to the HC-LC differences among participants. The LC participant relied heavily on the explicit code (written and spoken word) as the main means to convey thoughts, ideas, and feelings. The HC participant relied on implicit aspects of the communication. For example, many of the White conferees saw the Asian critiques as "wishy-washy" and lacking in critical analysis. They did not understand that the praises heaped on the person were more form than substance.

The key to understanding the basis of the Asian critiques was not in the words used, but in other factors such as (a) the amount of time used to praise the paper, (b) the amount of time spent to derogate the self, (c) the descriptors used, and (d) the questions that were asked at the end. A response such as "I would only ask Dr. Yamamoto two questions. First, how did he decide to use the particular research methodology, and second, how did he select the population to be researched." Those in the audience who understood the context (HC) knew that the questions indicated (a) the wrong methodology was used, and (b) the population was an unrepresentative one. These examples indicate how important it is for the counselor to understand racial/cultural communication styles.

SOCIOPOLITICAL FACETS OF NONVERBAL COMMUNICATION

There is a common saying among Black Americans, "If you really want to know what White folks are thinking and feeling, don't listen to what they say, but how they say it." In most cases, such a statement refers to the biases, stereotypes, and racist attitudes that Whites are believed to possess, but that they consciously or unconsciously conceal.

Rightly or wrongly, many minority individuals through years of personal experience operate from three assumptions. The first assumption is that all Whites in this society are racist. Through their own cultural conditioning, they have been socialized into a culture that espouses the superiority of White culture over all others (Helms, 1984; Katz, 1985; Ponterotto, 1988; Subnani, Ponterotto & Borodovsky, in press). The second assumption is that most Whites find such a concept disturbing and will go to great lengths to deny that they are racist or biased. Some of this is done deliberately and with awareness, but in most cases one's racism is largely unconscious. The last of these assumptions is that nonverbal behaviors are more accurate reflections of what a White person is thinking or feeling than "what they say."

There is considerable evidence to suggest that these three assumptions held by various racial/ethnic minorities are, indeed, accurate. Counselors and mental health practitioners need to be very cognizant of nonverbal cues from a number of different perspectives.

In the last section, we discussed how nonverbal behavior is culture-bound, and that the counselor cannot make universal interpretations about it. Likewise, nonverbal cues are important because they often (a) unconsciously reflect our biases, and (b) trigger off stereotypes we have of other people.

Nonverbals as Reflections of Bias

Some time back, a TV program called "Candid Camera" was the rage of the U.S. audiences. It operated from a unique premise, which involved creating very unusual situations for naive subjects who were then filmed as they reacted to them. One of these experiments involved interviewing housewives about their attitudes toward Black, Hispanic, and White teenagers. The intent was to select a group of women who, by all standards, appeared sincere in their beliefs that Blacks and Hispanics were no more prone to violence than their White counterparts. Unknown to them, they were filmed by a hidden camera as they left their homes to go shopping at the local supermarket.

The creator of the program had secretly arranged for a Black, Hispanic, and White youngster (dressed casually but nearly identically) to pass these women on the street. The experiment was counterbalanced; that is, the race of the youngster was randomly assigned as to which would approach the shopper first. What occurred was a powerful statement on unconscious racist attitudes and beliefs.

All the youngsters had been instructed to pass the shopper on the purse side of the street. If the woman was holding the purse in her right hand, the youngster would approach and pass on her right. If the purse was held with the left hand, the youngster would pass on her left. Studies of the film revealed consistent outcomes. Many women when approached by the Black or Hispanic youngster (approximately 15 feet away) would casually switch the purse from one arm to the other! This was an infrequent occurrence with the White subject. Why?

The answer appears quite obvious to us. The women subjects who switched their purses were operating from biases, stereotypes, and preconceived notions about what minority youngsters are like: they are prone to crime, more apt to snatch a purse or rob, more apt to be juvenile delinquents, and more likely to engage in violence. The disturbing part of this experiment was that the selected subjects were, by all measures, sincere individuals who on a conscious level denied harboring racist attitudes or beliefs. They were not liars, nor were they deliberately deceiving the interviewer. They were normal, everyday people. They honestly believed that they did not possess these biases, yet when tested, their nonverbal behavior (purse switching) gave them away.

The power of nonverbal communication is that it tends to be least under conscious control. Studies support the conclusion that nonverbal cues operate primarily on an unawareness level (Argyle, 1975; Wolfgang, 1985), that they tend to be more spontaneous and difficult to censor or falsify (Mehrabian, 1972), and that they are more trusted than words. In our society, we have learned to use words (spoken or written) to mask or conceal our true thoughts and feelings. Note how our politicians and lawyers are able to address an issue without revealing much of what they think or believe. This is very evident in controversial issues such as gun control, abortion, and issues of affirmative action.

Nonverbal behavior provides clues to conscious deceptions and/or unconscious bias. There is evidence that the accuracy of nonverbal communication varies with the part of the body used: facial expression is more controllable than the hands, followed by the legs and the rest of the body (Hansen et al., 1982). The implications for cross-cultural counseling are obvious. A counselor who has not adequately dealt with his or her own biases and racist attitudes may unwittingly communicate them to his or her culturally different client.

Minority clients will often "test the counselor" through a series of challenges. Many of these challenges are aimed at getting the counselor to self-disclose. The intent is to ascertain the counselor's level not only of expertness, but of trustworthiness as well. "How open and honest are you about your own racism and will you allow it to interfere with our relationship?" The minority client, in an attempt to seek an answer to the question, will create situations aimed at getting the counselor to reveal himself or herself. Some very common verbal tests are posed in questions like, "How can you possibly understand the minority experience? Have you ever laughed at racist jokes? How do you feel about interracial relationships? Are you a racist? Do you really care what happens to Blacks (Hispanics, etc.)?" How you answer the challenge (verbal and nonverbal) will either enhance or diminish your credibility.

If counselors are unaware of their own biases, the nonverbals are most likely to reveal their true feelings. Studies suggest that women and minorities are better readers of nonverbal cues than White males (Hall, 1976; Jenkins, 1982; J. C. Pearson, 1985; Weber, 1985). Much of this may be due to their HC orientation, but another reason may be *survival*. For a Black person to survive in a predominantly White society, he or she has to rely on nonverbal cues more often than verbal ones.

One of our male Black colleagues gives the example of how he must constantly be vigilant when traveling in an unknown part of the country. Just to stop at a roadside restaurant may be dangerous to his physical well-being. As a result, when entering a diner, he is quick to observe not only the reactions of the staff (waiter/waitress, cashier, cooks, etc.) to his entrance, but the reactions of the patrons as well. Do they stare at him? What type of facial expressions do they have? Do they fall silent? Does he get served immediately or is there an inordinate delay? These nonverbal cues reveal much about the environment around him. He may choose to be himself or play the role of a "humble" Black person who leaves quickly if the situation poses danger.

Interestingly, this very same colleague talks about tuning in to nonverbal cues as a means of *psychological survival*. He believes it is important for minorities to accurately read where people are coming from in order to prevent invalidation of the self. For example, a minority person driving through an unfamiliar part of the country may find himself or herself forced to stay at a motel overnight. Seeing a vacancy light flashing, the person may stop and knock on the manager's door. Upon opening the door and seeing the Black person, the White manager may show hesitation, stumble around in his/her verbalizations, and then apologize for having forgotten to turn off the vacancy light. The Black person is faced with the dilemma of deciding whether the White manager was telling the truth or is simply not willing to rent to a Black.

Some of you might ask, "Why is it important for you to know? Why don't you simply find someplace else? After all, would you stay at a place where you were unwelcome?" Finding another place to stay might not be as important as the psychological well-being of the minority person. Minorities have encountered too many situations in which double messages are given to them. For the Black individual to accept the simple statement, "I forgot to turn off the no-vacancy light" may be to deny one's own true feelings at being the victim of discrimination. This is especially true when the nonverbals (facial expression, anxiety in voice, and stammering) may reveal other reasons.

Too often minorities are placed in situations where they are asked to deny their true feelings in order to perpetuate *White deception.* Statements that minorities are oversensitive (paranoid?) may represent a form of denial. When a minority colleague makes a statement such as "I get a strange feeling from John," I feel some bias against minorities coming out," White colleagues, friends, and others are sometimes too quick to dismiss it with statements like "You're being oversensitive." Perhaps a better approach would be to say, "What makes you feel that way?" rather than to negate or invalidate what might be an accurate appraisal of nonverbal communication.

Thus, it is clear that minorities are very tuned in to nonverbals. For the counselor who has not adequately dealt with his or her own racism, the minority client will be quick to assess such biases. In many cases, the minority client may believe that the biases are too great to be overcome and will simply not continue in counseling. This is despite the good intentions of the White counselor who is not in touch with his/her own biases and assumptions about human behavior.

Nonverbals as Triggers to Our Biases/Fears

Oftentimes people assume that being an effective cross-cultural counselor is a straightforward process that involves the acquisition of knowledge about the various racial/ethnic groups. If we know that Asian Americans and Blacks have different patterns of eye contact than their White counterparts and if we know that these patterns signify different things, then we should be able to eliminate biases and stereotypes that we possess. Were it so easy, we might have eradicated racism years ago. While increasing our knowledge base about the lifestyles and experiences of minority groups is important, it is not a sufficient condition in itself. Our racist attitudes, beliefs, and feelings are deeply ingrained in our total being. Through years of conditioning they have acquired a strong irrational base, replete with emotional symbolisms about each particular minority. Simply opening a text and reading about Blacks and Hispanics will not deal with our deep-seated fears and biases.

Let us return to the example of Black/White interactions given at the beginning of the chapter to illustrate our point. Recall that many of the White faculty members believed that their Black colleague was "out of control," "too emotional," "irrational," "angry," and that the meeting should be terminated until such time that the topic could be addressed in an objective manner. On the other hand, the Black faculty member denied being angry and believed that the White faculty members were "fronting," deliberately concealing their true thoughts and feelings. Much of the confusion seemed linked to a difference in communication styles, and how these differences trigger off fears and biases we may possess.

One of the major barriers to effective understanding is the common assumption that different cultural groups operate according to identical speech and communication conventions. In the United States, it is often assumed that distinctive racial, cultural, and linguistic features are deviant, inferior, or embarrassing (Kochman, 1981; Stanback & Pearce, 1985). These value judgments then become tinged with beliefs we hold about Black people (Smith, 1981): racial inferiority, being prone to violence and crime, quick to anger, and a threat to White folks (Weber, 1985). The communication style of Black folks (manifested in nonverbals) can often trigger off these fears. We submit that the situation presented at the beginning of the chapter represents just such an example.

Black styles of communication are often high-keyed, animated, heated, interpersonal, and confrontational. Much emotion, affect, and feelings are generated (Hall, 1976; Weber, 1985). In a debate, Blacks tend to act as advocates of a position, and ideas are to be tested in the crucible of argument (Kochman, 1981). White middle-class styles, however, are characterized by being detached and objective, impersonal and nonchallenging. The person acts not as an *advocate* of the idea, but as a *spokesperson* (truth resides in the idea). A discussion of issues should be devoid of affect, because emotion and reason work against one another. One should talk things out in a logical fashion without getting personally involved. Blacks equate their own style of communication as indicating that the person is sincere and honest, while Whites equate their own style as reasoned and objective.

Many Blacks readily admit that they operate from a point of view and, as mentioned previously, are disinclined to believe that White folks do not. Smith (1981) aptly describes the Black orientation in the following passage:

> When one Black person talks privately with another, he or she might say: "Look, we don't have to jive each other or be like White folks; let's be honest with one another." These statements reflect the familiar Black saying that "talk is cheap," that actions speak louder than words, and that Whites beguile each other with words . . . In contrast, the White mind symbolizes to many Black people deceit, verbal chicanery, and sterile intellectivity. For example, after long discourse with a White person, a Black individual might say: "I've heard what you've said, but what do you really mean?" (p. 154)

Such was the case with the Black professor, who believed his White colleagues were "fronting" and being insincere.

While Blacks may misinterpret White communication styles, it is more likely that Whites will misinterpret Black styles. The direction of the misunderstanding is generally linked to the activating of unconscious "triggers" or "buttons" about racist stereotypes and fears they harbor. As we have repeatedly emphasized, one of the dominant stereotypes of Blacks in our society is that of the hostile, angry, prone-to-violence Black male. The more animated and affective communication style, closer conversing distance, prolonged eye contact when speaking, greater bodily movements, and the tendency to test ideas in a confrontational/argumentative format, lead many Whites to believe "their lives are in danger." It is not unusual for White mental health practitioners to describe their Black clients as being "hostile and angry." We have also observed White trainees who work with Black clients, nonverbally respond in such a manner as to indicate anxiety, discomfort, or fear (leaning away from their Black clients, tipping their chairs back, crossing their legs or arms, etc.) These are nonverbal distancing moves that may reflect the unconscious stereotypes they hold of Black Americans. While we would entertain the possibility that a Black client is angry, most occasions we have observed do not justify such a descriptor.

It appears that many Whites operate from the assumption that when an argument ensues, it may lead to a ventilation of anger with the outbreak of a subsequent fight. When the Black professor was told to "calm down," such may have been the fear of the White colleague. When the Black professor stated, "Don't worry, I'm not going to hit you!" it was obvious he knew what was going on in the head of his White colleague. What many Whites fail to realize is that Blacks distinguish between an argument used to debate a difference of opinion and one that ventilates anger and hostility (Kochman, 1981). In the former, the affect indicates sincerity and seriousness, there is a positive attitude toward the material, and the validity of ideas is challenged. In the latter, the affect is more passionate than sincere, there is a negative attitude toward the opponent, and the opponent is abused.

To understand Black styles of communication and to adequately relate to Black communication would require much study in the origins, functions, and manifestations of Black language (Jenkins, 1982). Weber (1985) believes that the historical and philosophical foundations of Black language have led to several verbal styles among Blacks. "Rappin," not the White usage (rap session), was originally a dialogue between a man and a woman where the intent was to win over the admiration of the woman. Imaginary statements, rhythmic speech, and creativity are aimed at generating interest in the woman for hearing more of the rap. It has been likened to a mating call, an introduction of the male to the female, and a ritual expected by many Black women.

Another style of verbal banter is called "woofing," which is an exchange of threats and challenges to fight. It may have derived from what Blacks refer to as "playing the dozens," which is the highest form of verbal warfare and impromptu speaking considered by many Blacks (Jenkins, 1983; Kochman, 1981; Weber, 1985). To the outsider, it may appear cruel, harsh, and provocative. Yet, to many in the Black community, it has historical and functional meanings. The term "dozens" was used during slavery by slavers to refer to Black persons with disabilities. Because he/she was "damaged goods," a disabled Black person would often be sold at a discount rate with eleven (one dozen) other "damaged slaves" (Weber, 1985). It was primarily a selling ploy where "dozens" referred to the negative physical features. Often played in jest, the game requires an audience to act as judge and jury over the originality, creativity, and humor of the combatants.

> Say man, your girlfriend so ugly, she had to sneak up on a glass to get a drink of water.
> Man, you so ugly, yo mamma had to put a sheet over your head so sleep could sneak up on you (Weber, 1985, p. 248).

> A: Eat shit.
> B: What should I do with your bones?
> A: Build a cage for your mother.
> B: At least I got one.
> A: She *is* the least. *(Labor, 1972, p. 321)*

> A: Got a match?
> B: Yeah, my ass and your face or my farts and your breath.
> (Kochman, 1981, p. 54)

Woofing and playing the dozens seem to have very real functional value. First, it allows training in self-control about managing one's anger and hostility in the constant face of racism. In many situations, it would be considered dangerous by a Black person to respond to taunts, threats, and insults. Second, woofing also allows a Black person to establish a hierarchy or pecking order without resorting to violence. Last, it can create an image of being fearless where one will gain respect.

This verbal and nonverbal style of communication has become a major aspect of Black interactions. Likewise, other minority groups have characteristic styles that may cause considerable difficulties for White counselors. One way of contrasting communication style differences may be in the overt activity dimension (the pacing/intensity) of nonverbal communication. Table 3.1 contrasts five different groups along this continuum. How these styles affect the counselor's perception and ability to work with culturally different clients is important for each and every one of us to consider.

COUNSELING AS COMMUNICATION STYLE

Throughout this text, we have repeatedly emphasized that counseling may be perceived as a process of interpersonal interaction and communication. As a result, it is not difficult to assume that *different* theories of counseling and psychotherapy represent *different* communication styles. There is considerable research support for this statement. The *Three Approaches to Psychotherapy* (Shostrom, 1966) and the *Three Approaches to Psychotherapy: II* (Shostrom, 1977) film series, which features Carl Rogers, Fritz Perls, and Albert Ellis in the former, and Rogers, Everett Shostrom, and Arnold Lazarus in the latter, has been the subject of much analysis. In

TABLE 3.1

Communication Style Differences (Overt Activity Dimension—Nonverbal/
Verbal)

American Indians	Asian Americans—Hispanics	Whites	Blacks
1. Speak softly/ slower	1. Speak softly	1. Speak loud/fast to control listener	1. Speak with affect
2. Indirect gaze when listening or speaking	2. Avoidance of eye contact when listening or speaking to high-status persons	2. Greater eye contact when listening	2. Direct eye contact (prolonged) when speaking, but less when listening
3. Interject less/ seldom offer encouraging communication	3. Similar rules	3. Head nods, non-verbal markers	3. Interrupt (turn taking) when can
4. Delayed auditory (silence)	4. Mild delay	4. Quick responding	4. Quicker responding
5. Manner of expression low-keyed, indirect	5. Low-keyed, indirect	5. Objective, task oriented	5. Affective, emotional, interpersonal

most cases, the studies have focused upon the first film and tried to identify differences in verbal response categories among the counselors (Hill, Thomas, & Rardin, 1979; Lee & Uhlemann, 1984; Weinrach, 1986, 1987), examined consistency and stability of the theorist (Dolliver, Williams, & Gold, 1980; Edwards, Boulet, Mahrer, Chagnon, & Mook, 1982; Weinrach, 1987), and compared perceived expertness, trustworthiness, and attractiveness of the sample counselors (Lee, Uhlemann, & Hasse, 1985; Uhlemann, Lee, & Hett, 1984). Some analyses have also been applied to the comparison of Rogers, Shostrom, and Lazarus as well (Meara, Pepinsky, Shannon, & Murray, 1981; Meara, Shannon, & Pepinsky, 1979; O'dell & Bhamer, 1981).

While internal consistency of the therapists has been questioned in several cases (Dolliver et al., 1980; Weinrach, 1987), some general conclusions may be tentatively drawn from all of these studies. Each theoretical orientation (Rogers, Person-Centered Counseling; Perls, Existential Counseling; Ellis, Rational-Emotive Counseling; Shostrom, Actualizing Therapy; and Lazarus, Multimodal Therapy) can be distinguished from the others, and the counseling styles/skills exhibited seem to be highly correlated with their theoretical orientation. For example, Rogers' style seemed to emphasize attending skills (encouragement to talk—minimal encouragers, nonverbal markers, paraphrasing, and reflecting feelings), Shostrom relied on direct guidance, providing information, and so forth, while Lazarus took an active, reeducative style. One study, for example, found that Rogers used minimal encouragers 53% of the time; restatements 11% of the time; interpretation, reflection, and information each 7% of the time (Hill et al., 1979). These results are highly consistent with person-centered counseling.

Rogers (1980) believes that clients have the innate capacity to advance and grow on their own. The reason they encounter problems in life is that significant others impose conditions of worth upon them. The result is that individuals try to live up to others' expectations, standards, and values while denying their innate actualizing tendency. Rogers' writings suggest his strong belief that people have the capacity to self-correct or grow in a positive direction if left on their own. It is almost like each and every one of us possesses a genetic blueprint. Counselors must avoid imposing conditions of worth upon their clients; avoid telling them what to do or how to solve problems; and avoid imposing their definition of the problem on them. Rather, counselors need to provide a nurturing and nutritious environment for their clients, accept them for what they are, and provide them with a way to view themselves (a mirror) as they are, and as they were meant to be. In this manner, clients will actively begin to change on their own.

The person-centered philosophy would be expected to be evident in the types of skills exhibited by the helping professional. For example, using Ivey's microcounseling language (Ivey et al., 1987) one would clearly see that Rogers would use primarily attending skills (minimal encouragers, paraphrasing, reflection of feelings, summarization, etc.) over influencing skills (giving advice and direction, expressing content/teaching, expressing feelings on the part of the counselor, and interpreting). Attending skills are person centered and provide a way for the client to see himself or herself. It is highly consistent with Rogerian philosophy. Influencing skills are active attempts to direct the client, and are considered counterproductive in counseling, because their use may be imposing conditions of worth—the precise dynamics which have led the client to suffer difficulties. Likewise, we see that if a theory assumes that the basis of problems resides in cognitions (irrational thoughts and processes), as does the rational-emotive approach, then the counselor would take a more active approach to directly attack the basis of the belief system and to teach the client new ways of thinking. Influencing skills would be highly used and, indeed, analysis of Ellis' style confirms this impression.

In the next chapter, we provide a strong rationale supported by research indicating that counselors who are perceived by their clients as expert, trustworthy, and attractive are more influential than those who are perceived to possess lower levels of these attributes. One question we have entertained is to what extent are these categories a function of the different counseling styles used by counselors? Limited studies have been conducted to address this question. Those that exist provide some support for the statement that differential verbal and nonverbal behavior affects percep-tions of expertness, trustworthiness, and attractiveness (Merluzzi, Banikiotes, & Missbach, 1978; Murphy & Strong, 1972; Uhlemann et al., 1984). For example, it was found that expertness was consistently the lowest for Rogers and the highest for Ellis and Lazarus in the previously mentioned film series.

Differential Skills in Cross-Cultural Counseling

Just as race, culture, ethnicity, and gender may affect communication styles, considerable support exists that theoretical orientations in counseling will likewise influence helping styles as well. D. W. Sue (1977, 1981) makes a strong case that different cultural groups may be more receptive to certain counseling/communication styles because of cultural and sociopolitical factors. And, indeed, the literature on cross-cultural counseling/ therapy strongly suggests that American Indians, Asian Americans, Black Americans, and Hispanic Americans tend to prefer more active-directive forms of helping than nondirective ones (Pedersen, Draguns, Lonner, & Trimble, 1981; Ruiz & Ruiz, 1983; D.W. Sue, 1981; Trimble, 1981; Vontress, 1981). Some actual studies of minority-group preference for helping styles support these assertions (Atkinson et al., 1978; Dauphinais et al., 1981; Peoples & Dell, 1975). We briefly describe two of these here to give the reader some idea of their implications.

Asian-American clients who may value restraint of strong feelings and believe that intimate revelations are to be shared only with close friends may cause problems for the counselor who is oriented toward "insight" or "feelings." It is entirely possible that such techniques as reflection of feelings, asking questions of a deeply personal nature, and making depth interpretations may be perceived as lacking in respect for the client's integrity. The process of insight into underlying processes may not be valued by an Asian-American client. For example, some clients who come for vocational information may be perceived by counselors as needing help in finding out what motivates their actions and decisions. Requests for advice or information from the client are seen as indicative of deeper, more personal conflicts. Although this might be true in some cases, the blind application of techniques that clash with cultural values seriously places many Asian Americans in an uncomfortable and oppressed position. Atkinson, Maruyama, and Matsui (1978) tested this hypothesis with a number of Asian-American students. Two tape recordings of a contrived counseling session were prepared in which the client's responses were identical, but the counselor's responses differed, being directive in one and nondirective in the other. Their findings indicated that counselors who use the directive approach were rated more credible and approachable than those using the nondirective counseling approach. Asian Americans seem to prefer a logical, rational, structured counseling approach over an affective, reflective, and ambiguous one. Similar conclusions have been drawn by other researchers as well (see the excellent review by Leong, 1986).

In another important study, Berman (1979) found similar results with a Black population. The weakness of the previous study was that there was failure to compare equal responses with a White population. Berman's study compared the use of counseling skills between Black and White male and female counselors. A videotape of culturally varied client vignettes was viewed by Black and White counselor trainees. They responded to the question, "What would you say to this person?" The data was scored and coded according to a microcounseling taxonomy that divided counseling skills into attending and influencing ones. The hypothesis made by the investigator was that Black and White counselors would give significantly different patterns of responses to their clients. Data supported the hypothesis. Black males and females tended to use the more active expressive skills (directions, expression of content, and interpretation) with greater frequency than their White counterparts. White males and females tended to use a higher percentage of attending skills. Berman concluded that the person's race/culture appears to be a major factor in the counselor's choice of skills, that Black and White counselors appear to adhere to a distinctive style of counseling. Berman (1979) concludes that the more active styles of the Black counselor tend to include practical advice and allow for the introjection of a counselor's values and opinions.

The implications for counseling become glaringly apparent. Mental health training programs tend to emphasize the more passive attending skills. Counselors so trained may be ill equipped to work with culturally different clients who might find the active approach more relevant to their own needs and values.

Implications for Cross-Cultural Counseling

Ivey's work (1981, 1986) in the field of microcounseling, cross-cultural counseling, and developmental counseling seems central to our understanding of counseling/communication styles. He believes that different theories are concerned with generating different sentences and constructs, and that different cultures may also be expected to generate different sentences and constructs. Counseling and psychotherapy may be viewed as special types of temporary cultures. When the counseling style of the counselor does not match the communication style of the culturally different client, many difficulties may arise: premature termination of the session, inability to establish rapport and/or cultural oppression of the client. Thus, it becomes clear that effective cross-cultural counseling occurs when the counselor and client are able to appropriately and accurately send and receive both verbal and nonverbal messages. When the counselor is able to engage in such activities, his or her credibility and attractiveness will be increased (see Chapter 4). Communication styles manifested in the counseling context may either enhance or negate the effectiveness of cross-cultural counseling. It appears that several major implications for counseling can be discerned.

Counseling Practice. As practicing counselors who work with a culturally diverse population, we need to move decisively in educating ourselves as to the differential meanings of nonverbal behavior, and the broader implications for communication styles. We need to realize that proxemics, kinesics, paralanguage, and high-low context factors are important elements of communication; that they may be highly culture-bound; and that we should guard against possible misinterpretation in our assessment of culturally different clients. Likewise, it is important that we begin to become aware of and understand our own communication/helping style: What is my counseling/communication style? What does it say about my values, biases, and assumptions about human behavior? How do my nonverbals reflect stereotypes, fears, or preconceived notions about various racial groups? What nonverbal messages might I not be aware of but might be communicating to my client? In what way does my helping style hinder my ability to work effectively with a culturally different client? What culturally/racially-influenced communication styles cause me greatest difficulty or discomfort? Why?

Ivey (1981; 1986) contends that counselors need to be able to shift their counseling styles to meet the developmental needs of clients. We contend further that effective counselors are those who can also shift their helping styles to meet the cultural dimensions of their clients. Ivey's work reveals that counselors of differing theoretical orientations will tend to use different skill patterns. These skill patterns may be antagonistic or inappropriate to the communication/helping styles of culturally different clients. In previously cited research, it was clear that White counselors (by virtue of their cultural conditioning and training) tended to use the more passive attending and listening skills in counseling, while non-White populations appear more oriented toward an active influencing approach. There are several reasons why this may be the case.

First, it is our contention that the use of more directive, active, and influencing skills is more likely to provide personal information about where the counselor is coming from. Giving advice or suggestions, interpreting, and telling the client how you, the counselor, feel are really acts of counselor self-disclosure. While the use of attending or more nondirective skills may also self-disclose, it tends to be minimal relative to using influencing skills. In cross-cultural counseling, the culturally different client is likely to approach the counselor with trepidation: "What makes you any different from all the Whites out there who have oppressed me?" "What makes you immune from inheriting the racial biases of your forebears?" "Before I open up to you (self-disclose), I want to know where you are coming from." "How open and honest are you about your own racism and will it interfere with our relationship?" "Can you really understand what it's like to be Asian, Black, Hispanic, American Indian, or the like?" In other words, a culturally different client may not open up (self-disclose) until you, the counselor, self-disclose first. Thus, to many minority clients, a counselor who expresses his/her thoughts and feelings may be better received in a counseling situation.

Second, the more positive response by minorities to the use of influencing skills appears related to diagnostic focus. In Chapter 7, we propose the concept of locus of responsibility. Studies support the thesis that White counselors are more likely to focus their problem diagnosis in individual, rather than societal, terms (Berman, 1979; Nwachuku & Ivey, in press).

In a society where individualism prevails, it is not surprising to find that White counselors tend to view their client's problems as residing within the individual rather than society. Thus, the role of the counselor will be person focused because the problem resides within the individual. Skills utilized will be individual centered (attending) aimed at changing the person. Many minorities accept the importance of individual contributions to the problem, but they also give great weight to system or societal factors that may adversely impact their lives. Minorities who have been the victims of discrimination and oppression perceive that the problem resides externally to the person (societal forces). Active systems intervention is called for, and the most appropriate way to attack the environment (stressors) would be an active approach. If the counselor shares their perception, he or she may take a more active role in the sessions, giving advice and suggestions, as well as teaching strategies (becoming a partner to the client).

Unfortunately, our counselor-training programs are very deficient in teaching counselors the appropriate influencing skills needed for effective cross-cultural counseling. Much of this resides in a philosophical belief that clients should solve problems on their own, that they are ultimately responsible for the outcomes in their lives, and that counselors who dispense advice/suggestions and disclose their thoughts or feelings are adversely influencing their clients or fostering "dependency." As one minority client said to us, "I'm not that weak, stupid, or fragile that what advice you give to me will be unquestioningly accepted."

Finally, what Ivey (1986) calls "style-shift counseling" may have personal limitations. We cannot be all things to everyone. That is, there are personal limits to how much we can change our communication styles to match those of our culturally different clients. The difficulty in shifting styles may be a function of inadequate practice, inability to understand the other person's world view, and/or personal biases or racist attitudes that have not been adequately resolved. In these cases, the counselor might consider several alternatives: (1) seek additional training/education, (2) seek consultation with a more experienced counselor, (3) consider the possibility of referring the client to another counselor, and (4) become aware of personal communication style limitations and try to anticipate their possible impact upon the culturally different client. Oftentimes, a counselor who is able to recognize the limitations of his/her helping style, and knows how it will impact the culturally different client can take steps to minimize possible conflicts. Interestingly, one of the authors has been involved in a study (Yao, Sue, & Hayden, in progress) which found that once rapport and a working relationship are established with a minority client, the counselor may have greater freedom in using a helping style quite different from that of the client. The crucial element appears to be the counselor's ability to acknowledge limitations in his/her helping style, and to anticipate the negative impact it may have on the culturally different client. In this way, the counselor may be saying to the client, "I understand your world view, and I know that what I do or say will appear very Western to you, but I'm limited in my communication style. I may or may not understand where you're coming from, but let's give it a try." For some minority clients, this form of communication may be enough to begin the process of bridging the communication-style gap.

Implications for Training and Research. With respect to training, counselor education programs need to do several things. First and most important is the recognition that no one style of counseling will be appropriate for all populations and situations. A program that is primarily psychoanalytically oriented, cognitively oriented, existentially oriented, person-centered oriented, or behaviorally oriented may be doing a great disservice to their trainees. The goals and processes espoused by the theories may not be those held by culturally different groups. The theories tend to be not only culture-bound, but also narrow in how they conceptualize the human condition. In an analysis of the previously mentioned film series (*Three Approaches to Psychotherapy*, Shostrom, 1966), Meara, Shannon, and Pepinsky (1979) concluded that Rogers taught his client her "feeling self"; Perls taught her to be her "fighting self"; and Ellis taught her to be her "thinking" self.

Each school of counseling has strengths, but they may be one-dimensional; they concentrate only on feelings, or only on cognitions, or only on behaviors. We need to realize that we are *feeling, thinking, behaving, social, cultural* and *political* beings. What we are advocating in training programs is an approach that calls for openness and flexibility both in conceptualizing the issues and in actual skill building. In many respects, it represents an eclectic approach similar to what Brammer and Shostrom (1982) refer to as "systematic eclecticism." Rather than being random, haphazard, and inconsistent, it is an attempt to use counseling strategies, techniques, and styles that consider not only individual characteristics, but cultural and racial factors as well. Such an approach has been advocated by Ponterotto (1987) in working with Mexican Americans.

Along with the above training, a number of people have advocated that training programs need a strong antiracism component (Carney & Kahn, 1984; Corvin & Wiggins, 1989; D. W. Sue et al., 1982). Simply acquiring information/knowledge of a racial minority, and expanding the repertoire of response is not enough. According to Corvin and Wiggins (1989), "White racism is not a result of cultural differences, but the consequences of White ethnocentrism." Attempts to teach effective cross-cultural counseling will be doomed to failure unless trainees address their own White racism. Unfortunately, programs seem very reluctant to implement antiracism training because it threatens the very foundations of the program. Racism is a very painful topic for many trainees, and they are likely to react negatively to it. More importantly, many faculty members seem equally threatened and may be a part of the problem, rather than the solution.

With respect to research implications, we would only mention a few. A most fruitful area to research would be to investigate counseling and communication styles with respect to such factors as race, culture, ethnicity, and gender. Most of the studies we have reviewed lend support to the notion that various racial groups do exhibit differences in communication style. What is missing is explicit research exploring the interaction of these styles with various theoretical counseling approaches. Do race and culture affect a culturally different client's receptivity to counseling style? In what ways? How does the style affect a client's perception of counselor expertness, attractiveness, and trustworthiness?

If we are to make progress in understanding these questions, evaluation of counseling approaches can begin only if relevant scoring systems are developed and a common framework is established. While cross-cultural research in this area has increased, there have been problems associated with the definition of skills that fall under the directive and nondirective divisions (Folensbee, Draguns, & Danish, 1986). In some cases, the skills identified in each category were found to be the same, resulting in contradictory findings.

Last, to develop truly relevant and effective culture-specific approaches may mean a completely different perspective: Before the advent of Western counseling/therapy approaches, how did members of a particular culture solve their problems? What were the intrinsic, natural, help-giving networks? Can we identify specific helping skills in the culture and use that as a frame of reference rather than Western concepts of mental health? Such a research approach would allow us to eventually develop counseling theories that are different from those we have learned.

In an important study aimed at these questions, Nwachuku & Ivey (in press) studied the African-Igbo culture in order to (a) identify culture-specific means of helping, and (b) test whether such helping approaches could be taught to counselor trainees. They systematically identified key behaviors, attitudes, and values of the culture, translated them into identifiable helping skills, and attempted to teach these strategies to counselor trainees. Their preliminary findings suggest that it is possible to identify culture-specific strategies in a given culture, and that these are teachable. Statements that we do not have the research base or technology can no longer be used as excuses for the counseling profession not to move in a direction that addresses cultural diversity in practice, training, and research.

CHAPTER 4

Sociopolitical Considerations of Mistrust in Cross-Cultural Counseling

"I have worked with very few Blacks during my tenure at the Counseling Center, but one particular incident left me with very negative feelings. It occurred in the fall when a Black student named Walter was given an appointment with me. Even though I'm White, I tried not to let his being Black get in the way of our session. I treated him like everyone else, a human being who needed help.

"At the onset, Walter was obviously guarded, mistrustful, and frustrated when talking about his reasons for coming. He spoke about his failing grades, about the need to obtain help with study skills, and about advice in changing majors. He was quite demanding in asking for advice and information. It was almost as if Walter wanted everything handed to him on a silver platter without putting any work into the counseling. Confronting him about his avoidance of responsibility would probably be counterproductive, so I chose to focus in on his feelings. Using person-centered techniques, I reflected his feelings, paraphrased his thoughts, and summarized his dilemmas. This did not seem to immediately help as I sensed an increase in the tension level, and he seemed antagonistic toward me.

"After several attempts by Walter to obtain direct advice from me, I stated, 'You're getting frustrated at me because I'm not giving you the answers you want.' It was clear that this angered Walter. Getting up in a very menacing manner, he stood over me and angrily shouted, 'Forget it, man! I don't have time to play your silly games.' For one brief moment, I felt in danger of being physically assaulted before he stormed out of the office.

"This incident occurred several years ago, and I must admit that I was left with a very unfavorable impression of Blacks. I know it sounds racist, but Walter's behavior only reinforces my belief that they have trouble controlling their anger, like to take the easy way out, and find it difficult to be open and trusting of others. If I am wrong on this belief, I hope this workshop (cross-cultural counseling) will help me to better understand the Black personality."

The above incident was supplied by a workshop participant and is used here because it illustrates some of the major issues addressed in this chapter. Repeatedly we have made the point that race relationships, and specifically Black/White relationships, are oftentimes reflected in the counseling/therapy interactions. We do not question the sincerity of the White counselor in his desire to help the Black client. However, it is obvious to us that the counselor is part of the problem and not the solution.

The counselor's preconceived notions and stereotypes about Blacks seemed to have affected his definition of the problem, assessment of the situation, and therapeutic intervention.

First, statements that Walter wants things handed to him on a "silver platter," his "avoidance of responsibility," and his "wanting to take the easy way out" are symbolic of social stereotypes that Blacks are "lazy and unmotivated." The counselor fails to entertain the possibility that requests for advice, information, and suggestions may be legitimate and not indicative of pathological responding.

Second, the counselor's statements that Blacks have difficulty "controlling their anger," that Walter was "menacing," and that the counselor was in fear of being assaulted seems to paint the picture of the hostile, angry, and violent Black male—a societal stereotype consciously and unconsciously subscribed to by many in this society. Is it possible that Walter has a legitimate reason for being angry? Is it possible that the counselor and the process of counseling are at the source of the Black student's frustration and anger? Is it possible that the counselor was never in physical danger, but that his own affectively based stereotype of "the dangerous Black male" caused his unreasonable fear? As discussed in the last chapter, are we witnessing a possible misinterpretation of communication styles?

The above questions lead us to our third point. The answers seem to lie with the oppressor, not the oppressed. In almost every introductory text on counseling and psychotherapy, lip service is paid to "counselor know thyself." In other words, we become better counselors the more we understand our own motives, biases, values, and assumptions about human behavior. Unfortunately, very few counselor-training programs have their students explore their values, biases, and preconceived notions in the area of racist attitudes, beliefs, and behaviors. We are taught to look at our clients, to analyze them, and to note their weaknesses, limitations, and pathological trends; less often do we look for positive healthy characteristics. As mental health professionals, we may find it difficult and unpleasant to explore our racism, and our training allows us a good means of avoiding it. When the counselor ends his story by stating that he hopes the workshop will "help me better understand the Black personality," who is really doing the avoidance of responsibility?

Fourth, the counselor states he tried to not let Walter's "blackness get in the way of counseling," and that he treated him like any other "human being." This is a very typical statement made by Whites who subscribe to the "myth of color blindness." Our contention is that it is nearly impossible to overlook the fact that a client is Black, Asian American, Hispanic, and so forth. When operating in this manner, however, the "color-blind" therapist may actually be obscuring his/her understanding of who the culturally different client really is. To overlook one's racial group membership is to deny an intimate and important aspect of one's identity. Those who advocate a "color-blind" approach seem to operate under the assumption that "Black is bad" and that to be different is to be deviant.

Last, and central to the thesis of this chapter, is the statement by the counselor that Walter appears "guarded and mistrustful" and has difficulty being "open" (self-disclosing). We have mentioned several times that the inability of a counselor to establish rapport and a relationship of trust with culturally diverse clients is a major counseling barrier. When the emotional climate is negative, and when little trust or understanding exists between the counselor and the client, counseling can be both ineffective and destructive. Yet, if the emotional climate is realistically positive and if trust and understanding exist between the parties, the two-way communication of thoughts and feelings can proceed with optimism. This latter condition is often referred to as "rapport" and sets the stage in which other essential conditions can become effective. One of these, self-disclosure, is particularly crucial to the process and goals of counseling, because it is the most direct means by which an individual makes himself/herself known to another (Greene, 1985; Mays, 1985).

This chapter attempts to discuss the issue of trust as it relates to minority clients. Our discussion does not deal with cultural variables among certain groups (Asian Americans, American Indians, etc.) that dictate against self-disclosure to strangers. This has already been presented in Chapter 2. This chapter first presents a brief discussion of the sociopolitical situation as it affects the trust-mistrust dimension of certain culturally different populations. Second, we look at factors that enhance or negate the cross-cultural counselor's effectiveness as it relates to the theory of social influence. Third, we systematically examine how counselor credibility and similarity affect a client's willingness to work with a counselor from another race/culture.

EFFECTS OF HISTORICAL/CURRENT OPPRESSION

The history of race relations in the United States has influenced us to the point of being extremely cautious in revealing our feelings and attitudes about race to strangers. In an interracial encounter with a stranger, each party will attempt to discern gross or subtle racial attitudes of the other while minimizing vulnerability. For minorities in the United States, this lesson has been learned well. While White Americans may also exhibit cautiousness similar to their minority counterparts, the structure of society places more power to injure and damage in the hands of the majority culture. In most self-disclosing situations, White Americans are less vulnerable than their minority counterparts.

As the individual chapters on American Indians, Asian Americans, Blacks, and Hispanics will reveal, the history and experiences of the culturally different have been those of oppression, discrimination, and racism. Institutional racism has created psychological barriers among minorities that are likely to interfere with the counseling process. Institutional racism is a set of policies, priorities, and accepted normative patterns designed to subjugate, oppress, and force dependence of individuals and groups to a larger society. It does this by sanctioning unequal goals, unequal status, and unequal access to goods and services. Institutional racism has fostered the enactment of discriminatory statutes, the selective enforcement of laws, the blocking of economic opportunities and outcomes, and the imposition of forced assimilation/acculturation on the culturally different. The sociopolitical system thus attempts to define the prescribed role occupied by minorities. Feelings of powerlessness, inferiority, subordination, deprivation, anger and rage, and overt/covert resistance to factors in interracial relationships are likely to result.

Several writers (Harrison, 1975; Kochman, 1981; Stanback & Pearce, 1985; Thomas, 1969; Willie, Kramer, & Brown, 1973) have pointed out how Blacks, in responding to their slave heritage, history of discrimination, and America's reaction to their skin color, have adopted behavior patterns toward Whites important for survival in a racist society. These behavior patterns may include indirect expressions of hostility, aggression, and fear. During slavery, in order to rear children who would fit into a segregated system and who could physically survive, Black mothers were forced to teach them (a) to express aggression indirectly, (b) to read the thoughts of others while hiding their own, and (c) to engage in ritualized accommodating-subordinating behaviors designed to create as few waves as possible (Willie et al., 1973). This process involves a "mild dissociation," where Blacks may separate their true selves from their role as "Negroes" (Pinderhughes, 1973). A dual identity is often used, where the true self is revealed to fellow Blacks, while the dissociated self is revealed to meet the expectations of prejudiced Whites. From the analysis of Black history, the dissociative process may be manifested in two major ways.

First, "playing it cool" has been identified as one means by which Blacks or other minorities may conceal their true feelings (Greene, 1985; Grier & Cobbs, 1971; Jones, 1985). The intent of this manner of behavior is to prevent Whites from knowing what the minority person is thinking/feeling and to express feelings/behaviors in such a way as to prevent offending or threatening Whites (White & Parham, 1990). Thus, a culturally different individual who may be experiencing conflict, explosive anger, and suppressed feelings will appear serene and composed on the surface. It is a defense mechanism aimed at protecting minorities from harm and exploitation.

Second, the "Uncle Tom syndrome" may be used by minorities to appear docile, nonassertive, and happy-go-lucky. Especially during slavery, Blacks learned that passivity is a necessary survival technique. To retain the most menial jobs, to minimize retaliation, and to maximize survival of the self and loved ones, many minorities have learned to deny their aggressive feelings toward their oppressors.

We are reminded of the skit performed by Richard Pryor, the Black comedian, in which the issue of Black awareness of personal vulnerability was sarcastically portrayed. In a monologue, Pryor mimiced how he recently purchased a brand-new Cadillac and was proudly driving about when he was pulled over by a White police officer. Aware that many White officers have preconceived notions about "dangerous Black males" and not wanting to be "blown away," Pryor humorously enacted how he immediately raised his arms loudly claiming, "Look, no hidden weapons!" When asked for his driver's license, Pryor states, "I will now take my right hand and use only two fingers to get my wallet located in the left breast pocket of the jacket." Pryor tips his body slightly to the left so his jacket flops open and pronounces "no hidden weapons there either." Ever so slowly, he advances his right hand toward the wallet to retrieve it. The skit continued in this very sarcastic but realistic statement about the nature of Black/White relations in our society.

The overall result of the minority experience in the United States has been to increase vigilance and sensitivity to the thoughts and behaviors of Whites in society. We mentioned earlier that Blacks have been forced to read the thoughts of others accurately in order to survive. This has resulted in some studies (Kochman, 1981; Smith, 1981; D. W. Sue, 1981) revealing that certain minority groups such as Black Americans are better readers of nonverbal communication. This was discussed in some detail in the last chapter. Many Blacks have oftentimes stated that Whites "say one thing, but mean another." This better understanding and sensitivity to nonverbal communication has allowed Blacks to enhance their survival in a highly dangerous society. As noted in the last chapter, it is important for the minority individual to accurately read nonverbal messages, not only for physical survival, but for psychological reasons as well.

In summary, it becomes all too clear that past and continuing discrimination against certain culturally diverse groups is a tangible basis for minority distrust of the majority society (Grier & Cobbs, 1968; Jones, 1985; Mays, 1985). White people are perceived as potential enemies unless proved otherwise. Under such a sociopolitical atmosphere, minorities may use several adaptive devices to prevent Whites from knowing their true feelings. Because cross-cultural counseling may mirror the sentiments of the larger society, these modes of behavior and their detrimental effects may be reenacted in the sessions.

The fact that many minority clients are suspicious, mistrustful, and guarded in their interactions with White counselors is certainly understandable in light of the foregoing analysis. In spite of their conscious desires to help, White counselors are not immune from inheriting racist attitudes, beliefs, myths, and stereotypes about Asian-American, Black, Hispanic, and American-Indian clients. For example, White counselors often believe that Blacks are nonverbal, paranoid, and angry and most likely to have character disorders (Evans, 1985; Jones, 1985; Willie et al., 1973) or to be schizophrenic (Pavkov, Lewis & Lyons, 1989). As a result, they view Blacks as unsuitable for counseling and psychotherapy. Counselors and social scientists who hold to this belief fail to understand the following facts.

1. As a group, Black Americans tend to communicate nonverbally and feel that nonverbal communication is a more accurate barometer of one's true feelings and beliefs (Hall, 1976; Kochman, 1981; Stanback & Pearce, 1985; Weber, 1985; Willie et al., 1973). Blacks have learned that intellectual interactions are less trustworthy than the nonverbal messages sent by participants. Hall (1976) observes that Blacks are better able to read nonverbal messages (high context) than their White counterparts and rely less on intellectual verbalizations than on nonverbal communication to make a point. Whites, on the other hand, tune in more to verbal than to nonverbal messages (low context). Because they rely less on nonverbal cues, Whites need greater verbal elaborations to get a point across. Being unaware of and insensitive to these differences, White counselors are prone to feel Blacks are unable to communicate in "complex" ways. This judgment is based on the high value that counseling places on intellectual/verbal activity.

2. Rightfully or not, White counselors are often perceived as symbols of the Establishment, and the minority client is likely to impute all the negative experiences of oppression to the counselor (Katz, 1985; Vontress, 1971). This may prevent the minority client from responding to the counselor as an individual. While the counselor may be possessed of the most admirable motives, the client may reject the counselor simply because he/she is White (Vontress, 1971). Thus, communication may be directly or indirectly shut off.

3. Some minorities may lack confidence in the counseling process because the White counselor often proposes White solutions to their concerns (Atkinson et al., 1989; Thomas & Sillen, 1972). Many pressures are placed on culturally diverse clients to accept an alien value system and reject their own.

4. The "playing it cool" and "Uncle Tom" responses of many minorities are also present in the counseling session. As pointed out earlier, these mechanisms are attempts to conceal true feelings, to effectively hinder self-disclosure, and to prevent the counselor from getting to know the client.

To summarize, the culturally different client entering cross-cultural counseling is likely to experience considerable anxiety about ethnic/racial/

cultural differences. Suspicion, apprehension, verbal constriction, unnatural reactions, open resentment and hostility, and "passive" or "cool" behavior may all be expressed. Self-disclosure and the possible establishment of a working relationship can be seriously delayed and/or prevented from occurring. In all cases, the counselor may be put to severe tests about his/her trustworthiness. A culturally effective counselor is one who is able to adequately resolve challenges to his/her credibility. We now turn our attention to an analysis of those dimensions that may enhance or diminish the minority client's receptivity to self-disclosure.

CREDIBILITY AND ATTRACTIVENESS IN CROSS-CULTURAL COUNSELING

In the last section, we presented a case to explain how the political atmosphere of the larger society affects the minority client's perception of a cross-cultural counseling situation. Minorities in the United States have solid reasons for not trusting White Americans. Lack of trust often leads to guardedness, inability to establish rapport, and lack of self-disclosure on the part of culturally different clients. What a counselor says and does in the sessions can either enhance or diminish his/her credibility and attractiveness. A counselor who is perceived by clients as highly credible and attractive is more likely to elicit trust, motivation to work/change, and self-disclosure. These appear to be important conditions for effective counseling to occur (S. Sue & Zane, 1987).

Theories of counseling and psychotherapy attempt to outline an approach designed to make them effective. It is our contention that cross-cultural helping cannot be approached through any one theory of counseling (Rogler, Malgady, Constantine, & Blumenthal, 1987). There are several reasons for such a statement. First, theories of counseling are composed of philosophical assumptions regarding the nature of "man" and a theory of personality (Belkins, 1988; Corsini, 1984; London, 1964). These characteristics, as pointed out earlier, are highly culture-bound (Ivey et al., 1987; Katz, 1985). What is the "true" nature of people is a philosophical question. What constitutes the healthy and unhealthy personality is also debatable and varies from culture to culture and class to class.

Second, theories of counseling are also composed of a body of therapeutical techniques and strategies. These techniques are applied to clients with the hope of effecting change in either behaviors or attitudes. A counseling theory dictates what techniques are to be used and, implicitly, in what proportions. In the last chapter we were able to see that client-centered counselors behave differently than rational-emotive ones. The fact that one school of counseling can be distinguished from another has implications: It suggests a certain degree of rigidity in working with culturally different clients who might find such techniques offensive or inappropriate. The implicit assumption is that these techniques are imposed according to the theory and not based on client needs and values.

It is very important for the counselor to be aware of the implications in regard to minority reading of nonverbal behavior. "Playing it cool" and the "Uncle Tom" syndrome, as well as other challenges to the counselor, are frequently given in order to assess the counselor's nonverbal message rather than the verbal one. When topics related to racism are brought up in the session, what the counselor says may oftentimes be negated by his/her nonverbal communication. If this is the case, the minority client will quickly pick up the inconsistency and conclude that this counselor is incapable of dealing with cultural/racial diversity.

Third, theories of counseling have oftentimes failed to agree among themselves about what constitutes desirable "outcomes" in counseling. This makes it extremely difficult to determine the effectiveness of counseling and therapy (Patterson, 1980). For example, the psychoanalytically oriented counselor uses "insight," the behaviorist uses "behavior change," the client-centered person uses "self-actualization," and the rational-emotive person uses "rational cognitive processes." The potential for disagreement over appropriate outcome variables is increased even further when the counselor and client come from different cultures. While the counseling outcome is extremely important, we attempt to concentrate our discussion on "process" elements. We are more concerned here with *how* change occurs (the process) during counseling rather than with *what* change (the outcomes) results from counseling.

Counseling as Interpersonal Influence

When people engage in interactions with one another, they inevitably attempt to exert influence. These social-influence attempts may be overt/covert or conscious/unconscious. Whether the intent is to create a favorable impression when meeting people, to toilet train a young child, to convince people that cigarette smoking is harmful, to gain acceptance from a desired group, or to sell goods, these social-influence attempts are all aimed at changing attitudes and/or behaviors.

Likewise, counseling may be conceptualized as an interpersonal-influence process in which the counselor uses his/her social power to influence the client's attitudes and behaviors (Strong, 1968). In reviewing the literature in social psychology on opinion change, Strong (1968) found parallels between this field and the counseling process. Specifically, communication attributes that had been established as important determinants of attitude change seemed similar to those that make an effective counselor. Counselors who are perceived by their clients as credible (expert and trustworthy) and attractive are able to exert greater influence than those perceived as lacking in credibility and attractiveness. There is a sufficient number of counseling analogue studies that support this contention

(Atkinson & Carskaddon, 1975; Barak & La Crosse, 1975; Merluzzi, Merluzzi, & Kaul, 1977; Schmidt & Strong, 1971; Spiegel, 1976; Strong & Schmidt, 1970). Using social-influence theory as a means to analyze counseling not only has empirical validity and concentrates on process variables, but also seems to be equally applicable to all approaches. Regardless of the counseling orientation (person-centered, psychoanalytic, behavioral, transactional analysis, etc.), the counselor's effectiveness tends to depend on his/her perceived expertness, trustworthiness, and attractiveness (Barak & Dell, 1977; Barak & La Crosse, 1975).

Most of the studies mentioned have dealt exclusively with a White population. Thus, findings that certain attributes contribute to a counselor's credibility and attractiveness may not be so perceived by culturally different clients. It is entirely possible that credibility, as defined by credentials indicating specialized training, may only mean to a Hispanic client that the White counselor has no knowledge or expertise in working with Hispanics. This assumption is based on the fact that most training programs are geared for White middle-class clients and are culturally exclusive.

Our focus in this section is twofold: (1) we outline the various ways clients perceive their counselor's attempts to influence them, and (2) we discuss the dimensions of counselor expertness, trustworthiness, and similarity as they relate to culturally different clients. We are then able to lay the foundation for a theory of cross-cultural counseling, which is presented and discussed later.

Psychological Sets of Clients

Credibility and attractiveness of the counselor is very much dependent on the psychological set or frame of reference for the culturally different client. We all know individuals who tend to value rational approaches to solving problems and others who value a more affective (attractiveness) approach. It would seem reasonable that a client who values rationality might be more receptive to a counseling approach that emphasizes the counselor's credibility. Thus, understanding a client's psychological set may facilitate the counselor's ability to exert social influence in counseling. Collins (1970) has proposed a set of conceptual categories that we can use to understand people's receptivity to pressures for conformity (change). We apply those categories here with respect to the counseling situation. These five hypothetical "sets" or "frames of mind" are elicited in clients for several different reasons. Race, ethnicity, and the experience of discrimination often affect the type of "set" that will be operative in a minority client.

1. *The Problem-Solving Set: Information Orientation.* In the problem-solving set, the client is concerned about obtaining correct information (solutions, outlooks, and skills) that has adaptive value in the real world.

The client accepts or rejects information from the counselor on the basis of its perceived truth or falsity; is it an accurate representation of reality? The processes used tend to be rational and logical in analyzing and attacking the problem: (a) the client may apply a consistency test and compare the new facts with information he/she already possesses; (b) the person may apply a corroboration test by actively seeking information from others for comparison purposes. The former test makes use of information the individual already has, while the latter requires him/her to seek out new information.

Advocates of a single school of thought do not realize that when they make statements about their counseling and therapeutic orientation (such as "I am Rogerian," "I am behavioral," "I am rational-emotive in orientation," etc.), they conceptualize people in the same way and respond toward them in a therapeutic mode that is similar regardless of race, color, creed, religion, and gender. Counselors and therapists who respond in such a manner fail to take into account that people differ in a number of ways along these dimensions.

Through socialization and personal experiences, we have learned that some people are more likely to provide accurate/helpful information (be credible) than others. Sources that have been dependable in the past, that have high status, possess great reputations, occupy certain roles, and are motivated to make accurate representations are more likely to influence us. Minorities may have learned that many Whites have little expertise when it comes to their lifestyles and that the information/suggestions they give are White solutions/labels.

It is highly possible that racial/ethnic groups may vary in their information orientation. For example, D. W. Sue (1981) has indicated that many Puerto Ricans who come for counseling and therapy expect information, advice, and direct suggestions. Likewise, it has been found that many Asian Americans tend not only to prefer a structured, direct, and practical orientation, but oftentimes seek advice, consolation, and suggestions from counselors. Counselors who do not value the problem-solving set and who may be affectively oriented may actually have great difficulties in relating to the client.

2. *The Consistency Set.* People are operating under the consistency set whenever they change an opinion, belief, or behavior in such a way as to make it consistent with other opinions, beliefs, or behaviors. This principle is best illustrated in Festinger's *A Theory of Cognitive Dissonance* (1957). Stated simply, the theory says that when a person's attitudes, opinions, or beliefs are met with disagreement (inconsistencies), cognitive imbalance or dissonance will be created. The existence of dissonance is psychologically uncomfortable and produces tension with drive characteristics. The result is an attempt to reduce the dissonance. Collins (1970) asserts that the consistency set may really be a byproduct of the problem-solving set. This is so because we assume that the real world is consistent. For example, since counselors are supposed to help, we naturally believe that they would not do something to hurt us. If they do, then it creates dissonance. To reduce this inconsistency, we may discredit or derogate the counselor (he/she is not a good person after all!) or in some way excuse the act (he/she did it unintentionally). The rules of the consistency set specify that "good people do good things" and "bad people do bad things." It is important to note that the consistency set states that people are not necessarily *rational* beings but *rationalizing* ones. A counselor who is not in touch with his/her prejudices/biases may send out conflicting messages to a minority client. The counselor may verbally state, "I am here to help you," but at the same time, nonverbally indicate racist attitudes/feelings. This can destroy the credibility of the counselor very quickly in the case of a minority client who accurately applies a consistency set: "White people say one thing, but do another. You can't believe what they tell you."

Generally, minority clients who enter counseling with a White therapist will tend to apply a consistency test to what the counselor says or does. That is because the client is trying to test the counselor as to whether he or she has the knowledge, understanding, and expertise to work with a minority individual. A minority client will actively seek out disclosures on the part of the client to compare them with the information he/she has about the world. Should the counselor pass the test, then new information may be more readily accepted and assimilated.

As we have seen earlier in this text, minority individuals apparently are better readers of nonverbal cues. As a result, the counselor who sends out conflicting verbal and nonverbal messages may easily be dismissed as being unable to help the client.

3. *The Identity Set.* In the identity set, the individual generally desires to be like or similar to a person or group he/she holds in high esteem. Much of our identity is formed from those reference groups to which we aspire. We attempt to take on the reference group's characteristics, beliefs, values, and behaviors because they are viewed as favorable. An individual who strongly identifies with a particular group is likely to accept the group's beliefs and conform to behaviors dictated by the group. If race or ethnicity constitutes a strong reference group for a client, then a counselor of the same race/ethnicity is likely to be more influential than one who is not.

There are a number of studies (see reviews by Atkinson, 1983, 1985; Atkinson & Schein, 1986) indicating that certain similarities between the counselor and client may actually enhance counseling longevity and counselor preference. For example, racial similarity between counselor and client may actually affect willingness to return for counseling and hopefully facilitate counseling effectiveness. The studies on this are quite mixed as there is considerable evidence that membership group similarity may not be as effective as belief or attitude similarity. Furthermore, a number of studies (Parham, 1989; Parham & Helms, 1981; 1985) suggest that the stage of cultural or racial identity affects which dimensions of similarities will be preferred by the minority client. We will have much more to say about this in the next chapter dealing with cultural identity development.

4. *The Economic Set.* In the economic set, the person is influenced because of perceived rewards and punishments the source is able to deliver. In this set, a person performs a behavior or states a belief in order to gain rewards and avoid punishments. In the case of the counselor, he/she controls important resources that may affect the client. For example, a counselor may decide to recommend the expulsion of a student from the school. In less subtle ways, the counselor may ridicule or praise a client during a group-counseling session. In these cases, the client may decide to change his/her behavior because the counselor holds greater power. The major problem with the use of rewards and punishments to induce change is that while it may assure "behavioral compliance," it does not guarantee "private acceptance." Furthermore, for rewards and coercive power to be effective, the counselor must maintain constant surveillance. Once the surveillance is removed, the client is likely to revert back to previous modes of behavior. For culturally different clients, counseling that operates primarily on the economic set is more likely to prevent the development of trust, rapport, and self-disclosure.

The economic set is probably the strongest indicator of cultural oppression in counseling (D. W. Sue, 1981). We in the mental health profession like to believe that counseling and psychotherapy is aimed at helping people, at freeing them, and allowing them greater autonomy and choice in life situations. Unfortunately, in working with culturally diverse clients whose lifestyles and values may differ from our own, we oftentimes engage in cultural oppression. That is, we attempt to make them conform to our standards and ways of behavior. In doing this, we can exercise the economic set strongly by making our clients feel inadequate for being different.

5. *The Authority Set.* Under this set, some individuals are thought to have a particular position that gives them a legitimate right to prescribe attitudes and/or behaviors. In our society, we have been conditioned to believe that certain authorities (police officers, chairpersons, designated leaders, etc.) have the right to demand compliance. This occurs via training in role behavior and group norms. Mental health professionals, like counselors, are thought to have a legitimate right to recommend and provide psychological treatment to disturbed or troubled clients. It is this psychological set that legitimizes the counselor's role as a helping professional. Yet, for many minorities, it is exactly the roles in society that are perceived to be instruments of institutional racism.

None of the five sets or frames are mutually exclusive. These sets frequently interact and any number of them can operate at the same time. For example, it is possible that you are influenced by a counselor you find highly credible. It is also possible that you like the counselor or find him/her very attractive. Are you accepting his/her influence because the counselor is credible (problem-solving set), attractive (identification set), or both?

It should be clear at this point that characteristics of the influencing source (counselor) are all-important in eliciting types of changes. In addition, the type of set placed in operation oftentimes dictates the permanency and degree of attitude change. For example, the primary component in getting compliance in the economic and authority set is the power that the person holds over you—the ability to reward or punish; in identification (the identity set), it is the attractiveness or liking of the counselor; and in internalization (the problem-solving and consistency set), credibility or truthfulness is important.

While these sets operate similarly for both majority and minority clients, their manifestations may be quite different. Obviously, a minority client may have great difficulty identifying (identification set) with a counselor from another race or culture. Also, what constitutes credibility to minority clients may be far different from what constitutes credibility to a majority client. We now focus on how counselor characteristics affect these sets as they apply to the culturally different.

Counselor Credibility

Credibility (that elicits the problem-solving, consistency, and identification sets) may be defined as the constellation of characteristics that makes certain individuals appear worthy of belief, capable, entitled to confidence, reliable, and trustworthy. Expertness is an "ability" variable, while trustworthiness is a "motivation" one. Expertness depends on how well-informed, capable, or intelligent others perceive the communicator (counselor). Trustworthiness is dependent on the degree to which people perceive the communicator (counselor) as motivated to make invalid assertions. In counseling, these two components have been the subject of much research and speculation (Barak & Dell, 1977; Barak & La Crosse, 1975; Dell, 1973; La Crosse & Barak, 1976; LaFromborse & Dixon, 1981; Spiegel, 1976; Sprafkin, 1970; Strong, 1968; Strong & Schmidt, 1970). The weight of evidence supports our commonsense beliefs that the counselor who is perceived as expert and trustworthy can influence clients more than one who is perceived to be lower on these traits.

Expertness. Clients often go to a counselor not only because they are in distress and in need of relief, but also because they believe the counselor is an expert; he/she has the necessary knowledge, skills, experience, training, and tools to help (problem-solving set). Perceived expertness is typically a function of (a) reputation, (b) evidence of specialized training, and (c) behavioral evidence of proficiency/competency. For culturally different clients, the issue of counselor expertness seems to be raised more often than in going to a counselor of one's own culture and race. As mentioned previously, the fact that counselors have degrees and certificates from prestigious institutions (authority set) may not enhance perceived expertness. This is especially true of clients who are culturally different and aware that institutional racism exists in training programs. Indeed, it may have the opposite effect by reducing credibility! Neither is reputation-expertness (authority set) likely to impress a minority client unless the favorable testimony comes from someone of his/her own group.

Thus behavior-expertness, or demonstrating your ability to help a client, becomes the critical form of expertness in cross-cultural counseling (problem-solving set). And as we discussed in an earlier chapter, using counseling skills and strategies appropriate to the life values of the culturally different client is crucial. We have already mentioned there is evidence to suggest that certain minority groups prefer a much more active approach to counseling. A counselor playing a relatively inactive role may be perceived as being inexpert (Peoples & Dell, 1975). The example presented next shows how the counselor's approach lowers perceived expertness.

ASIAN-AMERICAN MALE CLIENT: It's hard for me to talk about these issues. My parents and friends . . . they wouldn't understand . . . if they ever found out I was coming here for help . . .

WHITE MALE COUNSELOR: I sense it's difficult to talk about personal things. How are you feeling right now?

ASIAN-AMERICAN CLIENT: Oh, all right.

WHITE COUNSELOR: That's not a feeling. Sit back and get in touch with your feelings [pause]. Now tell me, how are you feeling right now?

ASIAN-AMERICAN CLIENT: Somewhat nervous.

WHITE COUNSELOR: When you talked about your parents' and friends' not understanding and the way you said it made me think you felt ashamed and disgraced at having to come. Was that what you felt?

While this exchange appears to indicate that the counselor (a) was able to see the client's discomfort, and (b) interpret his feelings correctly, it also points out the counselor's lack of understanding and knowledge of Asian cultural values. While we do not want to be guilty of stereotyping Asian Americans, many do have difficulty, at times, dealing with feelings. The counselor's persistent attempts to focus on feelings and his direct and blunt interpretation of them may indicate to the client that the counselor lacks the more subtle skills of dealing with a sensitive topic and/or is shaming the client (see chapter on Asian Americans).

Furthermore, it is possible that the Asian-American client in this case is much more used to discussing feelings in an indirect or subtle manner. A direct response from the counselor addressed to a feeling may not be as effective as one that deals with it indirectly. In many traditional Asian groups, subtlety is a highly prized art, and the traditional Asian client may feel much more comfortable when dealing with feelings in an indirect manner.

In many ways, behavioral manifestations of counselor expertness override other considerations. For example, many counselor educators claim that specific counseling skills are not as important as the attitude one brings into the counseling situation. Behind this statement is the belief that universal attributes of genuineness, love, unconditional acceptance, and positive regard are the only things needed. Yet the question remains, how does a counselor communicate these things to culturally different clients? While a counselor might have the best of intentions, it is possible that his/her intentions might be misunderstood. Let us use another example with the same Asian-American client.

ASIAN-AMERICAN CLIENT: I'm even nervous about others seeing me come in here. It's so difficult for me to talk about this.

WHITE COUNSELOR: We all find some things difficult to talk about. It's important that you do.

ASIAN-AMERICAN CLIENT: It's easy to say that. But, do you really understand how awful I feel, talking about my parents?

WHITE COUNSELOR: I've worked with many Asian Americans and many have similar problems.

In this sample dialogue, we find a distinction between the counselor's intentions and the effects of his comments. The counselor's intentions were to reassure the client that he understood his feelings, to imply that he had worked with similar cases, and to make the client not feel isolated (others have the same problems). The effects, however, were to dilute and dismiss the client's feelings and concerns, to take the uniqueness out of the situation.

Likewise, a counselor who adheres rigidly to a particular school of counseling, or who relies primarily on a few counseling responses is seriously limited in his/her ability to help a wide range of clients. While counseling theories are important, counselor-training programs have an equally strong responsibility to teach helping skills that cut across schools of counseling. Only in this way will future counselors be better able to engage in a wide variety of counseling behaviors when working with culturally diverse groups.

Trustworthiness. Perceived trustworthiness encompasses such factors as sincerity, openness, honesty, or perceived lack of motivation for personal gain. A counselor who is perceived as trustworthy is likely to exert more influence over a client than one who is not. In our society, certain roles like ministers, doctors, psychiatrists, and counselors are presumed to exist to help people. With respect to minorities, self-disclosure is very much dependent on this attribute of perceived trustworthiness. Because counselors are often perceived by minorities to be "agents of the Establishment," trust is something that does not come with the role (authority set). Indeed, it may be the perception of many minorities that counselors cannot be trusted unless otherwise demonstrated. Again, the role and reputation you have as being trustworthy must be demonstrated in behavioral terms. More than anything, challenges to the counselor's trustworthiness will be a frequent theme blocking further exploration/movement until it is resolved to the satisfaction of the client. These verbatim transcripts illustrate the trust issue.

WHITE MALE COUNSELOR: I sense some major hesitations . . . it's difficult for you to discuss your concerns with me.

BLACK MALE CLIENT: You're damn right! If I really told you how I felt about my coach [White], what's to prevent you from telling him? You Whities are all of the same mind.

WHITE COUNSELOR: Look, it would be a lie for me to say I don't know your coach [angry voice]. He's an acquaintance, but not a personal friend. Don't put me in the same bag with all Whites! Anyway, even if he was, I hold our discussion in strictest confidence. Let me ask you this question, what can I do that would make it easier for you to trust me?

BLACK CLIENT: You're on your way, man!

This verbal exchange illustrates several issues related to trustworthiness. First, the minority client is likely to constantly test the counselor regarding issues of confidentiality. Second, the onus of responsibility for proving trustworthiness falls on the counselor. Third, to prove that one is trustworthy requires, at times, self-disclosure on the part of the counselor. That the counselor did not hide the fact that he knew the coach (openness), became angry about being lumped with all Whites (sincerity), assured the client he would not tell the coach or anyone about their sessions (confidentiality), and asked the client how he would work to prove he was trustworthy (genuineness) were all elements that enhanced his trustworthiness.

The "prove to me that you can be trusted" ploy is a most difficult one for counselors to handle. It is difficult because it demands self-disclosure on the part of counselors, something counselor-training programs have taught us to avoid. It places the focus on the counselor rather than on the client and makes many uncomfortable. It is likely to evoke defensiveness on the part of many counselors. Here is another verbatim exchange in which defensiveness is evoked, destroying the counselor's trustworthiness.

BLACK FEMALE CLIENT: Students in my drama class expect me to laugh when they do 'steppin fetchin' routines and tell Black jokes . . . I'm wondering whether you've ever laughed at any of those jokes.

WHITE MALE COUNSELOR: [long pause] Yes, I'm sure I have. Have you ever laughed at any White jokes?

BLACK CLIENT: What's a White joke?

WHITE COUNSELOR: I don't know [nervous laughter]; I suppose one making fun of Whites. Look, I'm Irish. Have you ever laughed at Irish jokes?

BLACK CLIENT: People tell me many jokes, but I don't laugh at racial jokes. I feel we're all minorities and should respect each other.

Again, the client tested the counselor indirectly by asking him if he ever laughed at racial jokes. Since most of us probably have, to say "no" would be a blatant lie. The client's motivation for asking this question was (a) to find out how sincere and open the counselor was, and (b) whether the counselor could recognize his racist attitudes without letting it interfere with counseling. While the counselor admitted to having laughed at such jokes, he proceeded to destroy his trustworthiness by becoming defensive. Rather than simply stopping with his statement of "Yes, I'm sure I have," or making some other similar one, he defends himself by trying to get the client to admit to similar actions. Thus the counselor's trustworthiness is seriously impaired. He is perceived as motivated to defend himself rather than help the client.

The counselor's obvious defensiveness in this case has prevented him from understanding the intent and motive of the question. Is the Black female client really asking the counselor whether he has actually laughed at Black jokes before? Or, is the client asking the counselor if he is a racist? Both of these questions have a certain amount of validity, but it is our belief that the Black female client is actually asking the following important question of the counselor: "How open and honest are you about your own racism, and will it interfere with our session here?" Again, the test is one of trustworthiness, a motivational variable that the White male counselor has obviously failed.

To summarize, expertness and trustworthiness are important components of any counselor relationship. In cross-cultural counseling, however, the counselor may not be presumed to possess either. The counselor working with a minority client is likely to experience severe tests of his/her expertness and trustworthiness before serious counseling can proceed. The responsibility for proving to the client that you are a credible counselor is likely to be greater when working with a minority than a majority counselee. How you meet the challenge is important in determining your effectiveness as a cross-cultural counselor.

We have come quite a long way in terms of examining how credibility and trustworthiness on the part of the counselor are affected by racial-cultural factors. We have also briefly discussed similarity and the evocation of the identification set. Do minority clients actually prefer a member of their own race in counseling? This is a very important question where the findings seem to be mixed or varying.

It is quite obvious that we know minority individuals who prefer seeing people of their own race and cultural background and some who apparently do not care. We may also know some minority individuals who would prefer to see counselors not of their own race. What are the determining factors that affect this selection process? How important are membership group similarity and attitude similarity in a culturally differ- ent client's preference for members of his or her own race? It appears that certain types of similarities and dissimilarities may affect the credibility of the counselor differentially. Relevant similarities seem more powerful than irrelevant ones. Also, the minority individual's stage of cultural identity may cause him or her to interact quite differently with this question. In the next chapter, we will discuss cultural identity development and how it may affect a minority client's preference for a counselor of his or her own race.

CONCLUSIONS

Since counseling is a White middle-class activity, the factors that may enhance the social influence of the majority counselor might, indeed, lower his/her power base when working with certain culturally different clients. As we have seen, credibility is usually defined in terms of two general dimensions: expertness and trustworthiness. Perceived expertness is typi- cally a function of reputation, behavioral proficiency, or evidence of specialized training (degrees, certificates, and so on). Trustworthiness encompasses such factors as sincerity, openness, honesty, or perceived lack of motivation for personal gain. While majority clients may also be concerned with the counselor's credibility, cultural differences and/or experiences of oppression in U.S. society make the minority client more sensitive to these characteristics of the counselor. Tests of credibility may occur frequently in the counseling session, and the onus of responsibility for proving expertness and trustworthiness lies with the counselor.

In cross-cultural counseling, the counselor may also be unable to use the client's identification set (membership group similarity) to induce change. At times, racial dissimilarity may prove to be so much of a hindrance as to render counseling ineffective. Some have agreed that attitudinal similarity may be more important than racial similarity in counseling. Research in this area is inconclusive. It seems to depend on several factors: (a) the type of presenting problems, (b) the degree and stage of racial/ethnic identity, and (c) certain characteristics of the counse- lor that may override race differences. Indeed, the difficulties in cross- cultural counseling may not stem from race factors per se, but from the implications of being a minority in the United States that assigns secondary status to them. In any case, a broad general statement on this matter is oversimplistic. Cross-cultural counseling by virtue of its definition implies major differences between the client and counselor. How these differences can be bridged and under what conditions a counselor is able to work effectively with culturally different clients are key questions.

CHAPTER 5

Racial/Cultural Identity Development

A most promising approach to the field of cross-cultural counseling has been the increased interest and work in the field of racial/cultural identity development among minority groups (Atkinson et al., 1989; Carter & Helms, 1987, 1985; Helms, 1985; Oler, 1989; Parham, 1989; Parham & Helms, 1981). Most would agree that Asian Americans, Blacks, Hispanics, and American Indians have a distinct cultural heritage that makes each different from the other. Yet, such cultural distinctions can lead to a monolithic view of minority-group attitudes and behaviors (Atkinson et al., 1989). The erroneous belief that all Asians are the same, all Blacks are the same, all Hispanics are the same, or all American Indians are the same has led to numerous therapeutic problems.

First, therapists may often respond to the culturally-different client in a very stereotypic manner and fail to recognize within-group or individual differences. For example, research indicates that Asian-American clients seem to prefer and benefit most from a highly structured and directive approach rather than an insight/feeling-oriented one (Atkinson, Maruyama & Matsui, 1978; Kim, 1985; Mau & Jepson, 1988; Root, 1985; D. Sue & S. Sue, 1972; S. Sue & Morishima, 1982). While such approaches may generally be effective, they are often blindly applied without regard for possible differences in client attitudes, beliefs, and behaviors. Likewise, conflicting findings in the literature regarding whether a minority client prefers a counselor of his/her own race seem to be a function of our failure to make such distinctions (Atkinson & Schein, 1986; Parham & Helms, 1981; Ponterotto & Wise, 1987). Preference for a racially or ethnically similar counselor may really be a function of the cultural/racial identity of the minority person (within-group differences) rather than of race or ethnicity per se.

Second, the strength of racial/cultural identity models lies in their potential diagnostic value (Helms, 1985). In the previous chapters, we cited statistics indicating that premature termination rates among minority clients may be attributed to the inappropriateness of transactions that occur between the counselor and the culturally different client. Research now suggests that a minority individual's reaction to *counseling,* the *counseling process,* and to the *counselor* is influenced by his/her cultural/racial identity and not simply linked to minority-group membership. The high failure-to-return rate of many culturally different clients seem intimately linked to the mental health professional's inability to accurately assess the cultural identity of the client.

A third important contribution derived from racial identity models is their acknowledgment of sociopolitical influences in shaping minority identity. As mentioned previously, most therapeutic approaches often neglect their potential sociopolitical nature. The early models of racial identity development all incorporated the effects of racism and prejudice (oppression) upon the identity transformation of their victims. Vontress (1971), for instance, theorized that Afro-Americans moved through decreasing levels of dependence on White society to emerging identification with Black culture and society (Colored, Negro, and Black). Other similar models for Blacks have been proposed (Cross, 1971, 1972; Hall, Cross, & Freedle, 1972; Jackson, 1975; Thomas, 1970, 1971). The fact that other minority groups such as Asian Americans (Maykovich, 1973; D. W. Sue & S. Sue, 1972; S. Sue & D. W. Sue, 1972b), Hispanics (Szapocznik, Santiste-ban, Kurtines, Hervis & Spencer, 1982; Ruiz, 1990), and women (Downing & Roush, 1985; McNamara & Rickard, 1989) have proposed similar processes may indicate experiential validity for such models as they relate to various oppressed groups.

BLACK IDENTITY DEVELOPMENT MODELS

Early attempts to define a process of minority identity transformation came primarily through the works of Black social scientists and educators (Cross, 1971; Jackson, 1975; Thomas, 1971). Black identity models proposed by Cross (1970; 1971) and Jackson (1975) are discussed here because they represent the most highly developed of those proposed.

The Cross model (1971; 1972; Hall et al., 1972) delineates a four-stage process (originally five) in which Blacks in the United States move from a White frame of reference to a positive Black frame of reference: *preencounter, encounter, immersion-emersion,* and *internalization.* The *preencounter* stage is characterized by individuals (Blacks) who consciously or unconsciously devalue their own Blackness and concurrently value White values and ways. There is a strong desire to assimilate and acculturate into White society. In the *encounter* stage, a two-step process begins to occur. First, the individual encounters a profound crisis or event that challenges his/her previous mode of thinking and behaving; second, the Black person begins to reinterpret the world and a shift in world views results. Cross points out how the slaying of Martin Luther King was such a significant experience for many Blacks. The person experiences both guilt and anger over *being* "brainwashed" by White society. In the third stage, *immersion-emersion*, the person withdraws from the dominant culture and immerses himself or herself in Black culture. Black pride begins to develop, but internalization of positive attitudes toward one's own blackness is minimal. In the emersion phase, feelings of guilt and anger begin to dissipate with an increasing sense of pride. The final stage, *internalization*, is characterized by inner security as conflicts between the old and new identities are resolved. Global antiwhite feelings subside as the person becomes more flexible, more tolerant, and more bicultural/multicultural.

A similar four-stage model has been proposed by Jackson (1975). Like Cross and others, Jackson believed that a Black person's identity is strongly influenced by that person's experiences of racism and oppression. In the *passive-acceptance* stage, the person accepts and conforms to White social, cultural, and institutional standards. Feelings of self-worth come from a white perspective. In the *active-resistance* stage, the person is dedicated toward rejection of White social, cultural, and institutional standards. A great deal of anger (global anti-White feeling) is directed toward White society. The *redirection stage* sees the individual as attempting to develop uniquely Black values, goals, structures, and traditions. This is a period of isolationism in which anger dissipates and is channeled into pride in identity and culture. Once a sense of inner security develops, the person enters the *internalization* stage. The person can own and accept those aspects of U.S. culture that are seen as healthy and can stand against those things that are toxic (racism, sexism, and oppression). White and Black cultures are seen as not necessarily in conflict.

Although these identity development models pertain specifically to the Black experience, we have already pointed out how various other groups have proposed similar processes. Earlier writers (Berry, 1965; Stonequist, 1937) have observed that minority groups share similar patterns of adjustment to cultural oppression. In the past several decades, Asian Americans, Hispanics, and American Indians have experienced sociopolitical identity transformations so that a "Third World consciousness" has emerged with cultural oppression as the common unifying force. As a result of studying these models and integrating them with their own clinical observations, Atkinson, Morten, and Sue (1979; 1983; 1989) have proposed a five-stage Minority Identity Development Model (MID). We attempt to refine and elaborate on the MID, but prefer to call it the Racial/Cultural Identity Development Model (R/CID). As we shall see shortly, this model may also be applied to White identity development.

The R/CID model proposed here is not a comprehensive theory of personality, but rather a conceptual framework to aid counselors in understanding their culturally different client's attitudes and behaviors.

The model defines five stages of development that oppressed people experience as they struggle to understand themselves in terms of their *own culture*, the *dominant culture*, and the *oppressive relationship* between the two cultures: *conformity, dissonance, resistance and immersion, introspection*, and *integrative awareness*. At each level of identity, four corresponding beliefs and attitudes that may help counselors understand their minority clients better are discussed. These attitudes/beliefs are an integral part of the minority person's identity and are manifest in how he/she views (a) the self, (b) others of the same minority, (c) others of another minority, and (d) majority individuals. Table 5.1 outlines the R/CID model and the interaction of stages with the attitudes and beliefs.

Conformity Stage

Similar to individuals in the passive-acceptance stage (Jackson, 1975) and the preencounter stage (Cross, 1970), minority persons are distinguished by their unequivocal preference for dominant cultural values over their own. White Americans in the United States represent their reference group and the identification set is quite strong. Lifestyles, value systems, and cultural/physical characteristics most like White society are highly valued while those most like their own minority group are viewed with disdain or are repressed. Because the conformity stage represents, perhaps, the most damning indictment of White racism, and because it has such a profound negative impact upon minority groups, we spend more time discussing it than the other stages. Let us use a case approach to illustrate the social-psychological dynamics of the conformity process.

Who Am I? White or Black

A 17-year-old White student, Mary comes to counseling for help in sorting out her thoughts and feelings concerning an interracial relationship with a Black student. Although she is proud of the relationship and feels that her liberal friends are accepting and envious, Mary's parents are against it. Indeed, the parents have threatened to cut off financial support for her future college education unless she terminates the affair immediately.

During counseling, Mary tells of how she has rid herself of much bigotry and prejudice from the early training of parents. She joined a circle of friends who were quite liberal in thought and behavior. She recalls how she was both shocked and attracted to her new friends' liberal political beliefs, philosophy, and sexual attitudes. When she first met John, a Black student, she was immediately attracted to his apparent confidence and outspokenness. It did not take her long to become sexually involved with him and to enter into an intense relationship. Mary became the talk of her former friends, but she did not seem to care. Indeed, she seemed to enjoy the attention and openly flaunted her relationship in everyone's face.

TABLE 5.1

Racial/Cultural Identity Development

Stages of Minority Development Model	Attitude toward Self	Attitude toward Others of the Same Minority	Attitude toward Others of Different Minority	Attitude toward Dominant Group
Stage 1— Conformity	Self-depreciating	Group-depreciating	Discriminatory	Group-appreciating
Stage 2— Dissonance	Conflict between self-depreciating and appreciating	Conflict between group-depreciating and group-appreciating	Conflict between dominant-held views of minority hierarchy and feelings of shared experience	Conflict between group appreciating and group depreciating
Stage 3— Resistance and immersion	Self-appreciating	Group-appreciating	Conflict between feelings of empathy for other minority experiences and feelings of culturo-centrism	Group-depreciating
Stage 4— Introspection	Concern with basis of self-appreciation	Concern with nature of unequivocal appreciation	Concern with ethnocentric basis for judging others	Concern with the basis of group-depreciation
Stage 5— Integrative Awareness	Self-appreciating	Group-appreciating	Group-appreciating	Selective appreciation

Because Mary requested couple counseling, the counselor sees them together. John informs the counselor that he came solely to please Mary. He sees few problems in their relationship that cannot be easily resolved. John seems to feel that he has overcome many handicaps in his life, and that this represents just another obstacle to be conquered. When asked about his use of the term "handicap," he responds, "It's not easy to be Black, you know. I've proven to my parents and friends in high school, including myself, that I'm worth something. Let them disapprove—I'm going to make it into a good university." Further probing revealed John's resentment over his own parents' disapproval of the relationship. While his relations with them had worsened to the point of near-physical assaults, John continued to bring Mary home. He seemed to take great pride in being seen with a "beautiful blond-haired, blue-eyed White girl."

In a joint session, Mary's desire to continue and John's apparent reluctance becomes obvious. Several times when John mentions the prospect of a "permanent relationship" and both attending the same university, Mary does not seem to respond positively. She does not seem to want to look too far into the future. Mary's constant coolness to the idea and the counselor's attempt to focus on this reluctance anger John greatly. He becomes antagonistic toward the counselor and puts pressure on Mary to terminate this useless talk "crap." However, he continues to come for the weekly sessions. One day his anger boils over, and he accuses the counselor of being biased. Standing up and shouting, John demands to know how the counselor feels about interracial relationships.

There are many approaches to analyzing the above case, but we have chosen to concentrate on the psychological dynamics evidenced by John, the Black student. However, it is clear from a brief reading of this case that both John and Mary are involved in an interracial relationship as a means of rebellion and as attempts to work out personal identity issues. In Mary's case, it may be rebellion against conservative parents and parental upbringing, and the secondary "shock value" it has for her former friends and parents (appearing liberal). John's motivation for the relationship is also a form of rebellion. There are many clues in this case to indicate that John identifies with White culture and feels disdain for Black culture. First, he seems to equate his Blackness with a "handicap" to be overcome. Is it possible that John feels ashamed of who and what he is (Black)? While feeling proud of one's woman friend is extremely desirable, does Mary's being *White, blond-haired,* and *blue-eyed* have special significance? Would John feel equally proud if the woman was beautiful and Black? Being seen in the company of a White woman may represent affirmation to John that he has "made it" in White society. Perhaps he is operating under the belief that White ways are better and has been sold a false bill of goods.

While John's anger in counseling is multidimensional, much of it seems misdirected toward the counselor. John may actually be angry toward Mary who seems less than committed to a long-term or "permanent relationship." Yet, to acknowledge that Mary may not want a permanent relationship will threaten the very basis of John's self-deception (that he is not like the other Blacks and is accepted in White society). It is very easy to blame John for his dilemma and to call him an "Oreo" (Black outside and White inside). However, lest we fall prey to blaming the victim, let's use a wider perspective in analyzing this case.

John (and even Mary) is really a victim of larger social psychological forces operating in our society. The key issue here is the dominant-subordinate relationship between two different cultures (Atkinson et al., 1989; Brody, 1963; Clark & Clark, 1947; Derbyshire & Brody, 1964; Freire, 1970; Jackson, 1975). It is reasonable to believe that members of one cultural group tend to adjust themselves to the group possessing the greater prestige and power in order to avoid inferiority feelings. Yet, it is exactly this act that creates ambivalence in the minority individual. The pressures for assimilation and acculturation (melting-pot theory) are strong, creating possible culture conflicts. Jones (1972) refers to such dynamics as cultural racism: (a) belief in the superiority of one group's cultural heritage—its language, traditions, arts-crafts, and ways of behaving (White) over all others; (b) belief in the inferiority of all other lifestyles (non-White); and (c) the power to impose such standards onto the less powerful group.

The psychological costs of racism on minorities are immense, and John exemplifies this process. Constantly bombarded on all sides by reminders that Whites and their way of life are superior and all other lifestyles are inferior, many minorities begin to wonder whether they themselves are not somehow inadequate (Baldwin, 1963; Ellison, 1966; Kardiner & Ovesey, 1962; D. W. Sue, 1975), whether members of their own group are not to blame, and whether subordination and segregation are not justified. Clark and Clark (1947) first brought this to the attention of social scientists stating that racism may contribute to a sense of confused self-identity among Black children. In a study of racial awareness and preference among Black and White children, they found (a) Black children preferred playing with a White doll over a Black one, (b) the Black doll was perceived as being "bad," and (c) approximately one-third, when asked to pick the doll that looked like them, picked the White one. It is interesting to note that in the 1987 American Psychological Convention in New York City, a group of researchers reported finding similar results among cabbage-patch dolls.

It is unfortunate that the inferior status of minorities is constantly reinforced and perpetuated by the mass media through television, movies, newspapers, radio, books, and magazines. This contributes to widespread stereotypes that tend to trap minority individuals: Blacks are superstitious, childlike, ignorant, fun loving, or dangerous and criminals; Hispanics are dirty, sneaky, and criminals; Asian Americans are sneaky, sly, cunning, and passive; Indians are primitive savages. Such portrayals cause widespread harm to the self-esteem of minorities who may incorporate them. That preconceived expectations can set up self-fulfilling prophesies has been demonstrated by Rosenthal and Jacobson (1968). The incorporation of the larger society's standards may lead minority-group members to react negatively toward their own racial and cultural heritage. They may become ashamed of who they are, reject their own group identification, and attempt to identify with the desirable "good" White minority. In the *Autobiography of Malcolm X* (Haley, 1966), Malcolm X relates how he tried desperately to appear as White as possible. He went to painful lengths to straighten and dye his hair so he would appear more like White males. It is evident that many minorities do come to accept White standards as a means of measuring physical attractiveness, attractiveness of personality, and social relationships. Such an orientation may lead to the phenomenon of racial self-hatred in which people dislike themselves for being Asian, Black, Hispanic, or Native American. Like John, individuals operating from the conformity stage experience racial self-hatred and attempt to assimilate and acculturate into White society. People at the conformity stage seem to possess the following characteristics.

1. *Attitude and Beliefs toward Self.* Self-depreciating attitudes and beliefs. Physical and cultural characteristics identified with one's own racial/cultural group are perceived negatively, something to be avoided, denied, or changed. Physical characteristics (black skin color, "slant-shaped eyes" of Asians), traditional modes of dress and appearance, and behavioral characteristics associated with the minority group are a source of shame. There may be attempts to mimic what is perceived as "White mannerisms", speech patterns, dress, and goals. Low internal self-esteem is characteristic of the person. The fact that John views his own blackness as a "handicap," something bad, and something to deny is an example of this insidious, but highly damaging, process.

2. *Attitudes and Beliefs toward Members of the Same Minority.* Group-depreciating attitudes and beliefs. Majority cultural beliefs and attitudes about the minority group are also held by the person in this stage. These individuals may have internalized the majority of White stereotypes about their group. In the case of Hispanics, for example, the person may believe that members of his or her own group have high rates of unemployment because "they are lazy, uneducated, and unintelligent." Little thought or validity is given to other viewpoints such as unemployment being a function of job discrimination, prejudice, racism, unequal opportunities, and inferior education. Because persons in the conformity stage find it psychologically painful to identify with these negative traits, they divorce themselves from their own group. The denial mechanism most commonly used is "I'm not like them; I've made it on my own; I'm the exception."

3. *Attitudes and Beliefs toward Members of Different Minorities.* Discriminatory. Because the conformity-stage person most likely strives for identi-

fication with White society, he/she not only shares similar dominant attitudes and beliefs toward his/her own minority group, but toward other minorities as well. Minority groups most similar to White cultural groups are viewed more favorably, while those most different are viewed less favorably. For example, Asian Americans may be viewed more favorably than Blacks or Hispanics in some situations. While a stratification probably exists, we caution readers that such a ranking is fraught with hazards and potential political consequences. Such distinctions oftentimes manifest themselves in debates as to which group is more oppressed and which group has done better than the others. Such debates are counterproductive when used to (a) negate another group's experience of oppression; (b) foster an erroneous belief that hard work alone will result in success in a democratic society; (c) shortchange a minority group (i.e., Asian Americans) from receiving the necessary resources in our society, and (d) pit one minority against another (divide and conquer) by holding one group up as an example to others.

4. *Attitude and Beliefs toward Members of the Dominant Group.* Group-appreciating attitude and beliefs. This stage is characterized by a belief that White cultural, social, institutional standards are superior. Members of the dominant group are admired, respected, and emulated. White people are believed to possess superior intelligence. Some individuals may go to great lengths to appear White. In the *Autobiography of Malcolm X,* the main character would straighten his hair and primarily date White women (as in the case of John). Reports that Asian women have undergone surgery to reshape their eyes to conform to White female standards of beauty may (but not in all cases) typify this dynamic.

Dissonance Stage

No matter how much an individual attempts to deny his/her own racial/cultural heritage, he or she will encounter information or experiences inconsistent with culturally held beliefs, attitudes, and values. An Asian American who believes that Asians are inhibited, passive, inarticulate, and poor in people relationships may encounter an Asian leader who seems to break all these stereotypes. A Hispanic individual who may feel ashamed of his cultural upbringing may encounter another Hispanic who seems proud of his/her cultural heritage. A Black who may have deceived himself or herself into believing that race problems are due to laziness, untrustworthiness, or personal inadequacies of his/her own group, suddenly encounters racism on a personal level. Denial begins to break down, which leads to a questioning and challenging of the attitudes/beliefs of the conformity stage.

In all probability, movement into the dissonance stage is a gradual process. Its very definition indicates the individual is in conflict between disparate pieces of information or experiences that challenge his or her current self-concept. People generally move into this stage slowly, but a traumatic event may propel some individuals to move into dissonance at a much more rapid pace. Cross (1972) states that a monumental event such as the assassination of a major leader like Martin Luther King can oftentimes push people quickly into the ensuing stage.

1. *Attitudes and Beliefs toward Self.* Conflict between self-depreciating and self-appreciating attitudes and beliefs. There is now a growing sense of personal awareness that racism does exist, that not all aspects of the minority or majority culture are good or bad, and that one cannot escape one's cultural heritage. For the first time the person begins to entertain the possibility of positive attributes in the minority culture and, with it, a sense of pride in self. Feelings of shame and pride are mixed in the individual and a sense of conflict develops. This conflict is most likely to be brought to the forefront quickly when other members of the minority group may express positive feelings toward the person: "We like you because you are Asian, Black, American Indian, or Hispanic." At this stage, an important personal question is being asked: "Why should I feel ashamed of who and what I am?"

2. *Attitudes and Beliefs toward Members of the Same Minority.* Conflict between group-depreciating and group-appreciating attitudes and beliefs. Dominant-held views of minority strengths and weaknesses begin to be questioned, as new, contradictory information is received. Certain aspects of the minority culture begin to have appeal. For example, a Hispanic male who values "individualism" may marry, have children, and then suddenly realize how Hispanic cultural values that hold the "family as the psychosocial unit" possess positive features. Or, the minority person may find certain members of his group to be very attractive as friends, colleagues, lovers, and so forth.

3. *Attitudes and Beliefs toward Members of a Different Minority.* Conflict between dominant-held views of minority hierarchy and feelings of shared experience. Stereotypes associated with other minority groups become questioned and a growing sense of comradeship with other oppressed groups is shared. It is important to keep in mind, however, that little psychic energy is associated with resolving conflicts with other minority groups. Almost all energies are expended toward resolving conflicts toward the self, the same minority, and the dominant group.

4. *Attitudes and Beliefs toward Members of Dominant Group.* Conflict between group-appreciating and group-depreciating attitude. The person experiences a growing awareness that not all cultural values of the dominant group are beneficial to him/her. This is especially true when the minority person experiences personal discrimination. Growing suspiciousness and some distrust of certain members of the dominant group develops.

Resistance and Immersion Stage

The culturally different individual tends to completely endorse minority-held views and to reject the dominant values of society and culture. The person seems dedicated to reacting against White society and rejects White social, cultural, and institutional standards as having no validity for him or her. Desire to eliminate oppression of the individual's minority group becomes an important motivation of the individual's behavior. During the resistance and immersion stage, the three most active types of affective feelings are *guilt, shame,* and *anger.* There are considerable feelings of guilt and shame that in the past the minority individual has "sold out" his/her own racial and cultural group. The feelings of guilt and shame extend to the perception that during this past "sellout," the minority person has been a contributor and participant in the oppression of his/her own group and other minority groups. This is coupled with a strong sense of anger at the oppression and feelings of having been brainwashed by the forces in White society. Anger is directed outwardly in a very strong way toward oppression and racism. Movement into this stage seems to occur for two reasons. First, a resolution of the conflicts and confusions of the previous stage allows greater understanding of social forces (racism, oppression, and discrimination) and his/her role as a victim. Second, a personal questioning of why people should feel ashamed of themselves is asked. The answer to this question evokes feelings of guilt, shame, and anger.

1. *Attitudes and Belief toward the Self.* Self-appreciating attitudes and beliefs. The minority individual at this stage is oriented toward self-discovery of one's own history and culture. There is an active seeking out of information and artifacts that enhance that person's sense of identity and worth. Cultural and racial characteristics that once elicited feelings of shame and disgust become symbols of pride and honor. The individual moves into this stage primarily because he or she asks the question, "Why should I be ashamed of who and what I am?" The original low self-esteem engendered by widespread prejudice and racism most characteristic of the conformity stage is now actively challenged in order to raise self-esteem. Phrases such as "Black is beautiful," represent a symbolic relabeling of identity for many Blacks. Racial self-hatred becomes something actively rejected in favor of the other extreme, which is unbridled racial pride.

2. *Attitudes and Beliefs toward Members of the Same Minority.* Group-appreciating attitudes and beliefs. The individual experiences a strong sense of identification with and commitment to his/her minority group as enhancing information about the group is acquired. There is a feeling of connectedness with other members of the racial and cultural group and a strengthening of new identity begins to occur. Members of one's group are admired, respected, and often viewed now as the new reference group or ideal. Cultural values of the minority group are accepted without question. As indicated, the pendulum swings drastically from original identification with White ways to identification in an unquestioning manner with the minority-group's ways. Persons in this stage, are likely to restrict their interactions as much as possible to members of their own group.

3. *Attitudes and Beliefs toward Members of a Different Minority.* Conflict between feelings of empathy for other minority-group experiences and feelings of culturocentrism. While members at this stage experience a growing sense of comradeship with persons from other minority groups, a strong culturocentrism develops as well. Alliances with other groups tend to be transitory and based upon short-term goals or some global shared view of oppression. There is not so much an attempt to reach out and understand other racial-cultural minority groups and their values and ways, but more a superficial surface feeling of political need. Alliances generally are based upon convenience factors and/or are formed for political reasons such as combining together as a large group to confront a larger-perceived enemy.

4. *Attitude and Beliefs toward Members of the Dominant Group.* Group-depreciating attitudes and beliefs. The minority individual is likely to perceive the dominant society and culture as an oppressor and the group most responsible for the current plight of minorities in the United States. Characterized by both withdrawal from the dominant culture and immersion in one's cultural heritage, there is also considerable anger and hostility directed toward White society. There is a feeling of distrust and dislike for all members of the dominant group in an almost global anti-White demonstration and feeling. White people, for example, are not to be trusted for they are the oppressors or enemies. In extreme form, members may advocate complete destruction of the institutions and structures that have been characteristic of White society.

Introspection Stage

Several factors seem to work in unison to move the individual from the resistance and immersion stage into the introspection stage. First, the individual begins to discover that this level of intensity of feelings (anger directed toward White society) is psychologically draining and does not permit one to really devote more crucial energies to understanding themselves or to their own racial-cultural group. The resistance and immersion stage tends to be a reaction against the dominant culture and is not proactive in allowing the individual to use all energies to discover who or what he or she is. Self definition in the previous stage tends to be reactive (against White racism) and a need for positive self definition in a proactive sense emerges.

Second, the minority individual experiences feelings of discontent and discomfort with group views that may be quite rigid in the resistance and immersion stage. Oftentimes, in order to please the group, the culturally different individual is asked to submerge individual autonomy and individual thought in favor of the group good. Many group views may now be seen as conflicting with individual ones. A Hispanic individual who may form a deep relationship with a White person may experience considerable pressure from his or her culturally similar peers to break off the relationship because that person is the "enemy." However, the personal experiences of the individual may, indeed, not support this group view.

It is important to note that some clinicians often erroneously confuse certain characteristics of the introspective stage with the conformity stage. A minority person from the former stage who speaks against the decisions of his/her group may often appear similar to the conformity person. The dynamics are quite different, however. While the conformity person is motivated by global racial self-hatred, the introspective person has no such global negativism directed at his/her own group.

1. *Attitudes and Beliefs toward the Self.* Concern with basis of self-appreciating attitudes and beliefs. While the person originally in the conformity stage held predominately to majority-group views and notions to the detriment of his or her own minority group, the person now feels he or she has too rigidly held onto minority-group views and notions in order to submerge personal autonomy. The conflict now becomes quite great in terms of responsibility and allegiance to one's own minority group versus notions of personal independence and autonomy. The person begins to spend greater and greater time and energy trying to sort out these aspects of self-identity and begins to increasingly demand individual autonomy.

2. *Attitudes and Beliefs toward Members of the Same Minority.* Concern with unequivocal nature of group appreciation. While attitudes of identification are continued from the preceding resistance and immersion stage, concern begins to build up regarding the issue of group-usurped individuality. Increasingly, the individual may see his or her own group taking positions that might be considered quite extreme. In addition, there is now increasing resentment over how one's group may attempt to pressure or influence the individual into making decisions that may be inconsistent with the person's values, beliefs, and outlook. Indeed, it is not unusual for members of a minority group to make it clear to the member that if they do not agree with the group, they are against it. A common ploy used to hold members in line is exemplified in the questions: "How Asian are you?" "How Black are you?"

3. *Attitudes and Beliefs toward Members of a Different Minority.* Concern with ethnocentric basis for judging others. There is now greater uneasiness with culturocentrism and an attempt is made to reach out to other groups in finding out what types of oppression they experience, and how this has been handled. While similarities are important, there is now a movement into understanding potential differences in oppression that other groups might have experienced.

4. *Attitudes and Beliefs toward Members of the Dominant Group.* Concern with the basis of group depreciation. The individual experiences conflict between attitudes of complete trust for the dominant society and culture, and attitudes of selective trust and distrust according to the dominant individual's demonstrated behaviors and attitudes. Conflict is most likely to occur here because the person begins to recognize that there are many elements in U.S. American culture that are highly functional and desirable, yet there is confusion as to how to incorporate these elements into the minority culture. Would the person's acceptance of certain White cultural values make the person a sellout to his or her own race? There is a lowering of intense feelings of anger and distrust toward the dominant group but a continued attempt to discern elements that are acceptable.

Integrative Awareness Stage

Minority persons in this stage have developed an inner sense of security and now can own and appreciate unique aspects of their culture as well as those in U.S. culture. Minority culture is not necessarily in conflict with White dominant cultural ways. Conflicts and discomforts experienced in the previous stage become resolved, allowing greater individual control and flexibility. There is now the belief there are acceptable and unacceptable aspects in all cultures, and that it is very important for the person to be able to examine and accept or reject those aspects of a culture that are not seen as desirable. At the integrative awareness stage, the minority person has a strong commitment and desire to eliminate all forms of oppression.

1. *Attitudes and Beliefs toward Self.* Self-appreciating attitudes and beliefs. The culturally different individual develops a positive self-image and experiences a strong sense of self-worth and confidence. Not only is there an integrated self-concept that involves racial pride in identity and culture, but the person develops a high sense of autonomy. Indeed, the client becomes bicultural or multicultural without a sense of having "sold out one's integrity." In other words, the person begins to perceive his or her self as an autonomous individual who is unique (individual level of identity), a member of one's own racial-cultural group (group level of identity), a member of a larger society, and a member of the human race (universal level of identity).

2. *Attitudes and Beliefs toward Members of Same Minority.* Group-appreciating attitudes and beliefs. The individual experiences a strong sense of pride in the group without having to accept group values unequivocally. There is no longer the conflict over disagreeing with group goals and values. Strong feelings of empathy with the group experience are coupled with an awareness that each member of the group is also an individual. In addition, tolerant and empathic attitudes are likely to be expressed toward members of one's own group who may be functioning at a less adaptive manner to racism and oppression.

3. *Attitudes and Beliefs toward Members of a Different Minority.* Group-appreciating attitudes. There is now literally a reaching-out toward different minority groups in order to understand their cultural values and ways of life. There is a strong belief that the more one understands other cultural values and beliefs, the greater is the likelihood of understanding among the various ethnic groups. Support for all oppressed people, regardless of similarity to the individual's minority group, tends to be emphasized.

4. *Attitudes and Beliefs toward Members of the Dominant Group.* Attitudes and beliefs of selective appreciation. The individual experiences selective trust and liking from members of the dominant group who seek to eliminate oppressive activities of the group. The individual also experiences an openness to the constructive elements of the dominant culture. The emphasis here tends to be on the fact that White racism is a sickness in society and that White people are also victims who are in need of help as well.

COUNSELING IMPLICATIONS OF R/CID MODEL

Let us first point out some broad general counseling implications of the R/CID model before discussing specific meanings within each of the stages. First, an understanding of cultural identity development should sensitize counselors to the role that oppression plays in a minority individual's development. In many respects, it should make us aware that our role as counselors should extend beyond the office and should deal with the many manifestations of racism. While individual counseling is needed, combating the forces of racism means a proactive approach for both the counselor and client. For the counselor, systems intervention is often the answer. For the culturally different client, it means the need to understand, control, and direct those forces in society that negate the process of positive identity. Thus, a wider sociocultural approach to counseling is mandatory.

Second, the model will aid counselors in recognizing differences between members of the same minority group with respect to their cultural identity. It serves as a useful assessment and diagnostic tool for counselors to gain a greater understanding of their culturally different client (Helms, 1985). In many cases, an accurate delineation of the dynamics and characteristics of the stages may result in better prescriptive treatment. Those counselors familiar with the sequence of stages are better able to plan intervention strategies most effective for a culturally different client. For example, a client experiencing feelings of isolation and alienation in the conformity stage may require a different approach than he/she would in the introspection stage.

Third, the model allows counselors to realize the potentially changing and developmental nature of cultural identity among clients. If the goal of cross-cultural counseling is intended to move a client toward the integrative awareness stage, then the counselor is able to anticipate the sequence of feelings, beliefs, attitudes, and behaviors likely to arise. Acting as a guide and providing an understandable end-point will allow the client to more quickly understand and work through issues related to his/her own identity. We now turn our attention to the R/CID model and its implications for the counseling process.

Conformity Stage: Counseling Implications

Characteristics of conformity-stage individuals (belief in the superiority of White ways and inferiority of minority ways) suggest several counseling implications. First, the culturally different client is most likely to prefer a White counselor over a minority counselor. This flows logically from the belief that Whites are more competent and capable than members of one's own race. Such a racial preference can be manifested in the client's reaction to a minority counselor via negativism, resistance, or open hostility. In some instances, the client may even request a change in counselors (preferably someone White). On the other hand, the conformity individual who is seen by a White counselor may be quite pleased about it. In many cases, the culturally different client in identifying with White culture, may be overly dependent upon the White counselor. Attempts to please, appease, and seek approval from the counselor may be quite strong.

Second, most conformity individuals will find attempts to explore cultural identity or to focus in upon feelings very threatening. Clients in this stage generally prefer a task-oriented, problem-solving approach. That is because an exploration of identity may eventually touch upon feelings of low self-esteem, dissatisfaction with personal appearance, vague anxieties, racial self-hatred, and challenge the client's self-deception that he/she is not like the other members of his/her own race. In our earlier case of John, for example, when threatened by the idea that Mary may not want a "permanent" relationship, he uses the counselor as a scapegoat for his feelings of anger toward Mary. To recognize that he is really angry at Mary means a breakdown in his denial system and the need to confront his feelings of racial self-hatred, along with the realization that *he is a Black person!*

Whether you are a White or minority counselor working with a conformity individual, the general goal may be the same. There is an obligation to help the client *sort out* conflicts related to racial/cultural identity through some process of reeducation. Somewhere in the process of counseling, issues of cultural racism, majority-minority group relations, racial self-hatred, and racial cultural identity need to be dealt with in an integrated fashion. We are not suggesting a lecture or solely a cognitive approach to which clients at this stage may be quite intellectually receptive, but exercising good clinical skills that take into account the client's socioemotional state and readiness to deal with feelings. Only in this manner will the counselee be able to distinguish the difference between positive attempts to adopt certain values of the dominant society and a negative rejection of one's own cultural value (a characteristic of the Integrative awareness stage).

While the goals for the White and minority counselor are the same, the way a counselor works toward them may be different. In the case of the minority counselor, he/she is likely to have to deal with hostility from the culturally similar client. The counselor may symbolize all that the client is trying to reject. Because counseling stresses the building of a coalition, establishment of rapport, and to some degree a mutual identification, the counseling process may be especially threatening. The opposite may be true of work with a White counselor. The culturally different client may be overeager to identify with the White counselor in order to seek approval. However, rather than being detrimental to cross-cultural counseling, these two processes may be used quite effectively and productively. If the minority counselor can aid the client in working through his/her feelings of antagonism, and if the majority counselor can aid the client in working through his/her need to overidentify, then the client will be moved closer to awareness rather than self-deception. In the former case, the counselor can take a nonjudgmental stance toward the client and provide a positive minority role model. In the latter, the White counselor needs to model positive attitudes toward cultural diversity. Both need to guard against unknowingly reinforcing the client's self-denial and rejection.

Dissonance Stage: Counseling Implications

As individuals begin to become more aware of inconsistencies between dominant-held views and those of their group, a sense of dissonance develops. Preoccupation and questions concerning self, identity, and self-esteem are most likely brought in for counseling. More culturally aware than their conformity counterparts, dissonance clients may prefer a counselor who possesses good knowledge of the client's cultural group, although there may still be a preference for a White counselor. However, the fact that minority counselors are generally more knowledgeable of the client's cultural group may serve to heighten the conflicting beliefs and feelings of this stage. Since the client is so receptive toward self-exploration, the counselor can capitalize upon this orientation in helping the client come to grips with his/her identity conflicts.

Resistance and Immersion Stage: Counseling Implications

Minority clients at this stage are likely to view their psychological problems as products of oppression and racism. Only issues of racism are legitimate areas to explore in counseling. Furthermore, openness or self-disclosure to counselors other than one's own group is dangerous because White counselors are enemies and members of the oppressing group.

Resistance-and-immersion-stage clients believe society is to blame for their present dilemma and actively challenge the Establishment. They are openly suspicious of institutions, such as counseling services, because they view them as agents of the Establishment. Very few of the more ethnically conscious and militant minorities will use counseling because of its identification with the status quo. When they do, they are usually suspicious and hostile toward the counselor. Before counseling can proceed effectively, the counselor will have to deal with certain challenges from these students, such as the following:

HISPANIC CLIENT: First of all, I don't believe in counseling. I think it's a lot of bullshit. People in counseling are always trying to adjust people to a *sick* society, and what is needed is to overthrow this goddamned establishment. I feel the same way about those stupid tests. Cultural bias—they aren't applicable to minorities. The only reason I came in here was—well, I heard your lecture in Psychology 160, and I think I can work with you.

The male counselee in this case happened to be hostile and depressed over the recent death of his father. Although he realized he had some need for help, he still did not trust the counseling process.

CLIENT: Psychologists see the problem inside of people when the problem is in society. Don't you think White society has made all minorities feel inferior and degraded?

COUNSELOR: Yes, your observations appear correct. White society has done great harm to minorities.

The client was obviously posing a direct challenge to the counselor. Any defense of White society or explanations of the value of counseling might have aroused greater hostility and mistrust. It would have been extremely difficult to establish rapport without some honest agreement on the racist nature of American society. Later, the counselee revealed his father had just died. He was beginning to realize that there was no contradiction in viewing society as being racist and in having personal problems. Often, growing pride in self-identity in the extreme makes it difficult for clients who are having emotional problems to accept their personal difficulties.

A counselor working with a client at this stage of development needs to realize several important things. First, he or she will be viewed by the culturally different client as a *symbol* of the oppressive Establishment. If you become defensive and *personalize* the "attacks," you will lose your effectiveness in working with the client. It is important to not be intimidated or be afraid of the anger that is likely to be expressed; oftentimes, it is not personal and is quite legitimate. White, guilt and defensiveness can only serve to hinder effective cross-cultural counseling. It is not unusual for clients at this stage to make sweeping negative generalizations about White Americans. The White counselor who takes a nondefensive posture will be better able to help the client explore the basis of his/her racial tirades. In general, clients at this stage prefer a counselor of their own race. However, the fact that you share the same race or culture as your client will not insulate you from the "attacks." For example, a Black client may perceive the Black counselor as a "sellout" of his/her own race or as an "Uncle Tom." Indeed, the anger and hostility directed at the minority counselor may be even more intense than that directed at a White counselor.

Second, realize that clients in this stage will constantly test you. In earlier chapters, we described how minority clients will pose challenges to counselors in order to test their sincerity, openness, nondefensiveness, and competencies. Because of the active nature of client challenges, counseling sessions may become quite dynamic. Many counselors oftentimes find this stage the most difficult to deal with because counselor self-disclosure is often called for (see Chapters 2 and 3).

Third, individuals at this stage are especially receptive to counseling approaches that are more action oriented and aimed at external change (challenging racism). Also, group-counseling approaches with persons experiencing similar racial/cultural issues are well received. It is important that the counselor be willing to help the culturally different client explore new ways of relating to both minority and White persons.

Introspection Stage: Counseling Implications

Clients at the introspection stage may continue to prefer a counselor of their own race, but they are also receptive to counselors from other cultures as long as they understand their world view. Ironically, clients at this stage may, on the surface, appear similar to conformity persons. Introspection clients are in conflict between their need to identify with the minority group and their need to exercise greater personal freedom. Exercising personal autonomy may occasionally mean going against the wishes or desires of the minority group. This is often perceived by minority persons and their group as a rejection of their own cultural heritage. This is not unlike conformity persons who also reject their racial/cultural heritage. The dynamics between the two groups, however, are quite different. It is very important for counselors to distinguish the differences. The conformity person moves away from his/her own group because of perceived negative qualities associated with it. The introspection person desires to move away on certain issues, but perceives his/her group positively. Again, self-exploration approaches aimed at helping the client integrate and incorporate a new sense of identity are important. Believing in the functional values of U.S. society does not mean "selling out" or that you are against your own group.

Integrative Awareness Stage: Counseling Implications

Clients at this stage have acquired an inner sense of security as to self-identity. They have pride in their racial/cultural heritage yet can exercise a desired level of personal freedom and autonomy. Other cultures and races are appreciated, and there is a development toward becoming more multicultural in perspective. While discrimination and oppression remain a powerful part of their existence, integrative awareness persons possess greater psychological resources to deal with these problems. Being action or systems oriented, clients respond positively to the designing and implementation of strategies aimed at community and society change. Preferences for counselors are not based upon race, but those who can share, understand, and accept their world views. In other words, attitudinal similarity between counselor and client is a more important dimension than membership-group similarity.

WHITE IDENTITY DEVELOPMENT

Thus far we have described the stages of identity formation from the perspective of the minority client, with little consideration or regard to the cultural identity stage of the counselor. Whatever the race or cultural identity of the counselor, it makes sense that his/her stage is likely to have major implications for the client and the process of counseling (Clarey & Parker, 1989; Helms, 1984; Ponterotto, 1988). A minority counselor at the conformity stage may cause great harm to clients at other stages. The counselor may intentionally and unintentionally (a) reinforce a conformity client's feelings of racial self-hatred, (b) prevent or block a dissonance client from looking at inconsistent feelings/attitudes/beliefs, (c) dismiss and negate the resistance and immersion client's anger about racism (he or she is a radical), and (d) perceive the integrative awareness individual as having a confused sense of self-identity.

Other combinations of stages can lead to even greater confusion in counseling. What would counseling be like if the client was at the conformity stage while the counselor was at the resistance and immersion stage? Would the counselor feel negatively toward the client because he or she views the person as having sold out? We are obviously dealing with a highly complex and speculative area, which requires greater research and investigations. [See Helms' (1984) excellent analysis of dyad combinations.] Earlier admonitions for counselors to "know thyself" and grow culturally aware of their own biases, values, and assumptions about human behavior become more important.

Recently, a number of multicultural experts in the field have begun to emphasize the need for White counselors to deal with their concepts of Whiteness and to examine their own racism (Corvin & Wiggins, 1989; Helms, 1984; Ponterotto, 1988). These specialists point out that while racial/cultural identity development for minority groups proves beneficial in our work as counselors, more attention has to be devoted toward the White counselor's racial identity. Since the majority of counselors and trainees are White middle-class individuals, it would appear that White identity development and its implication for multicultural counseling would be important aspects to consider, both in the actual practice of counseling and in counselor training.

Three models of White identity development have been proposed. In 1980, Rita Hardiman (1982) proposed a White identity development model describing a developmental sequence of beliefs, values, feelings, and behaviors that White people pass in developing a nonracist, new White identity. The four-stage model parallels that developed by Bailey Jackson (1975) for Black Americans. The stages include acceptance, resistance, redefinition, and internalization. Following that publication, but working independently, Janet Helms (1984) published a major conceptual under-taking entitled "Toward a Theoretical Explanation of the Effects of Race on Counseling: A Black and White Model." She presented a five-stage process of White identity development: contact, disintegration, reintegra-tion, pseudoindependence, and autonomy. Her highly sophisticated model not only describes how Whites go through the process of defining themselves as racial beings, but describes how certain stage dyadic combi-nations affect the process and outcome of counseling. More recently, Joe Ponterotto (1988) and colleagues (Sabnani et al., in press) have applied their own model of White racial identity development to White counselor trainees. The stages they identified are pre-exposure/precontact, conflict, pro-minority/anti-racism, retreat into White culture, and redefinition and integration. Their work has attempted to identify the most effective learning experiences for trainees at each of the stages.

All three models seem to share some basic assumptions. First, racism is a basic and integral part of U.S. life and permeates all aspects of our culture and institutions. Second, Whites are socialized into U.S. society and, therefore, inherit the biases, stereotypes, and racist attitudes, beliefs, and behaviors of the society. In other words, all Whites are racist whether knowingly or unknowingly. Third, how Whites perceive themselves as racial beings seems to follow an identifiable sequence that can be called stages. Fourth, the stage of White racial identity development in a cross-cultural encounter (counseling minorities, counselor training, etc.) affects the process and outcome of an interracial relationship. Last, the most desirable stage is the one where the White person not only accepts his/her Whiteness, but defines it in a nondefensive and nonracist manner.

In our work with White trainees and practicing counselors, we have observed some very important changes they seem to move through as they work toward multicultural competence. Like Hardiman, Helms, and Ponterotto, we have been impressed with how Whites also seem to go through parallel racial/cultural identity transformations. Indeed, the racial/cultural identity model discussed earlier in this chapter seems equally applicable to White people as well. This is especially true if we accept the fact that Whites are as much victims of societal forces (socialized into racist attitudes and beliefs) as their minority counterparts. No child is born wanting to be a racist! Yet White people do benefit from the dominant-subordinant relationship evident in our society. It is this factor that Whites need to confront in an open and honest manner. Using the racial/cultural identity model proposed earlier, we would like to briefly describe how it may apply to identity transformation of Whites.

Conformity Stage (Whites)

The White person's attitudes and beliefs in this stage are very ethnocentric. There is minimal awareness of the self as a racial being (Ponterotto, 1988) and a belief in the universality of values and norms governing behavior. There is limited accurate knowledge of other ethnic groups, but a great deal of adherence to social stereotypes. Hardiman (1982) describes this stage as an acceptance of White superiority and minority inferiority. Consciously or unconsciously, the White person believes that White culture is the most highly developed, and all others are "primitive" or inferior. The conformity stage is marked by contradictory and oftentimes compartmentalized attitudes, beliefs, and behaviors. On the one hand a person may believe that he or she is not racist, yet believe that minority inferiority justifies discriminatory and inferior treatment; that minority persons are different and deviant, yet believe that "people are people" and that differences are unimportant (Helms, 1984). Like their minority counterparts at this stage, the primary mechanism operating here is one of denial and compartmentalization. For example, many Whites deny that they belong to a race. Katz & Ivey (1977) believe that such a denial allows Whites to avoid personal responsibility for perpetuating a racist system.

Dissonance Stage (Whites)

Movement into the dissonance stage occurs when the White person is forced to deal with the inconsistencies that have been compartmentalized or encounters information/experiences at odds with his/her denial. In most cases, a person is forced to acknowledge their Whiteness at some level, to examine their own cultural values, and to see the conflict between upholding humanistic nonracist values and their contradictory behavior. A major conflict is likely to ensue in people who recognize their racism and the part they play in oppressing minority groups. To act on this recognition may mean risking ostracism from other White relatives, friends, neighbors, and colleagues. Feelings of guilt, shame, anger, and depression may characterize this stage. Guilt and shame may be associated with the recognition of the White person's role in perpetuating racism in the past. Or, guilt may result from the person's being afraid to speak out on the issues or to take responsibility for his/her part in a current situation. For example, the person may witness an act of racism, hear a racist comment, or be given preferential treatment over a minority person but decide not to say anything for fear of violating racist White norms. Oftentimes, the person may delude himself or herself with rationalizations: "I'm just one person. What can I do about it?" This approach is one frequently taken by many White people in which they rationalize their behaviors by the belief that they are powerless to make changes. There is a tendency to retreat into White culture (Helms, 1984; Sabnani et al., in press).

Resistance and Immersion (Whites)

Should the White person progress to this stage, he/she will begin to question and challenge his/her own racism. For the first time, the person begins to realize what racism is all about, and his/her eyes are suddenly open. Racism is seen everywhere (advertising, television, educational materials, interpersonal interactions, etc.). There is likely to be considerable anger at family and friends, institutions, and larger societal values, which are seen as having sold him/her a false bill of goods (democratic ideals) that were never practiced. Guilt is also felt for having been a part of the oppressive system. Strangely enough, the person is likely to undergo a form of racial self-hatred at this stage. Negative feelings about being White are present and the accompanying feelings of guilt, shame and anger toward oneself and other Whites may develop. The "White liberal" syndrome may develop and be manifested in two complementary styles. The paternalistic protector role or the overidentification with another minority group (Helms, 1984; Ponterotto, 1988). In the former, the White person may devote his/her energies in an almost paternalistic attempt to protect minorities from abuse. In the latter, the person may actually want to identify with a particular minority group (Asian, Black, etc.) in order to escape his/her own Whiteness. The White person will soon discover, however, that these roles are not appreciated by minority groups and will experience rejection. Again, the person may resolve this dilemma by moving back into the protective confines of White culture (conformity stage), again experience conflict (dissonance), or move directly to the introspective stage.

Introspective Stage (Whites)

The White person who enters the introspective stage is likely to have gone between two extremes (White identity to rejection of Whiteness). Like a pendulum swinging from one end to the other, the person realizes that one's White identity cannot be defined by simple external forces. A need for greater individual autonomy is expressed. The standards used to judge one's White identity cannot come from one group or the other. Some compromise or middle ground needs to be developed. Feelings of guilt or anger that have motivated the person to identify with one or the other group are dysfunctional. An independent search for goals and direction beyond merely reacting to White racism is needed. The person no longer denies that he or she is White. But there is also a reduction of the defensiveness and guilt associated with being White.

Integrative Awareness Stage (Whites)

Whites at this stage experience a sense of self-fulfillment with regard to racial/cultural identity. A nonracist White identity begins to emerge.

Exploring White culture and those aspects that are nonexploitative and self-affirming are an intimate aspect of this stage. The person no longer denies personal responsibility for perpetuating racism, but tends not to be immobilized by guilt or prompted into rash acts by anger. There is increased knowledge of sociopolitical influences as they affect race relations, increased appreciation for cultural diversity, and an increased social commitment toward eradication of racism.

CAUTIONS/LIMITATIONS IN THE FORMULATION OF RACIAL/CULTURAL IDENTITY MODELS

In proposing the R/CID model, we have been very aware of some major cautions and possible limitations that readers need to take into account. First, the R/CID model should not be viewed as a global personality theory with specific identifiable stages that serve as fixed categories. Cultural identity development is a dynamic process, not a static one. One of the major dangers that counselors can fall into is to use these stages as fixed entities. In actuality, this should serve as a conceptual framework to help us understand development. Most culturally different clients may evidence a dominant characteristic, but there are mixtures of the various stages as well. Furthermore, situations and the types of presenting problems may make some characteristics more manifest than others. It is possible that culturally different clients may evidence conformity characteristics in some situations, but resistance and immersion characteristics in others. A question often raised in the formulation of cultural identity development models is whether identity is a linear process. Is it possible for individuals not to begin at one of these stages, or that they may move from one stage to the other while skipping another. In general, our clinical experience has been that minority and majority individuals in this society do tend to move at some gross level through each of the identifiable stages. Some tend to move faster than others, and some tend to stay predominately at only one stage and some may regress. This, however, is a question that needs to be tested empirically through research. Recently, Parham (1989) has proposed a nigrescense identity model characterized by complex loops to the various stages.

Second, it has become increasingly clear that almost all cultural identity development models begin at a stage that involves interaction with an oppressive society. Most of these are weak in formulating a stage prior to conformity characteristics. Recent Asian immigrants to the United States are a prime example of the inadequacy of cultural identity development models. Many of the Asian immigrants to the United States tend to hold very positive and favorable views of their own culture. What happens when they encounter a society that views cultural differences as being deviant? Will they or their offspring move through the conformity stage as presented in this model? Again, this is an empirical question.

Third, there is an implied value judgment given in almost all development models. It is clear that all cultural identity development models assume that some cultural resolutions are healthier than others. For example, the R/CID model does believe that the integrative awareness stage represents a higher form of healthy functioning.

Fourth, we need to take into consideration sociocultural forces that impact upon identity development. Many of the early Black identity development models arose as a result of perceived and real experiences of oppression in our society. The Third World movement (Black power movement, Yellow power movement, Red power movement, and Brown power movement) occurred in a period of our society that heightened racial-cultural pride and awareness. In other words, identity transformations are seen as being triggered by social movements that have powerful effects on the culturally different individual's identity. Does this mean that if social situations change, many of the cultural identity development models would also change? What apparently needs to be done is for us to explore and investigate how interpersonal, institutional, societal, and cultural factors may either facilitate or impede cultural identity development.

Fifth, there is a strong need for us to understand and refine these models. Issues of possible class, age, gender, and so forth, have not been addressed adequately in these models. Furthermore, we have talked about identity in a very global manner. A great deal of evidence is mounting that while identity may sequentially move through identifiable stages, affective, attitudinal, cognitive, and behavioral components of identity may not move in a uniform manner. For example, it is entirely possible that the emotions and affective elements associated with certain stages do not have a corresponding one-to-one behavioral impact.

Last, we need to begin looking more closely at the possible counselor and client stage combinations. As mentioned earlier, therapeutic processes and outcomes are often the function of the identity stage of both counselor and client. White identity development (WID) of the counselor can either enhance or retard effective counseling. As yet, the complexity of WID in counseling is only in the infancy stages. For a sophisticated discussion, the reader is encouraged to read the works by Helms (1984) and Sabnani et al. (in press).

CHAPTER 6

Cross-Cultural
Family Counseling

Several years ago, a female school counselor sought the senior author's advice about a Hispanic family she had recently seen. She seemed quite concerned about the identified client, Elena Martinez, a 13-year-old student who was referred to her for alleged peddling of drugs on the school premises. The counselor had thought that the parents "did not care for their daughter," "were uncooperative," and "were attempting to avoid responsibility for dealing with Elena's delinquency." When pressed for how she arrived at these impressions, the counselor provided the following information.

Elena Martinez is the second oldest of four other siblings, ages 15, 12, 10, and 7. The father is an immigrant from Mexico and the mother is a natural citizen. The family resides in a blue-collar Hispanic neighborhood in San Jose, California.

Elena had been reported as having minor problems in school prior to the "drug-selling incident." For example, she had "talked back to teachers," refused to do homework assignments, and had "fought" with other students. Her involvement with a group of other Hispanic students (suspected of being responsible for disruptive school-yard pranks) had gotten her into trouble. Elena was well-known to the counseling staff at the school. Her teacher last year reported that she was unable to "get through" to Elena. Because of the seriousness of the drug accusations, the counselor felt that something had to be done, and that the parents needed to be informed immediately.

The counselor reported calling the parents in order to set up an interview with them. When Mrs. Martinez answered the telephone, the counselor had explained how Elena had been caught on school grounds selling marijuana by a police officer. Rather than arrest her, the officer turned the student over to the vice-principal, who luckily was present at the time of the incident. After the explanation, the counselor had asked that the parents make arrangements for an appointment as soon as possible. The meeting would be aimed at informing the parents about Elena's difficulties in school and coming to some decision about what could be done.

During the phone conversation, Mrs. Martinez seemed hesitant about choosing a time to come in and, when pressed by the counselor, excused herself from the telephone. The counselor reported overhearing some whispering on the other end, and then the voice of Mr. Martinez. He immediately asked the counselor how his daughter was and expressed his consternation over the entire situation. At that point, the counselor stated that she understood his feelings, but it would be best to set up an appointment for tomorrow and talk about it then. Several times the counselor asked Mr. Martinez about a convenient time for the meeting, but each time he seemed to avoid the answer and to give excuses. He had to work the rest of the day and could not make the appointment. The counselor stressed strongly how important the meeting was for the daughter's welfare, and that the several hours of missed work was not important in light of the situation. The father stated that he would be able to make an evening session, but the counselor informed him that school policy prohibited evening meetings. When the counselor suggested that the mother could initially come alone, further hesitations seemed present. Finally, the father agreed to attend.

The very next day, Mr. and Mrs. Martinez and a brother-in-law (Elena's godfather) showed up together in her office. The counselor reported being upset at the presence of the brother-in-law when it became obvious he planned to sit in on the session. At that point, she explained that a third party present would only make the session more complex and the outcome counterproductive. She wanted to see only the family.

The counselor reported that the session went poorly with minimal cooperation from the parents. She reported, "It was like pulling teeth," trying to get the Martinezes to say anything at all.

The case of Elena Martinez exemplifies some major possible misunderstandings that may occur in working with minority families. Most important is the counselor's obvious lack of understanding concerning Hispanic cultural values, and how they traditionally affect not only communication patterns, but the role relationships as well. This lack of knowledge and a degree of insensitivity to the minority family's experience in the United States can lead to negative impressions such as, "They are uncooperative, avoiding responsibility and do not care for their children." Let us briefly analyze this case from another perspective.

First, it is entirely possible that the incidents reported by the counselor mean something different, when seen from traditional Hispanic culture. Unlike U.S. culture, which is much more egalitarian in the husband-wife relationship, some Hispanic Americans tend to be more patriarchal. The husband assumes the role of the dominant decision-maker, while the wife is relegated to a more submissive role. In reality, division of roles (husband is protector/provider while wife cares for the home/family) allows both to exercise influence and make decisions. A wife would be remiss in publicly making a family decision (setting up an appointment time) without consulting or obtaining agreement from the husband. Mrs. Martinez's hesitation on the phone to commit a meeting time with the counselor may be a reflection of the husband-wife role relationship rather than a lack of concern for the daughter. The counselor's persistence in forcing Mrs. Martinez to decide may actually be asking her to violate cultural dictates about appropriate role behaviors.

Second, the counselor may have seriously undermined the Hispanic concept of the extended family by expressing negativism toward the godfather's attendance at the counseling session. Middle-class White Americans consider the family unit to be nuclear (husband/wife and children related by blood), while most minorities define the family unit as an extended one. A Hispanic child can acquire a godmother (madrina) and a godfather (padrino) through a baptismal ceremony. Unlike many White Americans, the role of godparents in the Hispanic culture is more than symbolic as they can become co-parents (compadre) taking an active part in the raising of the child. Indeed, the role of the godparents is usually linked to the moral, religious, and spiritual upbringing of the child. Who else would be more appropriate to attend the counseling session than the godfather? Not only is he a member of "the family," but the charges against Elena deal with legal, moral/ethical implications as well.

Third, the counselor obviously did not consider the economic impact that missing a couple of hours' work might have on the family. Again, she tended to equate Mr. Martinez's reluctance to take off work for the "welfare of his daughter" as evidence of the parents' disinterest in their child. Trivializing the missing of work reveals major class/work differences that often exist between mental health professionals and their minority clients. Most professionals (mental health practitioners, educators, white-collar workers) are often able to take time off for a dental appointment, teacher conference, or personal needs without loss of income. Most of us can usually arrange for others "to cover for us," or to make up the lost hours on some other day. If we are docked for time off, only a few hours are lost and not an entire afternoon or day's work. This, indeed, is a middle- or upper-class luxury not shared by those who face economic hardships or who work in settings that do not allow for schedule flexibility.

For the Martinez family, loss of even a few hours' wages has serious financial impact. Most blue-collar workers may not have the luxury or option to make up their work. How, for example, would an assembly-line worker make up the lost time when the plant closes at the end of the day? In addition, the worker often does not miss just a few hours, but must take a half or full day off. In many work situations, getting a worker to substitute for just a few hours is not practical. To entice replacement workers, the company must offer more than a few hours (in many cases a full day). Thus, Mr. Martinez may actually be losing an entire day's wages! His reluctance to miss work may actually represent *high concern* for the family rather than *lack of care*.

Fourth, the case of Elena and the Martinez family raises another important question. What obligation do educational and mental health services have toward offering flexible and culturally appropriate services to minority constituents? Mr. Martinez's desire for an evening or weekend meeting brings this issue into clear perspective. Does the minority individual or family always have to conform to system rules and regulations? We are not arguing with the school policy itself—in some schools there are very legitimate reasons for not staying after school ends (high crime rate, etc.). What we are arguing for is the need to provide alternative service deliveries to minority families. For example, why not home visits or sessions off the school premises? Social workers have historically used this method with very positive results. It has aided the building of rapport (the family perceives your genuine interest), increased comfort in the family for sharing with a counselor, and allowed a more realistic appraisal of family dynamics. Counselors frequently forget how intimidating it may be for a minority family to come in for counseling. The Martinez's lack of verbal participation may not only be a function of the conflict over the absence of the godfather, but the relative impersonal and formal nature of counseling relative to the personal orientation of the Hispanic family (personalismo).

FAMILY COUNSELING

Family counseling has been identified as one of the fastest-growing fields in psychology today. It encompasses many aspects of the family, which may include marriage counseling, parent-child counseling, or work with more than one member of the family. Its main goal is to modify relationships within a family so as to achieve harmony (Foley, 1984). Family counseling is based on three assumptions: (1) it is logical and economical to treat together all those who exist and operate within a system of relationships (in most cases, it implies the nuclear family); (2) the problems of the "identified patient" are only symptoms, and the family itself is the client; and (3) the task of the therapist is to modify relationships and/or improve communications within the family system.

Two primary approaches have been identified in family counseling, although there are a number of variations. One of these, the *communications approach* is based on the assumption that family problems are communication difficulties. Many family communication problems are both subtle and complex. Family counselors concentrate on improving not only faulty communications but also interactions and relationships among family members (Satir, 1967). The way in which rules, agreements, and perceptions are communicated among members may also be important (Haley, 1967). The counselor's role in repairing faulty communications is active, but not dominating. He or she must seek to show family members how they are now communicating with one another; prod them into revealing what they feel and think about themselves and other family members, and what they want from the family relationship; and convince them to practice new ways of responding.

The *structural approach* also considers communication to be important, but it especially emphasizes the interlocking roles of family members (Minuchin, 1974). Most families are constantly in a state of change; they are in the process of structuring and restructuring themselves into systems and subsystems. The health of a family is often linked to the members' abilities to recognize boundaries of the various systems—alliances, communication patterns, and so forth. Oftentimes unhealthy family functioning and the symptoms exhibited by members are caused by boundary disputes.

From a philosophical and theoretical perspective, both approaches appear appropriate in working with various minority groups. For example, they appear to highlight the importance of the family (vs. the individual) as the unit of identity, to focus on resolution of concrete issues, to be concerned with family structure and dynamics, to place the therapist in an expert position, and to attempt to understand the communication and/or alliances via reframing. Many of these qualities, as we have seen, would be consistent with the world view of minorities. The problem arises, however, in how these goals and strategies are translated into concepts of "the family" or what constitutes the "healthy" family. Some of the characteristics of healthy families, identified by Ebert (1978), may pose problems in counseling with various minority groups. Expressing emotions freely and openly, each member having a right to be his/her unique self (individuate from the emotional field of the family), equal division of labor, egalitarian role relationships, and holding the nuclear family as the standard are some of these values. As in the case of Elena Martinez, these translations in family counseling can cause great problems in working with minority clients. To escape from our cultural encapsulation, it is necessary for us to understand the sociopolitical forces that affect minority families, to be aware of major differences in the value system we possess when contrasted with racial/cultural family values, and to understand structural family relationships that are different from our own. Let us explore these three areas in greater detail.

ISSUES IN WORKING WITH ETHNIC MINORITY FAMILIES

Effective cross-cultural family counseling needs to incorporate the many racial/cultural/economic/class issues inherent in the Martinez family example. While not solely unique to minority families, there are distinguishing quantitative and qualitative life events and experiences that distinguish minorities from middle-class White families. Ho (1987) has identified six factors he believes culturally sensitive family therapies must take into consideration.

1. *Ethnic minority reality* refers to the racism and poverty that dominates the lives of many minorities. Lower family income, greater unemployment, increasing numbers falling below the poverty line, etc., have had major negative effects not only on the individuals, but on family structures

as well. D. W. Sue and Kirk (1973) point out how the relocation of 110,000 Japanese Americans into concentration camps during World War II drastically altered the traditional Japanese family structures and relationships. By physically uprooting these U.S. citizens, symbols of ethnic identity were destroyed, creating identity conflicts and problems. Furthermore, the camp experience disrupted the traditional lines of authority. The elderly male no longer had a functional value as head of household, family discipline and control became loosened, and women gained a degree of independence unheard of in traditional Japanese families.

Likewise, Black-American families have also been victims of poverty and racism that have done much harm to them. Nowhere is this more evident than in statistics (U.S. Bureau of the Census, 1982) revealing a higher incidence of Black children living in homes without the biological father present—82% as compared with Whites 43%. More Black families are classified as impoverished (46%) as compared to Whites (10%). And, many more Black males are single, widowed, or divorced (47%) compared to Whites (28%). The high mortality rate among Black males has led some to call them an "endangered species" in which societal forces have even strained and affected the Black male-female relationship (Gibbs, 1987).

2. *Conflicting value systems* imposed by White society upon minority groups have also caused great harm to them. The case of Elena Martinez reveals how the White counselor's conception of the nuclear family may clash with traditional Hispanic emphasis on extended families. It appears that almost all minority groups place greater value on families, historical lineage (reverence of ancestors), interdependence among family members, and submergence of self for the good of the family (Kim, 1985; Yamamoto & Kubota, 1983). Blacks are often described as having a kinship system in which relatives of a variety of blood ties (aunts, uncles, preachers, brothers, sisters, boyfriends, etc.) may act as the extended family (Boyd, 1982; Norton, 1983; Thomas & Dansby, 1985). Likewise, the extended family in the Hispanic culture as evidenced in the case of Elena Martinez includes numerous relatives and friends (Carrillo, 1982; Mizio, 1983). Perhaps most difficult to grasp for many mental health professionals is the American-Indian family network, which is structurally open and assumes villagelike characteristics (Red Horse, 1983; Red Horse, Lewis, Feit, & Decker, 1981). This "family" extension is inclusive of several to many households. Unless counselors are aware of these value differences, they may unintentionally mislabel behaviors they consider bizarre and/or make decisions detrimental to the family. We have more to say about this important point shortly.

3. *Biculturalism* refers to the fact that minorities in the United States inherit two different cultural traditions. We have already discussed, in Chapter 5, issues of cultural conflict, cultural racism, and the "melting-pot" concept as it affects identity development. How biculturalism influences the family structures, communications, and dynamics needs to be understood by the counselor. The reluctance of a 22-year-old Hispanic male to go against the wishes of his parents, not to marry a woman he loves, may not be a sign of immaturity. Rather, it may reflect a conflict between duality of membership in two groups. A culturally effective counselor is one who understands the possible conflicts that may arise as a result of biculturalism.

4. *Ethnic differences in minority status* refers to the life experiences and adjustment that occur as a result of their status in the United States. Ho (1987) provides several important examples for ethnic groups: (a) The history of slavery for Black Americans has not only negatively impacted on their self-esteem, but has contributed to disruption of the Black male/Black female relationship and the structure of the Black family; (b) Racism and colonialism have made American Indians immigrants in their own land, and the federal government has even imposed a definition of race upon them (they must be able to prove they are at least one-quarter Indian "blood"); (c) Immigration status among Hispanics and Asian refugees/immigrants (legal resident to illegal alien) and the abuses, resentments, and discrimination experienced by them are constant stressful events in their lives; (d) Skin color and obvious physical differences are also important factors that determine the treatment of minority individuals and their families.

5. *Ethnicity and language* refers to the "common sense of bonding" among members of a group that contributes to a sense of belonging. The symbols of the group (ethnicity) are most manifested in language. Language structures meaning, determines how we see things, is the carrier of our culture, and affects our world view. Many minority clients do not possess vocabulary equivalents to standard English and when forced to communicate in English may appear "flat," "nonverbal," "uncommunicative," and "lacking in insight" (Romero, 1985). The problem is linguistic and not psychological. We have already discussed many of these problems in Chapter 2. Suffice it to say, the bilingual family service programs should be made available to minorities.

6. *Ethnicity and social class* refers to aspects of wealth, name, occupation, and status. Class differences between mental health professionals and their minority clients can often lead to barriers in understanding and communication. This was clearly evident in the case of Elena Martinez where the counselor had difficulty relating to a missed day of work. Needless to say, class differences become even more important for counselors to understand when working with minority families because they are disproportionately represented in the lower socioeconomic classes.

CROSS-CULTURAL FAMILY COUNSELING: A CONCEPTUAL MODEL

Effective cross-cultural family counseling operates under principles similar to what was outlined in earlier chapters. First, counselors need to become culturally aware of their own values, biases, and assumptions about human behavior (especially as it pertains to the definition of family). Second, it is important to become aware of the world view of the culturally different client and how that client views the definition, role, and function of the family. Last, appropriate intervention strategies need to be devised that would maximize success and minimize cultural oppression. While in earlier chapters the focus was on individual clients and their ethnic/racial groups, our concern in this chapter is with the "family" unit as defined from the group's perspective. In attempting to understand the first two goals, we are using the Kluckhohn and Strodtbeck (1961) model outlined below. This model allows us to understand the world views of culturally different families by contrasting the value orientations of the four main groups we are studying (as illustrated in Table 6.1): Asian Americans, American Indians, Black Americans, and Hispanic Americans.

People–Nature Relationship

Traditional Western thinking believes in mastery and control over nature. As a result, most therapists operate from a framework which ascribes to the belief that problems are solvable, and that both therapist and client must take an active part in solving problems via manipulation and control. Active intervention is stressed in controlling and/or changing the environment. As seen in Table 6.1, the four other ethnic groups view "people" as harmonious with nature.

Asian Confucian philosophy, for example, stresses a set of rules aimed at promoting loyalty, respect, and harmony among family members (S. Sue & Morishima, 1982; Yamamoto & Kubota, 1983). Harmony within

TABLE 6.1

Cultural Value Preferences of Middle-Class White Americans and Ethnic Minorities: A Comparative Summary

Area of Relationships	Middle-Class White Americans	Asian Americans	American Indians	Black Americans	Hispanic Americans
People to Nature/ Environment	Mastery over	Harmony with	Harmony with	Harmony with	Harmony with
Time Orientation	Future	Past-present	Present	Present	Past-present
People Relations	Individual	Collateral	Collateral	Collateral	Collateral
Preferred Mode of Activity	Doing	Doing	Being-in-Becoming	Doing	Being-in-Becoming
Nature of Man	Good & Bad	Good	Good	Good & Bad	Good

From *Family Therapy with Ethnic Minorities* (p. 232) by M. K. Ho, 1987, Newbury Park, CA: Sage. Copyright 1987 by Sage Publications. Reprinted by permission.

the family and the environment leads to harmony within the self. In their analysis of the Japanese family, Kitano and Kimura (1976) go to great lengths to point out how dependence upon the family unit and acceptance of the environment dictates differences in solving problems. Western culture advocates defining and attacking the problem directly. Asian cultures tend to accommodate and/or deal with problems through indirection. In child rearing, it is believed better to avoid direct confrontation and to use deflection. A White family may deal with a child who has watched too many hours of TV by saying, "Why don't you turn the TV off and study?" Or, more threatening, the parent might say, "You'll be grounded unless the TV goes off!" An Asian parent may respond by saying, "that looks like a boring program; I think your friend John must be doing his homework now." Or, "I think father wants to watch his favorite program." Such an approach stems from the need to avoid conflict and to achieve balance and harmony among members of the family and the wider environment.

In an excellent analysis of family therapy for Asian Americans, Kim (1985) points out how current therapeutic techniques of confrontation and of having clients express thoughts and feelings directly may be inappropriate and difficult to handle. For example, one of the basic tenets of family therapy is that the identified patient (IP) typically behaves in such a way as to reflect family influences and/or pathology. Oftentimes, an acting-out child is symbolic of deeper family problems. Yet, most Asian American families come to counseling *for the benefit of the IP* and *not the family!* Attempts to directly focus in on the family dynamics as contributing to the IP will be met with negativism and possible termination. Kim (1985) states:

> A recommended approach to engage the family would be to pace the family's cultural expectations and limitations by (1) asserting that the IP's problem (therefore not the IP by implication) is indeed the problem; (2) recognizing and reinforcing the family's concerns to help the IP to change the behavior; and (3) emphasizing that each family member's contribution in resolving the problem is vitally needed, and that without it, the problem will either remain or get worse bringing on further difficulty in the family. (p. 346)

Thus, it is apparent that U.S. values that call for us to dominate nature (i.e., conquer space, tame the wilderness, or harness nuclear energy) through control and manipulation of the universe are reflected in family counseling. Family counseling theories attempt to describe, explain, predict, and control family dynamics. The therapist actively attempts to understand what is going on in the family system (structural alliances and communication patterns), identify the problems (dysfunctional aspects of the dynamics), and attack it directly or indirectly through manipulation and control (therapeutic interventions). Ethnic minorities or subgroups that view people as harmonious with nature or believe that nature may overwhelm people ("acts of God") may find the therapist's mastery-over-nature approach inconsistent or antagonistic to their world view. Indeed, attempts to actively intervene in changing family patterns and relationships may be perceived "as the problem" because it may potentially unbalance that *harmony* which existed.

Time Dimension

How different societies, cultures, and people view time exerts a pervasive influence on their lives. U.S. society may be characterized as preoccupied with the future (Katz, 1985; Kluckhohn & Strodtbeck, 1961; Spiegel & Papajohn, 1983). Furthermore, our society seems very compulsive about time in that we divide it into seconds, minutes, hours, days, weeks, months, and years. Time may be viewed as a commodity ("time is money" and "stop wasting time") in fixed and static categories rather than as a dynamic and flowing process. Condon and Youself (1975) point out how the United State's future orientation may be linked to other values as well: (a) stress on youth and achievement in which the children are expected to "better their parents," (b) controlling one's own destiny by future planning and saving for a rainy day, and (c) optimism and hope for a better future. The spirit of the nation may be embodied in the General Electric slogan, "Progress is our most important product." This is not to deny the fact that people are concerned about the past and the present as well, but rather to suggest that culture, groups, and people may place greater emphasis on one over the other. Nor do we deny the fact that age, gender, occupation, social class, and other important demographic factors may be linked to time perspective (Gonzalez & Zimbardo, 1985). However, our work with various racial/ethnic minority groups and much of the research conducted (Condon & Youself, 1975; Hall, 1959; Ho, 1987; Inclan, 1985; Kluckhohn & Strodtbeck, 1961) support the fact that race, culture, and ethnicity are powerful determinants of whether the group emphasizes the past, present, or future.

Table 6.1 reveals that both American Indians and Black Americans tend to value a present time orientation, while Asian Americans and Hispanic Americans have a combination past-present focus. Historically, Asian societies have valued the past as reflected in ancestor worship and the equating of age with wisdom and respectability. Contrast this with U.S. culture in which youth is valued over the elderly and the belief that once one hits the retirement years, one's usefulness in life is over. As the U.S. population ages, however, it will be interesting to note whether a shift in the status of the elderly will occur. As compared to Anglo middle-class norms, Hispanics also exhibit a past-present time orientation. Strong hierarchical structures in the family, respect for elders and ancestors, and the value of "personalismo" all combine in this direction. American Indians also differ from their White counterparts in that they are very grounded in the "here and now" rather than the future. American-Indian philosophy relies heavily on the belief that time is flowing, circular, and harmonious.

Artificial division of time (schedules) is disruptive to the natural pattern (Ho, 1987). Black Americans also value the present because of the spiritual quality of their existence and their history of racism. Several difficulties may occur when the counselor or therapist is unaware of the differences of time perspective.

First, if time differences exist between the minority family and the White counselor, it will most likely be manifested in a difference in the pace of time: Both may sense things are going too slowly or too fast. An American-Indian family who values "being in the present" and who values the "immediate experiential reality of being" may feel that the counselor lacks respect for them and is "rushing them" (Lewis, 1981; Red Horse et al., 1981) while ignoring the quality of the personal relationship. On the other hand, the counselor may be dismayed by the "delays," "inefficiency," and lack of "commitment to change" among the family members. After all, time is precious and the counselor has only limited time to impact upon the family. The result is frequently dissatisfaction among the parties, lack of establishing rapport, misinterpretation of the behaviors or situations, and probably discontinuance of future sessions.

Second, Inclan (1985) points out how confusions and misinterpretations can arise as a result of Hispanics', particularly Puerto Ricans', marking time differently than their U.S. White counterparts. The language of clock-time in counseling (50-minute hour, rigid time schedule, once-a-week sessions) can conflict with minority perceptions of time (Katz, 1985). The following dialogue illustrates this point clearly:

> "Mrs. Rivera, your next appointment is at 9:30 a.m. next Wednesday."
> "Good, it's convenient for me to come after I drop off the children at school."

> Or, "Mrs. Rivera, your next appointment is for the whole family at 3:00 p.m. on Tuesday."
> "Very good. After the kids return from school we can come right in." (Inclan, 1985, p. 328)

Since school starts at 8 a.m., the client is bound to show up very early while in the second example the client will most likely be late (school ends at 3 p.m.). In both cases, the counselor is most likely to be inconvenienced, but worse yet is the negative interpretation that may be made of the client's motives (anxious, demanding, or pushy in the first case, while resistant, passive-aggressive or irresponsible in the latter one). The counselor needs to be aware that many Hispanics may mark time by *events* rather than by the clock.

Third, Ho (1987) suggests that many minorities who overall are present-time oriented would be more likely to seek immediate, concrete solutions rather than future-oriented "abstract goals." We have already noted in earlier chapters that goals or processes that are insight oriented assume that the client has time to sit back and self-explore. Career/vocational counseling in which clients explore their interest, values, work temperaments, skills, abilities, and the world of work may be seen as highly future oriented. These approaches, while potentially beneficial to the client, may pose dilemmas for both the minority family and counselor.

Relational Dimension

In general, the United States can be characterized as an achievement-oriented society, which is most strongly manifested in the Protestant work ethic (Spence, 1985). Basic to the ethic is the concept of *individualism:* (a) the individual is the psychosocial unit of operation, (b) the individual has primary responsibility for his/her own actions, (c) independence and autonomy are highly valued and rewarded, and (d) one should be internally directed and controlled (Katz, 1985; Yamamoto & Kubota, 1983). In many societies and groups within the United States, however, this value is not necessarily shared. Relationships in Japan and China are often described as being lineal where identification with others is both wide and linked to the past (ancestor worship). Obeying the wishes of ancestors or parents long since passed, and perceiving your existence and identity as linked to the historical past are inseparable. Almost all racial/ethnic minority groups in the United States tend to be more collateral in their relationships with people. In an individualistic orientation, the definition of the family tends to be linked to a biological necessity (nuclear family), while a collateral and/or lineal view encompasses various concepts of the extended family. Not understanding this distinction and the values inherent in these orientations may lead the family counselor to erroneous conclusions and decisions. Below is a case illustration of an American Indian youngster.

> A younger probationer was under court supervision and had strict orders to remain with responsible adults. His counselor became concerned because the youth appeared to ignore this order. The client moved around frequently and, according to the counselor, stayed overnight with several different young women. The counselor presented this case at a formal staff meeting, and fellow professionals stated their suspicion that the client was either a pusher or a pimp. The frustrating element to the counselor was that the young women knew each other and appeared to enjoy each other's company. Moreover, they were not ashamed to be seen together in public with the client. This behavior prompted the counselor to initiate violation proceedings. (Red Horse et al., 1981, p. 56)

Were it not for the fact that a Minneapolis American-Indian professional accidentally came upon the case, a revocation order being initiated against the youngster would surely have caused irreparable alienation between the family and the social service agency. The counselor had failed to realize that the American-Indian family network is structurally open and may include several households of relatives and friends along both vertical and horizontal lines. The young women were all first cousins to the client and each was as a "sister," with all the households representing different units of "the family."

Likewise, Black Americans have strong kinship bonds that may encompass both blood relatives and friends. Traditional African culture valued the collective orientation over individualism (Franklin, 1988; Sudarkasa, 1988). This group identity has also been reinforced by what many Blacks describe as the sense of "peoplehood" developed as a result of the common experience of racism and discrimination. In a society that has historically attempted to destroy the Black family, near and distant relatives, neighbors, friends, and acquaintances have arisen in an extended family support network (Hines & Boyd-Franklin, 1982; Thomas & Dansby, 1985). Thus, the Black family may appear quite different from the ideal nuclear family. The danger is that certain assumptions made by a White counselor may be totally without merit or may be translated in such a way as to alienate or damage the self-esteem of Blacks.

For example, the absence of a father in the Black family does not necessarily mean that the children do not have a father figure. This function may be taken over by an uncle or male family friend. Thomas and Dansby (1985) provide an example of a group-counseling technique that was detrimental to several Black youngsters. Clients in the group were asked to draw a picture of the family dinner table and place circles representing the mother, father, and children in their seating arrangement. They report that even before the directions for the exercise were finished, a young Black girl ran from the room in tears. She had been raised by an aunt. Several other Black clients stated they did not eat dinners together as a family except on special occasions or Sundays—a typical routine in some affluent Black families according to Willie (1982).

The importance of family membership and the extended family system has already been illustrated in the case of Elena Martinez (see opening case study). We give one example here to illustrate that the moral evaluation of a behavior may depend on the value orientation of the subject. Puerto Ricans, because of the collective orientation, view obligations to the family to be primary over all other relationships. When a family member attains a position of power and influence, it is expected that he or she will favor the relatives over "objective criteria." Businesses that are heavily weighted by family members, and appointments of family members in government positions, are not unusual in many countries. Failure to hire a family member may result in moral condemnation and family sanctions (Inclan, 1985). This is in marked contrast to what we ideally believe in the United States. Appointment of family members over objective criteria of individual achievement is condemned.

It would appear that differences in the relationship dimension between the mental health provider and the minority family receiving services can cause great conflicts. While family counseling may be the treatment of choice for many minorities (over individual counseling), its values may again be antagonistic and detrimental to minorities. Family approaches that place heavy emphasis on individualism and freedom from the emotional field of the family may cause great harm. Our approach should be to identify how we might capitalize on collaterality to the benefit of minority families.

Activity Dimension

One of the primary characteristics of White U.S. cultural values and beliefs is an action (doing) orientation: (a) we must master and control nature, (b) we must always do things about a situation, and (c) we should take a pragmatic and utilitarian view of life. In counseling, we expect clients to master and control their own life and environment, to take action to resolve their own problems, and to fight against bias and inaction (Katz, 1985). The doing mode is evident everywhere and is reflected in how White Americans identify themselves by what they *do* (occupations), children are asked what they want to do when they grow up, and higher value is given to inventors over poets and to doctors of medicine over doctors of philosophy. One common exercise given to school children returning to school is "What I did on my summer vacation."

It appears that both American Indians and Hispanics prefer a being or being-in-becoming mode of activity. Numerous writers (Lewis, 1981; Lewis & Ho, 1985; Richardson, 1981; Trimble, 1981) have discussed the American-Indian concept of self-determination and "noninterference." Value is placed on the spiritual quality of being, as manifested in self-containment, poise, and harmony with the universe. Value is placed upon the attainment of inner fulfillment and an essential serenity of one's place in the universe. Because each person is fulfilling a purpose, no one should have the power to interfere or to impose values. Oftentimes those unfamiliar with Indian values perceive the person as stoic, aloof, passive, noncompetitive, or inactive. In working with families, the counselor role of active manipulator may clash with American-Indian concepts of being-in-becoming (noninterference).

Likewise, Hispanic culture may be said to have a more here-and-now or being-in-becoming orientation. Like their American-Indian counterparts, Hispanics believe that people are born with "dignadad" (dignity) and must be given "respecto" (respect). They are born with innate worth and importance; the inner soul and spirit are more important than the body. People cannot be held accountable for their lot in life (status, roles, etc.) for they are born into this life state (Inclan, 1985; Mizio, 1983). A certain degree of "fatalismo" (fatalism) is present, and life events may be viewed as inevitable ("'Lo que Dios manda"—What God wills). Philosophically, it does not matter what people have in life or what position they occupy (farm laborer, public official, or attorney). Status is possessed by existing and everyone is entitled to "respecto."

Since this belief system deemphasizes material accomplishments as a measure of success, it is clearly at odds with Anglo middle-class society. While a "doing"-oriented family may define a family member's worth via achievement, a "being" orientation equates worth by simply belonging. Thus, when a client complains that someone is not an effective family member, what do they mean? This needs to be clarified by the counselor. Is it a complaint that the family member is not performing and achieving (doing), or does it mean that the person is not respectful and accommodating to family structures and values (being)?

Ho (1987) describes both Asian Americans and Black Americans as operating from the doing orientation. However, it appears that "doing" in these two groups is manifested differently than in the White American lifestyle. The active dimension in Asians is related not to individual achievement, but to achievement via conformity to family values and demands. Controlling one's own feelings, impulses, desires, and needs to fulfill responsibility to the family is strongly ingrained in Asian children. The doing orientation tends to be more ritualized in the roles and responsibilities toward members of the family. Black Americans also exercise considerable control (endure the pain and suffering of racism) in the face of adversity to minimize discrimination and to maximize success.

Nature of People Dimension

Middle-class White Americans generally perceive the nature of people as neutral. Environmental influences such as conditioning, family upbringing, and socialization are believed to be dominant forces in determining the nature of the person. People are neither good nor bad but a product of environment. While several minority groups may share features of this belief with Whites, there is a qualitative and quantitative difference that may affect family structure and dynamics. For example, Asian Americans and American Indians tend to emphasize the inherent goodness of people. We have already discussed the American-Indian concept of "noninterference," which is based on the belief that people have an innate capacity to advance and grow (self-fulfillment) and problematic behaviors are the result of environmental influences that thwart the opportunity to develop. Goodness will always triumph over evil if the person is left alone. Likewise, Asian philosophy (Buddhism and Confucianism) believes in peoples' innate goodness and prescribes role relationships that manifest the "good way of life." Central to Asian belief is the fact that the best healing source lies within the family (Ho, 1987) and seeking help from the outside (like counseling and therapy) is nonproductive and against the dictates of Asian philosophy.

Hispanics may be described as holding the view that human nature is both good and bad (mixed). Concepts of "dignidad" and "respecto" undergird the belief that people are born with positive qualities. Yet, some Hispanics, like Puerto Ricans, spend a great deal of time appealing to the supernatural forces so that children may be blessed with a good human nature (Inclan, 1985). Thus, there may be more acceptance of a "bad" child as being destined and less seeking of help from educators or mental health professionals for such problems. The preferred mode of help may be religious consultations and ventilation to neighbors and friends who sympathize and understand the dilemmas (change means reaching the supernatural forces).

Black Americans may also be characterized as having a mixed concept of people, but in general, like their White counterparts, they believe that man is basically neutral. Environmental factors have a great influence on how people develop. This orientation is consistent with Black beliefs that racism, discrimination, oppression, and other external factors create problems in living for the individual. Emotional disorders and/or antisocial acts are caused by external forces (system variables) rather than internal intrapsychic psychological ones. For example, high crime rates, poverty, and the current structure of the Black family is the result of historical and current oppression of Black people. White Western concepts of genetic inferiority and pathology (Black people are born that way) hold little validity for the Black person.

CROSS-CULTURAL FAMILY COUNSELING: PRACTICAL IMPLICATIONS

It is extremely difficult to speak specifically about the application of cross-cultural strategies and techniques in minority families because of the great variations not only among Asian Americans, Blacks, Hispanics, American Indians, and White Americans, but we note that large variations exist within the groups themselves. For example, Wong (1981) observes that the term "Asian and Pacific American" covers some 32 distinct subgroups. To suggest principles of cross-cultural family counseling or counseling that would have equal validity to all groups may make our discussion too general and abstract. Worse yet, we may foster overgeneralizations that border on being stereotypes. Likewise, to attempt an extremely specific discussion would mean dealing with literally thousands of racial, ethnic, and cultural combinations, a task that is humanly impossible. What seems to be required for the counselor is a balance of these two extremes: A framework that would help us understand differences in communication styles/structural alliances in the family and at the same time help us more specifically pinpoint cultural differences that exist within a particular family. Once that is accomplished, the counselor can turn his or her attention to creatively developing approaches and strategies of family counseling appropriate to the lifestyle of the minority family. To aid counselors in developing competencies in cross-cultural family counseling, we would like to outline some general principles that may be helpful.

First, cross-cultural family counseling requires that the counselors be able to view minority families in a less prejudiced manner and free themselves from the cultural conditioning of their past. One model counselors have found useful in their work with minority families has been the use of the value-orientation framework described in this chapter. Values are generalized and interrelated conceptions (world views), which guide behavior along what is believed to be desirable and undesirable dimensions. As we saw, Kluckhohn and Strodtbeck (1961) proposed five general human questions to which they propose three potential values-orientation preferences. Whether groups value a lineal, collateral, or individualistic orientation has major implications for their definition of the family and what are considered appropriate goals and strategies (intervention) in family counseling. Other value preferences, like the time dimension, relationships to nature, and so forth, are equally important and influential. Thus, we believe that a counselor needs a conceptual framework of how to view differences among the various racial minority groups. Other models are the theory of world views (Chapter 7) and racial/cultural identity development (Chapter 5).

Second, the effective cross-cultural family counselor needs to be especially attentive to traditional cultural family structure and extended family ties. We have already seen in the case of Elena Martinez how the godfather is an intimate part of the extended family system and should have been included in the counseling session. Understanding husband-wife relationships, parent-child relationships, and sibling relationships from different cultural perspectives is crucial to effective work with minority families. A counselor who is unaware that Asian Americans and Hispanics have a more patriarchal spousal relationship, while White Americans and Blacks have a more egalitarian one may inappropriately intervene. For example, the concept of equal division of labor in the home between husband and wife or working to a more equal relationship may be a violation of Hispanic cultural norms. Another example, given by Ho (1987) and that contrasts sharply with White western norms, is that most minority families view the *wifely* role as *less important* than the *motherly* role. For instance, the existence of children validates and cements the marriage; therefore, motherhood is often perceived as a more important role. Counselors should not judge the health of a family on the basis of the romantic egalitarian model characteristic of White culture.

Third, family counselors would be well advised to utilize the natural help-giving networks and structures that already exist in the minority culture and community. It is ironic that the mental health field behaves as if minority communities never had anything like mental health "treatment" until it came along and invented it. As mentioned in Chapter 1, Western-European culture operates from a very ethnocentric framework by defining mental health concepts and by making it unethical and illegal to practice counseling or therapy without proper credentials. It destroys the natural help-giving networks that already exist in a particular culture (declaring them illegal or not recognizing them as being legitimate), sets up inappropriate services, waits for minority populations to come to them, and then wonders why minorities do not come for treatment. The mental health profession acts as if only Western-European countries have "therapy" and that other countries and cultures do not. If that were the case, we wonder how some of the most ancient countries like China and Japan survived through all those years.

It is important that we recognize the ability of helping to take many forms. These forms often appear quite different from our own, but they are no less effective or legitimate. In cross-cultural counseling, modifying our counseling goals and techniques to fit the needs of minority populations is called for. Granted, mental health professionals are sometimes hard-pressed in challenging their own assumptions of what constitutes "counseling and therapy," or they feel uncomfortable in roles they are not accustomed to. Yet, the need is great to move in this most positive direction. Atkinson, Morten, and Sue (1989) discuss some of these roles in detail (consultant role, ombudsman and change-agent roles, facilitator of indigenous support systems, outreach role, etc.).

In the *consultant role,* counselors attempt to serve as resource persons to mental health professionals and/or minority populations in developing programs that would improve their life conditions through prevention and remediation. The *outreach role* requires that counselors move out of their offices and into their clients' communities. For example, since many Blacks are deeply involved in their church and respect their Black ministers, outreach and preventive programs could be delivered through the support of interdenominational Black ministerial alliances or personnel in the churches (Thomas & Dansby, 1985). Home visits are another outreach tactic that has been used traditionally by social workers. Counselors who use this ploy would be meeting the needs of minority clients (financial difficulties with transportation), allowing the counselor to see the family in their natural environment, making a positive statement about their own personal commitment and involvement with the family, avoiding the intimidating atmosphere of large informal and unfamiliar institutions and perhaps allowing the counselor to directly observe the environmental factors that are contributing to the families problems. The *ombudsman role,* which originated in Europe, functions to protect citizens against bureaucratic mazes and procedures. In this situation, the family counselor would attempt to identify institutional policies and practices that may discriminate or oppress a minority constituency. As a *facilitator of indigenous support systems,* the family counselor would structure their activities to supplement, not supplant, the already existing system of mental health. Collaborative work with folk healers, medicine persons, or community leaders would be very much a part of the family counselor's role.

Last, but not least, the family counselor will need to be creative in the development of appropriate intervention techniques when working with minority populations. With traditional Asian Americans, subtlety and indirectness may be called for rather than direct confrontation and interpretation. Formality in addressing members of the family, especially the father (Mr. Lee rather than Tom), may be more appropriate. For Black Americans, a much more interactional approach (as opposed to an instrumental one) in the initial encounter (rather than getting to the goal or task immediately) may be dictated. What we are saying is that approaches are often determined by cultural/racial/system factors, and the more the counselor understands about these areas, the more effective he or she will become.

CHAPTER 7

Dimensions of World Views

It has become increasingly clear that many minority persons hold world views different from members of the dominant culture. In Chapter 5, we examined one specific aspect of world views—cultural identity. In a broader sense, we can define a world view (D. W. Sue, 1977, 1978) as how a person perceives his/her relationship to the world (nature, institutions, other people, etc.). World views are highly correlated with a person's cultural upbringing and life experiences (Ibrahim, 1985; Ivey et al., 1987; Katz, 1985; D. W. Sue, 1978). Ivey, Ivey, and Simek-Downing (1987) refer to world views as "one's conceptual framework," or "how you think the world works." Ibrahim (1985) refers to it as "our philosophy of life," or our "experience within social, cultural, environmental, philosophical, and psychological dimensions." Put in a much more practical way, world views are not only composed of our attitudes, values, opinions, and concepts, but also they may affect how we think, make decisions, behave, and define events.

For minorities in America, a strong determinant of world views is very much related to racism and the subordinate position assigned to them in society. While the intent of this chapter is to discuss racial and ethnic minorities, it must be kept in mind that economic and social class, religion, and gender are also interactional components of a world view. Thus, upper- and lower-socioeconomic class Asian Americans, Blacks, Hispanics, or American Indians do not necessarily have identical views of the world.

Counselors who hold a world view different from that of their clients and are unaware of the basis for this difference are most likely to impute negative traits to clients. Constructs used to judge "normality" and "healthy" or "abnormality" and "unhealthy" may be inadvertently applied to clients. In most cases, culturally different clients have a greater possibility of holding world views different from those of counselors. Yet many counse-

lors are so "culturally blind," they respond according to their own conditioned values, assumptions, and perspectives of reality without regard for
other views. What is needed for counselors is for them to become
"culturally aware," to act on the basis of a critical analysis and understanding of their own conditioning, the conditioning of their clients, and the
sociopolitical system of which they are both a part. Without this awareness,
counselors who work with the culturally different may be engaging in
cultural oppression. Let us begin our exploration of world views by
continuing with the value orientation model proposed by Kluckhohn and
Strodtbeck (1961).

VALUE ORIENTATION MODEL OF WORLD VIEWS

One of the most useful frameworks for understanding differences
among individuals and groups is the Kluckhohn and Strodtbeck model
(1961) presented in the last chapter. It assumes there exists a set of core
dimensions (human questions) that are pertinent for all peoples of all
cultures. Differences in value orientations can be ascertained by how we
answer them. These questions and the three possible responses to them are
given in Table 7.1.

Kluckhohn and Strodtbeck (1961) clearly recognized that racial/
ethnic groups vary in how they perceive *time*. Cultures may emphasize
history and tradition, the *here and now*, or the *distant future*. For example,
Inclan (1985) points out how Puerto Ricans tend to exhibit present time
value orientation behaviors that may be different from Anglo future
orientation. Puerto Ricans frequently comment on how Anglos do not seem
to know how to have fun because they will leave a party in order to prepare
for a meeting tomorrow. Likewise, Anglos will often comment on how
Puerto Ricans are "poor and disorganized planners." They may notify their
boss at the last minute about their need to travel home for the holidays.
Worse yet, they may attempt to make airline reservations December 20th
for the Christmas holidays only to be forced to fly standby because of "poor
planning." As we saw in the last chapter, Puerto Ricans and Anglos mark
time differently.

Cultures also differ in their attitudes toward activity. In White
culture, "*doing*" is valued over "*being*" or even "*being-in-becoming*. There is a
strong belief that one's own worth is measured by task accomplishments. In
White culture, statements like "do something" indicate the positive value
placed on action. Likewise, when someone is involved in *being*, it may be
described as "hanging out" or "killing time." In most cases these represent
pejorative statements. In counseling and therapy, the perceived "inaction"
of a client who may adhere to a "being" orientation is usually associated
with some form of personal inadequacy.

Another dimension of importance is our *relationship with others*. In
some cultures, relationships tend to be more *lineal*, authoritarian, and
hierarchical (traditional Asian cultures) in which the father is the absolute

TABLE 7.1

Value-Orientation Model

Dimensions	*Value Orientations*		
1. *Time Focus* What is the temporary focus of human life?	*Past* The past is important. Learn from history.	*Present* The present moment is everything. Don't worry about tomorrow.	*Future* Plan for the future: Sacrifice today for a better tomorrow.
2. *Human Activity* What is the modality of human activity?	*Being* It's enough to just be.	*Being & In-Becoming* Our purpose in life is develop our inner self.	*Doing* Be active. Work hard and your efforts will be rewarded.
3. *Social Relations* How are human relationships defined?	*Lineal* Relationships are vertical. There are leaders and followers in this world.	*Collateral* We should consult with friends/ families when problems arise.	*Individualistic* Individual autonomy is important. We control our own destiny.
4. *People/Nature Relationship* What is the relationship of people to nature?	*Subjugation to Nature* Life is largely determined by external forces (God, fate, genetics, etc.)	*Harmony with Nature* People and nature co-exist in harmony.	*Mastery over Nature* Our challenge is to conquer and control nature.

Adapted *from:* "Effective Cross-Cultural Counseling and Psychotherapy: A Framework" by F.A. Ibrahim, 1985, *The Counseling Psychologist, 13,* 625–638. Copyright 1985 by *The Counseling Psychologist.* Adapted by permission. *From: Variations in Value Orientations* by F.R. Kluckhohn and F.L. Strodtbeck, 1961, Evanston, IL: Row, Patterson & Co. Copyright 1961 by Row, Patterson & Co. Adapted by permission. *From: Handbook for Developing Multicultural Awareness* (p.256) by P. Pedersen, 1988, Alexandria, VA: AACD Press. Copyright 1988 by AACD Press. Adapted by permission.

ruler of the family. Some cultures may emphasize a horizontal, equal, and *collateral* relationship, while others, like U.S. society, value *individual* autonomy. In earlier chapters, we pointed out how a counseling relationship that tends to be more equal and individualistic (I-Thou) may prove uncomfortable for clients who may adhere to a much more formal hierarchical relationship.

The *nature of people* has often been addressed in psychology and philosophy. In theories of personality, for example, Freud saw humans as basically evil or bad; Rogers saw them as innately good; behaviorists tended to perceive human nature as neutral. There is no doubt that cultures, societies, and groups may socialize people into a trusting or suspicious mode. Third World groups, by virtue of their minority status in the United States, may develop a healthy suspiciousness toward institutions and people. Unfortunately, because many mental health professionals may operate from a different value orientation (man is basically neutral or good), they may see the minority clients as evidencing "paranoid" traits.

The Value-Orientation Model also states that people make assumptions about how they *relate to nature*. Many American Indians, for example, perceive themselves as harmonious with "Mother Earth" and nature (Richardson, 1981). Poor Puerto Ricans are governed more by a value of subjugation to nature (Inclan, 1985). White Anglos, however, value conquering and controlling nature (Katz, 1985; Pedersen, 1988). Such an orientation by the counselor may often lead to difficulties. This aspect of the value dimension presumes that barriers to personal success or happiness may be overcome through hard work and perseverance. Minority or poor clients, however, may perceive this strategy as ineffective against many problems created by racism or poverty. Clients who fail to act in accordance with their counselor's values may be diagnosed as being the source of their own problems. It is precisely this value dimension that we feel has been severely neglected in the mental health field. The reason may lie in its sociopolitical nature.

The remaining part of this chapter deals with a discussion of world views as it relates to this central concept. It discusses how race and culture-specific factors may interact in such a way as to produce people with different world views, and it presents a conceptual model that integrates research findings with the clinical literature.

First, we discuss two factors identified as important in understanding persons with different psychological orientations: (a) locus of control (Caplan, 1970; Caplan & Paige, 1968; Forward & Williams, 1970; Gore & Rotter, 1963; Gurin, Gurin, Lao, & Beattie, 1969; Rotter, 1966) and (b) locus of responsibility (Abeles, 1976; Avis & Stewart, 1976; Forward & Williams, 1970; Gurin et al., 1969; Turner & Wilson, 1976). Second, we look at how these variables form four different psychological outlooks in life and their consequent characteristics, dynamics, and implications for the counselor. Last, we set forth some conclusions and precautions.

LOCUS OF CONTROL

J. Rotter (1966) first formulated the concept of internal-external control or the internal-external (I-E) dimension. "Internal control" (IC) refers to people's beliefs that reinforcements are contingent on their own actions and that people can shape their own fate. "External control" (EC) refers to people's beliefs that reinforcing events occur independently of their actions and that the future is determined more by chance and luck. J. Rotter conceived this dimension as measuring a generalized personality trait that operated across several different situations.

Based on past experience, people learn one of two world views: The locus of control rests with the individual or the locus of control rests with some external force. Lefcourt (1966) and J. Rotter (1966, 1975) have summarized the research findings that correlated high internality with (a) greater attempts at mastering the environment, (b) superior coping strategies, (c) better cognitive processing of information, (d) lower predisposition to anxiety, (e) higher achievement motivation, (f) greater social action involvement, and (g) placing greater value on skill-determined rewards. As can be seen, these attributes are highly valued by U.S. society and constitute the core features of mental health.

Early research on generalized expectancies of locus of control suggests that ethnic group members (Hsieh, Shybut, & Lotsof, 1969; Levenson, 1974; Strickland, 1973; Tulkin, 1968; Wolfgang, 1973), lower-class people (Battle & Rotter, 1963; Crandall, Katkovsky, & Crandall, 1965; Garcia & Levenson, 1975; Lefcourt, 1966; Strickland, 1971), and women (Sanger & Alker, 1972) score significantly higher on the external end of the locus-of-control continuum. Using the I-E dimension as a criterion of mental health would mean that minority, poor, and female clients would be viewed as possessing less desirable attributes. Thus, a counselor who encounters a minority client with a high external orientation ("it's no use trying," "there's nothing I can do about it," and "you shouldn't rock the boat") may interpret the client as being inherently apathetic, procrastinating, lazy, depressed, or anxious about trying. As we see in the next section, all these statements tend to blame the individual for his/her present condition.

The problem with an unqualified application of the I-E dimension is that it fails to take into consideration the different cultural and social experiences of the individual. This failure may lead to highly inappropriate and destructive applications in counseling. While the social-learning framework from which the I-E dimension is derived may be very legitimate, it seems plausible that different cultural groups, women, and lower-class people have learned that control operates differently in their lives as opposed to how it operates for society at large. In the case of Third World groups, the concept of external control takes on a wider meaning.

Some early investigators (Crandall et al., 1965; Hersch & Scheibe, 1967) have always argued that the locus-of-control continuum must make clearer distinctions on the external end. For example, externality related to impersonal forces (chance and luck) is different from that ascribed to cultural forces and that ascribed to powerful others. Chance and luck operate equally across situations for everyone. However, the forces that determine locus of control from a cultural perspective may be viewed by the particular ethnic group as acceptable and benevolent. In this case, externality is viewed positively. Two ethnic groups may be used as examples to illustrate this point.

Hsieh, Shybut, and Lotsof (1969) found that Chinese, American-born Chinese, and Anglo Americans varied in the degree of internal control they felt. The first group scored lowest in internality followed by the Chinese Americans and finally by Anglo Americans. These investigators felt that the "individual-centered" American culture emphasizes the uniqueness, independence, and self-reliance of each individual. It places a high premium on self-reliance, individualism, and status achieved through one's own efforts. In contrast, the "situation-centered" Chinese culture places importance on the group (an individual is not defined apart from the family), on tradition, social roles-expectations, and harmony with the universe. Thus, the cultural orientation of the more traditional Chinese tends to elevate the external scores. Note, however, that the external orientation of the Chinese is highly valued and accepted (Leong, 1985).

Likewise, one might expect Native Americans to score higher on the external end of the I-E continuum on the basis of their own cultural values. Several writers (Bryde, 1971; Trimble, 1981; Trimble & LaFromboise, 1985) have pointed to American Indian concepts of "noninterference" and "harmony with nature" that may tend to classify them as high externals. Anglos are said to be concerned with attempts to control the physical world and to assert mastery over it. To American Indians, accepting the world (harmony) rather than changing it is a highly valued lifestyle.

Support for the fact that Rotter's I-E distinction is not a unidimensional trait has also come from other studies (Gurin et al., 1969; Mirels, 1970) that indicate the presence of a political influence (powerful others). For example, a major force in the literature dealing with locus of control is that of powerlessness. *Powerlessness* may be defined as the expectancy that a person's behavior cannot determine the outcomes or reinforcements he/she seeks. Mirels (1970) feels that a strong possibility exists that externality may be a function of a person's opinions about prevailing social institutions. For example, lower-class individuals and Blacks are not given an equal opportunity to obtain the material rewards of Western culture (Carter, 1988). Because of racism, Blacks may be perceiving, in a realistic fashion, a discrepancy between their ability and attainment.

In this case, externality may be seen as a malevolent force to be distinguished from the benevolent cultural ones just discussed. Gurin et al. (1969), on the basis of their study, have concluded that while high external people are less effectively motivated, perform poorly in achievement situations, and evidence greater psychological problems, this does not necessarily hold for minorities and low-income persons. Focusing on external forces may be motivationally healthy if it results from assessing one's chances for success against systematic and real external obstacles rather than unpredictable fate! Three factors of importance for our discussion were identified by Gurin et al.

The first factor, called "control ideology," is a measure of general belief about the role of external forces in determining success and failure in the larger society. It represents a cultural belief in the Protestant ethic; success is the result of hard work, effort, skill, and ability. The second factor, "personal control," reflects a person's belief about his/her own sense of personal efficacy or competence. While control ideology represents an ideological belief, personal control is more related to actual control. Gurin et al. cited data that indicates Blacks are equally internal to Whites on the control ideology, but when a personal reference (personal control) was used, they were much more external. What this indicates is that Blacks may have adopted the general cultural beliefs about internal control, but find these cannot always be applied to their own life situations (because of racism and discrimination). It is interesting to note that Whites endorse control ideology statements at the same rate as personal control ones. Thus, the disparity between the two forms of control does not seem to be operative for White Americans. A third interesting finding was that personal control, as opposed to ideological control, was more related to motivational and performance indicators. A student high on personal control (internality) had greater self-confidence, higher test scores, higher grades, and so on. Those subjects who were high on the ideological measure were not noticeably different from their externally oriented counterparts.

The I-E continuum is a useful one for counselors to use only if they make clear distinctions about the meaning of the external control dimension. High externality may be due to (a) chance-luck, (b) cultural dictates that are viewed as benevolent, and (c) a political force (racism and discrimination) that represents malevolent but realistic obstacles. In each case, it is a mistake to assume the former is operative for a culturally different client. To do so would be to deny the potential influence of cultural values and the effects of prejudice and discrimination. The problem becomes more complex when we realize that cultural and discriminatory forces may both be operative. That is, American Indian cultural values that dictate an external orientation may be compounded by their historical experience of prejudice and discrimination in America. The same may be true for poor Puerto Ricans who often perceive a subjugation to nature due to their poverty and religious beliefs (Inclan, 1985).

LOCUS OF RESPONSIBILITY

Another important dimension in world outlooks was formulated from attribution theory (Jones et al., 1972) and can be legitimately referred to as "locus of responsibility." In essence, this dimension measures the degree of responsibility or blame placed on the individual or system. In the case of Blacks, their lower standard of living may be attributed to their personal inadequacies and shortcomings; or the responsibility for their plight may be attributed to racial discrimination and lack of opportunities. The former orientation blames the individual, while the latter explanation blames the system.

The degree of emphasis placed on the individual as opposed to the system in affecting a person's behavior is important in the formation of life orientations. Such terms as "person-centered" or "person-blame" indicate a focus on the individual. Those who hold a person-centered orientation (a) emphasize the understanding of a person's motivations, values, feelings, and goals, (b) believe that success or failure is attributable to the individual's skills or personal inadequacies, and (c) believe that there is a strong relationship between ability, effort, and success in society. In essence, these people adhere strongly to the Protestant ethic that idealizes "rugged individualism." On the other hand, "situation-centered" or "system-blame" people view the sociocultural environment as more potent than the individual. Social, economic, and political forces are powerful; success or failure is generally dependent on the socioeconomic system and not necessarily on personal attributes.

Caplan and Nelson (1973), in discussing the causal attribution of social problems, state that Western society tends to hold individuals responsible for their problems. Such an approach has the effect of labeling that segment of the population (racial and ethnic minorities) which differs in thought and behavior from the larger society as "deviant." Defining the problem as residing in the person enables society to ignore situationally relevant factors and to protect and preserve social institutions and belief systems. Caplan and Nelson (1973) go on to say:

> What is done about a problem depends on how it is defined. The way a social problem is defined determines the attempts at remediation—problem definition determines the change strategy, the selection of a social action delivered system, and the criteria for evaluation . . . Problem definitions are based on assumptions about the causes of the problem and where they lie. If the causes of delinquency, for example, are defined in person-centered terms (e.g., inability to delay gratification, or incomplete sexual identity), then it would be logical to initiate person-change treatment techniques and intervention strategies to deal with the problem. Such treatment would take the form of counselor or other person-change efforts to "reach" the delinquent, thereby using his potential for self-control to make his behavior more conventional . . .
>
> If, on the other hand, explanations are situation centered, for example, if delinquency were interpreted as the substitution of extra legal paths for already preempted, conventionally approved pathways for achieving socially valued goals, then efforts toward corrective treatment would logically have a system-change orientation. Efforts would be launched to create suitable opportunities for success and achievement along conventional lines; thus, existing physical, social, or economic arrangements, not individual psyches, would be the targets for change. (pp. 200–201)

Avis and Stewart (1976) point out that a person-centered problem definition has characterized counseling. Definitions of mental health, the assumptions of vocational guidance, and most counseling theories stress the uniqueness and importance of the individual. As a result, the onus of responsibility for change in counseling tends to rest on the individual. It reinforces a social myth about a person's ability to control his/her own fate by rewarding the members of the middle class who "made it on their own" and increases complacency about those who have not "made it on their own."

Thus, the individual system-blame continuum may need to be viewed differentially for minority groups. An internal response (acceptance of blame for one's failure) might be considered "normal" for the White middle class, but for minorities, it may be extreme and intrapunitive.

For example, a Black male client who has been unable to find a job because of prejudice and discrimination may blame himself ("What's wrong with me?" "Why can't I find a job?" "Am I worthless?"). Thus, an external response may be more realistic and appropriate ("Institutional racism prevented my getting the job".) Gurin et al. (1969) cite research findings which indicate that those Blacks who scored external (blame system) on this dimension (a) more often aspired to nontraditional occupations, (b) were more in favor of group rather than individual action for dealing with discrimination, (c) engaged in more civil rights activities, and (d) exhibited more innovative coping behavior. It is important to note that the personal control dimension discussed in the previous section was correlated with traditional measures of motivation and achievement (grades), while individual system-blame was a better predictor of innovative social action behavior. This latter dimension has been the subject of speculation and studies about its relationship to militancy and racial identity (Caplan & Paige, 1968; Forward & Williams, 1970; Gore & Rotter, 1963; Helms & Giorgis, 1980; Marx, 1967; Oler, 1989; D. W. Sue, 1977).

FORMATION OF WORLD VIEWS

The two psychological orientations, locus of control (personal control) and locus of responsibility, are independent of one another. As shown in Figure 7.1, both may be placed on the continuum in such a manner that they intersect, forming four quadrants: internal locus of control-internal locus of responsibility (IC-IR), external locus of control-internal locus of responsibility (EC-IR), internal locus of control-external locus of responsibility (IC-ER), and external locus of control-external locus of responsibility (EC-ER). Each quadrant represents a different world view or orientation to life. Theoretically, then, if we know the individual's degree of internality or externality on the two loci, we could plot them on the figure. We would speculate that various ethnic and racial groups are not randomly distributed throughout the four quadrants. The previous discussion concerning cultural and societal influences on these two dimensions would seem to support this speculation. Indeed, several studies on Blacks (Helms & Giorgis, 1980; Oler, 1989) and therapists (Latting, 1986) offer partial support for this hypothesis. Because our discussion focuses next on the political ramifications of the two dimensions, there is an evaluative "desirable-undesirable" quality to each world view.

FIGURE 7.1
Graphic Representation of World Views

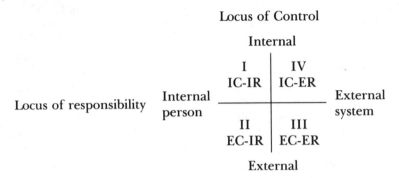

From "Eliminating Cultural Oppression in Counseling: Toward a General Theory" by D. W. Sue, 1978, *Journal of Counseling Psychology, 25,* p. 422. Copyright 1978 by the *Journal of Counseling Psychology.* Reprinted by permission.

Internal Locus of Control (IC)-Internal Locus of Responsibility (IR)

As mentioned previously, high internal personal control (IC) individuals believe they are masters of their fate and their actions do affect the outcomes. Likewise, people high in internal locus of responsibility (IR) attribute their current status and life conditions to their own unique attributes; success is due to one's own efforts, and the lack of success is attributed to one's shortcomings or inadequacies. Perhaps the greatest exemplification of the IC-IR philosophy is U.S. society. Pedersen (1988) describes U.S. American culture as the epitome of the individual-centered approach that emphasizes uniqueness, independence, and self-reliance. A high value is placed on personal resources for solving all problems: self-reliance, pragmatism, individualism, status achievement through one's own effort, and power or control over others, things, animals, and forces of nature. Democratic ideals such as "equal access to opportunity," "liberty and justice for all," "God helps those who help themselves," and "fulfillment of personal destiny" all reflect this world view. The individual is held accountable for all that transpires. Constant and prolonged failure or the inability to attain goals leads to symptoms of self-blame (depression, guilt, and feelings of inadequacy). Most White middle-class members would fall within this quadrant.

Stewart, Danielian, and Festes (1969) and Stewart (1971) have described in detail five American patterns of cultural assumptions and values. These are the building blocks of the IC-IR world view and typically guide our thinking about mental health services in Western society. As we have seen in the Kluckhohn and Strodtbeck model (1961), these values are manifested in the generic characteristics of counseling. The five systems of assumptions may be described as follows.

1. *Definition of Activity.* Western culture stresses an activity modality of "doing" and the desirable pace of life is fast, busy, and driving. A "being" orientation that stresses a more passive, experimental, and contemplative role is in marked contrast to American values (external achievement, activity, goals, and solutions). Existence is in action and not being. Activism is seen most clearly in the mode of problem solving and decision making. Learning is active and not passive. American emphasis is on planning behavior that anticipates consequences.

2. *Definition of Social Relations.* Americans value equality and informality in relating to others. Friendships tend to be many, of short commitment, nonbinding, and shared. In addition, the person's rights and duties in a group are influenced by one's own goals. Obligation to groups is limited, and value is placed on one's ability to actively influence the group. In contrast, many cultures stress hierarchical rank, formality, and status in interpersonal relations. Friendships are intense, of long term, and exclusive. Behavior in a group is dictated by acceptance of the constraints on the group and the authority of the leader.

3. *Motivation.* Achievement and competition are seen as motivationally healthy. The worth of an individual is measured by objective, visible, and materialistic possessions. Personal accomplishments are more important than place of birth, family background, heritage, or traditional status. Achieved status is valued over ascribed status.

4. *Perception of the World.* The world is viewed as distinctly separate from "humankind" and is physical, mechanical, and follows rational laws. Thus, the world is viewed as an object to be exploited, controlled, and developed for the material benefit of people. It is assumed that control and exploitation are necessary for the progress of civilized nations.

5. *Perception of the Self and Individual.* The self is seen as separate from the physical world and others. Decision making and responsibility rest with the individual and not the group. Indeed, the group is not a unit but an aggregate of individuals. The importance of a person's identity is reinforced in socialization and education. Autonomy is encouraged, and emphasis is placed on solving one's own problems, acquiring one's own possessions, and standing up for one's own rights.

Katz (1985) converts many of these characteristics into the components of counseling in Table 7.2.

Counseling Implications. It becomes obvious that Western approaches to counseling occupy the quadrant represented by IC-IR characteristics. Most counselors are of the opinion that people must take major responsibility for their own actions and can improve their lot in life through their

TABLE 7.2

The Components of White Culture: Values and Beliefs

Rugged Individualism:
Individual is primary unit
Individual has primary
  responsibility
Independence and autonomy
  highly valued and rewarded
Individual can control
  environment

Competition:
Winning is everything
Win/lose dichotomy

Action Orientation:
Must master and control nature
Must always do something about a
  situation
Pragmatic/utilitarian
  view of life

Communication:
Standard English
Written tradition
Direct eye contact
Limited physical contact
Control emotions

Time:
Adherence to rigid time
Time is viewed as a commodity

Holidays:
Based on Christian religion
Based on White history and male
  leaders

History:
Based on European immigrants'
  experience in the United States
Romanticize war

Protestant Work Ethic:
Working hard brings success

Progress & Future Orientation
Plan for future
Delayed gratification
Value continual improvement and
  progress

Emphasis on Scientific Method:
Objective, rational, linear thinking
Cause and effect relationships
Quantitative emphasis

Status and Power:
Measured by economic possessions
Credentials, titles, and positions
Believe "own" system
Believe better than other systems
Owning goods, space, property

Family Structure:
Nuclear family is the ideal social
  unit
Male is breadwinner and the head
  of the household
Female is homemaker and subor-
  dinate to the husband
Patriarchal structure

Aesthetics:
Music and art based on European
  cultures
Women's beauty based on blonde,
  blue-eyed, thin, young
Men's attractiveness based on
  athletic ability, power, economic
  status

Religion:
Belief in Christianity
No tolerance for deviation from
  single god concept

From *The Counseling Psychologist* (p. 618) by J. H. Katz, 1985, Beverly Hills, CA: Sage. Copyright 1985 by Sage Publications, Inc. Reprinted by permission.

own efforts. The epitome of this line of thought is represented by the numerous self-help approaches currently in vogue in our field.

Clients who occupy this quadrant tend to be White middle-class counselees, and for these counselees, such approaches might be entirely appropriate. In working with clients from different cultures, however, such an approach might be inappropriate. Diaz-Guerrero (1977), in his attempt to build a Mexican psychology, presents much data on how Mexicans and U.S. Americans differ with respect to their "views of life." To be actively self-assertive is more characteristic of Anglo-Saxon sociocultural premises than of the Mexican. Indeed, to be actively self-assertive in Mexican socioculture clinically, forecasts adjustment difficulties. Counselors with a quadrant I orientation are often so culturally encapsulated that they are unable to understand their minority client's (world view). Thus, the damage of cultural oppression in counseling becomes an ever-present threat.

External Locus of Control (EC)-Internal Locus of Responsibility (IR)

Individuals who fall into this quadrant are most likely to accept the dominant culture's definition for self-responsibility but to have very little real control over how they are defined by others. The term "marginal man" (person) was first coined by Stonequist (1937) to describe a person who finds himself/herself living on the margins of two cultures and not fully accommodated to either. Although there is nothing inherently pathological about bicultural membership, Jones (1972) feels that Western society has practiced a form of cultural racism by imposing its standards, beliefs, and ways of behaving onto minority groups. Marginal individuals deny the existence of racism; believe that the plight of their own people is due to laziness, stupidity, and a clinging to outdated traditions; reject their own cultural heritage and believe that their ethnicity represents a handicap in Western society; evidence racial self-hatred, accept White social, cultural, and institutional standards; perceive physical features of White men and women as an exemplification of beauty; and are powerless to control their sense of self-worth because approval must come from an external source. As a result, they are high in person-focus and external control. The same dynamics and characteristics of the conformity stage (see Chapter 5) seem to operate here.

In the past, mental health professionals have assumed that marginality and self-hatred were internal conflicts of the person almost as if they arise from the individual. In challenging the traditional notion of marginality, Freire (1970) states:

> . . . marginality is not by choice, marginal man has been expelled from and kept outside of the social system and is therefore the object of violence. In fact, however, the social structure as a whole does not "expel," nor is marginal man a "being outside of" . . .)

[Marginal persons] are "beings for another." Therefore the solution to their problem is not to become "beings inside of," but men freeing themselves; for, in reality, they are not marginal to the structure, but oppressed men within it. (pp. 10–11)

It is quite clear that marginal persons are oppressed, have little choice, and are powerless in the fact of the dominant-subordinate relationship between the middle-class WASP culture and their own minority culture. According to Freire (1970), if this dominant-subordinate relationship in society were eliminated, the phenomenon of marginality would also disappear. For if two cultures exist on the basis of total equality (an ideal for biculturalism), the conflicts of marginality simply do not occur in the person.

Counseling Implications. The psychological dynamics for the EC-IR minority client are likely to reflect his/her marginal and self-hate status. For example, White counselors might be perceived as more competent and preferred than counselors of the client's own race. To EC-IR minority clients, focusing on feelings may be very threatening, since it ultimately may reveal the presence of self-hate and the realization that they cannot escape from their own racial and cultural heritage. A culturally encapsulated White counselor who does not understand the sociopolitical dynamics of the client's concerns may unwittingly perpetuate the conflict. For example, the client's preference for a White counselor, coupled with the counselor's implicit belief in the values of U.S. culture, becomes a barrier to successive and effective counseling. A culturally sensitive counselor needs to (a) help the client understand the particular dominant-subordinate political forces that have created this dilemma, and (b) help the client distinguish between positive attempts to acculturate and a negative rejection of one's own cultural values.

External Locus of Control (EC)-External Locus of Responsibility (ER)

The inequities and injustices of racism seen in the standard of living tend to be highly damaging to minorities. For example, the standard of living for Asian Americans, Blacks, Hispanics, American Indians, and Puerto Ricans is much below that enjoyed by Whites. Discrimination may be seen in the areas of housing, employment, income, and education. In American cities, Black Americans are by far the most segregated of the minorities and the inferior housing they are confined to is not the result of free choice or poverty, but discrimination. This inequity in housing is also applicable to other minorities. D. W. Sue and D. Sue (1973) point out that contrary to popular belief, Chinatowns in San Francisco and New York City represent ghetto areas with high rates of unemployment, suicide, juvenile delinquency, poverty, and tuberculosis. Inferior jobs, high unemployment rates, and a much lower income than their White counterparts are also the plight suffered by other minorities. Lower income cannot be attributed primarily to less education. Blacks also suffer from segregated and inferior education: class size, qualification of teachers, physical facilities, and extracurricular activities all place them at a disadvantage. Furthermore, extreme acts of racism can wipe out a minority group. American Indians have witnessed widespread massacres that destroyed their leadership and peoples.

A person high in system-blame and external control feels that there is very little one can do in the face of such severe external obstacles as prejudice and discrimination. In essence, the EC response might be a manifestation of (a) having "given up," or (b) an attempt to "placate" those in power. In the former, individuals internalize their impotence even though they are aware of the external basis of their plight. In its extreme form, oppression may result in a form of "learned helplessness" (Seligman, 1982). Seligman believes that humans exposed to helplessness (underemployment, unemployment, poor quality of education, poor housing) via prejudice and discrimination may exhibit passivity and apathy (poor motivation), may fail to learn that there are events which can be controlled (cognitive disruption), and may show anxiety and depression (emotional disturbance). When minorities learn that their responses have minimal effects from the environment, a phenomenon results that can best be described as an expectation of helplessness. People's susceptibility to helplessness depends on their experience with controlling the environment. In the fact of continued racism, many may simply give up in their attempts to achieve personal goals. The basic assumption in the theory of learned helplessness is that organisms exposed to prolonged noncontrol in their lives develop expectations of helplessness in later situations. This expectation, unfortunately, occurs even in situations that are now controllable.

The dynamics of the placater, however, are not related to the giving-up response. Rather, social forces in the form of prejudice and discrimination are seen as too powerful to combat at that particular time. The best one can hope to do is to suffer the inequities in silence for fear of retaliation. "Don't rock the boat," "keep a low profile," and "survival at all costs" are the phrases that describe this mode of adjustment. Life is viewed as relatively fixed, with nothing much the individual can do. Passivity in the face of oppression is the primary reaction of the placater.

Smith (1977a; 1977b) notes that slavery was one of the most important factors shaping the social-psychological functioning of Black Americans. Interpersonal relations between Whites and Blacks were highly structured, placing Blacks in a subservient and inferior role. Those Blacks who broke the rules or did not show proper deferential behavior were severely punished. The spirits, however, of most Blacks were not broken. Conformance to White rules and regulations was dictated by the need to survive in an oppressive environment. Direct expressions of anger and resentment were dangerous, but indirect expressions were frequently seen.

Counseling Implications. EC-ER Black clients are very likely to see the White counselor as symbolic of any other Black/White relations. They are likely to show "proper" deferential behavior and to not take seriously admonitions by the counselor that they are the masters of their own fate. As a result, an IC-IR counselor may perceive the culturally different clients as lacking in courage and ego-strength and as being passive. A culturally effective counselor, however, would realize the bases of these adaptations. Unlike EC-IR clients, EC-ER individuals do understand the political forces that have subjugated their existence. The most helpful approach on the part of the counselor would be (a) to teach the clients new coping strategies, (b) to have them experience successes, and (c) to validate who and what they represent.

Internal Locus of Control (IC)-External Locus of Responsibility (ER)

Individuals who score high in internal control and system-focus believe in their ability to shape events in their own life if given a chance. They do not accept the fact that their present state is due to their own inherent weakness. However, they also realistically perceive that external barriers of discrimination, prejudice, and exploitation block their paths to the successful attainment of goals. There is a considerable body of evidence to support this contention. Recall that the IC dimension was correlated with greater feelings of personal efficacy, higher aspirations, and so forth, and that ER was related to collective action in the social arena area. If so, we would expect that IC-ER people would be more likely to participate in civil rights activities and to stress racial identity and militancy.

Racial Pride and Identity. Pride in one's racial and cultural identity is most likely to be accepted by an IC-ER person. The low self-esteem engendered by widespread prejudice and racism is actively challenged now by these people. There is an attempt to redefine a group's existence by stressing consciousness and pride in their own racial and cultural heritage. Such phrases as "Black is beautiful" represent a symbolic relabeling of identity from Negro and colored to Black or Afro-American. To many Blacks, Negro and colored are White labels symbolic of a warped and degrading identity given them by a racist society. As a means of throwing off these burdensome shackles, the Black individual and Blacks as a group are redefined in a positive light. Many racial minorities have begun the process in some form and banded together into what is called the "Third World Movement" (Asian Americans, Blacks, Hispanics, American Indians, and others). Since all minorities share the common experience of oppression, they have formed alliances to expose and alleviate the damage that racism has dealt. Problems like poverty, unemployment, housing, education, and juvenile delinquency, as well as emotional problems, are seen as arising from racism in society. Third World people have attempted to enhance feelings of group pride by emphasizing the positive aspects of their cultural heritage.

Militancy. Another area seemingly in support of the IC-ER world view was intimately related to the concept of militancy and collective social action. Between 1964 and 1968 there were 239 violent riots, with racial overtones, resulting in 8,000 casualties and 191 dead, mostly Black (National Commission on the Causes and Prevention of Violence, 1969). These events occurred in epidemic proportions that left the American people dazed and puzzled. Rochester in 1964, Chicago in 1965, Los Angeles in 1965, Cleveland in 1966, Detroit in 1967, and Newark in 1967, to name a few, were all struck by a seemingly senseless wave of collective violence in the Black ghettos. Confrontations between the police and Blacks, looting, sniping, assaults, and the burning of homes and property filled the television screens in every American home. In light of these frightening events, many people searched for explanations about what had happened. The basis of the riots did not make sense in terms of rising income, better housing, and better education for Blacks in America. After all, reasoned many, conditions have never been better for Black Americans. Why should they riot?

When the 1960s' riots are studied, two dominant explanations seem to arise. The first called the "riffraff theory" (person-blame) explained the riots as the result of the sick, criminal elements of the society: the emotionally disturbed, deviants, communist agitators, criminals, or unassimilated migrants. These agitators were seen as peripheral to organized society and possessing no broad social or political concerns. The agitators' frustrations and militant confrontation were seen as part of their own *personal* failures and inadequacies.

A second explanation referred to as the "blocked-opportunity theory" (system-blame) views riot participants as those with high aspirations for their own lives and belief in their ability to achieve these goals. However, environmental forces rather than their own personal inadequacies prevent them from advancing in the society and bettering their condition. The theory holds that riots are the result of massive discrimination against Blacks that has frozen them out of the social, economic, and political life of America. Caplan and Paige (1968) found that more rioters than nonrioters reported experiencing job obstacles and discrimination that blocked their mobility. Further probing revealed that it was not lack of training or education that accounted for the results. Fogelson (1970) presents data in support of the thesis that the ghetto riots are manifestations of grievances within a racist society. In referring to the riots he states that the rioting,

> was triggered not only because the rioters issued the protest and
> faced the danger together but also because the rioting revealed the
> common fate of Blacks in America. For most Blacks, and particu-

larly northern Blacks, racial discrimination is a highly personal experience. They are denied jobs, refused apartments, stopped-and-searched, and declared ineducable (or so they are told), they are inexperienced, unreliable, suspicious, and culturally deprived, and not because they are Black. (p. 145)

The recognition that ghetto existence is a result of racism and not the result of some inherent weakness, coupled with the rioters' belief in their ability to control events in their own lives, made a situation ripe for the venting of frustration and anger. Several studies support the contention that those who rioted have an increased sense of personal effectiveness and control (Abeles, 1976; Caplan, 1970; Caplan & Paige, 1968; Forward & Williams, 1970; Gore & Rotter, 1963; Marx, 1967). Indeed a series of studies concerning characteristics of the rioters and nonrioters failed to confirm the riffraff theory (Caplan, 1970; Caplan & Paige, 1968; Forward & Williams, 1970; Turner & Wilson, 1976). In general, the following emerged of those who engaged in rioting during the 1960s: (a) rioters did not differ from nonrioters in income and rate of unemployment, so they appear to be no more poverty stricken, jobless, or lazy, (b) those who rioted were generally better educated, so rioting cannot be attributed to the poorly educated, (c) rioters were better integrated than nonrioters in social and political workings of the community, so the lack of integration into political and social institutions cannot be used as an explanation, (d) long-term residents were more likely to riot, so rioting cannot be blamed on outside agitators or recent immigrants; (e) rioters held more positive attitudes toward Black history and culture (feelings of racial pride) and thus were not alienated from themselves. Caplan (1970) concluded that militants are not more socially or personally deviant than their nonmilitant counterparts. Evidence tends to indicate they are more "healthy" along several traditional criteria measuring mental health. Caplan also believes that attempts to use the riffraff theory to explain riots have an underlying motive. By attributing causes to individual deficiencies, the users of the riffraff theory relieve White institutions of the blame. Such a conceptualization means that psychotherapy, social work, mental hospitalization, or imprisonment should be directed toward the militants. Demands for systems-change are declared illegitimate because they are the products of "sick" or "confused" minds. Maintenance of the status quo rather than needed social change (social therapy) is reaffirmed.

Counseling Implications. There is much evidence to indicate that minority groups are becoming increasingly conscious of their own racial and cultural identities as they relate to oppression in U.S. society (Carter, 1988; Carter & Helms, 1987; Parham & Helms, 1981, 1985). If the evidence is correct, it is also probable that more and more minorities are most likely to hold an IC-ER world view. Thus, counselors who work with the culturally different will increasingly be exposed to clients with an IC-ER world view. And, in many respects, these clients pose the most difficult problems for the IC-IR White counselor. Challenges to the counselor's credibility and trustworthiness are likely to be raised by these clients. The counselor is likely to be seen as a part of the Establishment that has oppressed minorities. Self-disclosure on the part of the client is not likely to come quickly, and more than any other world view, an IC-ER orientation means that clients are likely to play a much more active part in the counseling process and to demand action from the counselor.

The theory being proposed here predicts several things about the differences between IC-IR and IC-ER world views in counseling. First, these two world views may dictate how a counselor and client define problems and how they use and are receptive to different styles of counseling. For example, IC-IR people will tend to see the problem as residing in the person, while IC-ER people will see the problem as being external to the individual. Furthermore, IC-ER counselors may use and are most receptive to counseling skills, styles, or approaches that are action oriented. This is in contrast to IC-IR counselors who may be more nondirective in their interactions with clients. Two particular studies seem to bear out these predictions.

Berman (1979) cites the example of a study which compared Black and White counselor trainees viewing videovignettes of Black and White clients. The clients presented problems related to vocational choice. To a question of "What would you say next?" White males tended to ask questions, White females tended to reflect feelings and to paraphrase, and Blacks tended to give advice and directions. More important, Blacks identified the problem as being in society rather than in the individual, whereas Whites tended to focus more on the individual. The assumption being made is that the Blacks in this study are most likely IC-ER counselor trainees. A similar study conducted by Atkinson, Maruyama, and Matsui (1978) with Asian Americans also revealed consistent findings. The more politically conscious Asian American (IC-ER) rated the counselor as more credible and approachable when using a directive (structure, advice, suggestions) rather than nondirective (reflection and paraphrase) approach.

CONCLUSIONS

The conceptual model presented in this chapter concerning world views and identity development among Third World groups is consistent with other formulations (Atkinson et al., 1989; Hall et al., 1972; Jackson, 1975; Parham, 1989; Parham & Helms, 1981, 1985; D.W. Sue, 1975). In all cases, these writers believe that cultural identity for minorities in America is intimately related to racism and oppression. Using this model in counseling culturally different clients has many practical and research implications.

1. It is obvious that counseling in the United States falls into the IC-IR quadrant. Clients are seen as able to initiate change and are held responsible for their current plights. A counselor operating from this framework will most likely be person centered. While such a view is not necessarily incorrect or bad, it may be inappropriately applied to clients who do not share this perception. When counselors are culturally-sociopolitically blind and impose their world views on clients without regard for the legitimacy of other views, they are engaging in a form of cultural oppression.

Therefore, what is needed is for counselors to become culturally aware, to understand the basis of their world views, and to understand and accept the possible legitimacy of others. Only when counselor education programs begin to incorporate cross-cultural concepts in their training (not from a White perspective, but from the perspective of each culture) will counseling possibly lose its oppressive orientation.

2. Another implication from this conceptual model is its use as an aid to understanding possible psychological dynamics of a culturally different client. Figure 7.2 presents a transactional analysis of the four quadrants.

For example, an EC-IR client who experiences self-hatred and marginality may be a victim of the dominant-subordinate relationship fostered in American society. The problem is not inherent or internal, and

FIGURE 7.2
Transactional Analysis of Sue's Cultural Identity Quadrants

IC-IR	IC-ER
I. (Assertive/Passive) I'm O.K. and have control over myself. Society is o.k., and I can make it in the system.	*IV. (Assertive/Assertive)* I'm O.K. and have control, but need a chance. Society is not o.k., and I know what's wrong and seek to change it.
EC-IR	**EC-ER**
II. (Marginal/Passive) I'm O.K., but my control comes best when I define myself according to the definition of the dominant culture. Society is o.k. the way it is; it's up to me.	*III. (Passive-Aggressive)* I'm not O.K. and don't have much control; might as well give up or please everyone. Society is not o.k. and is the reason for my plight; the bad system is all to blame.

From *Counseling and Development in a Multicultural Society* (p. 365) by J.A. Axelson. Copyright © 1985 by Wadsworth, Inc. Reprinted by permission of Brooks/Cole Publishing Company, Pacific Grove, California 93950, a division of Wadsworth, Inc.

counseling may be aimed at a reeducative process to get that client to become aware of the wider social-political forces at the basis of his or her plight.

An EC-IR person, whether he or she has given up or is placating, must be taught new coping skills to deal with people and institutions. Experiences of success are critically important for clients in this quadrant.

IC-ER clients are especially difficult for counselors to handle, because challenges to counseling as an act of oppression are most likely to arise. A counselor who is not in touch with these wider social-political issues will quickly lose credibility and effectiveness. In addition, IC-ER clients are externally oriented, and demands for the counselor to take external action on the part of the client will be strong (setting up a job interview, helping the client fill out forms, etc.). While most of us have been taught not to intervene externally on behalf of the client, all of us must look seriously at the value base of this dictate.

3. It is highly possible that problem definitions and specific counseling skills are differentially associated with a particular world view. One reason why Third World clients may prematurely terminate counseling (D. W. Sue, 1977) is the fact that counselors not only differ in world views, but also use counseling skills inappropriate to their clients' lifestyles. Our next step would be to research the following questions: Are there specific counseling goals, techniques, and skills best suited for a particular world view? If so, the implications for counseling training are important.

First, this indicates an overwhelming need to teach trainees the importance of being able to understand and share the world views of their clients. Second, it is no longer enough to learn a limited number of counseling skills. Ivey, Ivey, and Simek-Downing (1987) make a strong case for this position. The culturally effective counselor is one who is able to generate the widest repertoire of responses (verbal/nonverbal) consistent with the lifestyles and values of the culturally different client. Particularly for minorities, the passive approaches of asking questions, reflecting feelings, and paraphrasing must be balanced with directive responses (giving advice and suggestions, disclosing feelings, etc.) on the part of the counselor.

4. The counselor needs to understand that each world view has much to offer that is positive. While these four psychological orientations have been described in a highly evaluative manner, positive aspects of each can be found. For example, the individual responsibility and achievement orientation of quadrant I, biculturalism, and cultural flexibility of quadrant II, ability to compromise and adapt to life conditions of quadrant III, and collective action and social concern of quadrant IV need not be at odds with one another. The role of the counselor may be to help the client integrate aspects of each world view that will maximize his/her effectiveness and psychological well-being. Ivey, Ivey, and Simek-Downing (1987) call this person the "culturally effective individual." He/she is a "functional integrator" who is able to combine and integrate aspects of each world view into a harmonious union. To accomplish this goal, however, means the counselor is also able to share the world view of his/her clients. In essence, the culturally skilled counselor is also one who is a functional integrator.

SOME CAUTIONS

In closing, there are some precautions that should be exercised in using this model. First, the validity of this model has not been directly established through research although preliminary inquiries are promising (Helms & Giorgis, 1980; Latting, 1987; Oler, 1989). While much empirical and clinical evidence is consistent with the model, many of the assertions in the chapter remain at the speculative level. Second, the behavior manifestations of each quadrant have not been specifically identified. Regardless of a person's psychological orientation, we would suspect that individuals can adapt and use behaviors associated with another world view. This, indeed, is the basis of training counselors to work with the culturally different. Third, each style represents conceptual categories. In reality, while people might tend to hold one world view in preference to another, it does not negate them from holding variations of others. Most Third World people represent mixes of each rather than a pure standard. Fourth, whether this conceptual model can be applied to groups other than minorities in America has yet to be established. Last, we must remember that it is very possible for individuals from different cultural groups to be more similar in world view than those from the same culture. While race and ethnicity may be correlated with one's outlook in life, the correspondence certainly is not one to one.

CHAPTER 8

The Culturally Skilled Counselor

Increasingly, mental health practitioners and researchers have begun to turn their attention to the development of culture-specific techniques in counseling and therapy. As indicated in earlier chapters, this interest was generated by findings that various racial minorities tend to underutilize traditional mental health facilities or terminated prematurely after only one session (President's Commission on Mental Health, 1978; D. W. Sue, 1977b; S. Sue, 1977). These results were part of larger criticisms leveled at the mental health field for being culturally encapsulated (Pedersen et al., 1981; D. W. Sue, 1981; Wrenn, 1962), for failing to provide training experiences relevant to minorities (Bernal & Padilla, 1982; Carney & Kahn, 1984; Casas et al., 1986; Corvin & Wiggins, 1989), and for not addressing the issue of White racism in both trainers and practicing counselors (Carney & Kahn, 1984; Corvin & Wiggins, 1989; Helms, 1984; Katz & Ivey, 1977; D. W. Sue et al., 1982). These issues were the focus of numerous conferences in psychology and graduate education (Austin Conference, 1975; Dulles Conference, 1978; National Conference on Graduate Education in Psychology, 1987; Vail Conference, 1973), all noting the serious lack and inadequacy of psychology training programs in dealing with racial/cultural matters. As a result, the Education and Training Committee of Division 17 (Division of Counseling Psychology) developed minimal cross-cultural competencies that were subsequently endorsed by the Executive Committee for incorporation into psychology training programs (D. W. Sue et al., 1982). Among the standards adopted was a recommendation that culturally sensitive and relevant counseling strategies be developed, strategies that would fit the lifestyles, cultural values, and sociopolitical realities of minority clients.

Since the 1970s, it has been gratifying to witness the increase in literature addressing the need to develop culturally "sensitive," "relevant," and "appropriate" services for minority clients (Atkinson et al., 1989; Ivey, 1981, 1986; Lopez et al., in press; Ponterotto & Casas, 1987; Ridley, 1984). All seem to endorse the notion that various racial groups may require approaches or techniques that differ from those of White Anglo-Saxon middle-class clients. Indeed, the belief held by many cross-cultural scholars is that minority clients tend to prefer and respond better to directive rather than nondirective approaches, that counseling approaches which are active rather than "passive" are more effective, that a structured, explicit approach may be more effective than an unstructured, ambiguous one, and that minority clients may desire a counselor who self-discloses his/her thoughts or feelings (Atkinson et al., 1978; Berman, 1979; Dauphinais et al., 1981; Ivey, 1986; D. W. Sue, 1978; Szapocznik, Santisteban, Kurtines, Hervis, & Spencer, 1982).

Given all of these findings and ideas, we would like to "pull together" concepts presented in earlier chapters into an integrated picture of relevant processes/goals in cross-cultural counseling. We would like to (a) elucidate some important principles of cross-cultural counseling that may predict its effectiveness, and (b) describe characteristics of the culturally skilled counselor.

RELEVANT PROCESSES AND GOALS IN CROSS-CULTURAL COUNSELING

Thus far we have emphasized the necessity of the counselor working with a culturally different client to (a) be aware of the sociopolitical forces that have impacted the minority client, (b) understand that culture, class, and language factors can act as barriers to effective cross-cultural counseling, (c) point out how expertness, trustworthiness, and lack of similarity influences the minority client's receptivity to change/influence, (d) emphasize the importance of world views/cultural identity in the counseling process, (e) understand culture bound and communication style differences among various racial groups, and (f) become aware of one's own racial biases and attitudes. All these variables seem to imply one thing: counseling culturally different clients may require a different combination of skills (process) and goals. Yet, the question still remains, How do we determine relevant processes and goals in cross-cultural counseling? While a specific answer would not be possible, D. W. Sue (1977a, 1981) has presented a conceptual model that may be of help in answering this question.

To be more responsive to the culturally different, we must begin the much-needed task of systematically determining the appropriateness or inappropriateness of counseling approaches. Counselor education programs, mental health delivery systems, and counselors themselves must take major responsibility to examine and evaluate the relevance of their particular theoretical framework with respect to the client's needs and values. This statement implies several things. First, there must be a knowledge of minority group cultures and experiences. The earlier chapters were attempts to provide insights into this area for mental health practitioners. Furthermore, each of the individual chapters on American Indians, Asian Americans, Black-Americans, and Hispanic-Americans in this book is designed to address this point. Second, we must make clear and explicit the generic characteristics of counseling and the particular value assumptions inherent in the different schools of thought. Third, when these two aspects of our work are complete, we can compare and contrast them to see which approaches are (a) consistent, (b) conflicting, or (c) new to one another. Implicit in these statements is the assumption that different cultural and subcultural groups require different approaches. From there a decision can be made about how to work with a culturally different individual.

Figure 8.1 reveals four conditions that may arise when counseling a person from a different culture. This schema is proposed as one approach to looking at counseling and the culturally different. As Ivey and Authier (1978) point out, the model can also be used for examining the appropriateness of alternative theoretical models of counseling for different individuals within a single culture.

At the preentry level, culturally different clients inherit a whole constellation of cultural and class values, language factors, and life expe-

FIGURE 8.1

Processes and Goals in Counseling

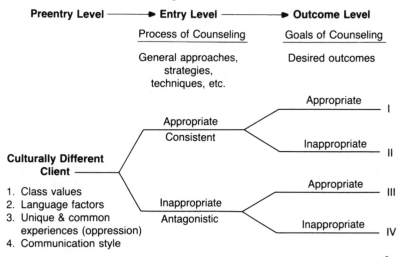

From *Counseling the Culturally Different: Theory and Practice,* 3d ed. (p. 99) by D. W. Sue, 1981, New York: John Wiley. Copyright 1981 by John Wiley. Reprinted by permission.

riences. Those factors form the person's cultural identity and his/her world view. Oftentimes, the minority client's communication style is a function of these factors. Further, the counselor is also a product of his or her culture, class, language, and experiences. In the case of a White helping professional, this is what may be referred to as White identity development. This will influence the counseling activity as well as the particular school of counseling chosen by the counselor. On entering the "process of counseling," counselors choose a general approach, style, or strategy in working with clients. All theories of counseling rely heavily on some basic techniques (existentialists may disagree) in the therapeutic session. Closely linked to the actual process of counseling are certain implicit or explicit goals such as insight, self-actualization, or behavior change. Or, there may be more specific goals, such as how to study better, deal with aggression, or interview for jobs. As can be seen in Figure 8.1, a culturally different client may be exposed to one of four conditions: (1) appropriate process, appropriate goals, (II) appropriate process, inappropriate goals, (III) inappropriate process, appropriate goals, (IV) inappropriate process, inappropriate goals.

Condition I—Appropriate Process, Appropriate Goals

In condition I the client is exposed to a counseling process that is consistent with his or her values, life experiences, and culturally conditioned way of responding. A Black male student from the ghetto who is failing in school and getting into fights with other students can be treated by the counselor in a variety of ways. Sometimes such a student lacks the academic skills necessary to get good grades. The constant fighting is a result of peers' teasing him about his "stupidity." A counselor who is willing to teach the student study and test-taking skills as well as give advice and information may be using an appropriate process consistent with the expectations of the student. The appropriate goals defined between counselor and client, besides acquisition of specific skills, may be an elevation of grades. Notice that this particular activity of counseling (teaching, giving advice, etc.) is not traditionally seen as a legitimate part of it. Calia (1968) points out that in working with the culturally different, counselors must break away from their narrow definition of counseling activities. Lorion (1974) concludes that the expectations of the lower-class client are different from those of therapists. Lower-class clients are more concerned with survival and making it on a day-to-day basis. They may expect immediate, concrete suggestions and advice. Getting job interviews for clients, teaching specific educational skills, and helping clients to understand and fill out unemployment forms may be the desired and preferred help. In addition, if the problem resides in the environment (racism, oppression, discrimination, etc.), it would appear appropriate that a more action-oriented approach to change the environment would be called for in this case. Thus, a counselor who uses counseling strategies that make sense to the client (consistent with his or her values) and defines suitable goals will be an effective and helpful one.

Condition II—Appropriate Process, Inappropriate Goals

Oftentimes, a counseling strategy may be chosen by the counselor that is compatible with the client's life experiences, but the goals are questionable. Again, let us take the aforementioned example of the Black ghetto student. Here the counselor may define the goal as the elimination of "fighting behavior." The chosen technique may be behavior modification. Since the approach stresses observable behaviors and provides a systematic, precise, and structured approach to the "problem," much of the nebulousness and mystique of counseling is reduced for the Black student. Rather than introspection and self-analysis, which many Third World people may find unappealing, the concrete tangible approach of behavioral counseling is extremely attractive.

While the approach may be a positive experience for many minorities, there is danger here regarding control and behavioral objectives. If the Black student is being teased and forced to fight because he is a minority-group member, then the goal of "stopping fighting behavior" may be inappropriate. The counselor in this situation may inadvertently be imposing his or her own standards and values on the client. The end goals place the problem in the hands of the individual rather than society, which produced the problem. Steiner (1975) and Bardo, Bryson, and Cody (1974) have termed these approaches "pacification programs."

To what extent does the client assume responsibility for deciding the direction of change? To what extent is the counselor forcing the client to adapt or adjust to a "sick" situation that ought to be changed? These are not easy questions to answer. They point out the complexity of certain social issues in counseling and the concern that many minorities express about cultural oppression in counseling.

Condition III—Inappropriate Process, Appropriate Goals

More often than not, counselors tend to use inappropriate strategies in working with the culturally different. Early termination of counseling is most likely to occur when the process is antagonistic to the values of the client and forces him or her to violate some basic personal values. The counselor, with the best of intentions and appropriate goals, may fail because the process is incompatible with values of the client. For example, many American Indians view the person as harmonious with nature. The world is accepted in its present form without undue attempts to change it (Edwards & Edwards, 1980; Everett et al., 1983). Unlike American-Indian society, Anglos are concerned with controlling and mastering the physical world. The more nature is controlled, the better. American Indians, who may operate under the principle of "noninterference," find coercion and the use of suggestion in counseling to be rude, ill-mannered, and hostile. Goodtracks (1973) states:

> The Indian child is taught that complete noninterference in interaction with all people is the norm, and that he should react with amazement, irritation, mistrust, and anxiety to even the slightest indication of manipulation or coercion. (p. 31)

The counselor who leans heavily on some form of intervention like the behavioral techniques may be seen as coercive and manipulative. American-Indian clients exposed to counselors who stress individual responsibility for changing and mastering the environment are, in effect, asking their client to violate a basic value. This may be one reason why American Indians have such a high dropout rate in our educational system.

Another example given by Ivey and Authier (1978) illustrates this condition with respect to person-centered counseling. The Rogerian conditions of respect for individuals, empathy, genuineness, and warmth may be very compatible with the values of many Third World people. However, the Rogerian process of paraphrasing, reflecting feelings, and summarizing can be incompatible with cultural patterns. Blacks, for example, may find the patient, waiting, and reflective type of a nondirective technique to be antagonistic to their values. Furthermore, empathy is difficult to establish when the counselor does not understand Black idioms, nonverbal modes of expression, and traditions and values of a Black lifestyle. In this case, other techniques to arrive at empathy may be called for. Some (Greene, 1985; Mays, 1985) contend that if a counselor is to be effective with Blacks, techniques that bring a client to a level of awareness and action would be best. Directive, confrontive, and persuasive approaches are more compatible.

There is some question about whether it is possible to use an inappropriate process to arrive at an appropriate goal. If a client, for whatever reason, stays in the counseling relationship, then does not his or her being exposed to a process that violates a basic value change the person? Can the client ever attain an appropriate goal? If we look only at the techniques and goals of different counseling theories, then the answer may appear to be yes. For example, Gestalt approaches emphasize the end goals of the "here and now" (present-time orientation) and getting in touch with bodily feelings. These goals may appear consistent with American-Indian values. Yet, the body of techniques used in Gestalt counseling tends to be confrontive and controlling—actions that may prove embarrassing to Indian clients.

The problem with looking solely at a particular theory is that doing so is "static." Counseling is a dynamic process, an activity that is ongoing. The relationships between process and goals are highly interrelated and complex. The question of whether condition III can ever exist cannot be easily answered. If the answer, however, is yes, then another issue presents itself: Do the ends justify the means?

Condition IV—Inappropriate Process, Inappropriate Goals

Approaches that are clearly inappropriate in terms of techniques and goals most generally lead to early termination of counseling. For example, Vietnamese clients who may value restraint of strong feelings and believe that intimate revelations are to be shared with only close friends may cause problems for the insight- or feeling-oriented counselor (Brower, 1980). Not only are the techniques inappropriate (reflecting feelings, asking questions of a deeply personal nature, making in-depth interpretations, and so on) and seen as lacking in respect for the client's integrity, but also the goal of insight into deep underlying processes may not be valued by the person. For example, Vietnamese clients who come for vocational information may be perceived by counselors as needing help in finding out what motivates their actions and decisions. Requests for advice or information from the client are seen as indicative of deeper, more personal conflicts. Although this may be true in some cases, the blind application of techniques that clash with cultural values and the rigid adherence to a goal such as insight seriously places many Vietnamese at a disadvantage. This analysis indicates three important things.

First, it is important for counselors to attend to group differences in working with racial or ethnic minorities. A culturally skilled counselor is one who is able to relate to minority-group experiences and has knowledge of cultural and class factors. Second, counselors need to recognize that working with individuals from different cultures does not dictate the same approach, but one that is differentially consistent with lifestyles. In counseling, *equal treatment may be discriminatory*. Third, it is important to systematically look at racial and ethnic differences as they relate to (a) the counselor's own approach and values, and (b) the various schools of counseling. One way we can do this is to more clearly understand what counselors do in counseling (process) and what particular goals counselors hold for their clients. It is hoped that a comparative analysis as proposed in Figure 8.1 will lead to a more realistic appraisal of the appropriateness of counseling approaches (psychoanalysis, Gestalt, behavior modification, person-centered approaches) in working with the culturally different.

CHARACTERISTICS OF THE CULTURALLY SKILLED COUNSELOR

Understanding of minority-group experiences and the issues raised throughout the text can be implemented only by enlightened, nondefensive, open and skilled counselors. Until recently, a systematic attempt to identify characteristics of the culturally skilled counselor was lacking (Bernal & Padilla, 1982; Ponterotto & Benesch, 1988; Ridley, 1984). This served as a major impediment to training programs that were receptive to cross-cultural training but had difficulty identifying what the program goals should be (Ivey, 1981; D. W. Sue & D. Sue, 1977b). It was not until 1980, that the Division of Counseling Psychology of the American Psychological Association directly addressed this issue (D. W. Sue et al., 1982) and outlined eleven characteristics of a culturally skilled counselor. Since its publication, it has been cited frequently and recommendations for developing training programs that address themselves to these skills have begun (Carney & Kahn, 1984; LaFramboise, Coleman, & Hernandez, 1989).

It is important to note that these proposed competencies were tentatively put forth with the encouragement that more concrete and sophisticated ones be developed. Since the senior author chaired the Committee that brought forth these recommendations and since extension and refinements are already underway, these are discussed in greater detail in this chapter. In addition, some liberty is taken in proposing new ones. Unlike their conceptual framework, which divides the competencies into the categories of beliefs/attitudes, knowledge, and skills, a broader division is used to incorporate all three. Consistent with the thesis stressed throughout this book, a culturally skilled counselor is seen as working toward these primary goals. First, a culturally skilled counselor is one who is actively in the process of becoming aware of his/her own assumptions about human behavior, values, biases, preconceived notions, personal limitations, and so forth. Second, a culturally skilled counselor is one who actively attempts to understand the world view of his/her culturally different client. In other words, what are the client's values and assumptions about human behavior, biases, and so on? Third, a culturally skilled counselor is one who is in the process of actively developing and practicing appropriate, relevant, and sensitive intervention strategies/skills in working with his or her culturally different client.

These three goals stress the fact that becoming culturally skilled is an *active process*, that it is *ongoing*, and that it is a process that *never reaches an end point*. Implicit is recognition of the complexity and diversity of the client and client populations, and acknowledgment of our own personal limitations and the need to always improve.

COUNSELOR AWARENESS OF OWN ASSUMPTIONS, VALUES, AND BIASES

In almost all human service programs, counselors, therapists, and social workers are familiar with the phrase, "Counselor, know thyself." Programs stress the importance of not allowing our own biases, values, or "hangups" to interfere with our ability to work with clients. In most cases, such warning stays primarily on an intellectual level with very little training directed at having trainees get in touch with their own values and biases about human behavior. In other words, it appears easier to deal with trainees' cognitive understanding about their own cultural heritage, the values they hold about human behavior, their standards for judging normality and abnormality, and the culture-bound goals they strive toward.

What makes examination of the self difficult is the emotional impact of attitudes, beliefs, and feelings associated with cultural differences and, in particular, *racism*. For example, as a member of the White group, what responsibility do you hold for the racist, oppressive, and discriminating manner by which you personally and professionally deal with minorities? This is a threatening question for White people to entertain. Yet, to be effective in cross-cultural counseling means one has adequately dealt with this question and worked through the biases, feelings, fears, guilt, and so forth, associated with it. It would appear, then, that a culturally skilled counselor will have developed beliefs and attitudes consistent with the following characteristics.

1. *The culturally skilled counseling psychologist is one who has moved from being culturally unaware to being aware and sensitive to his/her own cultural heritage and to valuing and respecting differences.* The counselor has begun the process of exploring his/her values, standards, and assumptions about human behavior. Rather than being ethnocentric and believing in the superiority of his/her group's cultural heritage (arts, crafts, traditions, language), there is acceptance and respect for cultural differences. Other cultures are seen to be as equally valuable and legitimate as his/her own. It is clear that a counselor who is culturally unaware is most likely to impose his or her values and standards onto a minority client. As a result, an unenlightened counselor may be engaging in an act of cultural oppression.

2. *The culturally skilled counselor is aware of his/her own values and biases, and how they may affect minority clients.* The counselor actively and constantly attempts to avoid prejudices, unwarranted labeling, and stereotyping. Beliefs that Blacks and Hispanics are intellectually inferior and will not do well in school, or that Asians make good technical workers but poor managers, are examples of widespread stereotyping that may hinder equal access and opportunity. Culturally skilled counselors try not to hold preconceived limitations/notions about their minority clients. As a check upon this process, they actively challenge the assumptions they are working on, they monitor their functioning via consultations, supervision, and/or continuing education.

3. *Culturally skilled counselors are comfortable with differences that exist between themselves and their clients in terms of race and beliefs.* Differences are not seen as being deviant! The culturally skilled counselor does not profess "color blindness" or negate the existence of differences that exist in attitudes and beliefs. The basic concept underlying "color blindness" is the humanity of all people. Regardless of color or other physical differences, each individual is equally human. While its original intent was to eliminate bias from counseling, it has served to deny the existence of differences in clients' perceptions of society arising from membership in different racial groups. The message tends to be, "I will like you only if you are the same," instead of, "I like you because of and in spite of your differences."

It is important that counselors begin to recognize the different levels of identity each possesses. Each counselor's *individual* identity makes him or her unique and unlike others. *Group* identity acts as a reference base that may incorporate such things as family, race, ethnicity, gender, religion, and so forth. *Universal* identity emphasizes those common aspects that all share as human beings. Counselors oftentimes deny the group identity of the client (race and culture) only to concentrate on the individual or universal level. While these levels do constitute aspects of the client, and while they are important and beneficial to consider, focusing on these to the exclusion of race or culture may be symbolic of discomfort in dealing with these issues (i.e., differences are deviant, negative, and create barriers).

4. *The culturally skilled counselor is sensitive to circumstances (personal biases, stage of ethnic identity, sociopolitical influences, etc.) that may dictate referral of the minority client to a member of his/her own race/culture or to another counselor, in general.* A culturally skilled counselor is aware of his/her limitations in cross-cultural counseling and is not threatened by the prospect of referring a client to someone else. This principle, however, should not be used as a "cop-out" for counselors who do not want to work with minority clients, or who do not want to work through their own personal hangups.

5. *The culturally skilled counselor acknowledges and is aware of his/her own racist attitudes, beliefs, and feelings.* A culturally skilled counselor does not deny the fact that he/she has directly or indirectly benefited from individual, institutional, and cultural racism and that he/she has been socialized in a racist society. As a result, the culturally skilled counselor possesses racist elements that may be detrimental to his/her minority client. Culturally skilled counselors accept responsibility for their own racism, and attempt to deal with it in a nondefensive, guilt-free manner. They have begun the process of defining a racist free, nonoppressive, and nonexploitative attitude. Addressing one's Whiteness as in the models of White identity development is crucial for effective cross-cultural counseling.

UNDERSTANDING THE WORLD VIEW OF THE CULTURALLY DIFFERENT CLIENT

It is crucial that counselors understand and can share the world view of their culturally different clients. This statement does not mean counselors have to *hold* these world views as their own, but rather that they can see and accept other world views in a nonjudgmental manner. Some have referred to it as cultural role-taking where the counselor acknowledges he/she has not lived a lifetime as an Asian, Black, Indian, or Hispanic person. It is almost impossible for the counselor to think, feel, react, and so forth, as a minority individual. Yet, cognitive empathy, as distinct from affective empathy, may be possible. It represents cultural role-taking where the counselor acquires practical knowledge concerning the scope and nature of the client's cultural background, daily living experience, hopes, fears, and aspirations. Inherent in cognitive empathy is the understanding of how counseling relates to the wider sociopolitical system that minorities contend with every day of their lives.

1. *The culturally skilled counselor must possess specific knowledge and information about the particular group he/she is working with.* He/she must be aware of the history, experiences, cultural values, and lifestyle of various racial ethnic groups. The greater the depth of knowledge of a cultural group and the more knowledge he/she has of many groups, the more likely that the counselor can be an effective helper. Thus, the culturally skilled counselor is one who continues to explore and learn about issues related to various minority groups throughout his/her professional career.

2. *The culturally skilled counselor will have a good understanding of the sociopolitical system's operation in the United States with respect to its treatment of minorities.* Understanding the impact and operation of oppression (racism, sexism, etc.), the politics of counseling, and the racist concepts that have permeated the mental health helping professions, is important. Especially valuable for the counselor is an understanding of the role cultural racism plays in the development of identity and world views among minority groups.

3. *The culturally skilled counselor must have a clear and explicit knowledge and understanding of the generic characteristics of counseling and therapy.* These encompass language factors, culture-bound values, and class-bound values. The counselor should clearly understand the value assumptions (normality and abnormality) inherent in the major schools of counseling and how they may interact with values of the culturally different. In some cases, the theories or models may limit the potential of persons from different cultures. Likewise, being able to determine those that may have usefulness to culturally different clients is important.

4. *The culturally skilled counselor is aware of institutional barriers that prevent minorities from using mental health services.* Such factors as the location of a mental health agency, the formality or informality of the decor, the language(s) used to advertise the services, the availability of minorities among the different levels, the organizational climate, the hours and days of operation, the offering of the services needed by the community, and so forth, are important.

DEVELOPING APPROPRIATE INTERVENTION STRATEGIES AND TECHNIQUES

Cross-cultural counseling effectiveness is most likely enhanced when the counselor uses counseling modalities and defines goals consistent with the life experiences/cultural values of the client. Throughout this chapter, this basic premise has been emphasized. Studies have consistently revealed that (a) economically and educationally disadvantaged clients may not be oriented toward "talk therapy," (b) self-disclosure may be incompatible with cultural values of Asian Americans, Hispanics, and American Indians, (c) the sociopolitical atmosphere may dictate against self-disclosure, (d) the ambiguous nature of counseling may be antagonistic to life values of the minority client, and (e) many minority clients prefer an active/directive approach to an inactive/nondirective one in counseling. Counseling has too long assumed that clients share a similar background and cultural heritage and that the same approaches are equally effective with all clients. This is an erroneous assumption that needs to be buried.

Because groups and individuals differ from one another, the blind application of techniques to all situations and all populations seems ludicrous. In the interpersonal transactions between the counselor and client, what is needed is differential approaches consistent with the life experiences of the person. In this particular case and as mentioned earlier, it is ironic that equal treatment in counseling may be discriminatory treatment! Counselors need to understand this. As a means to prove discriminatory mental health practices, Third World groups have in the past pointed to studies revealing that minority clients are given less preferential forms of treatment (medication, electroconvulsive shock therapy, etc.). Somewhere, confusion has occurred, and it was believed that to be treated differently is akin to discrimination. The confusion centered around the distinction between equal access and opportunities versus equal treatment. Third World groups may not be asking for equal treatment so much as they are for equal access and opportunities. This dictates a differential approach that is truly nondiscriminatory.

1. *At the skills level, the culturally skilled counselor must be able to generate a wide variety of verbal and nonverbal responses.* There is mounting evidence to indicate that minority groups may not only define problems differently from their Anglo counterparts, but respond differently to counseling therapy styles. It appears that the wider the repertoire of responses the counselor possesses, the better the helper he/she is likely to be. We can no longer rely on a very narrow and limited number of skills in counseling. We need to practice and be comfortable with a multitude of response modalities.

2. *The culturally skilled counselor must be able to send and receive both verbal and nonverbal messages accurately and "appropriately."* The key words "send," "receive," "verbal," "nonverbal," "accurately," and "appropriately" are important. These words recognize several things about cross-cultural counseling.

First, communication is a two-way process. The culturally skilled counselor must not only be able to communicate (send) his/her thoughts and feelings to the client, but also be able to read (receive) messages from the client. Second, cross-cultural counseling effectiveness may be highly correlated with the counselor's ability to recognize and respond not only to verbal, but also to nonverbal messages. Third, sending and receiving a message accurately means the ability to consider cultural cues operative in the setting. Fourth, accuracy of communication must be tempered by its appropriateness. This is a difficult concept for many to grasp. It deals with communication styles. In many cultures, subtlety and indirectness of communication is a highly prized art. Likewise, directness and confrontation are prized by others.

3. *The culturally skilled counselor is able to exercise institutional intervention skills on behalf of his/her client when appropriate.* This implies that help giving may involve out-of-office strategies (outreach, consultant, change agent, ombudsman roles, and facilitator of indigenous support systems) that discard the intrapsychic counseling model and view the problems/barriers as residing outside of the minority client.

4. *The culturally skilled counselor is aware of his/her helping style, recognizes the limitations he/she possesses, and can anticipate the impact upon the culturally different client.* All counselors have limitations in their ability to relate to culturally different clients. It is impossible to be all things to everyone; that is, no matter how skilled we are, our personal helping style may be limited. This is nothing to be ashamed of, especially if a counselor has tried and continues to try to develop new skills. As mentioned in the last chapter, when counseling-style adjustments appear too difficult, the next best thing to do may be to (a) acknowledge the limitations, and (b) anticipate your impact upon the client. These things may communicate several things to the culturally different client. First, that you are open and honest about your style of communication and the limitations or barriers they may potentially cause. Second, that you, the counselor, understand enough about the client's world view to potentially anticipate how this may adversely affect your client. Third, that you will communicate your desire to help despite your limitations. Surprisingly, for many culturally different clients, this may be enough to allow rapport building and greater freedom on the part of counselors to use techniques different from those of the client.

CONCLUSIONS

Some criticisms have been leveled at the advocacy of criteria that emphasizes differences between the counselor and the culturally different client. Indeed, characteristics of the culturally skilled counselor in this chapter stress dissimilarities between the counselor and client. Most of the criticisms seem to be of the following genre: (a) concentrating on differences fosters a backlash of racism, (b) by focusing on racial/cultural characteristics, the counselor may lose sight of the individual client, (c) there are so many differences and the field is so complex that one cannot possibly work with minorities, (d) counselors and therapists may be limited in their ability to adopt a different counseling style, (e) concentrating on culture-specific techniques may lead to a technique-oriented definition of counseling devoid of a conceptual framework, and (f) technique approaches may be distal to the goal of therapy (Helms, 1985; Margolis & Rungta, 1986; Ponterotto & Benesch, 1988; D. W. Sue, 1989; S. Sue & Zane, 1987).

There is much truth to many of these warnings, but let us not be guilty of "blaming the victim." Differences are not the problem. Being Asian American is not the problem. Being American Indian is not the problem. Being Black is not the problem. Being Hispanic is not the problem. The problem lies in the perception of what differences mean and in society's perception of the attributes attached to being a minority-group member! Cross-cultural counseling implies major differences between the counselor and client. Not only are there major differences, but those dissimilaries are associated with minority status in the United States. As a result, counselors who are afraid to face these facts squarely, who deny that they exist, who perceive these as "the problem," and who feel uncomfortable working out these differences will meet with failure. Counselors who are willing to address cultural differences directly are those who do not perceive them as impediments. Instead, counselors who view these differences as positive attributes will most likely meet and resolve the challenges that arise in cross-cultural counseling. Such an individual is a "culturally skilled counselor."

PART II

COUNSELING SPECIFIC POPULATIONS

In Part I we were concerned with providing a broad conceptual and theoretical base from which to analyze counseling and its relationship to the culturally different. While differences among minority groups have been mentioned, we have dealt mainly with concepts that seem equally applicable to minority experiences in the United States. This has been necessary to supply us with an analytical framework from which to view cross-cultural counseling. Yet it is equally important for us to recognize that while commonalities exist among varying cultural groups, differences are also present. These differences seem intimately correlated with (a) cultural values unique to an ethnic group, (b) historical experiences in the United States, and (c) U.S. treatment and stereotyping of the minority group.

The four groups described in the forthcoming chapters are American Indians, Asian Americans, Black Americans, and Hispanic Americans. We suggest that you apply concepts learned from Part I to each of these groups and ask yourself these questions:

1. What are the cultural values of the group?
2. What has been the historical experience of this group in the United States?
3. How may cultural values/historical experiences affect behavior, motivation, and the minority's perception of counseling?
4. Can you apply the concepts of racial/cultural identity and world views to each of the groups? What factors are important for consideration?

5. In reviewing the generic characteristics of counseling, which seem to be potential barriers? Why?

These questions as well as the ones at the end of each separate chapter will, hopefully, begin to help you address the field of cross-cultural counseling.

CHAPTER 9

Counseling American Indians

"I will die an Indian!" These words were spoken by Fred Coyote, an American-Indian writer, indicating that he had survived efforts by the U.S. government, government agencies, and school to try to get him to forget his heritage. Coyote is a Wailaki Indian whose group nearly became extinct in battles during the Gold Rush. As one of the few remaining Wailakis, he is intent upon passing the history of his tribe and tradition to his children. He is working to have all Indians feel proud of their own culture (Josephy, 1982).

In North America, the American-Indian population has been decimated due to contact with Europeans through wars and diseases. It is estimated that the large population of Indians was decreased to only 10% of its original number by the end of the eighteenth century (Richardson, 1981). Extermination and seizure of lands seemed to be the primary policy. Indians were forced from their lands onto reservations. During the 1930s, over 125,000 Indians from different tribes were forced from their homes in many different states to a reservation in Oklahoma. The move was traumatic for Indian families and, in many cases, disrupted their cultural traditions. Assaults against the Indian culture were also produced in attempts to "civilize" the Indians. Many of the Indian children were forced to be educated in English-speaking boarding schools. They were not allowed to speak their own language and had to spend eight continuous years away from their family and tribes (Blanchard, 1983). The negative impact was great on family and tribal cohesion.

In the past, the tribe, though the extended family, was responsible for the education and training of the children. The sense of identity developed through this tradition was undermined. In addition, even recent history is full of broken treaties, the seizure or misuse of Indian land, and battles (often led by the U.S. government) to remove fishing and hunting rights.

These acts have made the American Indians very suspicious of the motives of the majority culture.

THE AMERICAN INDIAN

American Indians form a highly heterogeneous group comprised of approximately 530 distinct tribes of which 478 are recognized by the U.S. government. Of these, 280 have a land base or reservation (Wise & Miller, 1983). The tribes vary in customs, language, and type of family structure. Tefft (1967) found that on some variables, differences between certain tribal groups are greater than between Indians and Caucasians. In addition, American Indians differ in their degree of acculturation and whether or not they live on reservations. Of the over 1 million American Indians living in the United States, approximately 50% live on reservations. Because of a birthrate that is twice that of the general population in the United States, the total population of American Indians has doubled in the past decade. The American Indians are a young population, with a modal age of 20 (Attneave, 1982).

What constitutes an Indian is often an area of controversy. As Trimble & Fleming (1989) point out, unlike other ethnic groups, American Indians have had a legal definition formulated for them by Congress. An individual has to have at least an Indian blood quantum of 25% to be considered an Indian. This definition has caused problems both within and outside the Indian community. Many in both groups feel that only an Indian who is of pure Indian blood is a true Indian. The arbitrary blood requirement established by the U.S. government has sometimes resulted in dissension among Indians due to the limited amount of funds available for social, economic, and educational development (Wise & Miller, 1983). Likewise, considerable controversy exists about whether the term "American Indian" or "Native American" should be used. We have chosen to use primarily the former because it appears to be the preferred usage by most Indians.

Indians are often thought to have specific physical characteristics such as black hair and eyes, brown skin, and high cheek bones. Trimble (1981) indicates that for many, it is difficult to accept as an Indian an individual who has light hair, blue eyes, and fair skin. However, American Indians display a wide range of phenotypic characteristics in terms of body size, skin and hair color, and facial features. Conflicts in identity are often great for individuals who do not fit the traditional physical stereotypes. They may meet with prejudice and rejection from Indians and non-Indians alike.

Tribe

For the many Indians living on reservations and for those living in urban areas, the tribe is of fundamental importance. The relationship that Indians have with their tribes is different from that between non-Indians and their society. Indians see themselves as an extension of their tribe. This identity provides them with a sense of belonging and security, with which they form an interdependent system. Status and rewards are obtained by adherence to tribal structure (Blanchard, 1983). Indians judge themselves in terms of whether or not their behaviors are of benefit to the tribe. Personal accomplishments are honored and supported if they serve to benefit the tribe. Indians who leave the reservation to seek greater opportunities often lose their sense of personal identity since they lose their tribal identity (Anderson & Ellis, 1988).

Family Characteristics

It is difficult to describe "the Indian family." Red Horse (1979) points out that only tribes exist and that the family structure varies from tribe to tribe. Some generalizations can be made, however. American Indians are characterized by a high fertility rate, a large percentage of out-of-wedlock births, and a strong role for women (U.S. Department of Health, Education & Welfare, 1980). For most tribes, the extended family is the basic unit. Children are often raised by relatives such as aunts, uncles, and grandparents who live in separate households (Staples & Mirande, 1980). In one tribe, over 90% of the grandparents lived in separate households but were involved and fulfilled traditional family roles on a daily basis with their children, grandchildren, and great-grandchildren. In a review of the literature on American Indian families, Staples and Mirande concluded that one-third are headed by females, approximately 25% receive public assistance, there is an average of three children per family, and inadequate income exists for over two-thirds of American Indians. The existence of high unemployment on reservations has forced many to move into urban areas. However, cultural conflict and the loss of contact with the extended family and tribe may be responsible for the fact that 40% return to the reservation (Miller, 1980).

The concept of the extended family is often misunderstood by those in the majority culture who operate under the concept of the nuclear family. The extended family often extends through the second cousin. For the American Indian, it is not unusual to have youngsters stay in a variety of different households. Misinterpretations can be made if one thinks that only the parents should raise and be responsible for the children. Red Horse (1982) presents a case of a 15-year-old girl who was doing very well in school. However, she chose not to live with her parents who had problems with alcohol but lived instead in five different households of relatives during a 3-year period. The White caseworker felt the pattern of moving around was an indication of irresponsibility on the part of the girl and neglect on the part of the parents. If the girl was a member of the majority culture, such an interpretation would not be out of line. At the age of 17, Linda requested a place of her own. This request was resisted by the social worker who cited her view that Linda was irresponsible and had displayed a pattern of instability. However, Indian professionals pointed out that Linda was doing very well in school and that many members of her extended family lived within an 8-block radius of her apartment. Further, she had the support of the school counselor and Indian professionals. It was also pointed out that a pattern of living in the households of the extended family was not uncommon. In this example, there are several factors to note. First, the pattern of behavior has to be considered in a cultural context. Second, the decision regarding Linda's request was based not only on cultural knowledge but also on her individual strengths and weaknesses. If she had not done well in school or had not displayed responsible behavior, the decision would most likely have been different. Red Horse cautions that in working with American Indians, the consideration of Indian values as well as specific problem behaviors should be reviewed before a treatment plan is developed.

Problems of Children and Adolescents

Indian children and adolescents not only face the developmental problems faced by all young people, they are also in a state of conflict over exposure to two very different cultures. They are caught between expectations of their parents to maintain traditional values and the necessity to adapt to the majority culture. These and other stressors may account for the fact that among Indian youth rates of truancy, school failure, drug use, and suicide are high (Red Horse, 1982; Shore, 1988).

VALUES

Because of the great diversity and variation among American Indians, it is difficult to describe a set of values that encompasses them all. Everett, Proctor & Cartmell (1980) and Wise and Miller (1983), however, feel that certain generalizations can be made regarding Indian values. Some of these values are as follows:

1. *Sharing.* Among Indians, honor and respect is gained by sharing and giving while in the dominant culture, status is gained by the accumulation of material goods. Trimble (1981) presents the case of a Lower Elwha Indian woman who sent her grandson to school with a large lunch. The teacher assumed that the lunch was for the child and had him consume all of it, not understanding that it was to be shared with other children. The child requested that his grandmother not prepare a large lunch for him again.

2. *Cooperation.* Indians believe that the family and group take precedence over the individual. Indian children may be seen as unmotivated in schools because of a reluctance to compete with peers in the

classroom. They may also feel it necessary to show their answers to another tribe member. Indians work hard to prevent discord and disharmony. In a counseling setting, they may find it easier to agree with the counselor, but will not follow through with the suggestions. In the majority culture, individual achievement and competition are seen as important.

3. *Noninterference.* Indians are taught not to interfere with others and to observe rather than react impulsively. Rights of others are respected. They are often seen as permissive in child rearing. In the majority culture, taking charge is valued.

4. *Time orientation.* Indians are very much involved in the present rather than the future. Ideas of punctuality or planning for the future may be unimportant. Life is to be lived in the here and now. Long-term plans such as going to college are seen as acts of egoism rather than future planning. Things get done according to a rational order and not according to deadlines. In the majority culture, delay of gratification and planning for future goals are seen as important qualities.

5. *Extended family orientation.* Interrelationships between a large number of relatives is important and there is strong respect for elders and their wisdom and knowledge. In the majority culture, the nuclear family is the basic unit of family structure and elders are not held in great esteem.

6. *Harmony with nature.* Rather than seeking to control the environment, Indians accept things as they are. In the majority culture, there are attempts to master and control the environment. The more nature that can be controlled, the better.

These value differences can produce certain problems, especially when Indian behaviors are interpreted from a non-Indian perspective. For example, Wise and Miller (1983) describe a case in which a teacher referred an Indian girl for counseling because of social anxiety and shyness. When asked the reason for the referral the teacher indicated that the girl would not look her in the eye when she spoke to her. This interpretation was premature, since the teacher was not aware that among many Indian groups, eye contact between a child and an elder indicated a lack of respect. There have been reported cases in which the lack of eye contact has been regarded as a deficit. A behavior modification procedure was employed to shape eye contact in a Navaho girl (Everett, Proctor & Cartmell, 1989). Anderson and Ellis (1980) point out some of the behavioral differences that can be observed as a result of value differences. Indian children tend to display sensitivity to the opinions and attitudes of their peers. They will actively avoid disagreements or contradictions. Most do not like to be singled out and made to perform in school unless the whole group would benefit. They are rarely future oriented.

Within-Group Differences

Although some of the value differences between Indians and non-Indians have been presented, many Indians are acculturated and hold the values of the larger society. The degree of assimilation should always be considered. For example, Lowrey (1983) points out differences within the Navaho people. Some have had minimal contact with the majority culture and are strongly oriented to their own culture. Others are acculturated, do not identify with Navaho values, and wish to move the Navaho nation into the modern world. Another group is able to move comfortably between the two cultures. They are also interested in "advancing" their tribe but want to be able to retain their traditional religious and family values. They want the freedom to choose from both cultures. Urban Indians are also going through a change. What appears to be emerging is a pan-Indian movement (Wise & Miller, 1983).

It is clear that within-group differences have to be considered in working with American Indians. Because of differences in acculturation, approaches that might be appropriate for a given individual might not be appropriate for "all Indians." Zitzow and & Estes (1981) have expressed concern that by presenting the cultural values of American Indians, counselors and mental health workers will develop a set of stereotyped notions about the appropriate method of counseling for members of this population. They suggest that it is necessary to assess the degree of assimilation of the specific American-Indian client. For example, the types of problems and the appropriate process and goals may be very different for an American Indian living on a rural reservation compared to an urbanized Indian who retains few of the traditional beliefs. Cultural knowledge helps but as they point out, "What is right for one 'Indian' may not be necessarily right for 'all Indians' " (Zitzow & Estes, 1981). The application of cultural knowledge inappropriately can mislead professionals in developing preconceived notions as how to counsel American Indians.

Zitzow and Estes emphasize the importance of recognizing individual differences in American Indians but also feel that it might be useful to develop a typology for conceptualizing this group. They offer suggestions to assess assimilation in American Indians and develop a two-point continuum. The first is the Heritage Consistent Native American (HCNA) whose predominant orientation is the American-Indian tribal culture. The second is the Heritage Inconsistent Native American (HINA) whose behaviors and lifestyles reflect the dominant American culture. These are not mutually exclusive and overlaps occur. Signs indicative of heritage consistency may include: growing up on or near a reservation, extended family orientation, involvement in tribal religious and cultural activities, education on or near a reservation, social activities primarily with other Native Americans, knowledgeable about or willing to learn about own culture, placing low priority on materialistic goals, and using shyness and silence as signs of respect.

Specific issues that may be involved in counseling the HCNA include: (a) the sense of security for the individual may be limited to the reservation and the extended family; (b) nonverbal communication may be more important, and the individual may have difficulty with the English language; (c) socialization may involve only other American Indians, and the individual may feel uncomfortable communicating with a non-Indian; (d) basic academic learning skills may be underdeveloped; (e) the value of education may not fit into the individual's belief system, and the individual might feel a conflict between motivation to learn and values on the reservation; (f) the individual might be concerned about failure and its impact on the extended family and the tribe; (g) they may have a difficult time establishing long-term goals; (h) the holding back of emotions may be perceived as a positive characteristic; (i) paternalism from government agencies may have diminished feelings of personal responsibility in decision making; and (j) the individual may be unfamiliar with the expectations of the dominant culture.

As opposed to HCNA individuals, issues that a HINA may face include: (a) denial and lack of pride in being a Native American; (b) pressure to adopt the majority cultural values; (c) guilt feelings over not knowing or participating in his/her culture; (d) negative views of Native Americans; and (e) a lack of a support and belief system.

Being able to identify the degree of acculturation or self-identity for an individual client is important. Zitzow and Estes (1981) present an example of two American Indian sisters, one of whom is adopted and raised by a White family away from the reservation. She is not knowledgeable about her culture and is not interested in participating in traditional activities. She is not totally comfortable with her White friends but is less comfortable with her native culture. The other sister was raised on the reservation within an extended family. She participates in tribal activities and is proud of her identity. However, she is uncertain and uneasy when interacting with the dominant culture. Each of the sisters would require a different intervention. The first would have to examine value and self-identity conflicts. The second requires skills in coping with the dominant society.

In addition, Zitzow and Estes feel that there are common counseling issues that should be explored with all American Indians, such as alcoholism, possible feelings of distrust toward mental health professionals (especially non-Native American), prejudice and discrimination, possible lack of strong self-identity, fear of failure and ridicule, a lack of exposure to successful American-Indian role models, feelings of frustration that others are responding to them in a stereotypic fashion rather than as an individual, and possible conflicts over commitment to long-term goals such as education, with feelings of alienation from tribal and extended family values. American Indians should be responded to as individuals first. Cultural knowledge only serves to indicate areas of potential difficulty and allows the mental health professional to be sensitive to cultural issues and values.

PROBLEM AREAS

Substance abuse is one of the greatest problems faced by the American Indian. Cases of terminal liver cirrhosis are 14 times greater among Indians than non-Indians between the ages of 25 and 34 (Indian Health Service, 1978). Death from alcoholism is 6½ times greater than in the general population (Westermeyer, 1972). Nearly one-third of all outpatient visits to the Indian Health Services involve alcohol abuse or dependence. In addition, drug abuse and dependence are very high among young Indian clients (Rhoades et al., 1980). In one survey, up to 70% of Indian adolescents in an urban school setting were involved in drug and alcohol abuse (Red Horse, 1982). Alcohol use is associated with fighting, vandalism, and delinquency (Manson, Tatum, & Dinges, 1982). Suicide rates for American Indians are twice that of the national average, with adolescence to adulthood as the time of greatest risk (Shore, 1988). Concern was expressed at the 1981 American Indian Child Conference over the increase in the number of alcoholics among young parents with an accompanying increase in child abuse. Tribal officials voiced distress with this finding and were also concerned about the increase in Fetal-Alcohol-Syndrome babies among American Indians.

A variety of explanations has been put forth to indicate possible reasons for the rise in alcohol abuse. Some have focused on the release of feelings of frustration and boredom, allowing Indians to express emotions that are normally under control, serving as a social event, and the acceptance of drinking in many tribal groups (Berlin, 1982). Manson, Tatum, and Dinges (1982) indicate that among many American Indians, drinking is an accepted practice and is encouraged among family members. Parents are often heavy drinkers and allow their children to drink. Manson and his colleagues feel that a major etiologic component of childhood abuse of alcohol is the Indian respect for autonomy and permissiveness, which then allows a child to determine how much alcohol to consume. Medicine (1982) describes drinking in the Lakota in which alcohol is part of a social event that includes small children and infants. Young children are taken to bars and by the early teen years have formed drinking groups of their own. The younger children are encouraged by adolescents to sniff glue and to drink. Peer pressure to drink is especially high for males. Thus, drinking patterns are established at an early age. Drinking tends to end for women when they are 35–40 years old and men tend to level off when they reach 40. Many individuals report problems following reduced alcohol consumption, including loneliness and feelings of not being part of the social group.

Anderson and Ellis (1980) feel that drinking among Indians is a different phenomenon than drinking in non-Indians. For the former, it is a social event that promotes sociability and a sense of tribe. It is done in groups and in binges. Turning down an offered drink is considered to be an act of individual autonomy and disruptive to group harmony. Alcoholics in the majority culture, however, tend to drink continuously, often in isolation, and as a means to escape responsibility.

Treatment of Substance Abuse

Schinke et al. (1985) indicate that prevention and treatment of substance abuse is best accomplished in groups of Indian youth, preferably led by Indian social workers, teachers, or school counselors. The process would involve six steps. The first would provide the students with accurate information on drugs and alcohol. Respected elders and older youth might be invited to talk about some of the dangers of drug use. Suggestions can be made that natural highs can be gained by spirit dancing, singing, and dancing. Medicine (1982) also indicates that tribal communities can gain information about the effects of alcohol abuse through workshops. Gaining the support of the tribal officials would be very important to reinforce efforts to curb drinking. It can also be pointed out that alcohol was an "introduced evil" and not a part of traditional tribal rituals. Second, problem-solving skills in rejecting alcohol would be developed. Schinke and his colleagues give an example of a teenager who would share a six-pack of beer with friends during the school lunch hour. He did not like the feelings of sleepiness in class after consuming the beer. He is asked to brainstorm solutions. Suggestions he comes up with are that he could drink only a little, pretend to drink, stay in class during the lunch break, pretend that he had a stomachache, or not drink at all. He chooses the latter solution but decides to stand beside his cousin who will not pressure him to drink. The development of alternative responses can be very helpful in reducing the chances of abuse. The third step would be to develop a cognitive rehearsal strategy. Coping statements can be thought of, expressed subvocally, and then aloud. The individual thinks of what he or she can say to refuse to participate and then rehearses it aloud. The fourth step involves behavioral rehearsal with coaching and reinforcement. For example, a student might be told to consider a situation in which a friend of yours wants you to smoke pot with her. How would you indicate that you do not wish to do so? In this situation another American-Indian student supports and reinforces the student who is practicing refusal skills.

PAT: Why don't you come over to my house, and we can get high?

PAULETTE: Uh . . . I don't know. I might have something to do.

PEER COACH [QUIETLY]: Real good start. Try to talk louder and more certain.

PAT: Come on, it's more fun to get high than anything else you have to do.

PAULETTE: It would be more fun to go to a movie.

PAT: We could get high at my place and watch television.

PEER COACH [*QUIETLY*]: Don't give in, Paulette.

PAULETTE: I don't want to get high. If that's all you want to do, I'll find something to do myself.

The fifth step would involve establishing a positive social network. Family and friends who will support nondrinking are identified and brought into the social network. Involvement in alternative activities such as dance, intertribal sports, and clan activities is encouraged. Pairs and groups of individuals are formed to assist one another in rejecting the use of alcohol and other drugs.

EDUCATION

American-Indian children appear to do well during the first few years of school. However, by the fourth grade, a pattern of decline and dropouts occurs. Y. Red Horse (1982) feels that the decline is due to the exposure to negative stereotypes as the children begin to identify themselves as Indians. These negative views produce feelings of hopelessness and despair. In the Seattle School District, nearly 59% of American-Indian students in middle school had a grade-point average below 2.00 (over 9% had GPAs above 3.00) as compared to 21% of White students. American-Indian students were also more likely to be suspended (34%) as compared to White students (17%). For adolescent Indian girls, a particular problem is pregnancies at school age. In one study in Minneapolis, 40% of all school pregnancies occurred in Indian girls. This figure did not include girls who had dropped out of school because of pregnancy (Y. Red Horse, 1982). The inability to complete an education perpetuates the cycle of poverty and lack of opportunities.

Approximately 40,000 Indian and Eskimo children attend boarding schools and the number is increasing (Kleinfeld & Bloom, 1977). Many of the children spend 8 months in schools each year and must learn and adapt to a foreign culture and language. The schools are often located in another state and mix a variety of students from other Indian tribes. In the Indian tribes, the youths learned by observing their elders and members of the extended family. In boarding schools, they are deprived of this opportunity and have only each other as models. This experience, along with the training and employment of adults off the reservation, has tended to further weaken the culture (Lowrey, 1983).

The boarding schools originated with the idea of turning the Indians away from their own culture to a more "civilized" one. Attempts were made to keep the youth away from the teaching of their tribe (Josephy, 1982). Missionary-dominated schools were also set up to indoctrinate the Indians with English or French cultures (Katz, 1981). Although many of the boarding schools have changed their philosophy and now focus on helping Indian students be aware of their heritage, it also appears that a large number of students suffer from loneliness, depression, and school failure (Berlin, 1982). Kleinfeld and Bloom (1977) studied a variety of boarding schools and found that the environment seemed to be responsible for social and emotional disturbances in the students. Forty-nine percent of high school freshman developed psychological problems that were school related. It is significant that 43% of the freshman dropped out or transferred before their sophomore year. High levels of emotional disturbance were also reported during students' sophomore years. However, some American Indians feel that the boarding school has improved to the point where it provides a worthwhile education (Berlin, 1982; Kleinfeld and Bloom, 1977).

COUNSELING AMERICAN-INDIAN CHILDREN AND YOUTH

Katz (1981) feels that one of the first steps in working with Native adolescents is to incorporate a discussion of the Indian/White relationship. This has several purposes. First, it allows the client to be aware of potential problems if the therapist is White. Second, it gets the client to consider his/her own feelings about values, self-identity, and relationship with the majority society. Problems involving identity formation may be great and swing back and forth, with the Indian youths sometimes seeing themselves as primarily Indian, and sometimes moving in the direction of White values. The therapist has to help recognize and clarify the conflicts so that the client can make an individual resolution. Trimble (1981) indicates that if a client has weak or negative value, self-identity can be improved by strengthening value preferences and by developing pride in their culture. Adolescents may also have conflicts between their values and those of the majority culture, and may have problems getting to work on time, saving money, and attending school regularly. The different set of values and expectations can be presented and compromises may have to be made.

Indian youths also have a difficult time with assertion or the expression of strong emotions. However, Katz feels that a major loophole occurs when the individual becomes drunk. In this condition, an individual is not considered to be responsible for his/her behavior and can openly express anger. A case study of a 17-year-old Cree male, Chris, was presented to illustrate this point. Chris was attempting to save money on the job that he had so he could buy a car. However, he found this difficult to do since he was supporting his unemployed brother who was living with him. His brother contributed nothing to the living expenses and did not seek employment. Chris was caught between his personal desire and the cultural expectation of sharing with others. He was unable to express his feelings of anger. However, one day he allowed himself to get drunk and then angrily denounced his brother. Within a few days, the brother moved out. Neither discussed the incident, and they remained close. Although the outcome was a success, a more meaningful solution would have been to make the conflict conscious and decide what would be possible alternatives to the problem.

Because of the importance of the extended family, counseling may be more successful in homes and with family members or friends present. Group counseling seems to be a promising modality, as can be seen in the pilot project described by Yvonne Red Horse (1982). This pilot prevention program involved increasing the interdependence of Indian girls with their extended family. Nine Indian girls between the ages of 15 and 17, who were having adjustment problems in school, participated. All came from dysfunctional families in which there were problems with alcohol and drug abuse, unemployment, and inadequate housing. However, they all had in common an intact extended family network.

The pilot project involved working on the strengths that existed in the families and using a culturally accepted group format to promote social cohesion. Culture was used to strengthen group ties. Group identity was built through the participation of the members in cultural activities such as powwows, feasts, and intertribal dancing. As trust was built up in the groups, exploration of feelings and frustrations could be explored. A problem-solving approach was used to determine solutions that could be implemented. Extended family ties were strengthened by having the girls share their feelings with aunts, uncles, cousins, parents, and grandparents. Members of the extended family were consulted whenever problems arose. Reliance on help from extended family members increased. The Indian adolescents developed confidence and learned to be more independent through becoming more interdependent with family members.

COUNSELING ISSUES

Before working with American Indians, it is important to be aware of our own cultural biases. Much of what we do is based on Western values and influences. We expect clients to establish good eye contact, to discuss inner feeling, and to verbalize concerns. American Indians often will not display these behaviors. In working with adolescents, we often work toward having them develop increasing independence from their parents. We also see the nuclear family as the basic unit. For American Indians, interdependence with the extended family might be the goal. As parents, they are often much more permissive in their childrearing practices. It is important to be aware of how cultural influences have shaped our perception of ideal situations. It is also important to avoid stereotypes of what an individual Indian is like. Instead, it is critical to respond to the individual and identify and explore his or her values. In discussing a typology regarding the degree of assimilation by American Indians, Zitzow and Estes (1981) indicate possible problems and issues faced by American Indians with different orientations. We also presented some of the value differences between American Indians and the majority culture. Cultural knowledge should not be used in a stereotypic fashion. The value of cultural knowledge is to help the counselor be more flexible in outlook and be able to generate more alternative definitions about possible problems with a specific individual.

Can current counseling skills that most counselors have learned be appropriate in working with members of the American Indian population? "Is it conceivable that a traditional Indian, one steeped in the culture of the tribe would respond to conventional techniques regardless of the theoretical underpinnings? If not, is it possible to modify conventional techniques to render them appropriate for use with traditional clients?" (Trimble & LaFramboise, 1985, pp. 129–130). There is controversy surrounding the answer to this question. Trimble feels that client-centered approaches are often "disastrous" in working with American Indians. In contrast, Wise and Miller (1983) feel that a nondirective approach would be more effective than directive counseling. These statements indicate the current confusion over attempts to develop culturally relevant approaches in working with American Indians.

Trimble, in his statement, is pointing out problems with expectations. Many American Indians are not socialized to express inner thoughts and feelings, while Wise and Miller are equating the directive approach to confrontation and forcing the client to reveal sensitive material before trust has developed. Part of the disagreement is over the matter of timing. American Indians cannot be expected to talk about issues in a meaningful manner until trust has developed. Qualities such as respect and acceptance of the individual, unconditional positive regard, understanding the problem from the individual's perspective, allowing the client to explore his or her own values, and arriving at an individual solution are core qualities that may transcend cultures. However, American-Indian clients may need more guidance than is usually offered by client-centered approaches. Expectations of rapid discussion of sensitive material will not be fulfilled. It may be more helpful to first talk about other matters until trust has developed. Bryde (1971) indicates that American Indians expect the counselor to offer alternatives and solutions to the problem. The appropriate combination of client-centered with behavioral approaches might be very effective.

Many American Indians do not understand what occurs in counseling or what their expectations are. One study examined the impact of role preparation on a high-risk immigrant population. Immigrants seeking psychotherapy were assigned to either a role-preparation or a control group. Clients in the former group were given information about: (a) the role of the client and therapist, (b) how talking can help lead to a solution, and (c) the general course of therapy. The researchers found that those who received the precounseling address were less likely to terminate therapy prematurely, were more satisfied with therapy, and perceived more change in themselves than the control group. It might be helpful to furnish the same sorts of information to American-Indian clients. However, the role preparation has to be presented in a way that does not force them into some type of mode or justify using techniques without input from the client.

In conclusion, in working with American Indians, issues of Indian/White relationships may need to be explored, the individual's value structure should be identified and issues of culture conflict and identity should be investigated. Bicultural families may do well with traditional therapies but traditional American Indians may first have to deal with the issue of trust and may respond best to a combination of client-centered with behavioral approaches. Family therapy and processes that involve the extended family may be very fruitful. Other recommendations include: (a) realize that many American Indians will have problems with the limits of a 50-minute session; (b) in dealing with a dysfunctional family, attempt to strengthen it by use of the extended family; (c) during the initial session, keep a low profile and do not press the client; (d) allow the client time to finish statements and thoughts—do not interrupt; (e) confrontation is considered to be rude and should be kept to a minimum; (f) whenever possible, use a family or group treatment modality, and (g) respect the values of the American Indians. Most importantly, it is crucial that mental health professionals remember to, "Respond to the Native American as an individual first . . ." (Zitzow & Estes, 1981, p. 138).

STUDY QUESTIONS

1. How have historical factors helped to shape American-Indian perceptions of White America? How might this impact their response to a White counselor?

2. How does the concept of family and tribe differ from Western familial relationships? Suggest how these differences in views might impact negatively in cross-cultural counseling.

3. How do the values of American Indians differ from Western values? As a counselor, how might you deal with these differences?

4. In working with American Indians, Zitzow and Estes caution the mental health worker to respond to him/her as an individual first. What do they mean by this?

5. How might you modify your counseling style in working with American Indians?

6. What nonverbal communication style differences in American-Indian culture are most likely to cause counselors problems in assessment and treatment? How may they be overcome?

CHAPTER 10

Counseling Asian Americans

The Asian-American population is growing rapidly and in 1985 stood at 5 million in the United States. The large increase is due to the 1965 changes in immigration laws and the entry of over 700,000 Indochinese refugees since 1975. In 1984 alone, over 282,000 Asians entered the United States, and the Asian population is expected to double by 2010. The immigration pattern is changing the characteristics of the Asian-American population. The Japanese-American population, which had constituted the largest Asian group in the United States (701,000), has dropped to third place behind the Chinese (806,000) and Filipinos (775,000). Demographers predict that within 30 years the Filipinos will be the largest group followed by the Chinese, Koreans, Vietnamese, Asian Indians, and Japanese (Doerner, 1985). Because of the large number of Chinese who are entering the United States, over 60% of the Chinese population are now recent immigrants (Lorenzo & Adler, 1984). In fact, with the exception of Japanese Americans, the other Asian populations are now principally comprised of foreign-born individuals (McLeod, 1986).

Between-group differences among the Asian-American population may be quite great since it is comprised of at least 29 distinct subgroups that differ in language, religion, and values (Yoshioka, Tashima, Ichew, & Maurase, 1981). Compounding the difficulty in making any generalization about the Asian-American population are within-group differences. Individuals diverge on variables such as migration or relocation experiences, degree of assimilation or acculturation, identification with the home country, facility with their native and English languages, family composition and intactness, amount of education, and degree of adherence to religious beliefs (Wong, 1985).

ASIAN AMERICANS: A SUCCESS STORY?

In contrast to many Third World groups, the contemporary image of Asian Americans is that of a highly successful minority who have "made it" in society. For example, the belief that Asian Americans represent a "model" minority has been played up by the popular press in such headlines as "Success Story: Outwhiting the Whites," "Success Story of One Minority Group in the U.S." (*U. S. News & World Report*, 1966, *Newsweek*, 1971), "Asian Americans: Are They Making the Grade?" and "The Oriental Express" (*U. S. News & World Report*, 1984; *Psychology Today*, 1986). Indeed, a close analysis of census figures (S. Sue, D. W. Sue, & D. Sue, 1975) seems to support this contention. The Chinese and Japanese in this country have exceeded the national median income, and even Filipinos, who in 1968 were far below the nation's median income level, have now attained parity. The same holds true for educational attainment, where Asian Americans complete a higher median number of grades than all other groups.

Even more striking evidence of "success" is the apparent reduction of social distance between Asians and Whites. Bogardus (1925) developed a Social Distance Scale that is presumably a measure of prejudice and/or discrimination against minority groups. If a minority group is allowed to marry and form intimate relationships with the dominant group, then a reduction in social distance is said to have occurred. The incidence of interracial marriages for Japanese Americans (mainly Japanese-White) in 1970 for areas like Los Angeles, San Francisco, and Fresno, California, has approached 50% (Kikumura & Kitano, 1973; S. Sue & Morishima, 1982; Tinker, 1973). The rates are astoundingly high among Japanese and Filipino youths. This is in marked contrast to the incidence of Black-White marriages for all married Blacks in 1970 that was well under 2% (Urban Associates, 1974).

Besides these economic and social indicators of success, other mental health statistics reinforce the belief that Asians in America are relatively well adjusted, function effectively in society, and experience few difficulties. Studies consistently reveal that Asian Americans have low official rates of juvenile delinquency (Abbott & Abbott, 1968; Kitano, 1969), low rates of psychiatric contact and hospitalization (Kimmich, 1960; Kitano, 1969; S. Sue & Kirk, 1975; S. Sue & McKinney, 1975; S. Sue & D. W. Sue, 1974; Yamamoto, James, & Palley, 1969), and low rates of divorce (S. Sue & Kitano, 1973). Indeed, there seems to be a prevalent belief that Asian Americans are somehow immune to the forces of prejudice and discrimination.

These facts seem ironic in light of the massive discrimination that has historically been directed at Asians. Denied the rights of citizenship, denied ownership of land, assaulted, murdered, and placed in concentration camps during World War II, Asians in America have at one time or another been subjected to the most appalling forms of discrimination ever perpetrated against any immigrant group (Daniels, 1971; Kitano, 1969a; D. W. Sue & Frank, 1973).

A closer analysis of the status of Asian Americans does not support their success story. First, reference to the higher median income of Asian Americans does not take into account (a) the higher percentage of more than one wage earner in Asian than in White families, (b) an equal prevalence of poverty despite the higher median income, (c) lower poverty assistance and welfare than the general population, and (d) a discrepancy between education and income. Disparity exists in that while Asian wage earners may have higher levels of education, their wages are not commensurate with their training (Atkinson et al., 1989; Kim & Hurk, 1983; Urban Associates, 1974).

Second, in the area of education, Asian Americans show a disparate picture of extraordinary high educational attainment and a large undereducated mass. This bimodal distribution when averaged out indicates how misleading statistics can be. Furthermore, there is evidence that Asian Americans do experience educational difficulties, and studies find Asian immigrants and refugees encountering major educational problems because of English (Bliatout, Ben, Bliatout, & Lee, 1985; Nguyen & Henkin, 1983). Less well known is the fact that Asians who have lived in the United States for several generations still suffer from lack of English mastery (Watanabe, 1973). It was found that over 50% of entering University of California–Berkeley Asian students failed a "bonehead" English examination and were required to make up their language deficits in remedial noncredit courses. Asian-American students are twice as likely to fail English examinations when compared to their Caucasian counterparts. Furthermore, the assumption that the direct teaching of language skills will correct this deficiency indicates a failure to understand the Asian's difficulty with the English language. This has made existing remedial programs generally ineffective. While a bilingual background is a major contributor to their difficulty with the English language, the Asians' strong cultural injunctions against assertiveness, the shame and disgrace felt by the students at having to take such courses, and the isolation imposed on this group by a racist society are equally strong forces in their performance.

Third, there is now widespread recognition that, apart from being tourist attractions, Chinatowns, Manilatowns, and Japantowns in San Francisco and New York represent ghetto areas with prevalent unemployment, poverty, health problems, and juvenile delinquency. People outside these communities seldom see the deplorable social conditions that exist behind the bright neon lights, restaurants, and quaint shops. Statistics support the fact that San Francisco's Chinatown has the second largest population density for its size in the country, second only to Harlem (Charnofsky, 1971). The Chinese community has an extremely high tuberculosis rate and a suicide rate three times that of the national average

(Jacobs, Landau, & Pell, 1971). Continuing and recent mass murders committed over the years have been traced to Chinese juvenile gangs operating in Chinatown, and recent news reports show this trend to be on the increase.

Fourth, whether underutilization of mental health facilities is due to low rates of socioemotional adjustment difficulties, discriminatory mental health practices, and/or cultural values inhibiting self-referral is not known. D. W. Sue and Kirk (1972, 1973) found that Asian-American students on one university campus expressed greater feelings of loneliness, isolation, and anxiety than the general student population. This finding is inconsistent with the explanation of lower prevalence of mental health problems among Asians (Leong, 1986). Some investigators (Brown, Stein, Huang, & Harris, 1973; Kimmich, 1960; Kitano, 1969b; D. W. Sue & Kirk, 1975; S. Sue & McKinney, 1975; S. Sue & Morishima, 1982; S. Sue & D. W. Sue, 1971b, 1972) suggest that much of the mental illness, the adjustment problems, and the juvenile delinquency among Asians is hidden. The discrepancy between official and real rates may be due to such cultural factors as the shame and disgrace associated with admitting to emotional problems, the handling of problems within the family rather than relying on outside resources, and the manner of symptom formation, such as low acting-out disorders.

One revealing study conducted by D. W. Sue & Kirk (1975) compared the use of counseling and psychiatric services on a large university campus over a four-year period for Asian-American and non-Asian students. These two investigators found that Chinese- and Japanese-American students, in keeping with previous studies, underutilize the campus psychiatric service. However, a significantly greater percentage of Asian Americans were seen at the counseling center when compared with the non-Asian counterparts. In one particular group (Chinese-American females), the rate approached 50%! These investigators concluded that (a) the need for counseling services among Asian Americans is no lower than that of the general population, (b) Asian Americans may have greater need for academic, career, and vocational counseling than other groups, and (c) the increased contact of Asian students at the counseling center represents a "runoff" of those who would ordinarily be seen at a psychiatric service.

The myths and stereotypes about Asians in America, such as the popular belief that they represent model minorities and that they experience no difficulties in society, must be dispelled. Asian Americans view these stereotypes as having functional value for those who hold power in society. First, these stereotypes reassert the erroneous belief that any minority can succeed in a democratic society if the minority-group members work hard enough. Second, the Asian-American success story is seen as a divisive concept used by the Establishment to pit one minority group against another by holding one group up as an example to others. Third, the success myth has shortchanged many Asian-American communities from receiving the necessary moral and financial commitment due them as a struggling minority with unique concerns. It is especially important for counselors, pupil personnel workers, and educators who work with Asian Americans to look behind the success myth and to understand the Asian experience in America. The matter is even more pressing for counselors when we realize that Asian Americans are more likely to seek help at a counseling service rather than at a psychiatric service.

The approach of this chapter is twofold. First, it attempts to investigate how certain forces have served to shape and define the lifestyle of recent immigrants/refugees and U.S.-born Asian Americans. Second, this chapter explores how an understanding of the Asian-American experience suggests major modifications in counseling and psychotherapeutic practices to fit the needs of Asians in America.

FORCES SHAPING THE IDENTITY OF ASIAN AMERICANS

It is widely accepted that sociopolitical forces have a strong impact on the behavioral expression of different racial/ethnic groups. While many investigators believe that Asian Americans possess distinct subcultural systems (Abbott, 1970; Cordova, 1973; DeVos & Abbott, 1966; Kitano, 1969b; D. W. Sue, 1973), little is known of how these values have interacted with Western values and how they have influenced Asians in America. Although most social scientists continue to pay lip service to the fact that psychological development is not an isolated phenomenon apart from sociocultural forces, most theories of human behavior tend to be culturally exclusive. It seems important, therefore, that to understand the Asian-American experience, it is necessary to discuss the wider social milieu in which behavior and identity originate.

Historical Experience in America

Many in the American public are unaware that Asians in America have suffered from some of the most inhumane treatment ever accorded any immigrant group. Beginning in the 1840s, the Chinese were the first Asian group to arrive in large numbers. Because of the high demand for cheap labor (the discovery of gold in the Sacramento Valley and building of the transcontinental railroad) and the political unrest and overpopulation in certain provinces of China, a large steady stream of Chinese male peasants began to immigrate to the United States (Daniels, 1971; DeVos & Abbott, 1966). In the 1860s nearly all the Chinese lived and settled on the West Coast, with the heaviest concentrations in California. Because their presence in the labor force served to fill a void in the labor market, these early Chinese peasants were not particularly mistreated.

However, a series of business recessions, coupled with the completion of the Union-Central Pacific Railroad in 1869, made competition for jobs fierce. Because the Chinese constituted a large fraction of the California population and labor force, White workingmen saw them as an economic threat. The Chinese were especially vulnerable as scapegoats because of their "strange" customs and appearance; that is, they wore their hair in queues (pigtails), spoke in a "strange tongue," and ate "unhealthy" food. As a result, labor began to agitate against the Chinese with rallying cries such as "the Chinese must go." Although based originally on economics, Daniels (1971) feels that "the movement soon developed an idealogy of White supremacy/Oriental inferiority that was wholly compatible with the mainstream of American racism" (p. 3).

The systematic harassment of the Chinese resulted in legal discrimination that denied them the rights of citizenship; Chinese testimony in court was ruled inadmissible as evidence. Indeed, the Chinese were seen as heathens and subhuman aliens who were detrimental to the well-being of America. Exclusionist legislation was passed at all levels of government and culminated in the passing of a racist immigration law, the Chinese Exclusion Act of 1882, which was not repealed until 1943. Kagiwada and Fujimoto (1973) point out that the phrase "not a Chinaman's chance" alludes to these conditions. They point out further that these actions did not seem to satisfy the racist elements of society. Individual and mob violence such as mass murder, physical attacks, and having homes and property destroyed were common occurrences. Large-scale massacres of the Chinese in Los Angeles in 1851 and Rock Springs, Wyoming, in 1885 are examples of such abuse (Daniels, 1951; Kitano, 1969b). In many cases, the treatment of the Chinese was no better than that of African slaves.

The next Asian group to immigrate in large numbers to the United States was the Japanese. By the time the Japanese came in numbers to the United States beginning in the 1890s, the "Chinese problem" had been relatively solved. Most of the early Japanese immigrants found employment in railroads, canneries, mining, and so on. Since many of the Japanese had previously come from a farming class, their gravitation toward farming and gardening could be predicted (Kitano, 1969b). The Japanese immigrants' knowledge of agriculture and their perseverance made them highly successful in these fields, where they subsequently became economic competitors. The now-familiar pattern of violence and harassment previously directed at the Chinese was now channeled toward the Japanese. This pervasive anti-Oriental feeling became labeled as "the Yellow Peril."

Because Japan was a rising international power, the anti-Japanese feeling did not manifest itself in direct governmental legislation to restrict immigration, but led to a "Gentlemen's Agreement" to seal the flow of Asians to the United States. To further harass the Japanese, California passed the Alien Land Law in 1913 that forbade aliens to own land. The discrimination and prejudice toward the Japanese was most blatantly evident in the World War II incarceration of 110,000 Japanese Americans into concentration camps. The effects of this atrocity, perpetrated against the Japanese, and its humiliating effects are still very much evident today in the suspiciousness that many Asians have for the American mainstream. Indeed, nothing in the Constitution forbids such an action from being taken again.

As an act of reparation to Japanese Americans and Alaska Natives interned during World War II, the Congress and President Reagan signed into law payments of $20,000 per survivor in 1988. To date, not a payment has been made, as eligible survivors die at a rate of 200 a month. Indeed, as of this writing President Bush has eliminated reparation funding in the 1990 budget.

Likewise, the historical treatment of Filipinos and Koreans was no better than that given their Chinese and Japanese counterparts. The Chinese Exclusion Act of 1882 and Gentlemen's Agreement eventually created another imbalance in the labor situation (Rabaya, 1971; Shin, 1971). The Hawaiian super-plantation owners (mainly White) and the mainland businesses were forced to find another cheap source of labor. The two potential reservoirs of labor were Puerto Rico and the Philippines.

The Filipino immigrants who came to the United States also encountered much prejudice and discrimination. Labor unions led by the American Federation of Labor condemned the Filipinos as "cheap labor" lowering the standard of living for other White workers. The blame, however, was misdirected, since it was White employers who set up the system in order to increase profits.

More recently, some 700,000 refugees have arrived in the United States since 1975. The majority are Vietnamese (66.6%), Khmer (20.5%), Laotian (13.5%), and Hmong (7.8%) (Office of Refugee Resettlement, 1984). In general, the Indochinese refugees are under more stress than the immigrants. As Liu and Cheung (1985) point out, immigrants are individuals who have had time to prepare to move to the United States. However, refugees are often not in control of their own fate. For example, the vast majority of Vietnamese, who left just before the fall of Saigon in 1975, had only a few days to decide whether or not to leave their country. Refugees often had to wait in camps for years before immigrating to countries such as the United States, Australia, and France. Many Cambodians have experienced death in their immediate family from starvation or conflict with the Vietcong since they had worked with the Central Intelligence Agency (Cheung, 1987). Over 92% of the Hmong have stress-related illnesses. In fact, 75% are unemployed and 86% indicate they would return to Laos if possible (Smalley, 1984).

Significant immigration increases in the Asian-American population have led to a swell in current anti-Asian sentiment. The killing of Vincent Chin in 1982, the murder of Jim Loo in 1989, the Stockton, California, school massacre of five Cambodian and Vietnamese children at Cleveland Elementary School (1989) by a White male who "hated and blamed" Asians for the loss of American jobs (see Chapter 1), increases in racial slurs and the portrayal of Asians as subhuman "gooks" in such award-winning movies as *Platoon* and *Full Metal Jacket* attest to the current tenor of the times.

Unfortunately, space limitations do not allow us to focus on the diversity of Asian groups in the United States. We first concentrate on recent immigrants/refugees and then on the large group of Asian Americans (Chinese, Filipino, Japanese, Korean, etc.) who have lived here for some time (many were born and raised in the United States) who have experienced long-term effects of cultural racism.

While the experiences of recent immigrants and refugees are similar to those who came here in the past, and while Asian immigrants share many similar cultural values with those born and raised here, there appears to be a qualitative difference in their experience of cultural racism in the United States. Let us turn our attention to the special problems faced by immigrants/refugees and then to the U.S.-born Asian Americans.

SPECIAL PROBLEMS OF RECENT IMMIGRANTS AND REFUGEES

Cheung (1987) indicates that three waves of Southeast-Asian refugees, each with their own set of problems, came to the United States. The first wave came in 1975 with the fall of Saigon. Many of them had worked for the U.S. government and were acquainted with Western culture. Many fled at a moment's notice and left family members and their possessions behind. Depression is very high among Vietnamese refugees because of the method of departure from Vietnam and life in refugee camps (ACMH, 1987; Atkinson, Ponterotto, & Sanchez, 1984). Over 40% of Vietnamese patients seen at the Oregon Health Sciences University Clinic have a major affective disorder.

The second wave occurred from 1979 and 1982 and included not only Vietnamese, but also Cambodians, Laotians, and Hmongs. Hundreds had escaped by cramming themselves into small boats. Many drowned, starved to death, or were killed by Thai pirates. Hundreds of thousands remain in camps set up along the borders of different countries. The second wave is different from the first and is more likely to have included those who are less educated, possess fewer job skills, were more rural, have little contact with Western culture, are less likely to be proficient in English, and more likely to have spent relatively long periods of time in relocation camps.

In a study of 40,000 Southeast-Asian refugees in San Diego County, Rumbaut (1985) found that nearly 80% of one group of Khmer were uncertain of the fate of family members left behind in their home country and have been unable to contact them. This compares to 29.5% of the Hmong, 20.7% of the Chinese, and 4.6% of the Vietnamese. During and after the exodus, 40% of the refugees reported one or two deaths, and 9% had from 3 to 6 deaths in their immediate family—usually due to violent circumstances. The Khmer and Hmong reported the greatest number of losses among close family members. Rumbaut (1985) found that among the Hmong, 75% had incomes below the poverty level in 1982. This latter group seems to be having the most difficult time adjusting and 80% indicated they would return to their home country if this were possible.

A study by Nguyen & Henkin (1983) of 285 heads of households among refugees found that 80% complained of homesickness, 72% indicated being worried about the future, 55% felt lonely, and 40% indicated feeling sad most of the time. Many of the problems facing the refugee appear to be related to personal losses and culture conflict. In a sample of 118 Southeast-Asian refugee clients, major concerns involved: (1) being separated from members of the family, (2) marital and family problems, (3) worries about the future, (4) problems with English, and (5) job dissatisfaction. Among this sample, 25% had made suicide attempts, and behavioral problems in the schools among their children have increased. Vietnamese refugees report that their children display less politeness and obedience, that respect for elders is fading, and that the changing role of women is producing problems (Nguyen & Henkin, 1983).

The third wave of refugees occurred after the Vietnamese initiated the Orderly Departure Program in 1982. These refugees are comprised mainly of the elderly and Amerasian and unaccompanied minors. Most are illiterate.

VALUE CONFLICTS AND COUNSELING

Although the Asian immigrants and refugees form very diverse groups, there are certain areas of commonality such as deference to authority, emotional restraint, specified roles and hierarchical family structure and family and extended family orientation (Tsui & Schultz, 1985). Kinzie has outlined areas in which the Southeast-Asian patient and the American-trained therapist may differ, as shown in Table 10.1.

Although cultural knowledge is important in helping the counselor identify potential conflict areas, one must be careful not to apply cultural information in a stereotypic manner. Ishisaka, Nguyen, and Okimoto (1985) point out that cultural difficulties, such as the degree of assimilation, socioeconomic background, family experiences, and educational level, impact each individual in a unique manner. Knowledge of cultural values can help generate hypotheses about the way an Asian might view a disorder and his or her expectations of treatment, but it must not be applied in a rigid fashion.

Mental health and psychotherapy is a foreign concept to the east-Asian countries. In Vietnam in 1980, there were only six psychiatrists (Wong, 1985). Because of the unfamiliarity with mental health concepts, many refugees and immigrants have limited faith in talking about problems. As opposed to Caucasian students, Vietnamese students in the United States were less likely to recognize the need for mental health services, more concerned about the stigma attached to counseling, less open about

TABLE 10.1

Areas of Difference Between Southeast-Asian Patients
and American-Trained Therapists

Indochinese Patient Values	*Western-Trained Psychotherapist*
Focus on interdependence.	Personal choice and independence.
Structured and appropriate social relationships.	Situational ethics, rejection of authority. Equality of family relationships.
Should live in harmony with nature.	Nature to be mastered.
Mental illness due to imbalance in cosmic forces or lack of will power.	Mental illness is a result of mental and physical factors.
No cultural conceptualization of psychotherapy.	Strong orientation to values of psychotherapy and personal growth.
Treatment should be short and rapid.	View that therapy could take a long time.
Healer should be active and give solutions to problems.	Therapist often passive. Best solution is one developed by the patient.
Mental illness represented a failure of the family.	Mental illness is the same as other problems.

"Overview of Clinical Issues in the Treatment of Southeast Asian Refugees" (p. 321) by J. D. Kinzie, 1985. In T. C. Owan (ed.) *Southeast Asian Mental Health Treatment, Preventive Services, Training, and Research,* Washington, DC: National Institute of Mental Health.

personal problems, and less confident that mental health professionals would be of any help (Atkinson et al., 1984). In many Southeast-Asian countries, having a psychological problem is the same as being insane (Nguyen, 1985). Because of these differences in values and orientation, a therapeutic alliance may not be formed. Nisio and Bilmer (1987) present several cases in which the traditional approach was not successful.

In the first case, a Vietnamese family was referred to a Western therapist after their daughter had displayed bizarre behaviors. As part of the assessment, the counselor began to explore the possibility that the daughter's behavior might be affected by the dynamics between the husband and wife. Questions were asked about their marital relationship. The couple did not return for the next session. They indicated a willingness to continue therapy as long as marital problems were not discussed. The parents felt that their relationship was a private matter and not related to their daughter's problem.

In another case, the patients were a Laotian couple whose husband was alcoholic and physically abusive to his wife. The Western therapist encouraged the wife to become more independent and to consider leaving her husband. The couple did not return and instead sought the help of an Asian therapist. The therapist understood that an unhealthy situation existed, but was also aware of cultural norms and expectations. Greater independence for the wife in certain areas was reframed as an opportunity for the husband to have more time for himself. The husband's initial objections were eliminated when the changes were presented in this manner. It was also determined that the problems of abuse and alcohol intake were related to the stresses he felt in the new culture and the loss of his status. As these frustrations were addressed and dealt with, the husband stopped abusing his wife and terminated his drinking.

Physical complaints are a common and culturally accepted means of expressing psychological and emotional stress. It is believed that physical problems cause emotional disturbances, and that these will disappear as soon as there is appropriate treatment of the physical illness. Instead of talking about anxiety and depression, the mental health professional will often hear complaints involving headaches, fatigue, restlessness, and disturbances in sleep and appetite. Even psychotic patients typically made somatic complaints and sought treatment for those physical ailments (Nguyen, 1985). In the following discussion, Tsui and Schultz (1985) indicate how the differences in perspective can produce problems for both the patient and the mental health worker.

A female client complained about all kinds of physical problems such as feeling dizzy, having a loss of appetite, an inability to complete household chores, and insomnia. She asked the therapist if her problem could be due to "nerves." The therapist suspected depression since these are some of the physical manifestations of the disorder and asked the client if she felt depressed and sad. At this point, the client paused and looked confused. She finally stated that she feels very ill and that these physical problems are making her sad. Her perspective is that it was natural for her to feel sad when sick. As the therapist followed up by attempting to determine if there was a family history of depression, the client displayed even more discomfort and defensiveness. Although the client never directly contradicted the therapist, she did not return for the following session. In working with clients who have somatic complaints, it would be helpful to acknowledge them and recommend physical treatments before dealing with possible emotional factors.

TREATMENT STRATEGIES

Treatment strategies for immigrants and refugees have many elements of similarity. The following suggestions are from Ishisaka et al. (1985), Lorenzo and Adler (1984), Nidorf (1985), and Tung (1985):

1. Use restraint when gathering information. Because of the stigma against mental illness, the norm against sharing private matters with

outsiders, the lack of client knowledge of the mental health field, the therapist should refrain from asking too many questions.

2. Prepare the clients for counseling by engaging in role preparation. Lambert and Lambert (1984) found that Asian immigrants who were told about (a) what happens in therapy, (b) the need for verbal disclosure, (c) problems typically encountered by clients in therapy, (d) the role of the therapist and client, (e) misconceptions of therapy, and (f) the need for attendance adjusted better to counseling than a control group who did not receive role preparation. The clients who were prepared developed more accurate perceptions of therapy, saw their therapist as more interested and respectful, perceived more positive changes in their part, and were more satisfied with their adjustment.

3. Focus on the specific problem brought in by the client, and help the client develop his or her goals for therapy. This allows the concerns of the client to be presented and reduces the chance that the world view of the therapist will be imposed on the client.

4. Take an active and directive role. Because of cultural expectations and a lack of experience with mental health therapy, the clients will rely on the counselor to furnish direction.

5. Do a thorough analysis of current environmental concerns, such as the need for food and shelter. The clients may need help filling out forms, need information on services that are available to them, and help in interacting with agencies. Assess financial and social needs.

6. In working with families, consider intergenerational conflicts especially due to changes in role, culture conflict, and differences in acculturation levels.

7. The therapy should be time limited, focus on concrete resolution of problems, and deal with the present or immediate future.

In addition to these suggestions, it is important to do a careful history on refugees and determine areas such as their family life and life in their home country, their escape or immigration and how this was experienced, reasons for leaving, losses and expectations, their life in camps, the method of sponsorship, and their expectations in the United States. Also important would be difficulties refugees have had in adjusting to the new culture, their methods of coping, and marital and family problems that have developed. Taking a good history is important to help the counselor understand some of the issues involved in working with Southeast-Asian refugees.

Many of the refugees suffered great personal losses involving property, business, identity, and family members. A great many have strong feelings of regret, especially in cases in which family members were left behind. Lin, Masuda, and Tazuma (1982) report the case of a 56-year-old

Vietnamese woman who was living with her husband, two sons, and daughter. She had been suffering from a large number of physical symptoms and was in a depressed mood for two years. On a wall in her house was a picture of a daughter who had died during the evacuation. The mother was especially upset that her daughter's body had to be thrown into the sea and did not receive a proper burial. It was clear that the family was still in active mourning.

Nidorf (1985) feels that adolescents are at special risk of suffering problems. Young women may have been attacked sexually during the escape process and may present suicidal symptoms or have become sexually promiscuous. Young males may also display a variety of affective responses that may have been related to their helpless observation of the victimization of family members. Careful analysis of the past history of immigrants and refugees may be very helpful in developing a treatment plan for the Asian clients.

SPECIAL PROBLEMS OF U.S.-BORN ASIAN AMERICANS

As Asians become progressively exposed to the standards, norms, and values of the wider society, increasing assimilation and acculturation are frequently the result (Arkoff, 1959; Fong, 1965; Kitano, 1962, 1967, 1969b). Bombarded on all sides by peers, schools, and the mass media upholding Western standards as better than their own, Asian Americans are frequently placed in situations of extreme culture conflict that may lead to much pain and agony. For example, restraint of strong feelings is highly valued in Asian culture. However, Westerners see an individual exhibiting this trait as passive and inhibited. As a result of attaching negative connotations to such values, many Asian Americans become confused about how they should behave.

Unfortunately, it is extremely difficult for one to reconcile loyalties to two different cultural traditions, especially if one's parents are strongly in favor of retaining ethnic values. S. Sue and D. W. Sue (1971a) proposed a conceptual scheme of three different ways used by Asian Americans to adjust to these conflicting demands.

First, individuals may remain "loyal" to their own ethnic group by retaining traditional values and living up to the expectations of the family. The "traditionalist" adheres closely to the norms, standards, and values of the traditional Asian family.

Second, the individuals who are caught up in a culture conflict may oftentimes attempt to become overwesternized by rejecting traditional Asian values. Their pride and self-worth are defined by the ability to acculturate into White society. In their attempts to assimilate and acculturate into White society, they are often forced to reject the Asian side of themselves and thus feel ashamed of anything that reminds them of being Chinese or Japanese. They come to view their ethnicity as a handicap that may lead to various forms of racial self-hatred. This type of adjustment leads to an identity crisis, because the minority individuals cannot completely rid themselves of certain traditional ways and may lead a marginal existence; that is, they exist between the margin of two different cultural traditions. The "marginal person" can become quite contemptuous of Asian customs, values, behaviors, and even physical appearances. They may sarcastically describe Asian females as "flat chested" and "short-legged" when compared to Caucasian females. An anthropological field study conducted by Weiss (1970) found that many Chinese-American females viewed their male counterparts as inhibited, passive, and lacking in sexual attractiveness.

Third, another mode of adjustment is the Asian-American movement sometimes referred to as the "Yellow Power Movement." Like the marginal person, the Asian American is rebelling against parental authority, as he or she attempts to develop a new identity that will enable him or her to reconcile viable aspects of his/her heritage with the present situation. The roots of the Asian-American movement spring from two main sources. The first lies in the need to attain self-pride in one's racial and cultural identity by reversing the trend of negativity instilled in them by White society. Second, the Asian-American movement has strong political connotations in that the problems of minorities are seen to reside in society. The Asian American may become extremely militant in his/her concern with racism and civil rights. He/she appears to be much more sensitive to the forces in society that have served to shape and define his/her limited identity. Problems such as the poverty, unemployment, and juvenile delinquency and the individual, institutional, and cultural racism of Asians must be exposed and changed.

IMPLICATIONS FOR COUNSELING ASIAN AMERICANS

We have just seen how important it is for us to understand the culture and history of an ethnic minority in order to explain that minority's lifestyle. Educators, counselors, and pupil personnel workers often do not have enough knowledge of the Asian-American experience to make enlightened decisions. These professionals' ignorance of minority experiences has greatly shortchanged Asians from obtaining needed help in the areas of mental health. The following discussion dwells on two aspects of Asian-American mental health. First, it attempts to reveal to counselors some typical adjustment problems often encountered by Asian Americans. Second, specific suggestions are given about how to make counseling and psychotherapy more consistent with the experiences of Asian Americans.

Asian Americans and Adjustment Difficulties

Not only are personality characteristics influenced by culture and its interaction with the host society, but the manifestation of behavioral problems among Asian Americans seems intimately linked to these forces. Counselors who work with Asian Americans need to be aware of these conflicts. These problems can best be understood if we briefly return to our earlier discussion of culture conflict and the three reactions that many Asians have exhibited in their attempts to cope with society. The following three case descriptions are typical of the kinds of problems that have been observed in the traditionalist, marginal person, and Asian American.

The Case of John C.

John C is a 20-year-old junior student majoring in electrical engineering. He is the oldest of five children born and raised in San Francisco. The father is 58 years old and has been a grocer for the past 20 years, and the mother is a housewife. The parents have always had high expectations for their eldest son and constantly transmitted these feelings to him. Ever since he can remember, John's parents had decided that he would go to college and become an engineer—a job they held in high esteem.

Throughout his early school years, John was an outstanding student and was constantly praised by his teachers. He was hard-working, obedient, and never gave his teachers any trouble. However, his parents seemed to take John's school successes for granted. In fact, they would always make statements such as, "You can do better still."

John first came to the counseling center during the latter part of his junior year because of severe headaches and a vague assortment of bodily complaints. A medical checkup failed to reveal any organic malfunctioning, which led the psychologist to suspect a psychophysiological reaction.

John exhibited a great deal of anxiety throughout the interviews. He seemed suspicious of the psychologist and found it difficult to talk about himself in a personal way. As the sessions progressed, it became evident that John felt a great deal of shame about having come to a therapist. John was concerned that this family not be told since they would be disgraced.

Throughout the interviews, John appeared excessively concerned with failing his parents' expectations. Further exploration revealed significant sources of conflict. First, his grades were beginning to decline, and he felt he was letting his parents down. Second, he had always harbored wishes about becoming an architect, but felt this to be an unacceptable profession to his parents. Third, increasing familial demands were being placed on him to quickly graduate and obtain a job in order to help the family's financial situation. The parents frequently made statements such as, "Once you are out of school and making good money, it would be nice if you could help your brothers and sisters through college." John's resentment of these imposed responsibilities was originally denied and repressed. When he was able to clearly see his anger and hostility towards his parents, much of his physical complaints vanished. However, with the recognition of his true feelings, he became extremely depressed and guilty. John could not see why he should be angry at his parents after all they had done for him. (S. Sue & D. W. Sue, 1971a, p. 39)

The counselor who works with John C. is most likely working with an individual with a strong traditional orientation. As such, John C.'s problems tend to be somewhat different from the other two types; that is, the marginal person and Asian American. First, the counselor must be aware that when the traditionalist seeks counseling or therapy, as in the case of John C., this person is most likely to experience intense feelings of shame and guilt at admitting that problems exist. Issues of confidentiality are important to deal with. The counselor who is not sensitive to such feelings can greatly increase John's discomfort and cause an early termination of counseling. Second, the traditionalist may find it difficult to directly admit to problems and will present them in an indirect manner—that is, psycho-physiological reactions such as declining grades, vocational indecisions, and so on. It may be wise for the counselor to initially respond to these superficial problems, since they are less threatening to the traditionalist, until a degree of rapport and trust can be formed. Third, it is imperative that the counselor recognize that vocational indecision, often presented by Asian Americans, may mask deeper conflicts. In the case of John C., it tends to be a conflict between his own desires for independence and the extremely strong obligations he feels toward his parents. Last, counselors working with a person of traditional background must be willing to alter their usual style of counseling and therapy. The actual practice of counseling and psychotherapy may be inherently discriminating to the ethnic minorities. Since the counseling-therapy situation is essentially a White middle-class activity that values verbal expressiveness, openness, and a certain degree of psychological-mindedness, these values may cause problems between the counselor and the minority client (Chien & Yamamoto, 1982; Kaneshige, 1973; S. Sue & Morishima, 1982). For example, the traditionalist may find it difficult to talk about feelings and may find counseling so ambiguous that the counselor must take a much more active approach in structuring the interview sessions. A study by Atkinson, Maruyama, and Matsui (1978) provides empirical support for this contention. These investigators found Asian Americans to prefer a logical, rational, structured, counseling approach over an affective, reflective, ambiguous one. Since Asians respond more to structured situations and direct suggestions, the counselor must make modifications to his or her counseling style to incorporate these in order to be therapeutically effective (Mau & Jepsen, 1988; Yuen & Tinsley, 1981).

The Case of Janet T.

Janet T. is a 21-year-old senior, majoring in sociology. She was born and raised in Portland, Oregon, where she had limited contact with members of her own race. Her father, a second generation Chinese American is a 53-year-old doctor. Her mother, age 44, is a housewife. Janet is the second oldest of three children and has an older brother (currently in medical school) and a younger brother, age 17.

Janet came for therapy suffering from a severe depressive reaction manifested by feelings of worthlessness, by suicidal ideation, and by an inability to concentrate. She was unable to recognize the cause of her depression throughout the initial interviews. However, much light was shed on problems when the therapist noticed an inordinate amount of hostility directed towards him.

When inquiries were made about the hostility, it became apparent that Janet greatly resented being seen by a Chinese psychologist. Janet suspected that she had been assigned a Chinese therapist because of her own race. When confronted with this fact, Janet openly expressed scorn for "anything which reminds me of Chinese." Apparently, she felt very hostile towards Chinese customs and especially the Chinese male, whom she described as introverted, passive, and sexually unattractive. Further exploration revealed a long-standing history of attempts to deny her Chinese ancestry by associating only with Caucasians. When in high school, Janet would frequently bring home White boyfriends which greatly upset her parents. It was as though she blamed her parents for being a Chinese, and she used this method to hurt them.

During her college career Janet became involved in two love affairs with Caucasians, both ending unsatisfactorily and abruptly. The last breakup occurred four months ago when the boy's parents threatened to cut off financial support for their son unless he ended the relationship. Apparently, objections arose because of Janet's race.

Although not completely consciously, Janet was having increasing difficulty with denying her racial heritage. The breakup of her last torrid love affair made her realize that she was Chinese and not fully accepted by all segments of society. At first she vehemently and bitterly denounced the Chinese for her present dilemma. Later, much of her hostility was turned inward against herself. Feeling alienated from her own subculture and not fully accepted by American society, she experienced an identity crisis. This resulted in feelings of worthlessness and depression. It was at this point that Janet came for therapy. (S. Sue & D. W. Sue, 1971a, p. 41)

This particular case represents some of the conflicts encountered by the marginal person. The phenomenon of self-hatred is clearly evident. In their perception that traditional Asian ways serve as a hindrance to their own development and growth, many Asians attempt to become overwesternized by adopting White standards and customs. They become ashamed of Chinese or Japanese ways and rebel strongly against them. Counselors need to have a wider perspective of what culture conflicts actually mean.

Although there is nothing inherently wrong in acculturation, Western society has frequently been so intolerant of other lifestyles that deviations from Western norms are seen as abnormal. No wonder many Asian Americans begin to accept these comparisons and feel ashamed of their own racial and cultural identity. Viewed in this light, cultural conflicts may be manifestations of cultural racism.

In working with the marginal person, the counselor has an obligation to help the client sort out his/her identity conflicts by some form of reeducation. That is, somewhere in the process of counseling, the counselor must deal with the issue of cultural racism and its potential effects on individuals of minority backgrounds. Only in this manner can the counselor clear up the two sources of confusion that the marginal person apparently experiences.

Specifically, the marginal person must be helped to distinguish between positive attempts to acculturate and a negative rejection of his or her own cultural values. Also, many Asians who desire independence from parental control are confusing independence for rejection of parental control. Such was the case of Janet T. In her attempts to show her independence, Janet had rebellion equated in her mind with independence. For the counselor to work effectively with such an individual, he or she must be conversant with the culture history and experiences of Asians in America. If not, this minority group is obligated to seek consultation from others more experienced in these matters or those who will refer them to more appropriate resources.

The Case of Gale K.

Gale K. is a 22-year-old first-year graduate student in biochemistry. His father, once employed in an engineering firm, recently died from cancer. His 52-year-old mother is currently employed at the San Francisco Airport as a receptionist. Gale was born and raised in Oakland, California. He has three sisters, all of whom are married.

Much of Gale's early life was filled with conflict and antagonism between him and his parents. Like Janet T., Gale did not confine his social life exclusively to other Chinese Americans. Being the only son, his parents were fearful that they would lose their son should he marry a Caucasian. Five years earlier, their eldest daughter had married a Caucasian which caused great turmoil in the family and the subsequent disowning of the daughter.

Throughout much of his life, Gale attempted to deny his racial identity because he felt shame about being Chinese. However, within the last four years, a phenomenal change occurred in Gale. He actively participated in the Third World Strike at the University and became involved in a number of community change committees. Gale recalled with great fondness the "esprit de corps" and contagion he experienced with other concerned Asians. His parents had been delighted about his reorientation to see him dating

Asian girls and volunteering his time to tutor educationally-deprived children in Chinatown. However, they did not understand his activist thinking and outspoken behavior towards authority figures.

Gale came for therapy because he had not fully resolved guilt feelings concerning the recent death of his father. Several weeks prior to his father's death, Gale had a violent argument with him over his recent participation in a demonstration. When his father passed away, Gale felt a great deal of remorse. He had often wished that his father would have understood the Asian American movement.

Throughout the sessions, Gale exhibited an understanding and awareness of economic, political, and social forces beyond that of the average student. He attributed the plight of Asian Americans to the shortcomings of society. He was openly suspicious of therapy and confronted the therapist on two different issues. The first objection dealt with the use of tests in therapy. Gale felt them to be culturally biased and somewhat inapplicable to ethnic minorities. The second issue concerned the relationship of therapy to the status quo. Since therapy had traditionally been concerned with the adjustment of individuals to society, Gale questioned the validity of this concept. "Do you adjust people to a sick society?" Only after dealing with these issues was it possible for Gale and the therapist to focus on his feelings regarding the death of his father. (S. Sue & D. W. Sue, 1971a, pp. 43–44)

Unlike the traditional who defines self-worth by one's ability to bring honor to the family name and unlike the marginal person who defines self-worth via his or her ability to acculturate and be accepted by White society, the politically aware Asian American attempts to throw off the shackles of society by defining for himself/herself a new identity. All remnants of this person's old identity such as the term "Oriental" are replaced by such terms as "Asian Americans." This may be seen as a symbolic redefinition of this group's entire existence. The Asian American is much more aware than the other two groups of the political, social, and economic forces that have shaped his or her identity. The Asian American's greater social awareness causes him/her to be somewhat more sensitive to the effects of racism and to often react with overt anger and militancy.

The emphasis on the inequities of society and the feeling that change must be instituted in racist institutions make many Asian Americans suspicious of counseling services. Many feel that counseling services are agents of the Establishment and that their primary goal is to adjust clients to society. This can cause difficulties for both the client, whose political beliefs may mask his/her problems, and for the counselor, who must deal appropriately with certain challenges before counseling can proceed effectively. In the former, growing pride in self-identity frequently makes it difficult for many Asian students to accept their difficulties as personal rather than external. The client should be led to realize that although many problems of minorities are rooted in the shortcomings of society, there is no inherent contradiction in viewing society as racist and having personal problems. On the other hand, the counselor must be sensitive enough to know that many problems encountered by his or her clients are caused by society and that he or she must act accordingly. Militancy and emphasis on group pride are not signs of maladjustment, as many individuals would have us believe. It is imperative, however, that counselors be able to distinguish between the two types of confusion.

CONCLUSIONS

Hopefully, the foregoing discussion has provided an idea of the complexity of human behavior and how futile it is to attempt an understanding of ethnic minorities without an adequate exploration of their historical background, subcultural values, and unique conflicts. The lack of knowledge and the insensitivity of Western society to the plight of minorities have done much harm to Asian Americans. Educators and social scientists have a moral obligation to enlighten themselves and others to the life experiences of disadvantaged groups. Only in an atmosphere of trust and understanding can different groups live together in health and harmony.

STUDY QUESTIONS

1. Statistics seem to support the myth that Asians in America are a successful minority with no great counseling needs. What factors may be creating this illusion?
2. What are some special life experiences suffered by recent Southeast-Asian immigrants and refugees that may affect counseling? What current life circumstances are they facing and with what effect?
3. How may the historical experiences of Asians in America affect their world views?
4. What cultural values of traditional Asians negate the effectiveness of Western counseling approaches?
5. How has cultural racism (culture conflict) affected the identity development of Asians in America?
6. What counseling approaches were suggested by the authors in working with Asian Americans? How may the use of the approaches depend on the cultural identity of the student?

CHAPTER 11

Counseling Black Americans

Black Americans currently constitute the largest minority group in the United States and number over 23 million. Of these, over 86% live in cities or census tracts that are over 50% or more Black (Norton, 1983). The disadvantaged status, racism, and poverty are responsible for the following statistics. Forty-two percent of the prison population is Black. Black unemployment rates are about twice as high as for the White population. In addition, studies have found that the Black unemployed tend to engage in self-blame for their lack of a job (Wolinsky, 1982). The largest cause of death for Black youth is homicide. The life expectancy for White males is 5 years greater than for Black males. Black males are overrepresented in homicides (Parham & McDavis, 1987). Juvenile delinquency rates in Black youth are high (Myers & King, 1983), and alcoholism is increasing among Black women at a higher rate than for White females (Smith, 1985). Blacks are also an economically distressed group. The average family income is $12,674 as compared to $21,904 for White families (U.S. Bureau of the Census, 1980). In 1984, nearly 34% of Black families lived below the poverty level as compared to 11.5% of White families (Grosgebauer, 1987).

Although these statistics are grim, Bass, Acosta & Evans (1982) point out that much of our literature is based on individuals of the lower social class who are on welfare or unemployed and not enough on other segments of the Black population. For example, approximately 10% of Blacks are members of the upper class, 40% are middle class, and 50% belong to the lower class. The focus on one segment of Black Americans masks the great diversity that exists among Black Americans who may vary greatly from one another on factors such as socioeconomic status, educational level, cultural identity, family structure, and reaction to racism (Jones & Gray, 1983). Distinctions are very important to make. For example, Neighbors (1984) found that low-income Blacks experienced problems as being more severe than middle-income Blacks and were more likely to feel that there was a physical cause for their psychological problems.

EDUCATION

The gap in educational attainment between Black and White children is evident in kindergarten and increases through high school to the university level (Parham & McDavis, 1987). This problem is evident in a report by the Disproportionality Task Force in examining the overrepresentation of Blacks and other minorities in low academic achievement and disciplinary actions (Seattle Public Schools, 1986). In the study of Black and White middle-school students, it was found that 56.3% of the former had grade-point averages below 2.0 versus 20.9% for the latter group. Only 9.67% of Black students had a grade-point average above 3.0 versus 43.5% for White students. This GPA difference was also found in Seattle high school students. In addition, Black students are more than twice as likely as White students to be suspended and expelled. At some grade levels, up to 56% of Black students are referred to special education classes. The task force identified several factors that they believed contributed to the findings. The school system has a predominantly White teaching staff and the student population has changed from a predominantly White to a predominantly minority population. Because of this, teaching skills effective in the past may no longer work. Many teachers are also not sensitive to cultural differences and may respond inappropriately to minority-group members. Curriculum may also not be meaningful to the experiences of minority-group children. Drug abuse and unconcerned parents may also contribute to the lack of achievement in Black children. The Seattle school district is currently working on a program that addresses itself to these problems.

The gap in educational attainment between White and Black Americans is also very evident in higher education and appears to be increasing. The percentage of Black enrollment has declined from a peak in 1978 and has been decreasing through the mid-1980s (U.S. Department of Education, State Task Force on Minority Student Achievement, 1987). Many feel that recent cutbacks in financial support and educational programs for minorities along with an erosion of moral support has led to this decrease (Cordes, 1985). There is a feeling that society is less interested in the plight of minorities. This has been accompanied by increasing numbers of reported instances of racism on major university campuses. Reasons for this were discussed by a panel of prominent individuals at the University of Michigan (Lockard, 1987). They concluded that racism on campuses has been affected by several factors including: (1) a decline in interest in the United States for civil rights issues, (2) a backlash to advances that have been made by minorities, (3) declining levels of financial support, (4) a university environment that does not provide emotional support for minority students, (5) a lack of Black faculty members and mentors. The University of Michigan did commit itself to the recruitment and retention of Black students and faculty members in hopes of increasing enrollment.

FAMILY CHARACTERISTICS

The Black family has been generally described as matriarchal and blamed for many of the problems faced by Black Americans today (Smith, 1982). Statistics do support the view that there is an increasing percentage of Black families that are headed by a female (37% versus 11% for White families (Norton, 1983). Among lower-class Black families, over 70% are headed by a female (Jenkins (1985). Black women who are unmarried account for nearly 60% of births and of these mothers, the majority are teenagers. Over 50% of Black children have working mothers and are therefore often cared for by relatives (Norton, 1983). In 1970, 64% of Black Americans who were over 18 were married as opposed to only 50% in 1982 (U.S. Bureau of the Census, 1983).

What is missed with these statistics, however, is an acknowledgment of the strengths that exist in the Black family structure. For many, there exists an extended family network that provides emotional and economic support. Among families headed by females, the rearing of children is often undertaken by a large number of relatives, older children, and close friends. Within the Black family there exists an adaptability of family roles, strong kinship bonds, a strong work and achievement ethic, and strong religious orientation (Bass et al., 1982; Boyd, 1982). Thomas and Dansby (1985) indicate that both Black men and women value behaviors such as assertiveness and that within a family, Black males are more accepting of Black women's work roles and more willing to share in the responsibilities traditionally done by women such as picking up children from school. In spite of the problems with racism and prejudice, Black families have been able to instill positive self-esteem in their children (Norton, 1983). In a review of the research, Powell (1983) found that the self-esteem of Black children was similar to that of White children. She suggests that research be directed toward delineating the factors that insulate many Black children from the effects of racism.

Thomas and Dansby (1985) indicate that much of our reaction to Black families is due to our nuclear family orientation. They relate an incident in which children were asked to draw a picture of their mother and father and the rest of the family eating dinner together. A Black girl left the room in tears. She had been raised by her aunt. Many forms of our assessment and evaluation still are based on the middle-class perspective of what constitutes a family. Thomas and Dansby indicate that some families do not eat dinner together because they both have to work and in many families the child is raised by someone other than the parent. The different family structures that exist indicate the need to consider various alternative treatment modes and approaches in working with Black Americans. In working with Black families, the counselor often has to assume various roles such as educator, advocate, problem solver and role model. In many cases the therapist not only has to intervene in the family but has to deal with community interventions as well. A number of Black families who go into counseling are required to do so by the schools, courts, or police. Issues that may have to be dealt with are feelings about differences in ethnicity between the client and counselor and clarification of his/her relationship to the referring agency. Clients should be told what to expect during the initial session. Assessment may have to be made to determine not only how community resources can be better utilized, but also socioeconomic issues such as food, housing, and areas of strengths of the family members (Grevious, 1985).

Thomas and Dansby also suggest several other options in working with Black families. First, if the family is heavily involved in church activities, resources such as the minister could be enlisted by the therapist to deal with problems involving conflicts within the family and health issues such as family planning. In addition, programs for the enrichment of family life may be developed jointly with the church. Second, school programs may be developed to discuss childrearing practices and to initiate a support group. It would be important to advertise the program in such a way as to obtain the participation of members of the extended family rather than a "parent effectiveness" group. Third, Black adults who have been successful in raising children and have demonstrated good communication skills can be recruited to talk about their experiences and assist other families. Fourth, counseling that involves home visits have often been found to be effective in producing more effective communication in problem families.

FAMILY THERAPY

On the whole, family therapy with low-income Blacks has not been very successful. In one study at a family treatment center, the dropout rate for Black families was 81% as opposed to about 50% for White middle-class families (Gwyn & Kilpatrick, 1981). Family therapy can be particularly difficult for many Black families who feel that issues such as illegitimate births, marital status of adult members of a family, and the paternity of children may be reacted to negatively by the counselor (Boyd, 1982). This is in addition to other trust issues that may be involved. Knowledge of the family structure can aid in therapy. Boyd (1982) suggests the use of a method of inquiry that allowed important information to be gathered about the extended family.

A mother, Mrs. J, brought in her 13-year-old son, Johnny, who she said was having behavioral problems at home and in school. During the interview, the therapist found out that Johnny had 5 brothers and sisters living in the home. In addition, his "stepfather," Mr. W, also lived in the house. The mother's sister, Mary, and three children had recently moved in with the family until their apartment was repaired. The question of "who is living in the home?" caught this. The mother was also asked about other children not living at home. The mother also had a daughter living with an aunt in another state. The aunt was helping the daughter raise her child. When asked, "who helps you out?" the mother responded that a neighbor watches her children when she has to work and that both groups of children had been raised together. Mrs. J's mother also assisted with her children.

Further questioning revealed that Johnny's problem developed soon after her sister and her children moved in. Before this, Johnny had been the mother's primary helper and took charge of the children until the stepfather returned home from work. The changes in the family structure that occurred when the sister and her children moved in produced additional stress on Johnny. Treatment included Mrs. J and her children, Mr. W, Mary and her children, Mrs. J's mother. Pressures on Johnny were discussed and alternatives were considered. Mrs. J's mother agreed to take in Mary and her children temporarily. To deal with the disruption in the family, follow-up meetings were conducted to help clarify roles in the family system. Within a period of months, behavioral problems in the home and school had stopped for Johnny. He once again assumed a parental role to help out his mother and stepfather.

Boyd's example points out several important considerations to make in working with Black families. Because of the possibility of an extended or nontraditional family arrangement, questions should be directed to finding out who is living in the home and who helps out. It is also important to work to strengthen the original family structure and to try to make it more functional rather than to try to change it. One of the strengths of the Black family is that men and women and children are allowed to adopt multiple roles within the family. An older child like Johnny could adopt a parental role while the wife might take on the role of the father. The grandmother may be a very important family member who also helps raise the children. Her influence and help should not be eliminated, but the goal should be to make more efficient the working alliance with the other caregivers. A family therapist should remember that flexibility of roles is a strength but could also produce problems if the roles conflict with one another.

BLACK YOUTH

For many urban Black adolescents, life is complicated by problems of poverty, illiteracy, and racism. Unemployment can range from 37% to nearly 50% among Black teenagers (Parham & McDavis, 1987). Many poor

Black adolescents have met with frustration by giving up and feel victimized by the school system. They can barely read and have had few positive interactions with authority figures or with society. They may feel overwhelmed and depressed or hostile and angry (Paster, 1985).

Black youth often do not come to counseling willingly. Often they do so because they have been referred. Because of this, cooperation may be difficult for the counselor to obtain. The client might adopt a variety of tactics in talking to the counselor. Franklin (1982) cautions that the counselor be vigilant and not be misled by information that is being provided. A streetwise youth might deliberately attempt to frighten or shock the counselor by describing use of drugs and sexual behaviors in graphic detail. Others might adopt a highly confrontive and aggressive stance or engage in "rapping" or telling tales as a means of "testing" out the therapist. To deal with the possible resistance of the client, the counselor should first discuss the relationship he or she has with the referring agency and what the expectations are.

Paster (1985) makes several recommendations in working with Black youth. First, the youth's expectations about the usefulness of counseling should be discussed. Second, a negotiated contract on counseling duration and goals should be obtained. Paster recommends making it a short-term- (6- to 8-week) trial period. Third, the counselor should set firm limits, especially when dealing with verbal abuse and indicate that he/she is aware of what is happening. In addition, Paster feels that it is important for the counselor to act as an advocate for the youth and deal as an intermediary with agencies such as the school and the court. When possible, community resources should be utilized.

Paster indicated how she used some of these suggestions in working with a 13-year-old boy, "J," who was referred for counseling by his probation officer.

> J had had a history of problems with the authorities since the age of 7. He had been involved in a number of gang fights, committed burglaries, and had been arrested carrying a weapon. In school, he spent most of his time wandering in the schoolyard and halls. The judge had given him the option of counseling or incarceration. The counselor indicated that J had the right not to attend the sessions but that she would have to communicate that decision to the judge. Negotiations were made concerning expectations, attendance, and goals. J indicated that he did not feel that counseling would be of any benefit but did agree to attend. Together, they decided that two absences in attendance would result in a report to the judge of this fact. J was asked to bring back a list of what he desired to achieve in treatment. He came back the next session with a list requesting food and candy, becoming a football hero, and winning the lottery. Paster discussed these seriously with the boy but also with a sense of humor and felt that the excitement of discussion helped to engage J in the counseling process. He remained in

treatment for three years and showed substantial gains. In working with J, Paster had been able to achieve gains even with the initial resistance. She had discussed expections, negotiated goals, and, most important, was able to get J involved in the counseling process.

VALUES

Black values have been shaped by cultural factors, social class variables, and experience with racism. As a group, Black Americans tend to be more group centered, sensitive to interpersonal matters, and to value cooperation (Jackson, 1983). Noble (1976) feel that some of these values are due to their African heritage, which stress groupness, community, cooperation and interdependence, and being one with nature. In contrast White middle-class values focus on individuality, uniqueness, competition, and control over nature.

Black Americans have also been influenced by exposure to racism and prejudice in American society and by their struggle for identity. Because of these difficulties, Black Americans often display a differential response according to the race of the individual that they are interacting with. With other Blacks, they are often open, responsive, playful, and expressive. In interacting with White Americans, Blacks are often more guarded, formal, and less verbal (Gibbs, 1980). However, these behavioral differences in Black-Black and Black-White interaction patterns are also influenced by social class and the degree to which Black Americans have accepted White middle-class values.

The existence of racism has produced a variety of defense and survival mechanisms among Black Americans. A. C. Jones (1985) feels that it is important for the counselor or therapist to acknowledge the existence of these factors and to help the client identify maladaptive means of dealing with racism. For example, an individual may have only a limited or reflexive response in dealing with these situations. In counseling with a client, in which racism plays a part, the counselor must assist the client in developing a wider range of options and encourage the development of a more conscious, problem-solving mode. The client must consider the way he/she usually deals with racism and consider other options that might be more productive. The following case example by Jones demonstrates this approach:

A recently divorced, 25-year-old Black medical student sought therapy for migraine headaches that were stress related. He felt that the racist environment of the training school and a particular professor was responsible for his problem. He proposed to deal with the problem by directly confronting his professor and accusing him of racism. It did appear that the professor had engaged in prejudicial behavior. However, it is very possible that directly confronting the professor in this manner would have led to the student's dismissal from the school. Jones also found that the choice of this strategy was at least partially related to his unresolved feeling of anger over his recent divorce. This event had made him feel more vulnerable and the resulting bitter feelings helped in his choice of directly confronting the professor. As the client understood the impact of his divorce, he was able to consider a wider range of options that were open to him. He decided that it would be best to file a complaint with the minority affairs office. Although the tension between himself and the professor remained high, the student felt that he had chosen the best option and remained in school.

Some researchers (Atkinson, Morten & Sue, 1989 and Cross 1971) feel that minorities go through several stages of racial identity or consciousness. As discussed in Chapter 5, Cross suggests that Black Americans go through the following stages: (1) a preencounter phase during which Black identity is not valued and the individual sees White values as positive, (2) an encounter phase during which the individual becomes aware of his/her "Blackness," suffers an identity conflict, and begins to seek a new identity, (3) an immersion-emersion phase during which the individual now actively identifies with Black values and rejects White middle-class values, and (4) an internalization phase during which self-identity is strong and the individual becomes comfortable interacting with other cultures.

Problems with identity may be much more significant in biracial adolescents. Since 1970, there has been an increase of over 150% in intermarriages between Black and White individuals. Gibb (1987) in a preliminary report, indicates that mental health clinics are reporting increasing referrals involving biracial adolescents and many of them indicate problems with racial identity.

Parham and Helms (1981) have found that the stage of racial identity does influence clients' responses to counselors. Blacks at the preencounter phase preferred a White counselor while those in the other stages preferred a Black counselor. Pomales, Claiborn, and LaFromboise (1986) also found a slight effect of stage of racial identity on counselor characteristics. However, the strongest finding was that Black students see a "culturally sensitive" counselor (one who acknowledges the possibility that race or culture might play a role in the client's problem) as more competent than a "culture-blind" counselor (one who focuses on factors other than culture and race when dealing with the presenting problem). Helms (1986), however, feels that no single measure of racial identity could capture the affective states, attitudes, and behaviors that comprise racial identity. Some assessment of racial identity may be useful to a counselor to allow him/her to hypothesize the types of conflict the client may be undergoing and the way the world is viewed.

Working with a slightly different perspective, A. C. Jones (1985) feels that in working with a Black client, four sets of interactive factors must be considered (see Figure 11.1). First is the reaction to racial oppression. Most Black Americans have faced racism, and the consideration that this factor might play a role in their present problem should be examined. Pomales, Claiborn, and LaFromboise (1986) found that Black undergraduate students felt that a culture-sensitive counselor who indicates an interest in the possible impact of race or culture on problems was more competent than a counselor who did not. Second is the influence of Afro-American culture on the client's behavior. Clients may vary greatly in their identification with Afro-American traditions. Third, the majority culture may have a distinct impact on the personal identities and values of Black Americans. The task of the therapist is to help the client understand his or her motivation and make conscious, growth-producing choices. Fourth, clients often differ significantly in their family and individual experiences. For some, this last category may be much more significant than an individual's being a Black American.

Although all four factors may influence a Black-American client, the degree of overlap or importance of each of the factors may vary greatly from individual to individual. A middle-class Black American living in a predominantly White neighborhood may show a different pattern than a lower-class Black American living in a Black neighborhood. A. C. Jones (1985) feels that the advantage of this model is that it includes the elements involved in the studies on identity and forces the counselor to more completely assess external and internal influences on a Black American's problem.

FIGURE 11.1

The Interaction of Four Sets of Factors in the Jones Model

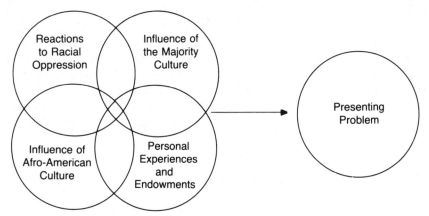

From "Psychological Functioning in Black Americans: A Conceptual Guide for Use in Psychotherapy" by A. C. Jones, 1985, *Psychotherapy, 22*, p. 367. Copyright 1982 by *Psychotherapy*. Reprinted by permission of the Editor, *Psychotherapy*.

COUNSELING ATTITUDES AND PROBLEMS

Black Americans who seek counseling are often thought to have a negative view of mental health services. Some support for this position is in the finding of the study by S. Sue et al. (1974) who found that 50% of Black patients terminate after the first session as opposed to 30% of White patients. Black clients also attended an average of 4.68 sessions versus 8.68 for White clients. However, it is also possible that Black Americans regard counseling positively but find a problem with the counseling process. Differences in the types of problems presented by Black and White clients do not appear to be responsible for the less favorable response by the former to counseling. Baum and Lamb (1983) found that of 170 Black students seeking help at a university counseling center, the majority of problems revolved around career and vocational choice, academic problems, anxiety, depression, and relationship problems. A comparison with White students found that they expressed very similar concerns. Few differences were also reported by Evans, Acosta, Yamamoto, and Hurwicz (1986) between reasons of Black and White patients for coming to a psychiatric outpatient clinic. The researchers did find that the former had a tendency to want the counselor to resolve the problem and felt that they had less to offer in this area.

The attitude Black Americans have of mental health clinics does not appear to be highly negative. In a representative sample of Black Americans, approximately 50% indicated neutral attitudes toward community mental health centers, 34% had positive attitudes, and less than 20% had negative attitudes (Gary, 1985). Parker and McDavis (1983) also found that most Black respondents were aware of the location of mental health agencies and had realistic views of their function. They believed that help could be obtained at the centers and that "normal" individuals utilize their services. They also felt that counseling could be helpful, that both Black and White counselors could be effective, that one of the goals of therapy is self-understanding, and that therapy involves more than just talking. Slight sex differences were found: Black females were somewhat more comfortable with a White counselor than Black males and the latter indicated a slightly greater preference than did Black females for seeing a Black counselor. Overall, it appears that Black Americans view counseling positively but may encounter difficulties during the counseling process itself.

BARRIERS TO EFFECTIVE CROSS-CULTURAL COUNSELING

Counselor Variables

A variety of factors involving the counselor, the Black client, their interaction, and expectations are probably responsible for the less-than-optimal outcome in counseling Black Americans. In discussing these variables, we first focus on problems that might occur in a White counselor. The majority counselor must deal with issues of racism and feelings of the Black client when working with him or her. It is important to examine one's own values when working with minorities. Greene (1985) indicates several areas that might have an impact on counseling. None of these stances is helpful to the Black client, and they necessitate a closer examination of one's motivation and personal feelings when working with Black clients.

1. *Racism or prejudice.* Feelings of superiority over another group may exist at either a conscious or unconscious level. Underlying this feeling may be the belief that Blacks are inferior and create their own problems. Cultural differences involving a different lifestyle may be viewed negatively and interpreted as an indication of pathology. A limited number of options may be discussed with the Black client and the focus is on intrapsychic conflicts without any examination of external influences on the problem. Positive aspects and strengths of the individual are not acknowledged or recognized. A "blaming the victim" approach is taken.

2. *Color blindness.* A counselor taking this stance argues that a Black client is the same as any client. Possible influences of culture and racism on the problem are not acknowledged or explored. Solutions that are suggested are based on a White middle-class perspective. As Kupers (1981) points out, many Black Americans have very different lifestyles as opposed to mainstream Americans. Minority-group status and experiences of and with racism must be acknowledged. Unless this occurs, realistic strategies to deal with real-life situations may not develop.

3. *Paternalism.* In this stance, the counselor interprets the clients' problems as always stemming from racism or prejudice. Severe disorders are excused as merely a reaction to racism or minority status. Possible personal contributions of the individual to his or her problem are not examined. The therapist may become the protector of the individual, which fosters dependence. In this event, clients are prevented from developing independent problem-solving skills or from understanding their own role in their problems.

4. *Unquestioning acceptance of Black power.* Associated with paternalism is a counselor who has the view that because of racism and prejudice, the client should have the right to achieve a personal goal without considering the rights and feelings of others. The Black client is allowed to freely express hostility or take any action since he/she is justified. This stance may involve feelings of racial guilt on the part of the counselor who is attempting to prove that he/she is open and accepting. This approach is also not helpful to the client.

Another barrier in cross-cultural counseling is that the process, goals, and expectations of the majority counselor might also not "fit" the world view of the client. Most therapies are directed toward the middle-class White client, who is educated and employed. Because of this, Black Americans may feel that the White therapist does not understand issues such as economic deprivation (Majors & Nikelly, 1983). The goals of personal growth and self-exploration may be insufficient since lower-class Blacks tend to focus more on external conditions than on intrapsychic concerns (Barbarin, 1984). Clients may need more help in dealing with socioeconomic issues such as housing, food stamps, and employment and may need concrete assistance rather than insight therapy (Grevious, 1985). E. E. Jones (1985) believes that behavioral approaches are more acceptable to Black clients.

Berman (1979) has found that Black counseling students used a different set of microskills than their White counterparts. The former tended to rely more on active expression skills such as giving directions and interpretation whereas White males and females used more attending skills and reflection of feelings. Berman reached several conclusions: (1) current counseling training programs place a heavy emphasis on nondirective attending skills, (2) the counseling style preferred by minorities may lie outside the narrow range of skills emphasized in the counseling profession, and (3) counseling programs may have to consider incorporating some of the more active elements if they wish to be sensitive to cultural differences. Counselors who work with Black clients will have to display a wider range of skills than they do in working with White clients.

Client Variables

Because of past experiences with racism and prejudice, Black clients are often distrustful of White counselors. To make headway in therapy, the therapist must establish a trusting relationship. Black clients are especially sensitive to interpersonal processes and will "size up" the counselor and test the relationship. They may directly challenge the therapist's values and qualifications or act in a very guarded and aloof manner. The counselor cannot merely sit back and expect a commitment to evolve. According to Jenkins (1985), these behaviors are part of protective mechanism. The nonresponsiveness is not "resistance" but an active means of evaluating the counselor. If the counselor is able to respond in a straightforward manner, a relationship may develop. It has to be understood that self-disclosure is very difficult for many Black clients since it leaves them vulnerable to racism.

Some self-disclosure is necessary for progress in counseling. Because of this, Ridley (1984) indicates the importance of determining the reasons for nondisclosure before treatment can occur. He feels that there are two major factors influencing disclosure in the Black client. The first is cultural paranoia, which is a healthy response to racism. Hesitancy about self-disclosure occurs because there is concern about being misunderstood, hurt, or taken advantage of if personal information is shared. The second factor is functional paranoia, which involves a behavioral pattern that stems from personal pathology. The individual displays pervasive suspicion and distrust of all therapists regardless of race. Ridley feels that Black clients can be high or low on these two factors and has developed a typology composed of four cells of Black client self-disclosure, as depicted in Figure 11.2.

In mode 1, the "intercultural nonparanoic discloser," the individual is able to self-disclose personal information, even to White counselors. Anxiety on the part of both parties may still exist with cross-cultural counseling. For example, many White counselors display some initial discomfort in working with a Black client. However, this anxiety is relatively easy to dissipate. In mode 2, "functional paranoiac," disclosure does not occur because of personal pathology. Race of the counselor has minimal effects on the willingness of the client to talk about personal matters. Ridley feels that this category has the greatest possibility of being misused. Assessment has to be carefully done to avoid the error of indicating personal pathology when none exists or when the individual is actually responding from cultural paranoia. Categorizing an individual as fitting into mode 2 should occur only after considering the other categories. In mode 3, the "healthy cultural paranoiac," the Black patient limits

FIGURE 11.2

Typology of Black Client Self-Disclosure

Functional Paranoia

	Low	High
Low	**MODE 1** Intercultural Nonparanoiac Discloser ————— ● Disclosive to either Black or White Therapist	**MODE 2** Functional Paranoiac ————— ● Nondisclosive to both Black and White Therapist
High	**MODE 3** Healthy Cultural Paranoiac ————— ● Disclosive to Black Therapist ● Nondisclosive to White Therapist	**MODE 4** Confluent Paranoiac ————— ● Nondisclosive to both Black and White Therapist

Cultural Paranoia (left axis label)

From "Clinical Treatment of the Nondisclosing Black Client" by C.R. Ridley, 1984, *American Psychologist, 39,* p. 1238. Copyright 1984 by American Psychological Association. Reprinted by permission.

self-disclosure because of past experiences with racism or due to the present attitude of the White counselor. The client may display suspiciousness and anticipate prejudice on the part of the counselor. This may be displayed by a "playing it cool" stance or by being aloof and passive. A danger exists in that the individual in this category will be evaluated as suffering from personal pathology. Ridley feels that most Black clients fall in mode 3. In mode 4, the "confluent paranoiac" involves both personal pathology and exposure to racism. Because both systems or factors are intermixed, it is very difficult to assess and treat. Separating these components will require a skillful therapist.

Ridley offers several recommendations in working with the different modes of nondisclosure. For the functional paranoiac, the most competent therapist for the specific problem should be obtained. The race of the therapist will play a lesser role in therapeutic outcome. For the healthy cultural paranoiac, two goals should be achieved. The first involves dealing with feelings of suspiciousness on the part of the client. Feelings of anger and frustration should be brought to the surface as well as feelings about working with a White counselor. The second is helping the client to discriminate when and when not to self-disclose. Generalizing to all Whites or situations is not adaptive. The modeling of self-disclosure by the White counselor can also help in establishing a relationship. In working with the confluent paranoiac, the optimal therapist would be of the same minority group and sensitive to issues involved in racism. The therapist must be able to acknowledge problems with racism but be able to differentiate normal from abnormal responses. This typology is helpful for the counselor in conceptualizing nondisclosure in Black clients. Self-disclosure has to occur before the presenting problems can be dealt with. However, such an approach can diminish within-group differences since clients are placed in four specific categories. Also, strategies for dealing with the presenting problems must still be initiated.

GROUP COUNSELING

Few studies in the use of group work with Black clients exist. McRoy & Oglesby (1984) indicated some modifications in procedures that had to be employed before a group approach developed for White couples in evaluating prospective adoptive couples could be used for a Black population. The orientation of the program was primarily a client-centered approach, which was combined with value clarification exercises, transactional analysis, and parent effectiveness training. The Black couples had wanted to adopt children and participated in this program. The group was comprised of five Black couples who had an average family income of $30,000 to $45,000. Most had at least some college education. The group was led by a White and a Black social worker.

Several problems occurred during the group sessions. First, most of the participants did not agree with the approach of the Parent Effectiveness Training. They perceived problems with what they interpreted as lengthy parent-child negotiations and also disagreed with the prohibition against the use of physical punishment. Most of the couples had already successfully raised children and indicated their belief that PET principles did not reflect "Black values in child rearing." Second, the couples indicated discomfort with role-playing and felt that the activity was "childish." Because of these problems modifications were made. The couples who had reared children were asked to present their method of handling problems with children and to discuss alternative ways it could be done. In place of role-playing, the Black social worker gave examples of active listening from his own experiences with his wife and then encouraged feedback and discussion from the participants. The couples were also asked to practice active listening at home and to discuss how it worked.

The Black participants were distrustful of the adoption process and concerned about whether or not they would be evaluated fairly. All of them had experienced racism before and felt that the White social worker would make the decision as to whether a specific couple would make good adoptive parents. The interaction by group members was directed to the Black social worker. The White social worker was accepted after making a humorous self-disclosure and when the roles and expectations were more clearly explained. Cohesiveness in the group was strong. Phone numbers and addresses were exchanged after the first meeting and all indicated the importance of a feeling of belongingness. The report by McRoy and Oglesby (1980) indicates the importance of discussing with Black participants the purpose of the group and roles of the group leaders. In addition, group goals and processes may have to be modified with Black participants because of differences in cultural values. Because of experiences with racism, Black participants in a group setting may be suspicious, especially when there might be an element of evaluation. Cohesiveness and good interpersonal relationships can quickly develop in the group and serve as a support for the participants.

CONSULTATION

Consultation practices might also have to be modified in working with Black consultees. Gibbs (1980) describes some of her experiences in school consultation. She observes that Blacks tend to focus more on interpersonal factors while Whites respond more to the instrumental skills demonstrated by the consultant. Her observations are based on a presentation of a proposed school project made to both Black and White teachers at an inner city school. She found that the same five-stage consultation phase occurred but that each group focused on separate issues. The stages involved:

1. *Appraisal stage.* During this stage, both Black and White teachers evaluated the consultant. Gibbs observed that Black teachers tended to be aloof and cool. They responded minimally and did not indicate interest through questions about the project. They wanted to know about the potential harm of the project for the Black children in the school. White teachers were much more attentive and asked questions related to the methods and goals of the project.

2. *Investigation stage.* During this stage, the consultant was checked out. The Black consultees focused on the consultant's personal life and her backgroup and values. For example, the Black principal asked Gibbs personal questions and then also related her own experiences with teaching. After this discussion, the Black principal said she would support Gibbs because she "liked her." Another Black teacher who was initially critical about the project became friendlier and supportive after a discussion during which they discovered areas of commonality. White teachers continued to focus on the technical aspects about the project and did not seek personal information except about the expertise and experiences of the consultant.

3. *Involvement stage.* If a favorable evaluation occurred during stages 1 and 2, the consultees became involved. For Black teachers it revolved around whether or not a personal relationship had been established. Part of their involvement included exchanges of personal information and social interactions during coffee breaks and lunch. White teachers maintained a formal professional relationship and were interested about what they would gain from their involvement. One teacher indicated that the approach could be used in working with emotionally disturbed children. Another indicated the belief that the project might help the school achieve goals.

4. *Commitment stage.* During this stage, Black teachers exhibited more interest in the goals of the project and less in the consultant's personality. White consultees also expressed willingness to participate.

5. *Engagement stage.* Final commitment was made by the teachers to support the project. For Black teachers this commitment was based on interpersonal qualities of the consultant, and for White teachers it was based on the instrumental competence displayed.

Because Black teachers focused on interpersonal relationship, Gibbs feels that it is important for the consultant to be genuine, down to earth, and establish an equal relationship. The consultant must also be open to interpersonal approaches and questioning by Black consultees. Gibbs's observations are useful in (1) helping understand the ways Black and White individuals differ during the consultation stages, (2) pointing out the differences between instrumental and interpersonal orientations, (3) providing training models for consultants who will work with Black Americans, and (4) providing a cross-cultural orientation useful in training both Black and White consultants in working with different cultural groups.

CONCLUSIONS

In working with Black Americans in counseling situations, certain suggestions can be made about the elements necessary during the vital first few sessions. Although these elements can be shifted around and some omitted, these steps may helpful to the counselor and client.

1. Identify the expectations of the Black clients, find out what they believe counseling is, and explore their feelings about counseling.

2. Indicate what you feel counseling is and what you do during counseling. Find out if they feel that will be useful to them.

3. Indicate the limits of confidentiality. If the client was referred, explain your relationship with that agency and the information, if any, that you will share with the agency.

4. If you are not Black, find out how the client feels about working with an individual from a different ethnic group.

5. If there is difficulty with self-disclosure, attempt to identify the reasons for this.

6. Find out information on the history of the problem and the client's perception of the causes. Also, what would the client see as a valuable outcome of counseling?

7. Gather information on the family (nuclear or extended). It is important to determine who helps out and who is living with the family.

8. Identify the strengths of the clients and their families. What resources are available to them? How have they handled problems successfully before?

9. Examine external factors that might be related to the presenting problem, including the impact of racism and concerns for health, education, employment. Identify agencies they come in contact with. Identify any additional stressors.

10. If appropriate, examine issues revolving around racial identity and associated personal conflicts.

11. After information about the problem has been gathered, establish mutually agreed-upon goals.

12. Talk about and consider the means to achieve the goals.

13. Discuss the number of sessions necessary to achieve the goals and the responsibilities of the counselor and the client.

14. Determine whether the client feels the two of you can work together. Also, consider other options that are available.

As we mentioned earlier, the first sessions are crucial in determining whether or not the client will return. The steps above help by explaining what counseling is and by enlisting the assistance of the client. Because of experiences, issues of trust may become very important. The counselor can deal with these issues by discussing them directly and by being open, authentic, and empathetic. The Black client will often make a decision by making an interpersonal evaluation of the counselor. The role of the counselor may have to be much broader for the Black as opposed to the White client. He or she may have to be more directive, help the client deal with agencies, and serve in an educative function. Although these steps may be helpful in working with most Black clients, it must be remembered that large within-group differences exist in the Black population. As A. C. Jones points out:

> Knowing that a client is black fails to inform adequately about his views of psychotherapy, about his personality and psychological conflict, and about his aspirations and goals in therapy, let alone about educational level, social background, or environmental context. There is enormous within-group variability. The question is not how to treat the black client, but how to treat *this* black client. (p. 175)

STUDY QUESTIONS

1. How may the Black family structure differ from the White family structure? In what ways might this influence assessment and the counseling process?

2. How would a counselor determine if a Black youth was deliberately attempting to control the counseling session? What steps might you take to deal with this?

3. Racism is a fact in American life. How would this impact on the counselor and the client? Indicate how you would assess its influence during the first session?

4. Some theorists believe that minorities go through stages of racial identity. Why would you need to consider this possibility in working with Black clients?

5. Self-disclosure is necessary in counseling. What are some reasons for hesitancy to do so among many Black clients? Suggest means of increasing self-disclosure.

6. What are some attitudinal barriers to cross-cultural counseling that might exist in working with a Black client? How would you identify these?

CHAPTER 12

Counseling Hispanic Americans

In this chapter, the term "Hispanic" is used to encompass individuals living in the United States who come or are of ancestry from Mexico, Puerto Rico, Cuba, El Salvador, the Dominican Republic, and other Latin American countries. However, the term is not accepted by all groups, and references such as "Latinos" or "La Raza" (the race) are preferred by some individuals. Even within specific subgroups, there are different opinions on the appropriate terms of identification. Some Hispanics from Mexico may refer to themselves as "Mexicano," "Mexican-American," "Chicano" or "Spanish-American" (Padilla & DeSnyder, 1985). The designation "Chicano" often produces a mixed reception. It is used by some Mexican Americans to indicate racial pride and consciousness but rejected by others, primarily older Mexican Americans, who consider it to be an insulting reference (Munoz, 1982). Even the term "Hispanic," is controversial since it does not indicate the influence of the indigenous cultures. However, the term will be employed in this chapter indicating the common background of Spanish language and customs. Although Hispanics share common characteristics, there are distinct differences between and within the different groups.

In physical characteristics, the appearance of Hispanics varies greatly, including resemblance to North-American Indians, Blacks, or Latins and Europeans. Mexican Americans are mostly of Mestizo ancestry (mixed Spanish and native Aztec-Indian blood). In Mexico, it is estimated that 55% are of Mestizo, 29% Indian, and 15% European background (Avila & Avila, 1980). Among Cuban Americans, most are of Spanish descent with the rest of Black or mixed ancestry. In Latin America, the immigration of African and Asian population with the resulting mixtures has resulted in a wide range of physical characteristics of individuals from these countries.

Puerto Ricans generally are of Spanish descent but influences from Indians and Blacks can also be seen.

DEMOGRAPHICS

According to the U. S. Census (U. S. Department of Commerce, 1980), Hispanic Americans comprise a population of 14.6 million, of whom nearly 9 million are of Mexican descent. Over 3 million are from Puerto Rico (Puerto Rico became a commonwealth on July 25, 1952 and its residents are U. S. citizens who can move between the Island and the mainland without any restrictions), and nearly 1 million are from Cuba. The rest are from Latin-American countries. However, LeVine and Padilla (1980) point out that the census counts traditionally tend to underrepresent the Hispanic population due to ongoing legal and undocumented immigration. It is estimated that 20 million (of whom two-thirds are of Mexican descent) is a closer approximation of the actual number of Hispanics currently residing in the United States (Ponterotto, 1987). Because of the high birthrate and ongoing immigration patterns, it is estimated that Hispanics will be the largest minority group in the United States by the year 2000 (Newton & Arciniega, 1983).

As a group, Hispanic Americans are a very young population, with an average age almost 10 fertile years younger than White Americans and two years younger than Black Americans (Odin, 1987). Because of their religious background as well as strong emphasis on large families and youth, nearly twice as many Hispanic households (54%) are comprised of four or more people as compared to 28% for the country as a whole (Church et al., 1985).

The vast majority of Hispanic Americans are situated in metropolitan areas of the United States and populate every state including Alaska and Hawaii. In certain states and cities, they make up a substantial percentage of the population. Arizona is 16% Hispanic; New Mexico, 36%; Denver, Colorado, 19%; Hartford, Connecticut, 20%; and Miami, Florida, 64%. Mexican Americans reside primarily in the Southwest and Great Lakes regions and in various metropolitan areas throughout the United States. Cubans populate the Miami Beach area of Florida in addition to other large cities in Florida. Puerto Ricans reside primarily in the large Northeastern cities. Approximately, one-third of all Hispanic Americans reside in California. In Los Angeles, alone, there are approximately 2 million individuals of Mexican descent and 300,000 Salvadorians, a number equal to one-half of the population of San Salvador (Church et al., 1985).

Hispanics are overrepresented among the poor, have high unemployment, and often live in substandard housing. Most are blue-collar workers and hold semiskilled or unskilled occupations (Carillo, 1982). There is a significant discrepancy between the annual incomes of Hispanics and Caucasians. According to the 1980 census, the median annual salary for a full-time Hispanic worker was $11,650 compared to $15,572 for a Caucasian worker. Median family income for Hispanics was $16,960 compared to $25,760 for Caucasians. However, differences between Hispanics occur. Puerto Ricans appear to be the least successful, with more than 40% living below the poverty level while Cubans have an average annual salary of $25,000 in Dade County, Florida (Church et al., 1985).

EDUCATION

Educationally, Hispanic Americans have not been faring well in the public schools. Hispanic students have a very high dropout rate, which rises with age. Nearly half drop out before completing high school. This is more than double the rate for Blacks and three times higher than that for White students (Odin, 1987). Among Hispanic groups, Puerto Rican students have the highest dropout rate. Over 70% do not complete high school (Mizio, 1983). Although there has been a great deal of emphasis on the importance of nondiscriminatory assessment, in Texas, Mexican Americans are overrepresented by 300% in the special education programs under the learning disabilities classification (Cummins, 1986).

Many of the educational difficulties faced by Hispanics relate to their varied proficiency with English. According to the 1970 census, Spanish is the primary language spoken in over half of the homes of Hispanic Americans, with a much larger percentage who regularly listen to or speak Spanish on a more limited basis. Second generation Hispanics are often bilingual. However, their command of the English language is often limited. Many are exposed first to Spanish in the home and then to English in the school. Immigrant parents may speak in Spanish and be responded to by their child in a combination of Spanish and English. A 1974 Supreme Court case (*Lau v. Nichols*) mandated that public schools provide a program that would not prevent non-English-speaking students from receiving a meaningful education. Subsequently, a document, popularly called the Lau Remedies, was developed by the U. S. Office of Civil Rights in 1975, dictating bilingual education as an appropriate means of correcting past practices. Bilingual education programs, which have been in effect for more than a decade, have been and continue to be the subject of much controversy and debate.

Cummins (1986) feels that a variety of factors, including intergroup power relationships, has much to do with the lack of educational success of Hispanic Americans. For example, Finnish students have a relatively poor academic performance in Sweden where they are considered a low-status group but are successful academically in Australia where they are a high-status group. Since change of status is not possible in the United States, Cummins feels that it is possible to "empower" students in schools through four components: (1) incorporation of the language and culture of the minority group into the school programs, (2) participation of the ethnic community in the children's education, (3) implementation of methods to increase motivation in students by having them use their own language to achieve greater knowledge, and (4) emphasis on having the professionals involved in assessment become advocates for the students instead of using tests to legitimize localizing the problem "in the student." A preschool Spanish-only program involving the Carpenteria School District located near Santa Barbara, California, incorporated the preceding factors. In the past, incoming Spanish-speaking students entering kindergarten scored approximately 14.5 on the School Readiness Inventory (scores of 20 or better are associated with success in kindergarten), which was about 8 points lower than English-speaking students. The parents of the students entering the experimental program approximated the characteristics of adults in the school district. The vast majority occupied the lower socio-economic class and the average educational level of the parents was sixth-grade completion.

In the Spanish-only preschool program in Carpenteria, the students developed language skills first in Spanish and used this to generate new ideas, understand concepts, and solve problems. Parents were involved and encouraged to provide specified experiences in the home. Community support was strong. After completion of the program, students scored approximately 21.6 on the School Readiness Inventory. An evaluation of the program indicated that although the children were less exposed to English, the enhanced Spanish skills allowed them to learn English better. It also indicated that a comprehensive program to counteract the effects of being a low-status minority group can be implemented and be successful.

FAMILY AND VALUES

For Hispanic Americans, family tradition is an important aspect of life. Family unity is seen as very important, as is respect for and loyalty to the family. Cooperation rather than competition among family members is stressed. Interpersonal relationships are maintained and nurtured within a large network of family and friends. For the family, a critical element is to develop and maintain interpersonal relationships. There is deep respect and affection among friends and family. The extended family includes not only relatives but often includes nonblood relatives such as the best man (*padrino*), maid of honor (*madina*), and godparents (*compadre* and *comadre*). The extended family is often seen as a resource, and help is generally not sought until advice is obtained from the extended family and close friends (Carillo, 1982). However, Padilla and DeSnyder (1985) point out that although there are many positive features of the extended family, emotional involvement and obligations with a large number of family and friends may also function as an additional source of stress.

The Catholic religion often has a major influence in Hispanic groups and is a source of comfort in times of stress. There is strong belief in the importance of prayer, and most participate in Mass. This religious belief is related to the view that: (1) sacrifice in this world is helpful to salvation, (2) being charitable to others is a virtue, and (3) one should endure wrongs done against you (Yamamoto & Acosta, 1982). The consequences of these beliefs are that many Hispanics have difficulty behaving assertively. They feel that problems or events are meant to be and cannot be changed. The strong reliance on religion can be a resource. Sometimes a priest can help deal with counseling issues. Acosta and Evans (1982) report the case of a 35-year-old, Spanish-speaking Mexican American, Jose, who came into the clinic complaining of anxiety attacks. The precipitating event appeared to be his impending marriage, which would necessitate reducing the amount of money he could send to his parents in Mexico. He felt that it would be a sin to reduce his assistance. The counselor suggested that Jose talk to his priest about this issue. With short-term counseling, along with assurance from the priest that he would not be committing a sin, Jose was able to marry and reconcile sending less to his parents. In addition to an extended family orientation and a fatalistic outlook, Hispanics also hold values that differ from those held by middle class Americans. For example, Inclan (1985) compares the latter with the values of traditional Puerto Ricans (see Table 12.1).

Middle-class Americans are usually concerned with time and planning for the future. Puerto Ricans often find humorous the need for Anglos to leave a party because they have to be ready for the coming day. Puerto Ricans prefer to enjoy the present activities. Activity is also viewed differently; being is valued more than doing. Middle-class Americans tend to stress the importance of doing something during a vacation. For the Puerto Rican, being with the family and experiencing this is more important than doing something. Among White middle-class families, individual achievement in the workplace is important, while for Puerto Rican families prestige and status are gained by demonstrating respect and cooperation in the family. Family members are given priority. If a member is in a position to hire someone, it is expected that the relative will be selected. In the

TABLE 12.1

Comparison of Value-Orientation Profiles for First-Generation Poor Puerto Ricans and Middle-Class Anglo Americans

Dimension	First-Generation Poor Puerto Rican	Middle-Class American
Time	Present > Future > Past	Future > Present > Past
Activity	Being > Doing > Being-in-Becoming	Doing > Being > Being-in-Becoming
Relational	Lineal > Collateral > Individual	Individual > Collateral > Lineal
Person-Nature	Subjugated > Harmony > Dominant Over	Dominant Over > Subjugated > Harmony
Basic Human Nature	Mixed > Evil > Good	Neutral > Evil > Good

From "Variations in Value Orientations in Mental Health Work with Puerto Ricans" by J. Inclan, 1985, *Psychotherapy, 22*, p. 328. Copyright 1985 by *Psychotherapy*. Reprinted by permission of the Editor, *Psychotherapy*.

person-nature dimension, the view is that humans must accommodate to nature and are not able to change events versus the White middle-class view that nature can and should be changed. Puerto Ricans feel that human nature is mixed and that whether an individual is good or bad is dependent upon supernatural forces. In the White middle class it is felt that basic human nature is neutral and can be changed. The orientation of Hispanics to the family and values produces certain consequences. First, the family is valued over the individual. Second, divorce is much less acceptable and less often seen as an alternative to marital difficulties. Third, conflicts in values can occur between family members at different levels of acculturation. Fourth, life's misfortunes are seen as inevitable, and Hispanics often feel resigned to their fate.

Inclan presents a case in which knowledge of a family's value orientation was helpful in treating a problem.

> During family therapy, a Puerto Rican mother indicated to her son, "You don't care for me anymore. You used to come by every Sunday and bring the children. You used to respect me and teach your children respect. Now you go out and work, you say, always doing this or that. I don't know what spirit (que diablo) has taken over you" (p. 332). In response the son indicated that he is working hard and sacrificing for the children; that he wants to be a success in the world and an individual that his children can be proud of. In examining the case, it is clear that the mother is expressing disappointment. She defines love as being with her, having the family gather together, and the subordination of individual desires for the family. The son has adopted a middle class set of values stressing individual achievement, doing, and the future. The clash in value differences was at the root of the problem.

In working with the family, the therapist provided an alternative way of viewing the conflict instead of using terms such as right or wrong. He explained that our views are shaped by the values that we hold. He asked about the socialization process that the mother had undergone. She emphasized the "good old days" and the socialization and values of her childhood. The son indicated the pain he felt in losing the understanding of the parents, but he felt he had to change in order to succeed in the United States. The therapist pointed out that different adaptive styles may be necessary for different situations and what is right is dependent upon the social context. Both of them began to acknowledge that they still loved one another but might have to show it in different ways. As a result of the sessions, the mother and son accepted one another and understood the nature of the original conflict.

FAMILY STRUCTURE

Traditional Hispanic families are hierarchical in form with special authority given to the elderly, the parents, and males. Within the family, the father assumes the role of the primary authority figure. Sex roles are clearly delineated (Acosta & Evans, 1982; Carillo, 1982; Green, Trankina, & Chavez, 1976; Mejia, 1983; Mizio, 1983). Children are expected to be obedient and are usually not consulted on family decisions. The sexual behaviors of adolescent females are severely restricted and sexual topics are rarely discussed with the children. Male children are afforded greater freedom to come and go as they please. Children are expected to contribute financially to the family when possible. Parents reciprocate by providing for them through young adulthood and even during marriage. This type of reciprocal relationship is a lifelong expectation (Mizio, 1983). Older children are expected to take care of and protect their younger siblings when away from home. The older sister may function as a surrogate mother. Adolescent children are expected to take responsibility at an early age. Even though they may be adolescents, many think of themselves and function as young adults. Marriage and parenthood are entered into early in life and are seen as stabilizing influences. Children are welcome and a source of pride. However, youthful marriages are vulnerable to dissolution (Vega, Hough, & Romero, 1985).

SEX-ROLE CONFLICTS

In working with Hispanic Americans, the counselor will often face problems dealing with conflicts over sex roles. In their traditional culture, men are expected to be strong, dominant, and the provider for the family whereas women are expected to be nurturant, submissive to the male, and self-sacrificing. As head of the family, the male expects the members to be obedient to him. However, the following pattern of migration among Hispanics has produced strain and stress with this role expectation. The male leaves the family in search of work, leaving behind his wife and children. This forced separation often becomes permanent, with the wife becoming the head of the household (Carillo, 1982). This change in family structure and exposure to the majority culture with differing sex-role expectations can produce problems. Carillo (1982) indicates areas in which males may have sex-role conflicts:

1. Submissiveness or assertion in the area of authority. The Hispanic male may have difficulty interacting with agencies and individuals outside of the family and may feel that he is not fulfilling his role. In addition, changes involving greater responsibility of the wife and children may produce problems related to his authority.

2. Feelings of isolation and depression because of the need to be strong. Talking about or sharing views of problems with others may be seen as a sign of weakness. With the additional stress of living in a very different culture, the inability to discuss feelings of frustration and anxiety produces isolation.

3. Conflicts over the need to be consistent in his role. As ambiguity and stresses increase, the need to adjust and to seek security in a more rigid adherence to the role produces anxiety.
4. Anxiety over questions of sexual potency.

The traditional feminine role in the Hispanic family is to be submissive to the male, self-sacrificing, and restrained (Mejia, 1983; Mizio, 1983). For females, conflicts may involve (1) expectations to meet the requirement of her role, (2) anxiety when unable to live up to these standards, (3) depression over not being able to live up to these standards, and (4) the inability to act out her feelings of anger. Espin (1985) feel that Hispanic women are socialized to feel that they are inferior and that suffering and being a martyr are characteristics of a good woman. With greater exposure to the dominant culture, such views may be questioned. Certain roles may change more than others. For example, Espin indicates that some women are very modern in their views of education and employment, but remain traditional in the area of sexual behavior and personal relationships. Others remain very traditional in all areas. Other writers (McCurdy & Ruiz, 1980; Ruiz, 1981) caution that Hispanic sex roles are not as inflexible and rigid as has often been described. For example, the concept of masculinity or machismo was described in terms of being a good provider by Hispanic respondents (Church et al., 1985). Mizio (1983) also points out that the double standard is decreasing rapidly in the urban class. Part of the reason for the change is that many women are required to act independently in the work setting and to deal with schools and other agencies. In some cases, women may become the wage earner, which produces problems since this role traditionally belongs to the male. Conversely, as the wife becomes more independent, the husband may feel anxiety. Both may feel that the man is no longer fulfilling his role. The counselor must be able to help the family deal with the anxiety and suspiciousness associated with role change (Green et al., 1976).

For both males and females, role conflict is likely to occur if the male is unemployed, if the female is employed, or a combination of the two. Especially tragic is the pattern of the male leaving his family behind to seek employment, which might last for long periods of time. The strain involved in the separation is responsible for the fact that very high rates of separation and divorce occur in Hispanic families (Ventura & Heuser, 1981). In addition, it may be easier for the female to obtain a job than for the male to do so. Since both feel that the male should be the provider for the family, an additional source of stress can occur.

In dealing with sex-role conflicts, the counselor faces a dilemma and potential value conflict. If the counselor believes in equal relationships should he or she move the clients in this direction? Green et al. (1976) points out some of the aspects of the situation that have to be taken into consideration.

If clearly differentiated sex roles are accepted as desirable in the culture, too much deviance will obviously cause rejection. A therapist working with cultural mores different from his own must be particularly careful not to impose his views on the patient. Rather, he must try to help the patient achieve change to the degree that the patient seeks it but not to a degree that will cause alienation from the ethnic group. (p. 232)

Green and his colleagues make a valuable point in that the consequences of too much of a change might be a rejection of the individual by the ethnic group. The degree of change should be left to the client. The responsibility of the counselor is to let the client know the consequences of the change. For example, Espin (1985) cautions that in working with women, changes in their role may be perceived as threatening to their family. Any counselor who works to help a female client achieve more independence without apprising her of potential problems within her family and community is not fulfilling his/her obligations.

Espin points out that Hispanic culture allows a certain range of behaviors and that a Hispanic woman may place herself anywhere within this range. A determination should also be made to see if a specific behavior is a result of personal choice or adherence to norms. An error can be made by a counselor in interpreting behaviors as personal choice when they might be merely adherence to cultural norms. Behaviors that are being maintained only at the cost of high anxiety and frustration can be interpreted as a matter of personal choice and not due to cultural factors. If cultural norms are used to explain behavior, it is possible that other factors influencing the individual's life will not be explored. Appropriate reactions to norm violations may be interpreted as neurotic behavior. As Espin puts it ". . . although there is a danger of being insensitive to cultural differences, there is also a danger of accepting as 'cultural' some behaviors or attitudes that might be self-defeating and damaging" (pp. 169–170). Therefore a careful assessment must be made to determine and distinguish between personal choice within a cultural context.

ACCULTURATION

Under the heading of Hispanic Americans, we have included a group of very distinct subpopulations that often have very large differences in customs and values. In addition, large differences exist within specific groups in terms of degree of acculturation, language spoken, and physical appearance. All of these factors make any generalization about Hispanics difficult. In addition, in many cities, Black culture has had an influence on Mexican-American values (Vega, 1983). All of these variables make it important to assess the influence of these factors on individual clients.

For example, Ponterotto (1987) indicates that the level of acculturation is related to variables such as dropout rate, experienced level of stress, and attitude toward counselor. In addition, the degree of acculturation may influence the possible types of problems faced by a Hispanic American, the way the problems are interpreted, and the appropriate process and goals in counseling. For example, second-generation Hispanic Americans are usually bilingual, but are usually only functional in English. They are often exposed to Spanish at home and exposed to English in the school and on television. Second-generation Hispanic Americans are often marginal to both native and majority cultures (Vega, 1983). Besides knowledge of possible problems faced by different generations of Hispanic Americans, acculturation also may influence perceptions of counseling and responses to counseling. For example, Sanchez and Atkinson (1983) found that Mexican Americans with a strong traditional orientation may have more difficulty being open and self-disclosing than those with a strong orientation toward the dominant culture. In their study, they also found that women held more positive attitudes toward counseling and are more likely to self-disclose. A study has also found that acculturated Hispanic-American wives were more likely to perceive themselves as equal partners in making decisions (O'Guinn, et al, 1987). Because of this, the impact of the level of acculturation on the individual and the entire family (in family therapy) would be important to take into consideration.

Because knowledge of acculturation level is important, a variety of acculturation measures has been developed. Formal assessment measures include: The Acculturation Rating Scale for Mexican Americans (ARSMA) (Cuellar, Harris, & Jasso, 1980). Scores on this 20-item questionnaire allow for categorizing on a five-point scale ranging from "Very Mexican," "Bicultural, Mexican oriented," "True Bicultural," "Bicultural, Anglo oriented," and "Very Anglicized." Measures of acculturation also exist for Puerto Ricans (Inclan, 1979) and Cubans (Szapocznik, Scopetta, Kurtines, and Aranalde, 1978). If the counselor feels uncomfortable using a formal measure, it is also possible to inquire about the specific Hispanic group that they are from, length of time in the country or generational status, primary language, religious orientation and strength of religious beliefs, whether they live in a barrio, the reason for immigration (if immigrants), if they are in an extended family situation, and other information related to acculturation (Dominguez-Ybarra & Garrison, 1977; Juarez, 1985). However, it must be remembered that acculturation is often not a straightforward process. On values such as family solidarity, ethnic identification, religious orientation, and sex roles, a single individual might score very traditional in some areas and more Anglicized (Espin, 1985; Vega et al., 1983). What this means is that even though acculturation information is helpful, it is the responsibility of the counselor to examine individual patterns of acculturation and to develop individual counseling plans. The danger exists that acculturation measures will be given and that the client will be seen in a stereotypical manner. Cultural information is important in alerting the counselor to possible issues and conflicts. As with any client, information can be obtained that assists in the conceptualization of problems. However, an individual treatment plan must be developed on the basis of all information available.

CLIENT PROBLEMS

It is important to remember that many of the problems of Hispanic Americans are from external sources. Because the majority are poor, they often suffer the stresses involved in situations without adequate food and shelter and in dealing with bureaucracies and in employment (De la Cancela, 1985; Munoz, 1982). LeVine and Padilla (1980) point out that symptoms of stress displayed by Hispanics to external factors are often similar to those caused by personal conflicts. "If extrapsychic conflict is predominant, therapy aimed at social action and the alleviation of discrimination and poverty may be appropriate. If intrapsychic conflict is more basic, introspective or behavioral therapy is the treatment of choice" (p. 256). The careful assessment of the source of the emotional disturbance is necessary before the appropriate action can be taken, and this should be done very early in the counseling session. For example, Ruiz (1981) presents the case of a married, migrant worker in his mid-fifties who comes into therapy complaining of hearing threatening voices. He refuses to leave his home because of anxiety. In working with many Hispanics, Ruiz recommends an analysis of external causes first. In this case, it is suggested that the worker undergo a complete physical with special attention to exposure to pesticides and other agricultural chemicals that might result in mental symptoms. It is also possible that the feelings of fear displayed by the individual stem from factors such as suspiciousness of outside authorities, fear of deportation of self or others in the family or recent encounters with creditors. External factors that are specific to the experience of Hispanic Americans must first be examined.

Recent immigrants often have feelings of estrangement and displacement in the United States due to culture conflict and disruption of the extended family. For example, Cuban elders expected that they would be accorded a high status later in life and be the ultimate authority in the family. This expectation has not been met. Instead, they are often considered to be burdens to the family, resulting in feelings of isolation and depression (Szapocznik, et al., 1982). Intergenerational conflicts due to differences in rates of acculturation are common. *Verguenza* (shame) is a common problem among Mexican Americans and is evident during the initial process of acculturation. Dominguez-Ybarra and Garrison (1977) feel that it is important to provide a link with Mexican values in working with these clients and to help them understand the conflict as a function of differences between Mexican and Anglo values. However, Green et al. (1976) indicate that in working with an *agringado* (acculturated Mexican American) the counselor should not attempt to reinstate traditional values but rather should indicate potential areas of conflict and the consequences of their stance. LeVine and Padilla (1980) feel that the pressures in acculturation versus the pressures to remain ethnically loyal are common in Hispanics. They recommend that a determination has to be made with the client in terms of how much acculturation or separation from the dominant culture will produce personal growth.

COUNSELING CONSIDERATIONS, STRATEGIES, AND MODALITIES

Because of the fact that many Hispanics suffer from factors beyond their control such as prejudice, discrimination, and poverty, some professionals have argued for social change. Rivera (1984) argues that the goal in working with Puerto Rican patients should be to help them become more aware of the oppression they face and to attain personal and collective liberation. Espin (1985) feels that oppression also exists against women in the Hispanic culture and that the counselor should help women "empower" themselves. Ponterotto (1987) believes that an important part of counseling Hispanics is the consideration of psychosocial, economic, and political needs of the clients.

In working with traditional Hispanics, the most appropriate counselor would be bilingual and bicultural. Unfortunately, there are few therapists who fit this description. It is important that the counselor be knowledgeable and understanding of both minority and majority cultural values and beliefs. Objectivity and the ability to integrate the different value systems as they relate to the problems presented by the client are critical. Because of the lack of bilingual counselors, problems in communication occur with Hispanic clients who are not conversant in English. For example, Marcos (1973) found that Mexican-American patients were seen as suffering from greater psychopathology when interviewed in English than when interviewed in Spanish. However, interpreters may present difficulties themselves in the counseling process. They are often responsible for distortions in communication. Marcos (1979) found that distortions may result from (1) the interpreter's language competence and translation skills, (2) the interpreter's lack of psychiatric knowledge, and (3) the attitudes of the counselor. For example, relatives used as interpreters often answer the questions put to the client without waiting for a response. The following example occurred in an actual exchange:

CLINICIAN (*TO SPANISH-SPEAKING PATIENT*): What about worries, do you have many worries?

INTERPRETER (*TO PATIENT*): Is there anything that bothers you?

PATIENT: I know, I know that God is with me, I'm not afraid. They cannot get me [pause]. I'm wearing these new pants and I feel protected. I feel good, I don't get headaches anymore.

INTERPRETER (*TO CLINICIAN*): He says he is not afraid, he feels good, he doesn't have headaches anymore. (Marcos, 1979, p. 173)

To reduce some of these errors, Marcos recommends that the mental health professional meet with the interpreter to discuss goals, areas to be assessed, and possible sensitive areas that may need to be explored. The language proficiency of the interpreter should also be assessed. It might also be helpful to have as part of the team, an indigenous worker who is knowledgeable about the community and can provide help in contacting social service agencies or assistance when this is needed in working with a client.

In developing treatment strategies it is important to consider the expectation of the clients. Traditional Hispanic Americans are accustomed to being treated by physicians. They are unclear as to the purpose of counseling and may expect medication, a quick solution to their problem, and advice as to what to do (Acosta & Evans, 1982; Green et al., 1976). To increase the "fit" between expectations and techniques, the counselor should (1) carefully explain the difference between the physician and the counselor, (2) indicate the role of the counselor and client in counseling, (3) discuss the goals for counseling, and (4) select techniques that are appropriate to the cultural norms of Hispanics.

Most mental health professionals (De la Cancela, 1985; De Snyder, 1985; Juarez, 1985; Ponterotto, 1987; Ruiz & Casas, 1981; Yamamoto & Acosta, 1982) feel that techniques should be employed that are active, concrete, and problem solving in their orientation. Juarez feels that behavior therapy has these characteristics and fits client expectations of direct intervention and guidance to change behaviors. Specific tasks are assigned and counselors take a very active and directive role. Other advantages are a focus on the impact of the environment on behavior and a here-and-now emphasis. Ponterotto also feel that these procedures and methods of treatment and goal selection work well with Hispanics. Boulette (1976) found that behavioral approaches such as assertive training are more effective for Mexican-American women than nondirective therapy. Montijo (1985) feels that a cognitive behavioral approach would be effective with Puerto Ricans in raising self-esteem by eliminating self-defeating thoughts and promoting more accurate perceptions of the environment. In terms of length, Yamamoto and Acosta recommend short-term therapy lasting four to five sessions.

Because of the importance of the extended family and the relationships among its members, family therapy is often recommended in working with Hispanics. This is especially important since changes in the client in an individual session may have profound effects on the family (De la Cancela, 1985; Padilla & DeSnyder, 1985). Structural family approaches are useful since the hierarchical structure is considered along with the impact of socioeconomic and cultural factors. This approach has been used effectively with Puerto-Rican families (Canino & Canino, 1982).

Counseling Children and Adolescents

Counselors working with Hispanic students must determine if a complaint is real or imagined (Ruiz & Casas, 1981). For example, if a student feels that he/she is encountering prejudice, intervention will depend on the reality of the complaint. If it is real, several steps may be taken. The source of the prejudice can be directly confronted and/or the individual can learn to respond appropriately when treated unfairly. If, however, it is due to feelings of inferiority and only imagined, a cognitive behavior approach to correct perceptions would be appropriate. The same type of determination has to be made for all complaints.

Relationship problems with family members are often presented. In working with the child or adolescent, it must be remembered that attempts to deal with the problem can produce additional problems in the family. In this situation, the use of family therapy would be a possibility. In a case that Ruiz and Casas present, a student stated "My father never asks me for help around the home . . . but expects me to be around every weekend in case there's something to be done. He doesn't understand that studying is a full-time job" (pp. 197–198). Assertive training was employed but modified in that it was performed to present the student's view in a manner that did not show disrespect. The son stated that he was willling to help but needed advance notice because of school obligations. This was practiced in a manner that would show no disrespect to the father. There was no attempt to state personal desires in all areas. In using assertive training it should emphasize the importance of situational assertiveness to the student, indicating that it might be appropriate to be assertive in a classroom or on job interviews but that it may not be necessary to do so with parents.

Cuento (folklore therapy), an interesting program that involved a culturally sensitive approach, was used in working with at-risk Puerto Rican children (Rogler et al., 1987). The program attempted to reduce the stress and anxiety felt by second-generation Hispanic children who were marginal to both cultures. The Cuento involved reading folktales to the children. The stories were then discussed in terms of cultural values and the specific ways that the characters encountered and solved problems. It was hoped that pride in culture as well as developing means of dealing with the environment would occur. To develop this second aspect, children were asked to role-play the various characters in the story and to role-play positive solutions to the situations faced. In another group, the same procedures were involved. However, an additional feature was present in that adapted folktales were used. The cultural values remained the same but contemporary situations were presented. The setting of the stories approximated the actual environment that the children lived in and the types of problems presented were urban in nature. Again, the values and problems were discussed and the children role-played solutions. Both of these groups produced greater reduction in anxiety in the children than traditional group therapy and a no-treatment control. The most effective group involved the adapted story. This approach appears promising since cultural values are maintained and stressed, and children learn to develop adaptable behaviors in stressful situations.

Initial Interviews

Several writers (Munoz, 1982; Padilla & DeSnyder, 1985; Yamamoto & Acosta, 1982) have made several suggestions as to how to conduct the initial session with Hispanic Americans:

1. It is important to engage in a respectful, warm, and mutual introduction with the client. Be sure to pronounce the client's name correctly. As Munoz points out, it is difficult to establish rapport when the client winces every time you say his or her name.

2. Give a brief description of what counseling is and the role of each participant. Also explain the notion of confidentiality.

3. Have the client state in his/her own words the problem or problems as he/she sees it.

4. Use paraphrasing to summarize the problem as you understand it and make sure that the client knows you understand it.

5. Have the client prioritize the problems.

6. Determine the client's expectations and develop appropriate goals with the help of the client. Discuss possible consequences of achieving the goals.

7. Discuss the possible participation of family members and consider family therapy.

8. Evaluate the role of environmental factors in the problem.
   (a) Determine country, reason for immigration (if immigrant), degree of acculturation. Also assess degree of level of acculturation in involved family members. Determine possible problems because of conflicts produced by acculturation.
   (b) Assess possible problems from external sources such as need for food, shelter, employment, or stressful interactions with agencies.
   (c) Provide necessary assistance in developing and maintaining environmental supports.

9. Explain the treatment to be used, why it was selected, and how it will help achieve the goals.

10. With the client's input, determine a mutually agreeable length of treatment.

Conclusion. In working with Hispanic populations, it must be remembered that there are large between- and within-group differences in terms of values, acculturation level, and problems faced. These differences must be examined before counseling can proceed. Although this information is vital, it can also be misused if generalizations are made in a stereotypic fashion. Background information only provides the counselor with potential issues and problems faced by the client. An individual treatment plan must be developed. With Hispanics and other minority-group members, the assessment of possible environmental factors is critical. Problems presented in response to the stresses of poverty, poor housing, lack of facility with English, and dealing with agencies often produce symptoms that are similar to those produced by intrapsychic conflicts. The more traditional the Hispanic, the more likely the necessity for treatment strategies that are concrete, goal oriented, and structured. Family and group therapy are other useful modalities. In considering goals, it is important to consider and discuss with the client the consequences of changes on the individual, his/her family, and the relationship with his/her cultural group.

STUDY QUESTIONS

1. What are some value differences between Hispanic and Western culture? How might these affect the process and goals of counseling?

2. If you were a counselor working with a Hispanic client, how would you determine the degree of acculturation or assimilation? Why would this be important?

3. Describe traditional sex-role expectations among Hispanics. How would you deal with a situation in which one spouse has a narrower definition of appropriate sex roles than the other?

4. In working with Hispanics, what external factors should be assessed? Why?

5. Suggest how you might structure the initial counseling interview with an immigrant or unacculturated Hispanic individual?

6. What images or stereotypes do you hold of Hispanics? How might these interfere with your ability to work with Hispanic clients?

PART III

CRITICAL INCIDENTS IN CROSS-CULTURAL COUNSELING

In this final chapter, we present a series of case vignettes on various racial/ethnic minorities. We have added many new cases since the first edition was published. Each is presented in some counseling, education, or work-related context, and raises cross-cultural or multicultural issues described in Parts I and II. We encourage students to also review appropriate chapters in Part II that correlate with the cases.

CHAPTER 13

Critical Incident Cases

Critical incidents have been shown to be an effective means of highlighting and illustrating crucial issues, concerns, and decision points likely to arise in certain characteristic situations. They represent simulation techniques in the broadest sense. Almost all the cases contained in this chapter possess three similarities:

1. the situation or incident represents an area of *conflict* of cultures, values, standards, or goals;

2. the solution is not always obvious, or there may be considerable *controversy* as to the most appropriate or effective action to take; and

3. the vignette includes important conditions under which the situation occurred.

While critical incidents may be criticized on the grounds that they over-simplify the issues, and that they may not be realistic, we have found them very useful with students and helping professionals. Their usefulness and benefits include the following:

1. Trainees can begin to become potent agents of change for culturally different clients early in training. They can begin the task of identifying cultural or sociopolitical forces operating in a situation so that understanding and awareness of issues are enhanced.

2. In a laboratory setting, trainees have the opportunity to examine potentially troublesome situations that may hinder their functioning with clients. World-view differences and value differences can be explored and contrasted with other trainees. For example, increas-

ing awareness and sensitivity to client reactions, communications, and the meaning of differences often result. What is more important is to discuss trainee reactions and distortions (value judgments) that may have detrimental impact on culturally different clients.

While the first two sections of this text have been devoted mainly to providing general and specific information about counseling and the culturally different, this chapter is concerned with analysis and application. In the following pages, you will be exposed to several cross-cultural situations that involve people from different cultural/racial backgrounds. Each case is briefly described in some counseling, educational, or mental health framework. Your task is to do three things as enumerated here:

1. Identify as many cross-cultural issues in the case vignettes as possible. Do not stop with one or two! Your ability to see the situations from as many perspectives as possible is important. In most cases, listing your answers with brief elaborations is all that is needed.

2. Identify as many possible value differences between the interaction of the characters or the values of the characters and institutions. For example, restraint of strong feelings may be highly valued by certain Asian groups, but not by many White Americans. A possible value conflict may arise between individuals from each group. Conflicts can also arise between an individual and institution or another society. In this case, institutional and societal values need to be identified. Again, listing these conflicts with some elaboration to clarify your analysis is all you need do.

3. Committing yourself to a course of action in each case vignette forces you to examine your own values/priorities and those presented in the case. Address yourself to what you would do, how you would do it, and why? In other words, it is important to define your goals, approach, and rationale.

USING THE CASE VIGNETTES

These case vignettes, when used as a teaching/training tool by a skilled and knowledgeable leader, can (a) help you become culturally aware of your own values, (b) expand your awareness of other world views, (c) anticipate possible cultural barriers in counseling, and (d) generate and suggest alternative counselor intervention strategies more consistent with the life experiences of minorities.

The instructor or workshop leader may wish to use the case vignettes in several ways. For example, these cases may be used to stimulate group discussion among participants or be used for individual study and learning.

Some of these cases are also conducive to role-playing rather than purely cognitive exercises. The cases may be used prior to reading the text, during each chapter as may be appropriate, or after the complete study of Parts I and II. The benefits derived from the critical incidents depend on the ingenuity and effectiveness of the facilitator. In our classes and workshops, we have found that if a systematic approach is used for the express purpose of accomplishing these objectives, any combination will aid in learning. We have even used critical incidents to assess the effects of a course or workshop on participants (mid-term examinations, take-home assignments, final examinations, etc.). A typical outline we follow in leading discussions and having students write an analysis of a case is shown in Figure 13.1. This same form, or some variant of it, may be reproduced and used by students to study the cases.

Learning can also occur when trainees are asked to create a cross-cultural counseling situation. Creation of a good critical incident requires that you understand (a) alternative world views, (b) the generic characteristics of counseling, (c) value systems of the culturally different, and (d) social-institutional dynamics. Creating a critical incident requires active integration rather than isolated learning. Furthermore, these can be shared with other participants to enhance further learning. You may like to use the form outlined in Figure 13.2.

FIGURE 13.1

CRITICAL INCIDENT ANALYSIS

Name _____

Critical Incident No. _____   **Date** _____

1. In the case vignette just read, please identify as many cross-cultural issues as possible. Please be brief, and list them (1, 2, 3, etc.) when possible.

2. Identify potential value differences/conflicts occurring or likely to occur in this case.

3. Suppose you are a counselor or mental health worker who finds himself/herself in the situation. What would be (a) your goals, (b) your course of action, and (c) your rationale for the goals and action you have chosen?

   (a) Goals

   (b) Course of action

   (c) Rationale

FIGURE 13.2

CREATING A CROSS-CULTURAL COUNSELING
CRITICAL INCIDENT

Name_____ **Date**_____

    As one aspect of cross-cultural counselor training, we are interested in compiling several counseling cases that deal with cultural/racial issues. These critical incidents may be used in future training. All of you are being asked to describe a cross-cultural counseling encounter that raises cross-cultural counseling issues. We are especially interested in the counselor-client interaction, but a broader description (teaching, colleague relationships, institutional dilemmas, etc.) is also permissible. The specific purposes of this assignment are to (a) identify cultural points of view and responses, (b) show how two cultural dictates may lead to misunderstandings, (c) reveal how traditional counseling may clash with cultural values, and (d) suggest alternative ways of dealing with the critical incident.

    Your brief description should involve an actual or hypothetical event that took place over a limited period of time. The situation should be cross-cultural involving people from two different cultures, and should place the counselor in an ambiguous position with no easy solution.

    Please describe such a situation and answer the following questions. All information will be treated as confidential. If more space is required, use the reverse side to elaborate.

1. Describe a cross-cultural counseling situation you experienced, witnessed, or heard about.

_____

_____

_____

2. Describe the events in sequence, indicating what, when, where, how, and why they occurred.

_____

_____

_____

3. List the race/culture of the persons involved, giving their relationship to one another.

_____

_____

_____

4. Describe how the counselor or main character handled the situation.

_____

_____

_____

5. What cross-cultural issues did this situation raise?

_____

_____

_____

6. How should the counselor have handled the situation and why?

_____

_____

_____

7. Please describe any additional information we might need in order to use this case as a training one.

_____

_____

_____

CRITICAL INCIDENTS

Since publication of the first edition of _Counseling the Culturally Different: Theory and Practice,_ we have added many new cases illustrating cross-cultural and sociopolitical issues. Some of the previous cases have been deleted and woven into the main body of the text, but a few of them remain in this chapter. All cases are real, in that they represent hypothetical or composite examples submitted by workshop participants or were the direct experiences of the authors in teaching, supervision, and practice. They were chosen for several reasons. First, each was strong in cross-cultural counseling themes that seem to occur with high frequency. Second, the issues in many of the cases transcend the specific situations. For example, several of the cross-cultural cases do not occur in a counseling and mental health setting, but they have important implications for it. Last, many of the case vignettes present issues that cut across not only settings, but population, age, and gender. While a situation may involve a college student, the themes may also apply to elementary school students as well.

The cases cover a diversity of racial/cultural minorities and raise general and specific counseling issues. Each is presented uninterrupted without commentary or analysis. These are followed by a series of questions intended to raise issues that students may not have considered, or to provoke thought and controversy. At the end of _all cases,_ the last section contains a revealing look at issues/conflicts keyed to the specific vignette.

We suggest readers first attempt to analyze the cases before studying the last section. We hope readers will find these cases helpful in integrating greater understanding of cross-cultural/multicultural counseling.

List of Cases

Case	Population
1. The Language "Problem"	Black American/Hispanic American
2. Can Culture Justify the Practices?	Vietnamese
3. I'm Not a Racist	Black American
4. Equality of Relationships	Hispanic American
5. Assert Yourself	American Indian
6. Culture Conflict	Asian American
7. Fitting In	Black American
8. Fair Grading	Hispanic American
9. Winning Isn't Everything—It's the Only Thing	American Indian
10. Stereotypes or Truths?	Asian American
11. Who's to Blame?	Hispanic American
12. Helping These People	Hispanic American
13. Burning Out	Black American
14. Dormitory Living	Laotian
15. Who Am I: Asian or White?	Asian American
16. Express Your Thoughts and Feelings	Asian American/Black American
17. Who Is the Victim?	Asian American/Black American
18. What They Want Is Not What They Need!	Black American

THE CASES

1. THE LANGUAGE "PROBLEM"

Mr. Bill Smith, a teacher of English, was having difficulty with many of the minority students in his section. Several of the Black and Hispanic students had done poorly in an essay test, and he was concerned about it. Mr. Smith had always emphasized to his students that learning proper English was vital to success in this society. Part of the minority students' problem was the constant emphasis on bilingual programs. It prevented them from acquiring the necessary language tools to succeed. Unless Hispanic students were able to overcome their Spanish-speaking background and Blacks get off their ridiculous "Black language" trip, they would always occupy the lower rungs of the ladder.

An especially poignant example of the "minority problem" occurred in his classroom one day. A Black student was having a casual conversation with another when the teacher overheard the student say, "What it is, man?" Mr. Smith immediately corrected the student by saying that the proper form was, "What is it, man?" Both students appeared offended and stated that they (a) knew what they meant, (b) were speaking Black language, and (c) were not interested in "White man's" talk. The teacher became angry and lectured the two on how their perverted form of English would doom them to failure. "You're not in Africa! You are in America, and in America we speak English. No wonder you people always do poorly in school."

Questions

1. Shouldn't minorities in the United States learn to speak "good" English if they want to succeed in this society?
2. What effect does the teacher's beliefs have upon minority students (self-image and self-esteem)?
3. Did Mr. Smith misunderstand the phrase, "What it is, man?" Is there such a thing as Black language?
4. If minority students are at a disadvantage in high school English courses, what can be done to rectify this inequity?
5. Where does responsibility for change lie? With the teacher? With the minority students? What needs to be done in this case?

2. CAN CULTURE JUSTIFY THE PRACTICES?

Mr. and Mrs. Nguyen and their four children left Vietnam in a boat with 36 other people. Several days later, they were set upon by Thai pirates. The occupants were all robbed of their belongings; some were killed, including two of the Nguyen's children. Nearly all the women were raped repeatedly. The trauma of the event is still very much with the Nguyen family who now reside in St. Paul, Minnesota. The event was most disturbing to Mr. Nguyen who had watched two of his children drown and his wife being raped. The pirates had beaten him severely and tied him to the boat railing during the rampage. As a result of his experiences, he continued to suffer feelings of guilt, suppressed rage, and nightmares.

The Nguyen family came to the attention of the school and social service agencies because of suspected child abuse. Then oldest child, Phuoc (age 12) had come to school one day with noticeable bruises on his back and down the spinal column. In addition, obvious scars from past injuries were observed on the child's upper and lower torso. His gym teacher had seen the bruises and scars and reported it to the school counselor immediately. The school nurse was contacted about the possibility of child abuse and a conference was held with Phuoc. He denied he had been hit by his parents and refused to remove his garments when requested to do so. Indeed, he became quite frightened and hysterical about taking his shirt off. Since there was still considerable doubt about whether this was a case of child abuse, the counselor decided to let the matter drop for the moment. Nevertheless, school personnel were alerted to this possibility.

Several weeks later, after four days of absence, Phuoc returned to school. The homeroom teacher noticed bruises on the forehead and nose bridge of Phuoc. When the incident was reported to the school office, the counselor immediately called the Child Protective Services to report a suspected case of child abuse.

Because of the heavy caseload experienced by the Child Protective Services, a social worker was unable to visit the family until weeks later. The social worker, Mr. P., had called the family and visited the home on a late Thursday afternoon. Mrs. Nguyen greeted Mr. P. upon his arrival. She appeared nervous, tense, and frightened. Her English was poor, and it was difficult to communicate with her. Since Mr. P. had specifically requested to also see Mr. Nguyen as well, he inquired about his whereabouts. Mrs. Nguyen answered that he was not feeling well and in the room downstairs. She said he was having "a bad day," had not been able to sleep last night, and was having flashbacks. In his present condition, he would not be helpful.

When Mr. P. asked about the bruises on her son, Phuoc, Mrs. Nguyen did not seem to understand what he was referring to. The social worker explained in detail the reason for his visit. Mrs. Nguyen explained that the scars were due to the beating given her children by the Thai pirates. She became very emotional about the topic and broke into tears.

While this had some credibility, Mr. P. explained that there were fresh bruises on Phuoc's body as well. Mrs. Nguyen seemed confused, denied there were new injuries, and denied they would hurt Phuoc. The social worker persisted in pressing Mrs. Nguyen about the new injuries when she suddenly looked up and said, "Thùôc Nam." It was obvious that Mrs. Nguyen now understood what Mr. P. was referring to. When asked to clarify what she meant by the phrase, Mrs. Nguyen pointed at several thin bamboo sticks and a bag of coins wrapped tightly in a white cloth. It looked like a blackjack! She then pointed downstairs in the direction of the husband's room. It was obvious from the gestures of Mrs. Nguyen that her husband had used these to beat her son.

Questions

1. Was this a clear case of child abuse? What evidence do we have that Phuoc was being beaten at home?

2. Can you argue in the opposite direction that it was not a case of child abuse? What are some possible explanations?

3. Can you think of any cultural factors that might affect your assessment of the case? What is "Thùôc Nam?"

4. In looking at this case, what impact do you believe their experience in leaving Vietnam may have on their current adjustments and reactions?

5. In reading this vignette, what other information would you like to obtain in order to properly assess that case? Why would you want that information?

6. If it is found that there are culturally accepted practices that resulted in the bruises, would it make any difference to you? In other words, if a practice produces injuries to a child, can it be justified on a cultural basis?

3. I'M NOT A RACIST

Miriam Cohen, a young, single, attractive White counselor had recently graduated from a prestigious Eastern university in Counseling Psychology. Because of her expressed desire to work with the "disadvantaged," she accepted a position as a psychologist in a community mental health center, whose catchment area included a heavy concentration of Black clients. Some of her White friends had suggested that she accept one of numerous other positions she had been offered. Ms. Cohen decided against going elsewhere, because "these people need help." Her professors commended her public service interest and "social justice" commitment.

Within a period of several weeks, Ms. Cohen experienced two rather disturbing experiences in working with Black clients. The first involved a Black couple who had come in because of "marital difficulties." She found it extremely difficult to establish rapport with them and to get them to open up about their problems. They seemed to view her with suspicion and implied that she could not possibly understand them since she was White. During one session, the husband mentioned that he played in a local jazz band, which took him away from home frequently. His wife did not like his being away at night, and she was fearful that he was "fooling around" with a female member of the band.

Since Ms. Cohen's undergraduate major had been dramatic arts (she even had a course on Contributions of Black Entertainers), she saw this as a good opportunity to establish a sense of commonality between herself and her Black clients. She directed the conversation toward Black movie stars, singers, and athletes. At this juncture, the wife became noticeably agitated and stated, "Stop that shit, honey! You're not Black and you never will be."

Ms. Cohen was surprised at the wife's reaction and apologized to the couple for offending them. She tried to explain that she was just trying to establish a working relationship with them and that she was not unfamiliar with Black experiences. "After all, I'm a Jew, and I know what oppression is. I'm also a woman, like you, and have experienced sex discrimination as well." At this point, the couple rose from their seats, stated that they were wasting time, and left the room.

The second incident occurred with a young Black male client who had been ordered by the court to undergo counseling for "wife beating." He was a handsome muscular individual who obviously prided himself on his physical appearance. He had been divorced from his wife for nearly a year and had consistently denied that he physically abused her. He stated that he had pleaded guilty and accepted probation and counseling because "those Whites will give me a bum rap if it goes to trial." He had been married to a White woman who he claimed had "used him," and who he had discovered was a racist.

"All of you Whites are racist. What do you care about me?" At these statements Ms. Cohen tried to assure the client that she did care about Black people and that she wouldn't be here unless she cared. The anger and agitation seemed to drain from the client when this was said, and he seemed to open up more fully.

He talked about his boyhood experiences of discrimination, how he had been hurt by his ex-wife, how he couldn't find a good job because of racism, and how he felt so lonely and isolated. "Sometimes I feel like I'm worthless, that no one cares about me. What woman would want an unemployed Black man?" Again, Ms. Cohen reassured the client that everyone was worthwhile, and that he was no different.

Looking up at Ms. Cohen, the Black client asked, "Do you really mean that?" Ms. Cohen responded in the affirmative. This was followed by a series of other questions, "Do you think women would find me attractive? Do you find me attractive?"

While Ms. Cohen answered all of these questions honestly, she felt very uncomfortable at this point. She was totally unprepared for what happened next. The client moved his chair next to her, placed his right hand on her knee and asked, "Do you really like me?" Ms. Cohen recalls that she felt frozen and trapped. She did not answer the question, but firmly removed the hand from her knee and shifted her chair away. At these actions, the following exchange took place.

CLIENT: You Whites are all the same, say one thing, mean another! You're just another racist bitch!

Ms. COHEN: I'm not racist. This is a counseling relationship . . .

CLIENT: You think I'm hitting on you. Well, maybe I am, what's wrong with a man liking a woman. I'm not against interracial relationships, but you seem to be!

Ms. COHEN: There's nothing wrong with it, but our relationship is strictly professional . . . I mean, it would not be therapeutic.

CLIENT: [*Lowering voice*] You mean if we didn't have a counseling relationship you would consider going out with a Black man?

Ms. COHEN: Yes, well . . . maybe.

CLIENT: Well, then I'd like to request seeing another counselor. That way our counseling relationship won't get in the way!

Questions

1. Why did Ms. Cohen's attempt to relate to the Black couple fail? Why did her mention of Black entertainers and use of Black phrases seem to turn the couple off?

2. Doesn't Ms. Cohen have a valid point that Jews and women are also oppressed groups? Shouldn't this allow us to understand and relate to one another in a more meaningful fashion? Why did it seem to have the opposite effect?

3. How did the "prove to me you're not racist" issues get played out by both Ms. Cohen and the Black clients? What type of testing is going on in the two incidents described above? How did the counselor fail both of them?

4. What attitudes and insights are needed by Ms. Cohen in order to work effectively with Black clients? Is it possible for a White counselor not to be racist?

5. As a counselor working with these cases, what would you have done and why?

4. EQUALITY OF RELATIONSHIPS

Esteban and Carmen O., a Puerto Rican couple, sought help at a community mental health clinic in the Miami area. Mr. O. had recently come to the United States with only a high school education, but had already acquired several successful printing shops. Carmen, his wife, was born and raised in Florida. The two had a whirlwind courtship that resulted in a marriage after only a three-month acquaintance. She described her husband as being handsome, outspoken, confident, and a strong person who could be affectionate and sensitive. Carmen used the term "machismo" several times to describe Esteban.

The couple had sought counseling after a series of rather heated arguments over his long work hours and his tendency to "go drinking with the boys" after work. She missed his companionship, which was constantly present during their courtship, but now seemed strangely absent. Carmen, who had graduated from the local college with a BA in business, had been working as a secretary and was on the verge of being promoted to an administrative assistant when she met Esteban. She resigned her position prior to her marriage, with the urging of Esteban who stated that "it was beneath her" and that he was capable of supporting both of them.

Both had agreed to seek outside help with their marital difficulties, and they had been assigned to Dr. Carla B., a White woman psychologist.

The initial session with the couple was characterized by Esteban doing most of the talking. Indeed, Dr. B. was quite put off by what she characterized as Esteban's arrogant attitude. He frequently spoke for his wife and interrupted Dr. B. often, not allowing her to finish questions or make comments. Esteban stated that he understood his wife's desire to spend more time with him, but that he needed to seek financial security for "my children." While the couple did not have any children at the present time, it was obvious that Esteban expected to have many with his wife. He jokingly stated, "After three or four boys, she won't have time to miss me."

It was obvious that his remark had a strong impact on Carmen as she appeared quite surprised. Dr. B., who during this session had been trying to give Carmen an opportunity to express her thoughts and feelings, seized the opportunity. She asked Carmen how she felt about having children. As Carmen began to answer, Esteban blurted out quickly, "Of course, she wants children. All women want children."

At this point Dr. B. (obviously angry) confronted Esteban about his tendency to answer or speak for his wife and the inconsiderate manner in which he kept interrupting everyone. Esteban became noticeably angry and stated, "No woman lectures Esteban. Why aren't you at home caring for your husband? What you need is a real man."

While Dr. B. did not fall for what she considered to be a baiting tactic she was, nevertheless, quite angry. The session was terminated shortly thereafter.

During the next few weeks, Carmen came alone to the sessions without her husband, who refused to return. Their sessions consisted of dealing with Esteban's sexist attitude and the ways she could be her "own person." Dr. B. stressed the fact that Carmen had an equal right in the decisions made in the home, that she should not allow anyone to oppress her, that she did not need her husband's approval to return to her former job, and that having children was an equal and joint responsibility.

During this period, the couple separated from one another. It was a difficult period for Carmen who came for therapy regularly to talk about her need "to be my own person," a phrase used often by Dr. B. Carmen and Esteban finally divorced after only a year of marriage.

Questions

1. What egalitarian attitude held by the therapist may be in conflict with Puerto Rican values concerning male-female relationships and the division of responsibilities in the household? Are these values sexist?

2. Is it right to impose one's values and beliefs upon a culturally different group no matter how strongly we believe in them (women should have equal rights and not be oppressed)?

3. How might the gender of the counselor affect his/her credibility when working with culturally different clients? In this case, what Puerto Rican cultural values might make it difficult for Esteban to see a White female psychologist?

4. What does the concept "machismo" mean?

5. If you were the counselor, what course of action would you take? Why?

5. ASSERT YOURSELF

Sylvia Echohawk is a 29-year-old American Indian woman who works for one of the major automobile manufacturing companies in the United States. The company has recently implemented an affirmative action program designed to open up jobs for minorities. The personnel director, a White male counseling psychologist, is in charge of it. Sylvia, who was hired under the affirmative action program, is referred to him by her immediate supervisor because of "frequent tardiness." Also, the supervisor informs the psychologist that other employees take advantage of Sylvia. She goes out of her way to help them, shares her lunches with them, and even lends them money. Several times during the lunch hours, other employees have borrowed her car to run errands. The supervisor feels that Sylvia needs to actively deal with her passive-aggressive means of handling anger (tardiness), to set limits on others, and to be able to assert her rights.

In an interview with Sylvia, the psychologist notices several things about her behavior. She is low-keyed, restrained in behavior, avoids eye contact, and finds it difficult to verbalize her thoughts and feelings. After several meetings, the psychologist concludes that Sylvia would benefit from assertion training. She is placed in such a group during regular working hours but fails to show up for meetings after attending the first one. Additionally, Sylvia's supervisor informs the psychologist that she has turned in a two-week resignation notice.

Questions

1. Is it possible that American-Indian communication styles are leading to inaccurate assumptions made by the counselor?

2. In what ways would the following values shared by American Indians affect both the work setting and counseling approach (cooperation, sharing, temporal perspective, and harmony)?

3. What does an affirmative action program mean? What does it mean to you? How do you feel about it?

4. What obligations do organizations have in adapting their practices to fit the needs of culturally different workers? What obligations does the culturally different worker have to adjust?

5. What can be done on both an individual and institutional level to help Sylvia?

6. CULTURE CONFLICT

David Chan is a 21-year-old student majoring in electrical engineering. He first sought counseling because he was having increasing study problems and was receiving failing grades. These academic difficulties became apparent during the first quarter of his senior year and were accompanied by headaches, indigestion, and insomnia. Since he had been an excellent student in the past, David felt that his lowered academic performance was caused by illness. However, a medical examination failed to reveal any organic disorder.

During the initial interview, David seemed depressed and anxious. He was difficult to counsel because he would respond to inquiries with short, polite statements and would seldom volunteer information about himself. He avoided any statements that involved feelings and presented his problem as strictly an education one. Although he never expressed it directly, David seemed to doubt the value of counseling and needed much reassurance and feedback about his performance in the interview.

After several sessions, the counselor was able to discern one of David's major concerns. David did not like engineering and felt pressured by his parents to go into this field. Yet, he was unable to take responsibility for any of his own actions, was excessively dependent on his parents, and was afraid to express the anger he felt toward them. Using the Gestalt "empty chair technique," the counselor had David pretend that his parents were seated in empty chairs opposite him. The counselor encouraged him to express his true feelings toward them. While initially he found it very difficult to do, David was able to ventilate some of his true feelings under constant encouragement by the counselor. Unfortunately, the following sessions with Dave proved unproductive in that he seemed more withdrawn and guilt-ridden than ever.

Questions

1. What cultural forces may be affecting David's manner of expressing psychological conflicts?

2. What possible unwarranted interpretations are being made about David Chan?

3. What stereotypes do you have about Asian-Americans? How may stereotypes affect the holder of the stereotypes' attitudes and behaviors? How may they affect the minority individual?

4. How may the counseling techniques used by the counselor clash with the traditional Asian cultural values? With what effect?

5. If you were the counselor, what course of action would you take? Why?

7. FITTING IN

Sonya Johnson is a 15-year-old Black female student attending a predominantly White high school. Her parents had recently moved to a new community because her father had been offered a promotion in a national computer firm. Prior to her move, Sonya and her parents had lived in a middle-class racially mixed neighborhood, where she attended a school with many other Blacks. The parents had been apprehensive about the move because the new community was primarily White. They were very concerned about the potential isolation they would experience as a family. Yet, Mr. Johnson's promotion was too good an opportunity to turn down, so he reluctantly accepted.

While Sonya's grades dropped significantly in the new school, the parents felt that they would improve once she became acclimated. Indeed, they were heartened when Sonya came home one day and stated she was considering tryouts for the cheerleading team. Up until then, Sonya had appeared very isolated from school activities and occasionally appeared depressed. She had found it difficult to make friends, seldom expressed interest in outside activities, and had recently become involved with a small group of students who called themselves "The Shakers." Mr. and Mrs. Johnson disapproved of the group, but found it difficult to talk with Sonya about them; they appeared to be her only friends.

During the next few days, Sonya conscientiously practiced her cheerleading yells and choreographic moves. She was not unfamiliar with these activities because her older sister had been a cheerleader. Thus, she appeared to have a distinct advantage over some of her fellow classmates.

Several days before the tryouts, Sonya abruptly stopped practicing. When asked about her sudden change, Sonya mentioned that she was no longer interested in competing for one of the "stupid" positions. The parents were quite surprised, and pressed her for the reasons. The daughter refused to elaborate and became quite angry at her parents. The parents decided to drop the matter, but contacted the school for a parent/counselor conference about their daughter.

Mr. and Mrs. Johnson were referred to Sonya's freshman counselor who seemed reluctant to see both of them. Mrs. Beale, the counselor, greeted both of them upon their arrival at the school office. She appeared slightly tense and nervous as she inquired about the reasons they requested a conference. When the Johnsons expressed some of their concerns about Sonya, Mrs. Beale stated, "I'm not surprised. We've been having problems with Sonya from the first day."

She went on to explain that Sonya did not "fit in" at the school, that she was frequently disruptive in her classes, that she was argumentative and intimidating to other students, and that she was disrespectful and prone to use abusive language with her teachers. At this point, Mrs. Johnson asked why they had not been informed of these problems earlier, to which Mrs. Beale responded, "I would never have guessed that Sonya would have such concerned parents. My experience . . . well . . . some parents don't care, and it's useless to talk to them anyway."

As the session progressed, it became clear that Sonya had taken up with a group of other students (The Shakers) who were considered the fringe elements of the school. They were responsible for schoolyard pranks, baiting other students into fights, and suspected of peddling drugs. Their name, "The Shakers," was derived from their stated desire to "shake up the school."

In addition, the parents discovered through the counselor that Sonya had been advised by the activity's director that she should withdraw from the cheerleading competitions. When pressed for why this advice was given, Mrs. Beale stated that the director felt Sonya did not have the qualities required to make a "good cheerleader."

These statements enraged Sonya's father, who demanded to see the principal immediately. He confronted the counselor about her insensitivities, about the activity director's bias, and about the school's need to change. Mrs. Beale, who now appeared quite frightened, pleaded with Mr. Johnson to calm down. They had to discuss this in a rational manner if help was to be given to the daughter.

Questions

1. What must it be like for a Black student in a predominantly White school? What are some of the sources of stress and strain that a minority student might encounter? Could some of these account for Sonya's behavior?

2. What unwarranted assumptions about Blacks or Black families might the school staff be harboring? How might they be acted out in Sonya's case?

3. How might communication-style differences affect teachers' and students' perception of Sonya (intimidating, argumentative, abusive language, not the right personality for cheerleading, etc.)?

4. When the counselor said Sonya "did not fit in," what did it mean? Is it always the sole responsibility of the minority person to "fit in?"

5. If you were the counselor, how would you handle this situation from an individual and institutional perspective? Why?

8. FAIR GRADING

Many minority students are at a disadvantage when competing with White students for higher grades. Most White students are accustomed to the grading system, objective and essay exams, and are more fluent in standard English. In addition, minority students must often contend with the cultural adjustments inherent in a predominantly White university.

While these factors are not directly related to the student's academic performance, they certainly have an effect. Some well-meaning faculty, who are aware of this inequity, attempt to compensate for it by giving minority students higher grades than their work would ordinarily merit; other minority students sometimes use this argument in trying to have their grades changed. Other faculty feel they have no choice but to hold *all* their students accountable for the same level of academic achievement.

An example of this situation occurred recently with a Hispanic student who received a failing grade in her course. She was a freshman student already on academic probation. An "F" would result in having the student dropped from the university.

The student went to her professor asking to receive a "C" or "D" in the course. The student believed that she knew the material even though she did badly on both exams. The professor refused to change the grade unless the student had a legitimate excuse.

As a result of the impasse, the Hispanic student's EOP advisor interceded on her behalf. The male counselor explained that the new student was having extreme difficulties adjusting to the university, that she had come through the university's affirmative action program, and that she needed more time to work out these adjustment difficulties. Although reluctant at first, the professor offered the student the option of (a) withdrawing retroactively even though the deadline had passed, or (b) doing extra work to elevate her grade.

Questions

1. Did this minority student get more help than a White student might have received under similar circumstances? If yes, how can it be justified?

2. Should minority students receive "special treatment" in helping them adjust to university requirements?

3. What were the other alternatives that could have been followed by the minority student, EOP advisor, faculty member, or faculty adviser?

4. Why do you suppose the student didn't seek out help earlier than she did, and how would you encourage minority students to seek help?

5. If you had the power to determine the course of action, what would you have done? Why?

9. WINNING ISN'T EVERYTHING—IT'S THE ONLY THING

Janet Myers was having problems with Johnny Lonetree and Peter Echohawk, two American-Indian students in her class. They did not appear unintelligent, but were quite withdrawn, sullen, and passive. What irked her most was their tendency to always appear late, thereby interrupting her lectures. They seldom participated in class and when called upon would make irrelevant and tangential contributions.

Because Ms. Myers graded on contributions and discussions from students, both Johnny and Peter did poorly in point accumulations. Even her attempts to explain the "bell"-shaped curve to them for grading failed to change their lack of involvement in the course. The point totals and grades were always posted in a notebook open to student inspection.

Ms. Myers knew the two students would fail unless a miraculous change occurred. The next half of the course consisted of a series of debates among "hypothetical philosophers" role-played by groups of students. For example, the class would be divided into teams representing philosophers like Aristotle, Socrates, Plato, and so forth, who would debate each other over issues of life. Scores obtained by teams were dependent upon an individual student's being able to win a point over his/her classmate counterpart. Perhaps Johnny and Peter will be able to do better in this method of learning.

Questions

1. What American-Indian cultural values may be in direct conflict with educational values?

2. How would you characterize the teaching method by Ms. Myers? Is it representative of our education system?

3. What form of teaching might the teacher consider that would be more consistent with American-Indian values?

4. What responsibilities should professors and our education institutions exercise to provide alternative methods of learning in our pluralistic society?

5. If you could devise a culturally sensitive educational approach for American Indians, what would it consist of?

10. STEREOTYPES OR TRUTHS?

Mr. Marcus Wilson, Director of Personnel for Lazertech, was greatly disturbed by a recent study commissioned by his office. The career survey was initiated to determine employee satisfaction with their work and careers within the firm. Because a large number of workers were Asian Americans, Mr. Wilson noticed that many of them responded in a similar manner. For example, many of the Asian workers were unhappy about the lack of promotion within the company, felt they were victims of discrimination, felt they were not promoted when otherwise qualified, and felt that stereotypes from White peers/management were used as reasons to prevent their promotion to the managerial ranks.

As a result of the survey, Mr. Wilson shared the findings with several of the management team, who all happened to be White. The team tended to downplay the importance of bias in merit reviews and promotion. While they all agreed that Asian workers made good technical workers and team members, they thought that the reasons were real and objective. For example, they pointed out how some Asians seemed to have major difficulty communicating in oral and written form. Also: (1) They tend to be passive and make poor leaders. (2) They were not skilled in interpersonal relationships. (3) They had difficulty being open and frank in talking about their thoughts and feelings.

Although greatly reassured that the company was not biased in their review process, Mr. Wilson felt that such widespread dissatisfaction among Asian workers was counterproductive to the goals of the company. He felt a need to initiate some follow-up action to deal with these concerns, but was unsure of what course to take.

Questions

1. In your own knowledge and experiences, how justified are the concerns of the Asian-American workers?

2. Do you agree or disagree with the evaluation of the management team? Why?

3. How would you define stereotypes, and how may they affect merit reviews and promotion decisions?

4. What cultural factors may account for the reaction of management?

5. If you were the director of personnel, what course of action would you take? Why?

11. WHO'S TO BLAME

Felix Sanchez is a second-generation, 19-year-old freshman attending a major university in northern California. He is the oldest of five siblings, all currently residing in Colorado. Felix's father works as a delivery driver for a brewery, and his mother is employed part-time as a housekeeper. Both parents have worked long and hard to make ends meet and have been instrumental in sending their eldest son to college.

Felix is the first in his entire family (including relatives) to have ever attended an institution of higher education. It is generally understood that the parents do not have the financial resources to send Felix's other brothers and sisters to college. If they are to make it, they would need to do it on their own or obtain help elsewhere. As a result, Felix found a part-time job without the knowledge of his parents in order to secretly save money for his siblings' future education.

During the last two quarters, Felix has been having extreme difficulties in his classes. Felix's inability to obtain grades better than C's or D's greatly discouraged him. Last quarter, he was placed on academic probation and the thought of failing evoked a great sense of guilt and shame in him. While he had originally intended to become a social worker and had looked forward to his coursework, he now felt depressed, lonely, alienated, and guilt-ridden. It was not so much his inability to do the work, but the meaninglessness of his courses, the materials in the texts, and the manner in which his courses were taught. Worse yet, he just could not relate to the students in his dormitory and all the rules and regulations.

At the beginning of his last quarter, Felix was referred by his EOP adviser to the university counseling center. Felix's counselor, Mr. Blackburne, seemed sincere enough but only made him feel worse. After several sessions, the counselor suggested possible reasons for Felix's inability to do well in school. First, it was possible that he was "not college material" and had to face that fact. Second, his constant "sacrificing" of his time (part-time work) to help his siblings contributed to his poor grades. Third, Felix's depression and alienation was symptomatic of deeper more serious intrapsychic conflicts.

Questions

1. In what ways may the counselor be blaming Felix (as an individual) rather than external forces as the cause of his problems?

2. How may teaching styles, material and text used, and so forth, be the source of Felix's feeling of loneliness, isolation, depression, and meaninglessness?

3. How may institutional rules and regulations clash with concepts of "personalismo?"

4. Is the counselor perceiving traditional Hispanic family obligation as a source of deficit? What evidence do we have of this, and what effect might it have on Felix?

5. If you were the counselor, what course of action would you take? Why?

12. HELPING THESE PEOPLE

One of the most difficult cases I have ever treated was that of a Mexican-American family in southern California. Fernando M. was a 56-year-old recent immigrant to the United States. He had been married some 35 years to Refugio, his wife, and had fathered ten children. Only four of his children, three sons and one daughter, resided with him.

Fernando was born in a small village in Mexico and resided there until three years ago when he moved to California. He was not unfamiliar with California, having worked as a "bracero" for most of his adult life. He would make frequent visits to the United States during annual harvest seasons.

The M. family resided in a small, old, unpainted, rented house on the back of a dirt lot that was sparsely furnished with their belongings. The family did not own a car nor was public transportation available in their neighborhood. While their standard of living was far below poverty levels, the family appeared quite pleased at their relative affluence when compared with their life in Mexico.

The presenting complaints concerned Fernando. He heard threatening voices, was often disoriented, stated the belief that someone was planning to kill him, and that something evil was about to happen. He became afraid to leave his home, was in poor physical health, and possessed a decrepit appearance, which made him essentially unemployable.

When the M. family entered the clinic, I was asked to see them because the bilingual therapist scheduled that day had called in sick. I was hoping that either Fernando or Refugio would speak enough English to understand the situation. As luck would have it, neither could understand me, nor I them. It became apparent, however, that the two older children could understand English. Since the younger one seemed more fluent, I called upon him to act as a translator during our first session. I noticed that the parents seemed reluctant to participate with the younger son and for some time the discussion between the family was quite animated. Sensing something wrong and desiring to get the session underway, I interrupted the family and asked the son who spoke the best English, what was wrong. He hesitated for a second, but assured me everything was fine.

During the course of our first session, it became obvious to me that Fernando was seriously disturbed. He appeared frightened, tense, and, if the interpretations from his son were correct, hallucinating. I suggested to Refugio that she consider hospitalizing her husband, but she was adamant against this course of action. I could sense her nervousness and fear that I would initiate action in having her husband incarcerated. I reassured her that no action would be taken without a follow-up evaluation and suggested that she return later in the week with Fernando. Refugio said that it would be difficult since Fernando was phobic about leaving his home. She had had to coerce him into coming this time and did not feel she could do it again. I looked at Fernando directly and stated, "Fernando, I know how hard it is for you to come here, but we really want to help you. Do you think you could possibly come one more time? Dr. Escobedo (the bilingual therapist) will be here with me, and he can communicate with you directly." The youngest son interpreted.

The M. family never returned for another session and their failure to show up has greatly bothered me. Since that time I have talked with several Hispanic psychologists who have pointed out cross-cultural issues that I was not aware of then. Some questions which I have since asked myself are listed below for your consideration.

Questions

1. Was it a serious blunder for me to see the M. family or to continue to see them in the session when I could not speak Spanish? Should I have waited until Dr. Escobedo returned?

2. At the time it seemed like a good idea to have one of the children interpret for me and the family. What possible cultural implications might this have in the Mexican-American family? Do you think one can obtain an accurate translation through family interpreters? What are some of the pitfalls?

3. I tried to be informal with the family in order to put them at ease. Yet, some of my colleagues have stated that how I address clients (last names or first names) may be important. When I used the first names of both husband and wife, what possible cultural interpretation from the family may have resulted?

4. I saw Mr. M.'s symptoms as indications of serious pathology. What other explanations might I have entertained? Should I have so

blatantly suggested hospitalization? How do Hispanics perceive mental health issues?

5. Knowing that Mr. M. had difficulty leaving home, should I have considered some other treatment avenues? If so, what may they have been?

13. BURNING OUT

Mark Bennett, a recent Black graduate of Michigan State University, received his M.A. in counseling last year. In September, he was offered a counseling position at a California high school. The school had been under recent pressures from students and a few educators to hire a member of a minority group.

During his first months of counseling, Mark became painfully aware that approximately one-half of the faculty had resented his being hired, and another one-fourth seemed indifferent to him. While the others appeared sympathetic to his concerns, most recommended that he "not rock the boat," because he did not have tenure.

While passing a fellow counselor's office one day, Mark overheard a conversation in which Mr. Jay, a senior White counselor, made some very disparaging racist remarks about Black students in the school. It was his contention the Blacks lacked abstract conceptual reasoning and could be expected to do poorly in school. The only way they could get into college was through reverse racism quotas.

Angered by these statements, Mark confronted his colleague, but was only accused of eavesdropping and being too biased and idealistic to make adequate judgments. When Mark appealed to the principal, whom he had considered highly liberated and enlightened, he suddenly realized that he was really quite rigid and opinionated.

Mark's anger became so intense that he decided to voice his opinions strongly at a faculty meeting. Although the principal and faculty listened cordially and promised assessment of the "bias in the counseling program," nothing was done during that quarter. All inquiries were met during the following quarter with, "We are studying the situation." Besides this state of affairs, Mark's proposals for community outreach programs to the minority students were delayed for action or critically evaluated as "unworkable." Mark became increasingly isolated by faculty members, was often criticized at meetings, and was placed on many innocuous committees. When he turned down several "useless" appointments, the principal called him to task for not being more involved in the counseling program and the school.

When Mark received a negative year-end evaluation, he made an appointment to see the principal. The principal outlined Mark's disinterest in serving on committees and recounted his lack of cooperation with faculty as reasons for his poor evaluation. When told that his continued employment would prove nearly impossible unless he changed his "attitude," Mark became angry and threatened to resign. In a cold tone, the principal asked for his resignation in writing. The following night, several Black students came to his home and begged him to stay.

Questions

1. What should Mark do? Should he resign or heed the pleas of the students? Why?

2. Is Mark's predicament a common experience encountered by many minority professionals?

3. How were Mark's concerns, values, and beliefs being invalidated?

4. What were some of the things Mark did that made his desires to effect change difficult?

5. What other strategies could Mark have implemented in achieving his goals? What type of systems approach could he take in order to gain power?

14. DORMITORY LIVING

In many ways the dorm provides an ideal atmosphere for maximizing the nonformal educational experiences for White students through conversation and contact with international and minority students. In many cases, however, dorm living presents its own serious problems for the student's adjustment. The setting may be too radically different from back home for the student to make the adjustment. The dorm food may be unacceptable, either for religious reasons or because it is simply too different from the food back home. Sometimes students cook in their rooms, which is usually not encouraged by the dorm. Some students make other adjustments to improve dorm living for themselves, but in some cases the student becomes even more intensely lonely in the midst of bustling dorm activity around him/her. Often the minority or international student responds not by seeking counseling, advice, or help, but by withdrawing and seeing few persons. The student will sometimes almost drop out of sight and not even be noticed in his or her absence by the very busy students around him/her.

A White U.S. male student rooming with a Laotian immigrant in a university residence hall went to the resident advisor requesting a room change. The Laotian student had already had two previous roommates who had moved out, so the advisor was very concerned. The Laotian student was always having persons from his home country come in to eat strange-smelling food. They would cook in the room and then talk for hours each evening in their own language. The U.S. student didn't want to hurt his roommate's feelings, but it was impossible to live or study in that setting. He couldn't get used to the weird-smelling food and did not understand the Laotian language. The White student felt that the Laotian students were occasionally talking about him, and he became irritated and angry. Every time he tried to get a conversation going with his roommate, there would be awkward and embarrassing pauses since the roommate was normally very quiet. The U.S. student was ready to give up and wanted to move in with another White student where he would feel more at home. The resident advisor had tried talking with the Laotian student previously, but he insisted that everything was fine.

Questions

1. Why might the Laotian student hang onto fellow country persons as friends rather than go out and meet more White students? Likewise, why would the student cook in his room when the cafeteria provided all meals?

2. What possible cultural factors would account for the Laotian student's denial that anything was wrong between him and his roommate?

3. When you see a group of minorities clustered together, how do you react when they are speaking another language? How did the White student react?

4. Is it sufficient for an institution to accept minority students without adequate preparation for the possible impact of this?

5. What educational changes need to be made in order to sensitize students, staff, faculty, and administrators to the impact of cultural diversity?

6. If you were the resident advisor, what course of action would you take? Why?

15. WHO AM I: ASIAN OR WHITE?

Janet T. is a 21-year-old senior majoring in sociology. She was born and raised in Portland, Oregon, where she had limited contact with members of her own race. Her father, a second-generation Chinese American, is a 53-year-old doctor. Her mother, age 44, is a housewife. Janet is the second oldest of three children and has an older brother (currently in medical school) and a younger brother, age 17.

Janet came for counseling suffering from a severe depressive reaction manifested by feelings of worthlessness, suicidal ideation, and an inability to concentrate. She was unable to recognize the cause of her depression throughout the initial interviews. However, much light was shed on the problem when the counselor noticed an inordinate amount of hostility directed toward him. When inquiries were made about the hostility, it became apparent that Janet greatly resented being seen by a Chinese psychologist. Janet suspected that she had been assigned a Chinese counselor because of her own race. When confronted with this fact, Janet openly expressed scorn for "anything which reminds me of Chinese." Apparently, she felt very hostile toward Chinese customs and especially the Chinese male, whom she described as introverted, passive, and sexually unattractive.

Further exploration revealed a long-standing history of attempts to deny her Chinese ancestry by associating only with Caucasians. When in high school, Janet would frequently bring home White boyfriends, which greatly upset her parents. It was as though she blamed her parents for being born a Chinese, and she used this method to hurt them.

During her college career, Janet became involved in two affairs with Caucasians, both ending unsatisfactorily and abruptly. The last breakup occurred four months before, when the boy's parents threatened to cut off financial support for their son unless he ended the relationship. Apparently, objections arose because of Janet's race.

Although not completely conscious of it, Janet was having increased difficulty denying her racial heritage. The breakup of her last affair made her realize that she was Chinese and not fully accepted by all segments of society. At first, she vehemently and bitterly denounced the Chinese for her present dilemma. Later, much of her hostility was turned inward against herself. Feeling alienated from her own subculture and not fully accepted by American society, she experienced an identity crisis. This resulted in feelings of worthlessness and depression. It was at this point that Janet came for counseling.

Questions

1. What negative attitudes and/or assumptions did Janet make concerning her own race? Where do you think they came from?

2. Is there any connection between Janet's hostility toward the Chinese counselor and her associating mainly with Caucasians? Would she prefer a White counselor? Why?

3. Can you apply minority identity development theory in explaining Janet's behavior?

4. What is the cause of Janet's dilemma? Does it reside in her or in the sociopolitical environment?

5. If you were the counselor, what course of action would you take? Why?

16. EXPRESS YOUR THOUGHTS AND FEELINGS

A White female high school counselor has just undergone some group-dynamics training seminars and received specialized training in conducting group counseling. She has decided to run several groups in her own school along certain topical areas—study groups, career planning, and personal problems. While the first two groups are voluntary, the last one is formed on the basis of referrals from teachers. Since the counselor's high school is racially mixed, most of the groups also reflect this composition. However, the counselor noticed that very few Asian-American students were represented in the last group.

After several months of running two study skills, two career planning, and three personal-problem groups, the counselor began to see a pattern emerging.

While the Black and White students tended to be fairly verbal in their groups, the Asian-American students did not participate (verbally) as often. This was especially true of groups dealing with personal problems. Another observation was that the Asian-American students were not cooperating with her request that they confront others in the group and freely express their feelings in order to avoid misunderstandings.

As a result, the counselor redoubled her efforts to force participation from the Asian-American students. This, she felt, would help them get over their shyness and inhibitions. To implement this goal, she devised several role-playing situations in the group.

Questions

1. What might be some cultural factors affecting Asian-American students' response to the types of group (personal versus career) being offered?

2. How might communication-style differences among the three groups affect the *process* and *outcome* of the group experiences?

3. Can you identify "group-counseling values" or characteristics that may clash with the traditional cultural upbringing of Asian-Americans?

4. Will role-playing help the counselor achieve her goal?

5. If you were the counselor, what course of action would you take? Why?

17. WHO IS THE VICTIM?

A male international student who had just arrived at the university from an extremely conservative culture was welcomed by a group of U.S. and international students and invited to move into their International House. One of the U.S. female students was particularly warm toward him, and the two of them enjoyed talking with one another alone for hours at a time. The female student felt sorry for the international student and wanted to help him feel more at home. He, on the other hand, had never been alone with any other female outside his family and was encouraged by her friendliness.

One night after he had been here for about a week, he knocked on her door late at night and asked to talk with her. She had been sleeping and was wearing only a nightgown. Because he sounded so distressed, she let him into her room to find out what was bothering him. Without a great deal of preliminary explanation, he began to put his arms around hers and pushed her back on her bed. The more she resisted, the more excited he became until finally another resident, wakened by the noise, came into the room and intervened. The girl was both frightened and angry, threatening to charge the international student with attempted rape. The international student was also angry and felt she had trapped him into an embarrassing situation. By letting him into the room at that hour, he assumed she wanted to have sex with him. The other residents in the International House threatened to expel both persons.

Questions

1. Who is the victim in this case study? The White female student? The international student? Why?
2. What unwarranted assumptions did each student make?
3. How did the international student interpret the female student's behavior? How did the female student interpret the international student's behavior?
4. How might verbal/nonverbal communication influence the student's interpretation?
5. If you were in charge of the international exchange program, what might you do to prevent misunderstandings such as these?

18. WHAT THEY WANT IS NOT WHAT THEY NEED!

Supposing that you are a newly hired White counseling psychologist at a large public university working in their counseling center. It is nationally known as a fertile training ground for interns doing work in the area of socioemotional problems. The orientation of the center is heavily clinical (personal/emotional counseling) and uses the traditional one-to-one counselor-client model. Indeed, you quickly sense that a status hierarchy exists among the staff. At the top of the pecking order are those who do predominantly clinical work and at the bottom are the educational/vocational counselors. While the university is comprised of 10% Asians, 7% Blacks, and 2% others, very few Third World students are ever seen at the service.

One day, a Black student is given an appointment with you. He appears guarded, mistrustful, and frustrated when talking about his reasons for coming. He talks about his failing grades and the need to get some help in learning study skills or some advice about changing majors. Being trained in a nondirective approach, you feel both uncomfortable and resentful that he is demanding advice and information from you. You do not feel that your role is as an information-giver or a teacher. You see his attempts and requests as avoiding responsibility for making decisions. Instead, you decide to focus on his feelings and help him clarify them.

As taught by your professor, you begin to adroitly reflect his thoughts and feelings. As the hour progresses, you can sense an increasing tension between the two of you. When you decide to reflect his apparent tension and feelings of antagonism, the Black student angrily retorts, "Forget it, man! I don't have time to play your silly games." He then abruptly gets up and leaves the office.

Questions

1. What differential impact might the center's traditional one-to-one and clinical orientation have on minority students?
2. Why are minority students not coming to the center? Are the services appropriate or inappropriate?

3. What sociopolitical forces might be affecting the Black student's and White counselor's interaction?

4. What generic characteristics of counseling may be interfering with the session?

5. If you were the counselor, what institutional and counseling changes would you recommend? Why?

A discussion of the Issues and Conflicts involved in the preceding cases follows, starting on page 274.

ISSUES AND CONFLICTS

1. THE LANGUAGE "PROBLEM"

1. *The English teacher's strong emotional reaction.* Was the teacher really concerned about helping the minority students speak better English, or was he reacting from bias? Why did he feel a need to correct the students? After all, wasn't it a private conversation and not a classroom assignment?

2. *English teacher's perception of minorities as foreigners.* When the teacher stated, "You're not in Africa!" was he not viewing the minority students as not belonging in this country? Is not speaking "good English" equated with being "un-American"?

3. *Speaking "good English" equated with success.* There is no doubt that being able to learn and use English well is important for minorities. However, does it imply one should give up one's native language?

4. *Inferiority of non-English languages.* When teachers, counselors and others react negatively toward people who speak another language or speak with an accent, how does it affect the self-esteem of the minority individual?

5. *Student's perception of "White man's talk."* What were the students referring to?

6. *"Minority problem" or "White problem."* Teacher seems to be blaming the victim.

7. *Learning to speak English—forced compliance.* Most minorities would agree that speaking good English is important. However, teachers and others often use punitive, forced compliance methods reflecting their biases. Minorities, therefore, react against this aspect, which interferes with English acquisition.

8. *Individual change versus system change.* Is it always the responsibility of minorities to do the changing? Shouldn't institutions and those in the majority culture also take responsibility for change?

9. *Black language versus perverted form of English.* The teacher obviously misunderstood the question, "What it is, man?" In Black language it might translate into "How are things?" or "What's happening?" Many do not believe there is such a thing as Black language. What are your thoughts on the subject?

2. CAN CULTURE JUSTIFY THE PRACTICES?

1. *The trauma suffered by the Nguyen family.* Many immigrants and refugees suffered immensely in the war that tore their country apart and during their escape. What effect might the harrowing experience of the family have on them? Could they still be suffering from post-traumatic stress? How?

2. *Fresh bruises on Phuoc*. When Mrs. Nguyen stated, "Thùôc Nam," she was referring to traditional medical practice in Vietnam. Massage treatments are common and many involve coin rubbing (Cao Giò) or pressure massage (Giac Hòi). The latter uses bamboo tubes as suction tubes. The technique often leaves bruises on the person. Phuoc's 4-day absence from school was due to illness, and he was treated by the parents.

3. *Misunderstanding of teachers and social workers*. Apparently, the social worker thought Mr. Nguyen used the bamboo sticks and bag of coins to beat Phuoc.

4. *Cultural factors concerning disrobing*. Phuoc's reluctance to disrobe in front of strangers (nurse) may have been prompted by cultural taboos rather than by attempts to hide the injury.

5. *Language barriers*. It was obvious that Mrs. Nguyen had difficulty understanding the social worker. The social worker might have avoided much of the misunderstanding if an interpreter had been present.

6. *Mrs. Nguyen's denial of injuries*. To Mrs. Nguyen, the bruises were not injuries. Indeed, their physical presence indicated the "poison" had been sucked out by the treatment. It is a positive sign, not a negative one.

7. *Traditional medical practice versus child abuse*. Those who practice massage treatments believe in them. Is it considered child abuse if bruises result from these traditional medical practices? How does one tell the differences between bruises of the treatment and bruises left by abuse?

8. *Keeping family issues within the family*. Many Asians believe that family affairs are not disclosed publicly and especially to strangers. Disrobing publicly, telling others about the scars, or the trauma of the Thai pirates are not done readily. Yet, such knowledge is required by educators and social service agencies who must make enlightened decisions.

9. *Embarrassment of not being able to speak English well*. Many Vietnamese elders are embarrassed about their lack of proficiency in English. The thought of public humiliation (shame/disgrace) is strong. The conflict can be so great that they give up attempting English at all.

10. *Culturally accepted practice versus negative outcome*. Pressure massage seldom produces injuries in the recipients. Yet, if a practice had cultural sanctions but resulted in serious injuries, could it be justified?

3. I'M NOT A RACIST

1. *Ms. Cohen's motivations for working with minorities*. Altruistic or paternalistic?

2. *Establishing rapport with Black clients.* How did Ms. Cohen try to establish rapport with the Black clients? What were the results? Why?

3. *Black perceptions of White counselor.* Black clients are often suspicious of White helping professionals. How would you work through these suspicions?

4. *Testing Ms. Cohen's credibility.* Was Ms. Cohen aware that she was being tested in the counseling sessions? What were the tests? How did she do? What should she have done?

5. *We've all experienced discrimination.* Ms. Cohen equated the Black experience with being a "woman" and a "Jew." Is this a valid comparison? Why did it turn the Black couple off?

6. *Manipulation of Ms. Cohen.* Ms. Cohen was easily manipulated by the Black male client. How much did her attempts to "prove she was not racist" get in the way of effective counseling?

7. *White liberalism versus lack of self-understanding.* Ms. Cohen seemed wrapped up in her White liberalism. Consciously, she wanted to "help these people." Was she really a biased person? How much do you think she really understood about her motives and values?

8. *All Whites are racist.* A common perception held by many Blacks is that all Whites are racist. Ms. Cohen, for one, might disagree. Where do you stand on this debate? Can someone with racist attitudes and beliefs work effectively with a Black client? How?

9. *Negativism versus validation.* Ms. Cohen's emphasis on her being a "woman" and "Jew" did not seem to validate her clients' Black experience. Rather, it seemed to negate it. Why and how?

4. EQUALITY OF RELATIONSHIPS

1. *Lack of knowledge concerning Puerto Rican male-female relationships.* Egalitarian or patriarchal?

2. *In Hispanic culture, the term "machismo" also means protector.* Is the psychologist perceiving it in mainly negative terms (sexist, etc.)?

3. *Significance of male children in Puerto Rican culture.* Why is Esteban so desirous of having male children? Is he a sexist? Is Hispanic culture sexist?

4. *Educational level of wife.* Could Esteban feel threatened by his wife's higher educational level?

5. *White woman therapist.* Besides being of a different culture, how would gender of the therapist affect Esteban's receptivity to counseling? If women are held in lower esteem in Hispanic culture, would Esteban be threatened or humiliated by a female counselor?

6. *Individualism versus family focus.* The psychologist encouraged Carmen to be "her own person." The psychosocial unit of identity

among Puerto Ricans is the family. Children cement and validate the marriage. What should be Carmen's goals?

7. *Carmen's desire to work versus her role in the traditional Hispanic family.* How do Carmen and Esteban resolve this conflict? What role should the counselor play?

8. *Family counseling assumptions versus Puerto Rican family values.* What are some of the assumptions of family counseling that may clash with Hispanic family/cultural values? Nuclear family versus extended family? Male-female role relationships? Husband-wife relationships?

5. ASSERT YOURSELF

1. *Definition of "frequent tardiness."* What does Sylvia's immediate supervisor consider to be "frequent tardiness"?
    a. Is he picking on her because of his disapproval of affirmative action?
    b. If Sylvia does have a different perception of her "punctuality," will it
        (i) cost her her job?
        (ii) make her responsible for changing to meet the company's rules and time perspective?

2. *Sylvia's generosity versus "jealousy" of supervisor.* Are Sylvia's fellow employees taking advantage of her generosity and "naiveness," or is the supervisor jealous of Sylvia's popularity and comraderie with her fellow employees? The employees may respect and admire her willingness to help others and do not feel the same way toward the supervisor.

3. *Sylvia's idea of psychologists.* What are Sylvia's ideas and attitudes regarding psychologists and being referred by her supervisor? What does she think of their diagnosis? Does this shame her?

4. *Cultural enlightenment of psychologist and supervisor.* Are the supervisor and psychologist aware of cultural differences (Indian versus White) that could help them explain Sylvia's actions and more accurately understand her?

5. *Resignation.* Why did Sylvia resign?

6. *Restraint of behavior, avoidance of eye contact, nonverbalness, White versus Indian culture.* What does restraint of behavior, avoidance of eye contact, and nonverbalization of thoughts and feelings mean in an Indian versus White society?

7. *Affirmative action.* Do Sylvia's supervisor and personnel director approve of affirmative action hiring or not? Are they sincerely trying to help minority employees by referring them? If they disapprove, what may be the effects?

8. *Cooperation and sharing versus "I" orientation.* Sylvia's culture may value sharing and cooperation with fellow employees. The supervisor

values keeping what you have to yourself and not going out of your way to help others.

9. *Punctuality.* White culture values being on time/punctuality. Indian culture does not have the same time perspective. It does not value punctuality as much as the white culture does.

10. *Generic counseling characteristics.* Psychologist values verbalness, expression of feelings. Sylvia does not value or is not accustomed to this type of encounter.

11. *Assertiveness.* White culture in general values being assertive. Indian culture may not value asserting oneself to others, but rather being in harmony with others.

12. *Eye contact.* White society views eye contact as positive, attentive behavior; it is highly valued. Indian culture may view eye contact as a form of chastisement or disrespect, something negative; it is not valued as it is in White culture.

13. *Affirmative action.* The supervisor may not value affirmative action and is harder on those employees hired under this policy. The psychologist may value the affirmative action program and may sincerely try to help minority employees survive in the White work situation.

6. CULTURE CONFLICT

1. *Technique of counselors—inappropriate.* How may the use of the Gestalt "empty chair technique" do more harm than good in the case of a traditional Asian client? It forces Dave to talk back to his parents, which he would not normally do (out of respect for them).

2. *Expectations.* What are David's expectations of the counselor and of the counseling sessions? Is he seeking advice from the counselor, or is he there to learn how to take responsibility for his decisions?

3. *Restraint of feelings.* Does the counselor understand why David does not openly disclose his personal feelings (respect for authority)?

4. *Individual versus family responsibility.* Does the counselor understand David's relationship to his parents and family (decisions include family—not solely an individual decision)?

5. *Resolution.* Can David and the counselor arrive at a resolution that will satisfy both David and his parents?

6. *The major—engineering.* What aspects of the major does David dislike, or what aspects of the major turn David off? Why do David's parents want him to become an engineer? Does David like any aspects of engineering?

7. *Maintenance of engineering major.* Can David remain in engineering without causing serious physical and emotional harm to his body (somaticizing)?

8. *Parental confrontation.* Can David confront his parents about his dislike of engineering, or will his parents refuse to hear him?

9. *Timing of symptoms.* Why did the headaches, insomnia, and indigestion begin to show up during his senior year in school and not earlier?

10. *Internal conflicts within David.* David valued his parents' approval of his major (do what his parents want). David values changing majors (do what David wants).

11. *Generic characteristics of counseling.* The counselor values openness and elaboration of personal feelings. This is a White value. David's Chinese culture values restraint of feelings; his "short and polite statements" reflect respect for elders and authority. David's culture also does not value telling personal problems to "strangers."

12. *"I" versus "we" decisions.* White culture values taking responsibility for one's life (individual responsibility and decisions). Chinese culture values a family decision; the family is harmonious, and one is part of the family, not separate from it. Decisions are joint ones (made with the family).

13. *Counselor versus client responsibility.* The counselor values the client helping himself. David may value the counselor giving him advice and telling him what to do.

14. *Confrontation of elders.* The counselor values expressing one's anger to one's parents via the open chair technique. David's Chinese culture does not value talking back to or criticizing elders; it is a sign of disrespect.

15. *David versus his parents.* David's parents value engineering. David is coming to value it less and less.

7. FITTING IN

1. *Being one of the few Black students on a predominantly White campus.* What impact would this have on Sonya? Could this account for her joining "The Shakers"? Why?

2. *Biases and false assumptions by counselor.* Counselor assumed that Blacks do not care for their children and that calling for a conference would not help.

3. *Fitting in school.* Were the teachers and White students wanting Sonya to act White? What did the counselor mean about not having the "qualities" to make a "good cheerleader?" She didn't act White? She wasn't blond, blue-eyed, and light-skinned?

4. *Definition of "argumentative," "intimidating," "disrespectful," and "abusive language."* Are we dealing with Black language or street language in comparison to standard English? Are we dealing with communication style?

5. *Fears associated with Blacks.* Was Mrs. Beale a victim of the belief that Black males are hostile, angry, and prone to violence?

6. *White communication style versus Black communication style.* How might this be contributing to the problem?

7. *Antagonisms.* Might not the biased attitudes directed by teachers and students toward minority groups result in undesirable behavior? If Sonya was acting out, might it not be a reaction to the environment rather than an individual defect?

8. *Need for a reference group versus isolation.* The parents of Sonya were concerned about possible isolation of their daughter. Could she have joined a marginal group because she was lonely and felt invalidated by the White students?

9. *Individual versus institutional change.* Do minorities always have to "fit in"? What might the school do that would benefit racial/cultural diversity?

8. FAIR GRADING

1. *Making up lost ground.* Many minorities do not have a family background involving the U.S. American educational system. Lack of experience or knowledge concerning test taking, grading, and use of standard English places them at a disadvantage. How can they make up for this and "compete on a level track"?

2. *Applying some grading standards to everyone.* Should everyone attain the same level of performance in earning grades? In light of this issue, is it fair to certain minorities? Why?

3. *Internal educational changes.* What type of changes or internal university programs may help minority students deal with the system? How do we maximize success?

4. *Perception of EOP students.* Many White students perceive EOP students as less competent and capable who got in only because of their minority status. What effects can this have on the student?

5. *Affirmative action versus reverse racism.* How would you differentiate between the two concepts? What are your thoughts and beliefs concerning affirmative action programs? Are they fair or unfair? Why?

6. *Equal treatment versus differential treatment.* In this case, the Hispanic student was treated differently. Was this preferential treatment or attempts to recognize disparities due to life circumstances? Can equal treatment be discriminatory?

7. *University's recognition of cultural diversity.* Simply changing standards for admission is oftentimes not enough to attract and retain minority students. There must also be educational policy changes, culturally

relevant support services, relevant curriculum, and alterations in teaching styles. What would some new policies and internal changes look like?

9. WINNING ISN'T EVERYTHING—IT'S THE ONLY THING!

1. *Teacher attitude.* Is the teacher's negative attitude toward Johnny and Peter affecting how the White students treat them? Could this be defeating the effectiveness of the program?

2. *Interpretation of Johnny's and Peter's actions by White and Indian cultures.* What do Johnny's "tardiness and tangential contributions" signify in Indian culture versus White culture?

3. *Johnny and Peter being a minority in the class.* What effect does being one of the few minorities, if not the only minority, in a class have on Johnny and Peter and the other students?

4. *Teacher's attitude and awareness of Johnny's and Peter's cultural differences.* How willing is the teacher to deal with Johnny and Peter's cultural differences? The teacher continues to set up class exercises that are competitive. What is the teacher's attitude about Johnny and Peter being in her class?

5. *What should happen when two cultures meet?* How, if at all, should the teacher's classroom teaching style change to meet the cultural belief system of Indian culture? Do minority students always have to do the adjusting?

6. *Psychological impact on Johnny and Peter.* What is the psychological impact on Johnny and Peter in trying to apply their Indian culture in a White-ruled school? Could they be receiving double messages regarding their Indian culture: good on the reservation, bad at the White school?

7. *Biculturalism.* Can Johnny and Peter maintain or achieve a positive bicultural attitude when the teacher sets up the class to be monocultural? If the aim of the program is to "acculturate," is this being fair to them by putting down Indian values?

8. *White versus Indian culture interpretations of behavior.* The teacher may value the White interpretations of behavior (withdrawn, sullen) over an Indian interpretation of the same behavior (respect for authority or elders). Thus, her evaluation would be a negative and a culturally biased one.

9. *Punctuality.* The teacher values punctuality in her students. Indian culture values a different time perspective; no strict adherence to time.

10. *Cooperation versus competition.* White culture values competition. Indian culture values cooperation.

11. *Class participation.* The teacher values individual contributions; she states that Johnny and Peter are "withdrawn, sullen, and passive." They may not value the same system of teaching the teacher does, and thus may not respond to this teaching system. The system may be more to blame than they are.

12. *Verbalness.* The teacher values verbalness and students' speaking up in class. Indian culture may not put such a high emphasis on class participation as does the White culture. It is possible that Indian culture does not speak to thinking aloud. Or, Johnny and Peter's culture may believe that one speaks only when spoken to.

13. *White versus Indian interpretation of class contribution.* Johnny and Peter's contributions may be very relevant from an Indian point of view, but tangential from a White point of view. Or, is it possible that their communication style is more subtle and indirect than that used by Whites? Conflict in interpretation of their contributions may be causing many of these difficulties.

14. *Teaching system.* The teacher values the White system of teaching and learning (competitive/verbal); she does not seem to value Indian methods of teaching and learning, or even want to know what would be the best method in reaching them. Johnny and Peter value the teaching system they had at the reservation.

10. STEREOTYPES OR TRUTHS?

1. *A White management team.* Can an organization adequately assess itself without bias? Shouldn't outside experts be called in?

2. *Definition of leadership.* Is a leader one who is outwardly forceful and assertive? Is this the only form of leadership? Can other forms be effective with people? Many companies in Asia have become quite successful using a more cooperative format.

3. *Stereotypes.* Differences in communication style often trigger stereotypes we have of different groups: Asian Americans are poor with words, but good with numbers. They make good scientists or technical workers, but poor managers.

4. *Bias in merit reviews.* How do stereotypes affect the evaluator's perception of minority groups?

5. *Self-fulfilling prophecy.* Expectations of White peers and managers may actually result in Asian workers' believing they are incapable of management duties.

6. *Asian-American communication style versus White Western style.* Asian workers may value indirectness and subtlety in solving problems. White workers value directness, being frank, and "saying what's on your mind."

7. *Demand for White management styles.* Asian-American workers may be placed in an unenviable position of having to "act White" in order to be considered "management material." How can an organization recognize the importance of diversity in problem solving?

8. *Belief that there is only one way to be effective.* This may hinder a company's ability to succeed. How can cultural diversity enhance a company's success?

11. WHO'S TO BLAME?

1. *Individual blame versus system blame.* The counselor tended to attribute Felix's academic difficulties to personal deficiencies. What other external variables (sociocultural forces) may be contributing to Felix's feelings of loneliness, isolation, depression, and meaningless-ness? Concentrate on the characteristics of White middle-class learning/teaching styles versus Hispanic ones. Can alienation come from the materials taught and the texts used? As a culturally different student, how might you feel in an environment that used material from a totally different perspective?

2. *Family obligations as a deficit.* The counselor may be distorting cultural value into a deficit. For example, what does it mean to be the oldest in a traditional Hispanic family? Certainly, it is a position of importance and responsibility. Yet, the counselor may be communi-cating to Felix that his values are outdated and pathological. What evidence do we have of this, and what effect might it have on Felix?

3. *Felix's living situation.* What is there about Felix's living situation that may clash with Hispanic values, traditions, and modes of behavior? Speculate freely.

4. *Feelings of alienation, guilt, and shame.* What are the possible cultural and sociopolitical ramifications of these feelings? How do the strong family influences affect these feelings?

5. *What would you do and why?*

6. *Individual-centered approach of counselor versus sociocultural view by Felix.* The counselor views individual responsibility (IC-IR world view) as solely applicable to Felix. The reasons the counselor entertains about why Felix is doing poorly may clash with the client's perceptions.

7. *Institutional rules and regulations may clash with concepts of "personalismo."* Felix's dormitory situation may seem impersonal and devoid of the affective human qualities. In many Hispanic groups, human rela-tionships take precedence over institutional policies.

8. *Individual competition versus group cooperation.* The alienation Felix experiences may be the direct result of the individual competitive elements in our educational system. Individual recognition and

achievement are highly valued. Among Hispanic groups, cooperation to achieve mutually shared goals for the benefit of the group as opposed to the individual is highly valued.

12. HELPING THESE PEOPLE

1. *Basis of Fernando's paranoid reaction.* Are there cultural, sociopolitical, or biological reasons for his symptoms? Can his fears symbolize realistic concerns (fear of deportation, creditors, police, etc.)? How do Hispanic cultures view hallucinations? Could his years of exposure to pesticides and other dangerous agricultural chemicals be contributing? These questions are important for the counselor to consider.

2. *Transportation difficulties.* Many poor clients have difficulties traveling to mental health facilities for treatment. How can the counselor make it easier for them to be seen?

3. *Use of family interpreters.* Might the use of a son, especially the younger one, as an interpreter alter and violate the role relationships of the Hispanic family?

4. *Informality in addressing clients.* Informality in greeting a client such as using the first name, "Fernando" as opposed to "Mr. M." may be considered a lack of respect in some Hispanic groups.

5. *In-the-office treatment versus home visit.* If clients are unable to travel to your office for treatment, why not consider a home visit? Or, a meeting point between the destinations. What fears make it difficult for us to leave our safe offices?

6. *Use of interpreters.* Can interpreters give an accurate translation? Are mental health concepts equivalent in both cultures? Many concepts in English and Spanish do not have equivalent meanings. Yet, how else may we communicate if a bilingual person is not present?

7. *Bilingual therapists.* There is no doubt that the need for bilingual therapists is great. How might we increase their representation in the mental health fields?

8. *Counseling strategies undermine cultural values.* Need to use the son as an interpreter to help the family can undermine the authority of the family. Also, can a client act as an interpreter for the family without being influenced by them?

9. *Denial by son that something was wrong.* If something was wrong and the family objected to the son's interpreting, why did he deny it? Are there cultural reasons for not airing personal issues?

13. BURNING OUT

1. *Ignore racism or not?* Should Mark have ignored the biases of the other counselors? What are some ways he might have handled it?

2. *Change in attitude.* Can a counselor, who is racially biased, be changed to be less so via awareness?

3. *Should counselors criticize each other's work?* Should counselors criticize each other's work, even when their intentions are solely constructive? If so, what in what tactful ways could this be done by Mark?

4. *Integrity, what price?* How much is an individual willing to risk for something he/she believes in, and how much is he/she willing to overlook? Mark felt he should speak up and as a result put himself in an uncomfortable position.

5. *Is it worth the job, head counselor supervision?* Does Mark really want to remain and work in this type of atmosphere, one of racial bias toward minority clients and of hostility toward him?

6. *Effectiveness after incident.* Can Mark continue to work effectively when teachers, fellow counselors, and the principal do not appear to be giving him support or respect?

7. *Who should Mark have seen first?* Should Mark have gone to his superior (principal) before confronting the counselor? What is the institution's policy on this matter? Could Mark have abided by this policy?

8. *Politics and tact.* Could Mark have voiced his feelings and gotten what he wanted without creating the hostile atmosphere that he did? Mark had several things against him.
   a. He is new to the staff, and his voice may not carry as much clout as that of a counselor who has been there for many years.
   b. He is newly graduated, which could affect his credibility.
   c. By threatening to resign, he is asking the principal to take sides with him. If the principal took sides with Mark, this might create uneasy feelings among the rest of the counselors and the principal. Also, is threatening to resign like throwing a temper tantrum?

9. *Higher education.* Mark values counseling minorities to their full potential. The White counselor may not value higher education for minorities and may blanketly recommend vocational training programs for them.

10. *Institution backs White counselor.* The principal and the institution value the White counselor and his actions (counseling recommendation, seniority) more than they value Mark's actions (confronting counselor, principal, school board, and threatening to resign).

11. *Mark's confrontation with the White counselor.* The White counselor does not value Mark, a new minority counselor, telling him/her how to counsel. Mark values telling the other counselor what he thinks in the interest of the minority student.

12. *Mark's approach.* The principal may not have valued the way Mark approached the problem. It put the principal in a situation where he had to choose between the other counselors and Mark.

14. DORMITORY LIVING

1. *Laotian student's feeling invalidated on a White campus.* Many things may make a minority student feel out of place. The buildings, coursework, food, and so forth, may be oriented to meeting the needs of only one segment of the population.

2. *Need for in-service training of staff, educators, and sensitivity training for White students.* The university has a responsibility to recognize cultural diversity not only in educational activities, but in housing (living) conditions as well. How might this be done?

3. *Laotian student's denial of problem.* Many Asians, when asked whether problems exist, will deny it out of politeness or a desire not to insult or hurt the feelings of others.

4. *Unreasonable reaction to another language.* Were the Laotian students talking about the White roommate? White people often become uneasy when they see a group of minorities communicating in their own language. Are they plotting against them? Where do these fears and feelings come from?

5. *Appropriate support services.* If minorities avoid traditional counseling services, how may they be reached? What approach could a counselor or institution take that would encourage minority students to use them?

6. *Perception of awkward pauses and quiet behavior.* Could the long pauses and quiet behavior be culturally conditioned rather than a lack of desire to communicate?

15. WHO AM I: ASIAN OR WHITE?

1. *Janet T.'s motivation for interracial relationships.* Was she attempting to prove she has "made it" in White society? To defy parents? To prove self-worth?

2. *Janet's hostility toward the Chinese counselor.* Why was she hostile? What did the counselor symbolize?

3. *Stereotypes of the Chinese male.* Where did Janet acquire these images? Does she believe them?

4. *What type of identity does Janet have of herself?* Is her identity White? Is her identity Chinese? What manifestations of self-hatred are present?

5. *Cultural oppression and racial self-hatred.* Janet may be the victim of cultural oppression.

6. *Stage of racial/cultural identity.* Janet seems to be in the conformity stage of development. Do the characteristics seem applicable to her?

7. *Janet's realization that she is Chinese.* How was Janet's denial system breaking down?

16. EXPRESS YOUR THOUGHTS AND FEELINGS

1. *Awareness of cultural differences (counselor).* Is the counselor aware of the cultural differences between White and minority groups and between minority groups themselves?

2. *Training workshop emphasis.* Does the counselor's training reflect (i.e., did it teach her) what would work best with the minority society, but not necessarily with minority-group members?

3. *Goals/techniques.* Are the goals and techniques used by the counselor appropriate to all minority students? How are they inappropriate?

4. *Cultural oppression.* Is the counselor culturally oppressing the Asian-American students by trying to force participation of the students (the "I know what's best for you" syndrome)?

5. *Lack of Asian Americans in the last group (personal problems).* Does the counselor know or understand the reasons for there being few Asian American students in the personal-problem group?

6. *Verbal/expressive.* The traditional counselor values client qualities of being verbal, confrontive, and freely expressive of feelings. The Asian-American students do not value or put as much value on these characteristics as does the counselor.

7. *Goals.* The counselor values assertiveness and being uninhibited as some of the goals of the workshops. The Asian-American students do not value these things in the same way as does the counselor. Assertiveness and being uninhibited among peers is not the primary goal these Asian-American students wish to achieve. These students may be able to benefit from the contents of the workshops without being verbal during the course of the workshop.

8. *Exposure to personal feelings.* The counselor values expressing personal feelings and discussing personal problems with group members. The Asian-American students do not value discussion of and sharing their personal feelings and problems with "nonfamily" members.

17. WHO IS THE VICTIM?

1. *Significance of verbal and nonverbal messages in each culture.* Were there inaccurate interpretations in the sending and receiving of both verbal and nonverbal messages between the foreign and the U.S. student (proxemics, eye contact, conversation, conventions)?

2. *Sending double messages.* How may the U.S. student consciously (or unconsciously) send double messages to the foreign student?
   a. Let's be merely friends.
   b. Sexual come-ons. Why did she single him out?

3. *University behaviors.* Did both students assume their own behaviors were understood universally rather than culturally?

4. *Experiences and attitudes.* What were the different experiences and attitudes regarding male/female relationships of the foreign student and of the U.S. student? He had not been alone with any other females outside his family. She had felt her actions were just part of being friendly to the foreign student.

5. *Distress.* Why did the foreign student seem distressed to the U.S. student when he came to her door late one night?

6. *Conservative culture.* What does "extremely conservative culture" mean? Is sex after knowing a woman for one week considered conservative in the foreign student's culture? Was he not acting out of character?

7. *Sexual versus hospitable.* The foreign student valued the U.S. student's friendliness and their male/female relationship in a sexual way. The U.S. student valued the friendliness she offered the foreign student and their male/female relationship in a hospitable way.

8. *Who's the victim?* What is the difference in opinion between the U.S. and the foreign student about who was the victim of the incident? The foreign student felt he was the victim. The U.S. student felt she was the victim.

9. *Verbal and nonverbal behavior.* The foreign student and the U.S. student do not interpret and value all verbal and nonverbal language in the same way.

18. WHAT THEY WANT IS NOT WHAT THEY NEED!

1. *Prejob knowledge.* How much of an idea of departmental politics, emphasis, and hierarchy should a job applicant have before the interview and before accepting the job offer?

2. *Generic versus cultural characteristics of counseling.* Is the "traditional counselor-client model" effective in counseling minorities (nontraditional clients)?

3. *Fellow counselor cooperation.* How much cooperation can you expect from the counselors, most of whom favor dealing with personal/emotional problems versus vocational/educational problems?

4. *Minority participation with personal problems.* Will minorities be inclined to see counselors for personal reasons, no matter what the enticement?

5. *Why few minorities come to the counseling center?* Is the staff of the counseling center aware of the reasons that minorities have not come in before?

6. *Actual influence of a newly hired counselor.* As a newly hired counselor, how much influence do you have in changing institutional policies if you see a policy change as a means of increasing minority utilization of counseling center services?

7. *Priority of institution.* Does the institution's reputation of being a clinical training center take precedence over minority needs and recruitment?

8. *Self-defeating.* How does the institution discourage minorities by virtue of its traditional counselor-client model?

9. *Generic versus cultural characteristics of counseling.* The majority of counselors value traditional counselor-client models of counseling. Minorities do not value the same generic counseling characteristics.

10. *Revealing personal problems to counselors.* In all, 85% of counselors value dealing with clinical (personal/emotional) problems. Many minorities do not value revealing their personal problems to strangers (counselors). They would more likely come with vocational/educational concerns.

11. *Clinical versus vocational/educational counseling.* While 85% of the counselors value clinical problems, 5% of the counselors value vocational/educational concerns.

12. *New counselor and the institution.* A newly hired counselor values minority utilization of the counseling center. The majority of counselors value clients with socioemotional problems. Will they value minorities with vocational/educational concerns?

13. *Initial rapport.* Does the Black client initially feel he can be helped by and work with the White counselor?

14. *Inflexibility of counselor.* How is the counselor inflexible in his approach? The counselor immediately becomes uncomfortable and resentful when the student asks for advice and information. He cannot get away from being a nondirective counselor. This negatively affects his counseling session.

15. *Clarify goals and expectations.* Is there a need to clarify what the client expects of the counselor and what the counselor expects of the client?

16. *Referral?* When should a counselor refer his/her client? When does a counselor feel he/she cannot work effectively with a client so that a referral would be proper? If you realized you were biased, would you refer?

17. *Client taking off—leaving physically.* Should the counselor follow and catch up to the client after he has gotten angry and left the counselor's office? Is it the responsibility of the counselor to see that the client gets help even if from another counselor?

18. *Approach.* The counselor values a nondirective counseling approach. The client values more a directive and structured approach.

19. *Needs of the client.* The client values getting advice and information from the counselor. The counselor values having the client find out information for himself and take responsibility for himself.

20. *Expression of feeling.* The counselor values focusing on personal feelings. The client values focusing on academic issues and not on revealing intimate feelings to the counselor.

References

Abad, V., Ramos, J., & Boyce E. (1974). A model for delivery of mental health services to Spanish-speaking minorities. *American Journal of Orthopsychiatry, 44,* 584–595.

Abbott, K. (1970). *Harmony and individualism.* Taipei: Orient Cultural Press.

Abbott, K., & Abbott, E. (1968). Juvenile delinquency in San Francisco's Chinese-American community. *Journal of Sociology, 4,* 45–56.

Abeles, R. P. (1976). Relative deprivation, rising expectations and black militancy. *Journal of Social Issues, 32,* 119–137.

ACMH. (1987). *The California Southeast Asian mental health needs assessment.* Oakland, California: Asian Community Mental Health Services.

Acosta, F. X. & Evans, L. A. (1982). Effective psychotherapy for low-income and minority patients. In F. X. Acosta, J. Yamamoto & L. A. Evans (Eds.), *Effective psychotherapy for low-income and minority patients* (pp. 51–82). New York: Plenum Press.

Acosta, F. X., & Sheehan, J. G. (1978). Self-disclosure in relation to psychotherapist expertise and ethnicity. *American Journal of Community Psychology, 6,* 545–553.

Adams, H. J. (1973). Progressive heritage of guidance: A view from the left. *Personnel and Guidance Journal, 1973, 51,* 531–538.

Adebimpe, V. R. (1981). Overview: White norms and psychiatric diagnosis of Black patients. *American Journal of Psychiatry, 138,* 279–285.

Allport, G. W. (1961). *Pattern and growth in personality.* New York: Holt, Rinehart & Winston.

Anderson, J. W. (1985). The effects of culture and social class on client preference for counseling methods. *Journal of Non-White Concerns, 11,* 84–88.

Anderson, M. J., & Ellis, R. H. (1980). Indian American: The reservation client. In N. A. Vacc & J. P. Wittmer (Eds.), *Let me be me* (pp. 105–127). Muncie: IN: Accelerated Development.

Anderson, M. J. & Ellis, R. (1988). On the reservation. In N. A. Vacc, J. W. Wittmer & S. DeVaney (Eds.), *Experiencing and counseling multicultural and diverse populations (2d Edition)* (pp. 107–126). Muncie, IN: Accelerated Development.

Arbonam, C. (1990). Career counseling research and Hispanics. A review of the literature. *The Counseling Psychologist, 18,* 300–323.

Argyle, M. (1975). *Bodily communication.* London: Methuen.

Arkoff, A. (1959). Need patterns of two generations of Japanese-Americans in Hawaii. *Journal of Social Psychology, 50,* 75–79.

Arrendondo, P. (1985). Cross-cultural counselor education and training. In P. B. Pedersen (Ed.), *Handbook of cross-cultural counseling and therapy.* Westport, CT: Greenwood Press.

Arrendondo-Dowd, & Gonzales, J. (1980). Preparing culturally effective counselors. *Personnel and Guidance Journal, 58,* 657–662.

Association on American Indian Affairs. (1976). *Indian child welfare statistical survey.* Report submitted to American Indian Policy Review Commission, Congress of the United States.

Atkinson, D., Morten, G., & Sue, D. W. (1989). *Counseling American minorities: A cross-cultural perspective.* Dubuque, IA: W. C. Brown.

Atkinson, D. R. (1985). Research on cross-cultural counseling and psychotherapy: A review and update of reviews. In P. B. Pederson (Ed.), *Handbook of cross-cultural counseling and therapy.* Westport, CT: Greenwood Press.

Atkinson, D. R., & Carskaddon, G. (1975). A prestigious introduction, psychological jargon, and perceived counselor credibility. *Journal of Counseling Psychology, 22,* 180–186.

Atkinson, D. R., Furlong, M. J., & Poston, W. C. (1986). Afro-American preferences for counselor characteristics. *Journal of Counseling Psychology, 33,* 326–330.

Atkinson, D. R., Maruyama, M., & Matsui, S. (1978). The effects of counselor race and counseling approach on Asian Americans' perceptions of counselor credibility and utility. *Journal of Counseling Psychology, 25,* 76–83.

Atkinson, D. R. (1983). Ethnic similarity in counseling psychology: A review of research. *The Counseling Psychologist, 11,* 79–92.

Atkinson, D. R., Morten, G., & Sue, D. W. (1989). A minority identity development model. In D. R. Atkinson, G. Morten, & D. W. Sue (Eds.), *Counseling American Minorities* (pp. 35–52). Dubuque, IA: W. C. Brown.

Atkinson, D. R., Ponterotto, J. G., & Sanchez, A. R. (1984). Attitudes of Vietnamese and Anglo-American students toward counseling. *Journal of College Student Personnel, 25,* 448–452.

Atkinson, D. R., & Schein, S. (1986). Similarity in counseling. *The Counseling Psychologist, 14,* 319–354.

Attneave, C. (1971). Mental health of American Indians: Problems, perspectives and challenge for the decade ahead. Paper presented at the meeting of the American Psychological Association, HI, August 1972.

Attneave, C. (1982). American Indians and Alaska Native families: Emigrants in their own homeland. In M. McGoldrick, J. K. Pearce, J. Giordano (Eds.), *Ethnicity and family therapy* (pp. 55–83). New York: Guilford Press.

Attneave, C. L. (1985). Practical counseling with American Indian and Alaska Native clients. In P. B. Pedersen (Eds.), *Handbook of cross-cultural counseling and therapy* (pp. 135–140). Westport, CT: Greenwood Press.

Aubrey, R. F. (1977). Historical development of guidance and counseling and implications for the future. *Personnel and Guidance Journal, 55,* 288–295.

Avila, D. L., & Avila, A. L. (1980). The Mexican-American. In N. A. Vacc & J. P. Wittmer (Eds.), *Let me be me* (pp. 225–281). Muncie, IN: Accelerated Development.

Avis, J. P., & Stewart, L. H. (1976). College counseling Intentions a d change. *The Counseling Psychologist, 6,* 74–77.

Axelson, J. A. (1985). *Counseling and development in a multicultural society.* Belmont, CA: Brooks/Cole.

Baker, J. N., Wingert, P., & Matsumoto, N. (1987, July 27). Battling the IQ-test ban. *Newsweek, 53.*

Baldwin, J. (1963). *The fire next time.* New York: Dial Press.

Banks, W. (1977). Group consciousness and the helping professions. *Personnel and Guidance Journal, 55,* 319–330.

Banks, W., & Marten, K. (1973). Counseling: The reactionary profession. *Personnel and Guidance Journal, 41,* 457–462.

Barak, A., & Dell, D. M. (1977). Differential perceptions of counselor behavior: Replication and extension. *Journal of Counseling Psychology, 24,* 288–292.

Barak, A., & La Crosse, M. B. (1975). Multidimensional perception of counselor behavior. *Journal of Counseling Psychology, 22,* 471–456.

Baratz, S., & Baratz, J. (1970). Early childhood intervention: The social sciences base of institutional racism. *Harvard Educational Review, 40,* 29–50.

Barbarin, O. A. (1984). Racial themes in psychotherapy with Blacks: Effects of training on the attitudes of Black and white psychiatrists. *American Journal of Social Psychology, 4,* 13–20.

Bardo, J., Bryson, S. L., & Cody, J. J. (1974). Black concerns with behavior modification. *Personnel and Guidance Journal, 53,* 334–341.

Baron, J. (1971). Is experimental psychology relevant? *American Psychologist, 26,* 713–716.

Baron, R. M., & Needel, S. P. (1980). Toward an understanding of the differences in the responses of humans and other animals to density. *Psychology Review, 87,* 320–326.

Bass, B. A., Acosta, F. S., & Evans, L. A. (1982). The Black patient. In F. X. Acosta, J. Yamamoto, & L. A. Evans (Eds.), *Effective psychotherapy for low-income and minority patients* (pp. 83–108). New York: Plenum Press.

Battle, E., & Rotter, J. (1963). Children's feelings of personal control as related to social class and ethnic group. *Journal of Personality, 31,* 482–490.

Baum, M. C., & Lamb, D. H. (1983). A comparison of the concerns presented by Black and white students to a university counseling center. *Journal of College Student Personnel, 24,* 127–131.

Belkins, G. S. (1988). *Introduction to counseling.* Dubuque, IA: W. C. Brown.

Berlin, I. N. (1982). Prevention of emotional problems among Native-American Children: Overview of developmental issues. *Journal of Preventive Psychiatry, 1,* 319–330.

Berman, J. (1979). Counseling skills used by Black and white male and female counselors. *Journal of Counseling Psychology, 26,* 81–84.

Bernal, M. E., & Padilla, A. M. (1982). Status of minority curricula and training in clinical psychology. *American Psychologist, 37,* 780–787.

Bernstein, B. (1964). Elaborated and restricted codes: Their social origins and some consequences. In J. J. Gumperz & D. Hymes (Eds.), The ethnography of communication, *American Anthropologist, 66,* 55–69.

Berry, B. (1965). *Ethnic and race relations.* Boston: Houghton Mifflin.

Billingsley, A. (1970). Black families and white social science. *Journal of Social Issues, 26,* 127–142.

Blanchard, E. L. (1983). The growth and development of American Indians and Alaskan Native children. In G. J. Powell, J. Yamamoto, A. Romero, & A. Morales (Eds.), *The psychosocial development of minority group children.* New York: Brunner/Mazel.

Blau, T. (1970). Commission on accelerating Black participation in psychology. *American Psychologist, 25,* 1103–1104.

Bliatout, B. T., Ben, R., Bliatout, H. Y., & Lee, D. T. T. (1985). Mental health and prevention activities targeted to Southeast Asian refugees. In T. C. Owan (Ed.), *Southeast Asian mental health treatment, prevention services, training, and research.* Washington, DC: National Institute of Mental Health.

Bogardus, E. (1925). Measuring social distance. *Journal of Applied Sociology, 9,* 229–308.

Boulette, R. R. (1976). Assertive training with low income Mexican-American women. In M. R. Mirand (Ed.), *Psychotherapy with the Spanish-speaking: Issues in research and service delivery* (pp. 67–71). Los Angeles: Spanish-Speaking Mental Health Center.

Boxley, R., & Wagner, N. N. (1971). Clinical psychology training programs and minority groups: A survey. *Professional Psychology, 2,* 75–81.

Boyd, N. (1982). Family therapy with Black families. In E. E. Jones & S. J. Korchin (Eds.), *Minority mental health* (pp. 227–249). New York: Praeger.

Brammer, L. (1985). Nonformal support in cross-cultural counseling and therapy. In P. B. Pedersen (Ed.), *Handbook of cross-cultural counseling and therapy.* Westport, CT: Greenwood Press.

Brammer, L. M. (1977). Who can be a helper? *Personnel and Guidance Journal, 55,* 303–308.

Brecher, R., & Brecher, E. (1961). The happiest creatures on earth? *Harpers, 222,* 85–90.

Brody, E. B. (1963). Color and identity conflict in young boys. *Psychiatry, 26,* 188–201.

Brower, I. C. (1980). Counseling Vietnamese. *Personnel and Guidance Journal, 58,* 646–652.

Brown, A. L. D., & Hernasy, M. A. (1983). The impact of culture on the health of American Indian children. In G. J. Powell, J. Yamamoto, A. Romero, & A. Morales (Eds.), *The psychosocial development of minority group children* (pp. 39–45). New York: Brunner/Mazel.

Brown, J. E. (1976). Parallels between Adlerian psychology and Afro-American value system. *Individual Psychologist, 13,* 29–33.

Brown, T. R., Stein, K. M., Huang, K., & Harris, D. E. (1973). Mental illness and the role of mental health facilities in Chinatown. In S. Sue & N. N. Wagner (Eds.), *Asian Americans: Psychological Perspectives.* Palo Alto: Science & Behavior Books.

Bruhn, J. G., & Fuentes, R. G., Jr. (1977). Cultural factors affecting utilization of services by Mexican Americans. *Psychiatric Annals, 7,* 20–29.

Bryde, J. F. (1971). *Indian students and guidance.* Boston: Houghton Mifflin.

Bryson, S., & Bardo, H. (1975). Race and the counseling process: An overview. *Journal of Non-White Concerns in Personnel and Guidance, 4*(1), 5–15.

Bulhan, H. A. (1985). Black Americans and psychopathology: An overview of research and theory. *Psychotherapy, 22,* 370–378.

Buss, A. H. (1966). *Psychopathology.* New York: John Wiley.

Calia, V. F. (1968). The culturally deprived client: A reformulation of the counselor's role. *Journal of Counseling Psychology, 13,* 81–84.

Canino, I., & Canino, G. (1982). Cultural syntonic family therapy for migrant Puerto Ricans. *Hospital and Community Psychiatry, 33,* 299–303.

Caplan, N. (1970). The new ghetto man: A review of recent empirical studies. *Journal of Social Issues, 26,* 59–73.

Caplan, N., & Nelson, S. D. (1973). On being useful—The nature and consequences of psychological research on social problems. *American Psychologist, 28,* 199–211.

Caplan, N., & Paige, J. M. (1968, August). A study of ghetto rioters. *Scientific American, 219,* 15–21.

Cardon, J. C., & Yousef, F. (1975). *An introduction to intercultural communication.* New York: Bobbs-Merrill Company.

Carkhuff, R. R. (1986). *The art of helping.* Amherst, MA: Human Resource Development Press.

Carkhuff, R. R., & Pierce, R. (1965). Differential effects of therapist race and social class upon patient depth of self-exploration in the initial clinical interview. *Journal of Consulting Psychology, 31,* 632–634.

Carillo, C. (1982). Changing norms of Hispanic families: In E. E. Jones & S. J. Korchin (Eds.), *Minority mental health* (pp. 250–266). New York: Praeger.

Carlin, J. E., & Sokoloff, B. Z. (1985). Mental health treatment issues for Southeast Asian refugee children. In T. C. Owan (Ed.), *Southeast Asian mental health treatment, prevention services, training, and research.* Washington, DC: National Institute of Mental Health.

Carney, C. G., & Kahn, K. B. (1984). Building competencies for effective cross-cultural counseling: A developmental view. *The Counseling Psychologist, 12,* 111–119.

Carter, R. T. (1988). The relationship between racial identity attitudes and social class. *Journal of Negro Education, 57,* 22–30.

Carter, R. T., & Helms, J. E. (1987). The relationship between black value-orientations to racial identity attitudes. *Evaluation & Measurement in Counseling and Development, 19,* 185–195.

Casas, J. M. (1982). Counseling psychology in the marketplace: The status of ethnic minorities. *The Counseling Psychologist, 10,* 61–67.

Casas, J. M. (1984). Policy, training, and research in counseling psychology: The racial/ethnic minority perspective. In S. Brown, & R. Lent (Eds.), *Handbook of counseling psychology* (pp. 785–831). New York: John Wiley.

Casas, J. M., Ponterotto, J. G., & Gutierrez, J. M. (1986). An ethical indictment of counseling research and training: The cross-cultural perspective. *Journal of Counseling and Development, 64,* 347–349.

Charnofsky, S. (1971). Counseling for power. *Personnel and Guidance Journal, 49,* 351–357.

Cheung, L.-R. L. (1987). *Assessing Asian language performance.* Rockville: Aspen Publishers.

Chien, C. P., & Yamamoto, J. (1982). Asian-American and Pacific-Islander patients. In F. X. Acosta, J. Yamamoto, & L. A. Evans (Eds.), *Effective psychotherapy for low-income and minority patients* (pp. 117–145). New York: Plenum.

Chin, R. (1971). New York Chinatown today: Community in crisis. *Amerasia Journal, 1,* 1–24.

Chinatown gangs. (1972, July 5). *San Francisco Chronicle.*

Christensen, E. W. (1975). Counseling Puerto Ricans. *Personnel and Guidance Journal, 55,* 412–415.

Church, G. J., Goodgame, D., Leavitt, R., & Lopez, J. (1985, July 8). Hispanics: A melding of cultures. *Time, 126,* 36–39.

Clark, K. B. (1963). Educational stimulation of racially disadvantaged children. In A. H. Passow (Ed.), *Education in depressed areas* (pp. 142–162). New York: Teachers College Press.

Clark, K. B., & Clark, M. K. (1947). Racial identification and preference in Negro children. In T. M. Newcomb & E. L. Hartley (Eds.), *Readings in social psychology.* New York: Holt, Reinhart & Winston.

Clark, K. B., & Plotkin, L. (1972). A review of the issues and literature of cultural deprivation theory. In K. B. Clark (Ed)., *The educationally deprived* (pp. 47–73). New York: Metropolitan Applied Research Center.

Cole, J. & Pilisuk, M. (1976). Differences in the provision of mental health services by race. *American Journal of Orthopsychiatry, 46,* 510–525.

Collins, B. E. (1970). *Social Psychology.* Reading, MA: Addison-Wesley.

Condon, J. C., & Yousef, F. (1975). *An introduction to intercultural communication.* New York: Bobbs-Merrill Co.

Cordes, C. (1985). At risk in America. *APA Monitor, 9–11,* 27.

Cordova, F. (1973). The Filipino-Americans: There's always an identity crisis. In S. Sue & N. N. Wagner (Eds.), *Asian americans: psychological perspectives.* Palo Alto: Science & Behavior.

Corsini, R. J. (1984). *Current psychotherapies* (3rd ed.). Itasca, IL: F. F. Peacock Publishers.

Corvin, S., & Wiggins, F. (1989). An antiracism training model for white professionals. *Journal of Multicultural Counseling and Development, 17,* 105–114.

Crandall, V., Katkovsky, W., & Crandall, V. (1965). Children's beliefs in their own control of reinforcements in intellectual achievement situations. *Child Development, 36,* 91–109.

Cross, W. E., Jr. (1971). The Negro-to-Black conversion experience: Towards a psychology of Black liberation. *Black World, 20,* 13–27.

Cuellar, I., Harris, L. C., & Jasso, R. (1980). An acculturation scale for Mexican American normal and clinical populations. *Hispanic Journal of Behavioral Sciences, 2,* 199–217.

Cummins, J. (1986). Empowering minority students: A framework for intervention. *Harvard Educational Review, 56,* 18–36.

Daniels, R. (1971). *Concentration camps USA: Japanese Americans and World War II.* New York: Rinehart & Winston.

Darwin, C. (1859). *On the origin of species by natural selection.*

Dauphinais, R., Dauphinais, L., & Rowe, W. (1981). Effects of race and communication style on Indian perceptions of counselor effectiveness. *Counselor Education and Supervision, 21,* 72–80.

de Gobineau, A. (1915). *The inequality of human races.* New York: Putnam.

De La Cancela, V. (1985). Toward a sociocultural psychotherapy for low-income ethnic minorities. *Psychotherapy, 22,* 427–435.

Dell, B. M. (1973). Counselor power base, influence attempt, and behavior change in counseling. *Journal of Counseling Psychology, 20,* 399–405.

Deloria, V. (1969). *Custer died for your sins.* New York: Macmillan.

Derbyshire, R. L., & Brody, E. B. (1964). Marginality, identity and behavior in the Negro: A functional analysis. *International Journal of Social Psychiatry, 10,* 7–13.

DeVos, G., & Abbott, K. (1966). *The Chinese family in San Francisco.* MSW dissertation, University of California, Berkeley.

Diaz-Guerrero, R. (1977). A Mexican psychology. *American Psychologist, 32,* 934–944.

Doerner, W. R. (1985). Asians: To America with skills. *Time,* July 8, 1985, 42–44.

Dolliver, R. H., Williams, E. L., & Gold, D. C. (1980). The art of Gestalt therapy or: What are you doing with your feet now? *Psychotherapy: Theory, Research & Practice, 17,* 136–142.

Dominguez-Ybarra, A., & Garrison, J. (1977). Toward adequate psychiatric classification and treatment of Mexican-American patients. *Psychiatric Annals, 7,* 86–89.

Dorfman, D. D. (1978). The Cyril Burt question: New findings. *Science, 201,* 1177–1186.

Douglis, R. (1987, November). The beat goes on. *Psychology Today.*

Downey, N. E., & Roush, K. L. (1985). From passive acceptance to active commitment: A model of feminist identity development for women. *The Counseling Psychologist, 13,* 695–709.

Draguns, J. G. (1981). Cross-cultural counseling and psychotherapy. In A. J. Marsella & P. B. Pedersen (Eds.), *Cross-cultural counseling and psychotherapy.* New York: Pergamon.

Dublin, F. (1973, May). *The problem, who speaks next? considered cross-culturally.* Paper presented at the meeting of TESOL, San Juan, Puerto Rico.

Dulles Conference Task Force (1978, June). *Expanding the roles of culturally diverse peoples in the profession of psychology.* Report submitted to the Board of Directors of American Psychological Association, Washington, DC: American Psychological Association.

Eakins, B. W., & Eakins, R. G. (1985). Sex differences in nonverbal communication. In L. A. Samovar & R. E. Porter (Eds.), *Intercultural communication: A reader.* Belmont, CA: Wadsworth.

Ebert, B. (1978). The healthy family. *Family therapy, 5,* 227–232.

Edwards, A. W. (1982). The consequences of error in selecting treatment for Blacks. *Social Casework, 63,* 429–433.

Edwards, E., & Edwards, M. (1980). American Indians: Working with individuals and groups. *Social Casework, 61,* 498–506.

Edwards, H. P., Boulet, D. B., Mahrer, A. R., Chagnon, G. J., & Mook, B. (1982). Carl Rogers during initial interviews: A moderate and consistent therapist. *Journal of Counseling Psychology, 29,* 14–18.

Effective use of cultural role-taking (in press). *Professional Psychology.*

Egan, G. (1982). *The Skilled Helper* (2nd ed). Monterey, CA: Brooks/Cole.

Ellison, R. (1966). Harlem is nowhere. In *Shadow and Act.* New York: Random House.

Espin, O. M. (1985). Psychotherapy with Hispanic women. In P. B. Pedersen (Ed.), *Handbook of cross-cultural counseling and therapy* (pp. 165–171). Westport, CT: Greenwood Press.

Evans, D. A. (1985). Psychotherapy and Black patients: Problems of training, trainees, and trainers. *Psychotherapy, 22,* 457–460.

Evans, L. A., Acosta, F. X., Yamamoto, J., & Hurwicz, M. L. (1986). Patient requests: Correlates and therapeutic implications for Hispanics, Black, and Caucasian patients. *Journal of Clinical Psychology, 42,* 213–221.

Everett, F., Proctor, N., & Cortmell, B. (1983). Providing psychological services to American Indian children and families. *Professional Psychology, 14,* 588–603.

Everett, F., Proctor, N. & Cortmell, B. (1989). Providing psychological services to American Indian children and families. In D. R. Atkinson, G. Morten & D. W. Sue (Eds.), *Counseling American minorities* (3d ed.) (pp. 53–71). Dubuque, IA: W. C. Brown.

Fenz, W., & Arkoff, A. (1962). Comparative need patterns of five ancestry groups in Hawaii. *Journal of Social Psychology, 58,* 67–89.

Festinger, L. (1957). *A Theory of Cognitive Dissonance.* Evanston, IL: Row & Peterson.

Fogelson, R. M. (1970). Violence and grievances: Reflections on the 1960's riots. *Journal of Social Issues, 26,* 141–163.

Folensbee, R., Draguns, J. G., & Danish, S. (1986). Counselor interventions in three cultural groups. *Journal of Counseling Psychology, 33,* 446–453.

Foley, V. D. (1984). Family therapy. In R. J. Corsini (Ed.), *Current psychotherapies.* Itasca, IL: F. F. Peacock Publishers.

Fong, S. L. M. (1965). Assimilation of Chinese in America. Changes in orientation and social perception. *American Journal of Sociology, 71,* 265–273.

Forward, J. R., & Williams, J. R. (1970). International external control and Black militancy. *Journal of Social Issues, 26,* 74–92.

Franklin, A. J. (1982). Therapeutic interventions with urban Black adolescents. In E. E. Jones & S. J. Korchin (Eds.), *Minority mental health* (pp 267–295). New York: Praeger.

Franklin, J. H. (1988). A historical note on black families. In H. P. McAdoo (Ed.), *Black families.* Newberry Park, CA: Sage.

Freire, P. (1970). *Cultural action for freedom.* Cambridge: Harvard Educational Review Press.

Freud, S. (1960). Psychopathology of everyday life. In *Standard Edition, 6.* London: Hogarth.

Fukuyama, M. A., & Greenfield, T. K. (1983). Dimensions of assertiveness in an Asian-American student population. *Journal of Counseling Psychology, 30,* 429–432.

Fulong, M. J., Atkinson, D. R., & Casas, J. M. (1979). Effects of counselor ethnicity and attitudinal similarity on Chicano students' perceptions of counselor credibility and attractiveness. *Hispanic Journal of Behavioral Sciences, 1,* 41–53.

Galton, F. (1869). *Hereditary genius: An inquiry into its laws and consequences.* London: Macmillan.

Garcia, D., & Levenson, H. (1975). Differences between black's and white's expectations of control by chance and powerful others. *Psychological Reports, 37,* 563–566.

Garfield, J. C., Weiss, S. L., & Pollock, E. A. (1973). Effects of a child's social class on school counselors' decision making. *Journal of Counseling Psychology, 20,* 166–168.

Gary, L. E. (1985). Attitudes toward human service organizations: Perspectives from an urban Black community. *Journal of Applied Behavioral Science, 21,* 445–458.

Gaw, A. (1982). *Cross-cultural psychiatry.* Boston: John Wright.

Gibbs, J. T. (1980). The interpersonal orientation in mental health consultation: Toward a model of ethnic variations in consultation. *American Journal of Orthopsychiatry, 45,* 430–445.

Gibbs, J. T. (1987). Identity and marginality: Issues in the treatment of biracial adolescents. *American Journal of Orthopsychiatry, 57,* 265–278.

Gillie, D. (1977). The IQ issue. *Phi Delta Kappan, 58,* 469.

Goering, J. M., & Cummins, M. (1970). Intervention research and the survey process. *Journal of Social Issues, 26,* 49–55.

Goldman, L. (1977). Toward more meaningful research. *Personnel and Guidance Journal, 55,* 363–368.

Goldman, M. (1980). Effect of eye contact and distance on the verbal reinforcement of attitude. *The Journal of Social Psychology, 111,* 73–78.

Gonzalez, A. & Zimbardo, P. G. (1985). Time in perspective. *Psychology Today,* March, 21–26.

Goodtracks, J. G. (1973). Native American noninterference. *Social Work, 18,* 30–34.

Gore, P. M., & Rotter, J. B. (1963). A personality correlate of social action. *Journal of Personality, 31,* 58–64.

Gossett, T. F. (1963). *Race: The history of an idea in America.* Dallas: Southern Methodist University Press.

Green, J. M., Trankina, F. J., & Chavez, N. (1976). Therapeutic intervention with Mexican-American children. *Psychiatric Annals, 6,* 227–234.

Greene, B. A. (1985). Considerations in the treatment of Black patients by white therapists. *Psychotherapy, 22,* 389–393.

Grevious, C. (1985). The role of the family therapist with low-income Black families. *Family Therapy, 12,* 115–122.

Grier, W., & Cobbs, P. (1968). *Black rage.* New York: Basic Books.

Grier, W. H., & Cobbs. P. (1971). *The Jesus bag.* San Francisco: McGraw-Hill.

Grosgebauer, C. (1987). Minorities seek the American dream. *Guidepost, 29,* 1, 6.

Gurin, P., Gurin, G., Lao, R., & Beattie, M. (1969). Internal-external control in the motivational dynamics of negro youth. *Journal of Social Issues, 25,* 29–54.

Gwyn, F., & Kilpatrick, A. (1981). Family therapy with low-income Blacks: A tool or turn-off? *Social Casework, 62,* 259–266.

Habemann, L., & Thiry, S. (1970). *The effect of socioeconomic status variables on counselor perception and behavior.* Unpublished master's thesis, University of Wisconsin.

Haley, A. (1966). *The autobiography of Malcolm X.* New York: Grove Press.

Haley, J. (1967). Marriage therapy. In H. Greenwald (Ed.), *Active psychotherapy,* pp. 189–223. Chicago: Aldine.

Hall, E. T. (1959). *The silent language.* Greenwich, CT: Premier Books.

Hall, E. T. (1969). *The hidden dimension.* Garden City, New York: Doubleday.

Hall, E. T. (1974). *Handbook for proxemic research.* Washington DC: Society for the Ontology of Visual Communications.

Hall, E. T. (1976). *Beyond culture.* New York: Anchor Press.

Hall, W. S., Cross, W. E., & Freedle, R. (1972). Stages in the development of Black awareness: An exploratory investigation. In R. L. Jones (Ed.), *Black Psychology.* New York: Harper & Row.

Halleck, S. L. (1971, April). Therapy is the handmaiden of the status quo. *Psychology Today, 4,* 30–34, 98–100.

Hansen, J. C., Stevic, R. R., & Warner, R. W. (1982). *Counseling: Theory and process.* Toronto: Allyn-Bacon.

Hardiman, R. (1982). White identity development: A process oriented model for describing the racial consciousness of white Americans. *Dissertation Abstracts International, 43,* 104A. (University Microfilms No. 82-10330)

Harrison, D. K. (1975). Race as a counselor-client variable in counseling and psychotherapy: A review of the research. *Counseling Psychologist, 5,* 124–133.

Harrison, R. P. (1983, May). Past problems and future directions in nonverbal research. Paper presented at the *Second International Conference in Nonverbal Behavior,* Toronto.

Helms, J. E. (1984). Toward a theoretical explanation of the effects of race on counseling: A Black and white model. *The Counseling Psychologist, 12,* 153–165.

Helms, J. E. (1985). Cultural identity in the treatment process. In P. B. Pedersen (Ed.), *Handbook of cross-cultural counseling and therapy.* Westport, CT: Greenwood Press.

Helms, J. E. (1986). Expanding racial identity theory to cover counseling process. *Journal of Counseling Psychology, 33,* 62–64.

Helms, J. E. (1989). Considering some methodological issues in racial identity counseling research. *The Counseling Psychologist, 17,* 227–252.

Helms, J. E. & Giorgis, T. W. (1980). A comparison of the locus of control and anxiety level of African, Black American, and White American college students. *Journal of College Student Personnel*, November, 503–509.

Henkin, W. A. (1985). Toward counseling the Japanese in America: A cross-cultural primer. *Journal of Counseling & Development, 63,* 500–503.

Herrnstein, R. (1971). IQ. *Atlantic Monthly,* 43–64.

Hersch, P., & Scheibe, K. (1967). Reliability and validity of internal-external control as a personality dimension. *Journal of Consulting Psychology, 31,* 609–613.

Herzog, E. (1971). Who should be studied? *American Journal of Orthopsychiatry, 41,* 4–11.

Hill, C. E., Thames, T. B., & Rardin, D. K. (1979). Comparison of Rogers, Perls, and Ellis on the Hill Counselor Verbal Response Category System. *Journal of Counseling Psychology, 26,* 198–203.

Hines, P., & Boyd-Franklin, N. (1982). *Black families.* In M. McGoldrick (Ed.), *Ethnicity and family therapy.* New York: Guildford.

Ho, M. K. (1987). *Family therapy with ethnic minorities.* Newbury Park, CA: Sage.

Hollingshead, A., & Redlich, F. (1958). *Social class and mental illness.* New York: John Wiley.

Hollingshead, A. R., & Redlich, F. C. (1968). *Social class and mental health.* New York: John Wiley.

Hraba, J., & Grant, G. (1969). Black is beautiful: A reexamination of racial preferences and identification. *Journal of Personality and Social Psychology, 16,* 398–402.

Hsieh, T., Shybut, J., & Lotsof, E. (1969). Internal versus external control and ethnic group membership: A cross-cultural comparison. *Journal of Consulting and Clinical Psychology, 33,* 122–124.

Hynes, K., & Werbin, J. (1977). Group psychotherapy for Spanish-speaking women. *Psychiatric Annals, 7,* 64–73.

Ibrahim, F. A. (1985). Effective cross-cultural counseling and psychotherapy: A framework. *The Counseling Psychologist, 13,* 625–638.

Ibrahim, F. A., & Arrendondo, P. M. (1986). Ethical standards for cross-cultural counseling: Counselor preparation, practice, assessment, and research. *Journal of Counseling and Development, 64,* 349–352.

Inclan, J. (1979). Adjustment to migration: Family organization, acculturation, and psychological symptomatology in Puerto Rican women of three socioeconomic class groups. Unpublished doctoral dissertation. New York University.

Inclan, J. (1985). Variations in value orientations in mental health work with Puerto Ricans. *Psychotherapy, 22,* 324–334.

Indian Health Service (1978). *Indian health trends and services.* Washington, DC: U.S. Government Printing Office.

Ishisaka, H. A., Nguyen, Q. T., & Okimoto, J. T. (1985). The role in the mental health treatment of Indochinese refugees. In T. C. Owan (Ed.), *Southeast Asian mental health treatment, prevention services, training, and research.* Washington, DC: National Institute of Mental Health.

Ivey, A., & Authier, J. (1978). Microcounseling: Innovations in interviewing training. Springfield, IL: Charles C. Thomas.

Ivey, A. E. (1981). Counseling and psychotherapy: Toward a new perspective. In A. J. Marsella and P. B. Pedersen (Eds.), *Cross-cultural counseling and psychotherapy.* New York: Pergamon.

Ivey, A. E. (1986). *Developmental therapy.* San Francisco: Jossey-Bass.

Ivey, A. E., & Gluckstern, N. B. (1976). *Systematic videotraining for beginning helpers.* Amherst, MA: Microtraining Associates.

Ivey, A. E., Ivey, M. B., & Simek-Downing, L. (1987). *Counseling and psychotherapy: Skills, theories, and practice.* Englewood Cliffs, NJ: Prentice-Hall.

Jackson, A. M. (1983). A theoretical model for the practice of psychotherapy with Black populations. *Journal of Black Psychology, 10,* 19027.

Jackson, B. (1975). Black identity development. *Journal of Education Diversity, 2,* 19–25.

Jacobs, P., Landau, S., & Pell, E. (1971). *To serve the Devil. Vol. 2 Colonials and sojourners.* New York: Vintage Books.

Jenkins, A. H. (1985). Attending to self-activity in the Afro-American client. *Psychotherapy, 22,* 335–341.

Jenkins, A. H. (1982). *The psychology of the Afro-American.* New York: Pergamon.

Jenkins, Y. M. (1985). The integration of psychotherapy-vocational interventions: Relevance for Black women. *Psychotherapy, 22,* 394–397.

Jensen, A. (1969). How much can we boost IQ and school achievement? *Harvard Educational Review, 39,* 1–123.

Jensen, J. V. (1985). Perspective on nonverbal intercultural communication. In L. A. Samovar & R. E. Porter (Eds.), *Intercultural communication: A reader.* Belmont, CA: Wadsworth.

Jones, A. C. (1985). Psychological functioning in Black Americans: A conceptual guide for use in psychotherapy. *Psychotherapy, 22,* 363–369.

Jones, A. C., & Seagull, A. A. (1977). Dimensions of the relationship between the black client and the white therapist: A theoretical overview. *American Psychologist, 32,* 850–855.

Jones, B. E., & Gray, B. A. (1983). Black males and psychotherapy: Theoretical issues. *American Journal of Psychotherapy, 37,* 77–85.

Jones, E. E. (1985). Psychotherapy and counseling with Black clients. In P. B. Pedersen (Ed.), *Handbook of cross-cultural counseling and therapy* (pp. 173–179). Westport, CT: Greenwood Press.

Jones, E. E., Kanouse, D., Kelley, H. H., Nisbett, R. E., Valins, S., & Weiner, B. (Eds.). (1972). *Attribution: Perceiving the causes of behavior.* Morristown, NJ: General Learning Press.

Jones, E. E., & Korchin, S. J. (1982). Minority mental health: Perspectives. In E. E. Jones and S. J. Korchin (Eds.), *Minority mental health.* New York: Praeger.

Jones, J. M. (1972). *Prejudice and Racism.* Reading, MA: Addison-Wesley.

Josephy, A. M. (1982). *Now that the buffalo's gone: A study of today's American Indian.* New York: Knopf.

Journard, S. M. (1964). *The transparent self.* Princeton, NJ: D. Van Nostrand.

Juarez, R. (1985). Core issues in psychotherapy with the Hispanic child. *Psychotherapy, 22,* 441–448.

Jung, C. G. (1960). The structure and dynamics of the psyche. In *Collected Works, 8.* Princeton, NJ: Princeton University Press.

Kagan, N. (1986). *Interpersonal process recall: A method for influencing human interaction.* Washington, D.C. APGA.

Kagiwada, G., & Fujimoto, I. (1973). Asian-American studies: Implications for education. *Personnel and Guidance Journal, 51,* 400–405.

Kamin, L. (1974). *The science and politics of I.Q.* Potomac, MD: Eribaum.

Kane, M. B. (1970). *Minorities in textbooks: A study of their treatment in social studies texts.* Chicago: Quadrangle.

Kaneshige, E. (1973). Cultural factors in group counseling and interaction. *Personnel and Guidance Journal, 51,* 407–412.

Kardiner, A., & Ovesey, L. (1962). *The Mark of oppression*. New York: Norton.

Karno, M., & Edgarton, R. B. (1969). Perception of mental illness in a Mexican-American community. *Archives of General Psychiatry, 20,* 233–238.

Katz, J. (1985). The sociopolitical nature of counseling. *The Counseling Psychologist, 13,* 615–624.

Katz, P. (1981). Psychotherapy with Native adolescents. *Canadian Journal of Psychiatry, 26,* 455–459.

Katz, J. & Ivey, A. (1977). White awareness: The frontier of racism awareness training. *Personnel and Guidance Journal, 55,* 485–489.

Kazalunas, J. R. (1979). Counseling and testing procedures for Chicano students. *Journal of Non-White Concerns, 7,* 108–113.

Kikumura, A., & Kitano, H. H. (1973). Interracial marriage: A picture of the Japanese Americans. *Journal of Social Issues, 29,* 67–81.

Kim, K. C., & Hurk, W. M. (1983). Asian Americans and the success myth. *Amerasia Journal, 10,* 3–21.

Kim, S. C. (1985). Family therapy for Asian Americans: A strategic structural framework. *Psychotherapy, 22,* 342–356.

Kimmich, R. A. (1960). Ethnic aspects of schizophrenia in Hawaii. *Psychiatry, 23,* 97–102.

Kinzie, J. D. (1985). Overview of clinical issues in the treatment of Southeast Asian refugees. In T. C. Owan (Ed.), *Southeast Asian mental health treatment, prevention services, training, and research*. Washington, DC: National Institute of Mental Health.

Kitano, H. H. L. (1962). Changing achievement patterns of the Japanese in the United States. *Journal of Social Psychology, 58,* 257–264.

Kitano, H. H. L. (1964). Inter- and intragenerational differences in maternal attitudes towards child rearing. *Journal of Psychology, 63,* 215–220.

Kitano, H. H. L. (1967). Japanese-American crime and delinquency. *Journal of Psychology, 66,* 253–263.

Kitano, H. H. L. (1969a). Japanese-American mental illness. In S. C. Plog & R. B. Edgarton (Eds.), *Changing perspectives in mental illness*. New York: Holt, Rinehart & Winston.

Kitano, H. H. L. (1969b). *Japanese-Americans: The evolution of a subculture*. Englewood Cliffs, NJ: Prentice-Hall.

Kitano, H. H. L. (1970). Mental illness in four cultures. *Journal of Social Psychology, 80,* 121–134.

Kitano, H. H. L., & Kimura, A. (1976). The Japanese American family. In C. H. Mindle & R. W. Haberstein (Eds.), *Ethnic families in America*. New York: Elsevier.

Klein, D. C. (1968). *Community dynamics and mental health*. New York: John Wiley.

Kleinfeld, J., & Boom, J. (1977). Boarding schools: Effects on the mental health of Eskimo adolescents. *American Journal of Psychiatry, 134,* 411–417.

Kluckhohn, F. R., & Strodtbeck, F. L. (1961). *Variations in value orientations*. Evanston, IL: Row, Patterson, & Co.

Knapp, M. I. (1972) *Nonverbal communication in human interaction*. New York: Holt, Rinehart & Winston.

Knapp, M. L. (1980). *Essentials of nonverbal communication*. New York: Holt, Rinehart & Winston.

Kochman, T. (1981). *Black and white styles in conflict*. Chicago: University of Chicago Press.

Korman, M. (1974). National conference on levels and patterns of professional training in psychology. *American Psychologist, 29,* 441–449.

Kupers, T. (1981). *Public therapy: The practice of psychotherapy in the public mental health clinic.* New York: Macmillan.

LaBarre, W. (1985). Paralinguistics, kinesics and cultural anthropology. In L. A. Samovar & R. E. Porter (Eds.), *Intercultural communication: A reader.* Belmont, CA: Wadsworth.

Labov, W. (1972). Language in the inner city, *Studies in the Black English vernacular.* Philadelphia: University of Pennsylvania Press.

La Crosse, M. B., & Barak, A. (1976). Differential perception of counselor behavior. *Journal of Counseling Psychology, 23,* 170–172.

LaFromboise, T. D., Coleman, L. K., & Hernandez, A. (1989, August). *Development and factor structure of the cross-cultural counseling inventory.* Paper presented at American Psychological Association, New Orleans, LA.

LaFromboise, T. D., & Coleman, H. L. K. (1989, August). *Development and factor structure of the cross cultural counseling inventory.* Paper presented at the meeting of the American Psychological Association, New Orleans, LA.

LaFromboise, T. D., & Dixon, D. N. (1981). American Indian perception of trustworthiness in a counseling interview. *Journal of Counseling Psychology, 28,* 135–139.

Laing, R. D. (1967). *The divided self.* New York: Pantheon.

Laing, R. D. (1969). *The politics of experience.* New York: Pantheon.

Lambert, R. G., & Lambert, M. J. (1984). The effects of role preparation for psychotherapy on immigrant clients seeking mental health services in Hawaii. *Journal of Community Psychology, 12,* 263–275.

Lass, N. J., Mertz, P. J., & Kimmel, K. (1978). The effect of temporal speech alterations on speaker race and sex identification. *Language and Speech, 21,* 279–290.

Latting, J. E. & Zundel, C. (1986). World view differences between clients and counselors. *Social Casework, 12,* 66–71.

Lau, S. (1982). The effect of smiling on person perception. *The Journal of Social Psychology, 117,* 63–67.

Laval, R. A., Gomez, E. A., & Ruiz, P. (1983). A language minority: Hispanics and mental health care. *The American Journal of Social Psychiatry, 3,* 42–49.

Lazarus, P. J. (1982). Counseling the Native American child: A question of values. *Elementary School Guidance and Counseling, 32,* 83–99.

Lee, D. Y., & Uhlemann, M. R. (1984). Comparison of verbal responses of Rogers, Shostrom, and Lazarus. *Journal of Counseling Psychology, 31,* 91–94.

Lee, D. Y., Uhlemann, M. R., & House, R. F. (1985). Counselor verbal and nonverbal responses and perceived expertness, truthworthiness, and attractiveness. *Journal of Counseling Psychology, 32,* 181–187.

Lefcourt, H. (1966). Internal versus control of reinforcement: A review. *Psychological Bulletin, 65,* 206–220.

Leong, F. (1985). Career development of Asian Americans. *Journal of College Student Personnel, 26,* 539–546.

Leong, F. T. (1985). Career development of Asian Americans. *Journal of College Student Personnel, 26,* 539–546.

Leong, F. T. (1986). Counseling and psychotherapy with Asian-Americans: Review of literature. *Journal of Counseling Psychology, 33,* 196–206.

Lerner, B. (1972). *Therapy in the ghetto.* Baltimore: Johns Hopkins University Press.

Levenson, H. (1974). Activism and powerful others. *Journal of Personality Assessment, 38,* 377–383.

LeVine, E. S., & Padilla, A. M. (1980). Crossing cultures in therapy: Pluralistic counseling for the Hispanic. Monterey, CA: Brooks/Cole.

Lewis, O. (1966). *La Vida: A Puerto Rican family in the context of poverty—San Juan and New York.* New York: Random House.

Lewis, R. (1981). Cultural perspectives on treatment modalities with native Americans. In R. H. Dana (Ed.), *Human services for cultural minorities.* Baltimore: University Park Press.

Lewis, R. G., & Ho, M. K. (1985). Social work with Native Americans. *Social Work, 20,* 379–382.

Lin, K.-M., Masuda, M. I., & Tazuma, L. (1982). Adaptational problems of Vietnamese refugees, Part III. Case studies in clinic and field: Adaptive and maladaptive. *The Psychiatric Journal of the University of Ottawa, 7,* 173–183.

Lin, W. T., & Cheung, F. (1985). Research concerns associated with the study of Southeast Asian refugees. In T. C. Owan (Ed.), *Southeast Asian mental health treatment, prevention, services, training, and research* (pp. 345–390). Washington, DC: National Institute of Mental Health.

Lin, W. T. & Cheung, F. (1985). Research concerns associated with the study of Southeast Asian refugees. In L. C. Owan (Ed.), *Southeast Asian mental health treatment, prevention, services, training and research* (pp. 487–516). Washington, D.C.: National Institute of Mental Health.

Lockard, J. O. (1987). Racism on campus: Exploring the issues. *Michigan Alumnus, 93,* 22–33.

London, P. (1964). *Modes and morals of psychotherapy.* New York: Holt, Rinehart & Winston.

London, P. (1989). *Modes and morals of psychotherapy.* New York: Holt, Rinehart & Winston.

Lonner, W. J., & Sundberg, N. D. (1985). Assessment in cross-cultural counseling and therapy. In P. B. Pedersen (Ed.), *Handbook of Cross-Cultural Counseling and Therapy.* Westport, CT: Greenwood Press.

Loo, C., & Ong, P. (1984). Crowding perceptions, attitudes, and consequences among the Chinese. *Environment and Behavior, 16,* 55–87.

Lopez, S. R., Grover, K. P., Holland, D., Johnson, M., Kain, C. D., Kanel, K., Mellins, C. A., Rhoner, M. C. (in press). The development of culturally sensitive therapists. *Professional Psychology.*

Lorenzo, M. K., & Adler, D. A. (1984). Mental health services for Chinese in a community health center. *Social Casework, 65,* 600–610.

Lorion, R. P. (1973). Socioeconomic status and treatment approaches reconsidered. *Psychological Bulletin, 79,* 263–280.

Lorion, R. P. (1974). Patient and therapist variables in the treatment of low-income patients. *Psychological Bulletin, 81,* 344–354.

Lowe, C. M. (1969). *Value orientations in counseling and psychotherapy.* San Francisco: Chandler.

Lowrey, L. (1983). Bridging a culture in counseling. *Journal of Applied Rehabilitation Counseling, 14,* 69–73.

Lum, R. G. (1982). Mental health attitudes and opinions of Chinese. In E. E. Jones and S. J. Korchin (Eds.), *Minority mental health.* New York: Praeger.

Lyman, S. M. (1970). *The Asian in the West.* Reno, NV: University of Nevada Press.

Mackler, B., & Giddings, M. G. (1965). Cultural deprivation: A study in mythology. *Teachers College Record, 66,* 608–613.

Majors, R., & Nikelly, A. (1983). Serving the Black minority: A new direction for psychotherapy. *Journal of Non-White Concerns, 11,* 142–152.

Malgady, R. G., Rogler, L. H., & Costantino, G. (1987). Ethnocultural and linguistic bias in the mental health evaluation of Hispanics. *American Psychologist, 42,* 228–234.

Manson, S. M., Tatum, E., & Dinges, N. G. (1982). Prevention research among American Indian and Alaska Native communities: Charting further courses for theory and practice in mental health. In S. M. Manson (Ed.), *New directions in prevention among American Indian and Alaska Native Communities* (pp. 1–61). Portland, OR: Oregon Health Sciences University.

Marcos, L., & Alpert, M. (1976). Strategies and risks in psychotherapy with bilingual patients: The phenomenon of language independence. *American Journal of Psychiatry, 133,* 1275–1278.

Marcos, L. R. (1973). The language barrier in evaluating Spanish-American patients. *Archives of General Psychiatry, 29,* 655–659.

Marcos, L. R. (1979). Effects of interpreters on the evaluation of psychopathology in non-English-speaking patients. *American Journal of Psychiatry, 136,* 171–174.

Margolis, R. L., & Rungta, S. A. (1986). Training counselors for work with special populations: A second look. *Journal of Counseling and Development, 64,* 642–644.

Marsella, A. J., Kinzie, D., & Gordon, P. (1971, March). *Depression patterns among American college students of Caucasian, Chinese, and Japanese ancestry.* Paper presented at the Conference on Culture and Mental Health in Asia and the Pacific. Honolulu, HI.

Martin, D. O., & Thomas, M. B. (1982). Black student preferences for counselors: The influence of age, sex, and type of problem. *Journal of Non-White Concerns, 10,* 143–153.

Marx, G. T. (1967). *Protest and prejudice: A study of belief in the Black community.* New York: Harper & Row.

Maslow, A. H. (1968). *Toward a psychology of being.* Princeton: Van Nostrand.

Matsumoto, G. M., Meredith, G., & Masuda, M. (1970). Ethnic identification: Honolulu and Seattle Japanese-Americans. *Journal of Cross-Cultural Psychology, 1,* 63–76.

Mau, W. C., & Jepson, D. A. (1988). Attitudes toward counselors and counseling processes: A comparison of Chinese and American graduate students. *Journal of Counseling and Development 67,* 189–192.

Maykovich, M. H. (1973). Political activation of Japanese American youth. *Journal of Social Issues, 29,* 167–185.

Mays, V. M. (1985). The Black American and psychotherapy: The dilemma. *Psychotherapy, 22,* 379–388.

McCurdy, P. C. & Ruiz, R. A. (1980). Sex role and marital agreement. In R. A. Ruiz & R. E. Cromwell (Eds.), *Anglo, Black, and Chicano families in the urban community.*

McDavis, R. J. (1978). Counseling Black clients effectively: The eclectic approach. *Journal of Non-White Concerns, 7,* 41–47.

McFadden, J., & Wilson, T. (1977). *Non-white academic training with counselor education, rehabilitation counseling and student personnel programs.* Unpublished research.

McLeod, B. (1986). The Oriental express. *Psychology Today, 20,* 565–570.

McNamara, K., & Rickard, K. M. (1989). Feminist identity development: Implications for feminist therapy with women. *Journal of Counseling and Development, 68,* 184–193.

McRoy, R. G., & Oglesby, Z. (1984). Group work with Black adoptive applicants. *Social Work with Groups, 7,* 125–134.

Meadow, A. (1982). Psychopathology, psychotherapy, and the Mexican-American patient. In E. E. Jones & S. J. Korchin (Eds.), *Minority Mental Health* (pp 331–361). New York: Praeger.

Meara, N. M., Shannon, J. W., & Pepinsky, H. B. (1979). Comparison of the stylistic complexity of the language of the counselor and client across three theoretical orientations. *Journal of Counseling Psychology, 26,* 181–189.

Meara, N. M., Pepinsky, H. B., Shannon, J. W., & Murray, Meredith, G. M. (1966). Amae and acculturation among Japanese-American college students in Hawaii. *Journal of Social Psychology, 70,* 171–180.

Meara, N. M., Pepinsky, H. B., Shannon, J. W., & Murray, W. A. (1981). Semantic communication and expectations for counseling across three theoretical orientations. *Journal of Counseling Psychology, 28,* 110–118.

Medicine, B. (1982). New road to coping: Siouan sobriety. In S. M. Manson (Ed.), *New directions in prevention among American Indian and Alaska Native communities* (pp. 189–212). Portland, OR: Oregon Health Sciences University.

Mehrabian, A. (1972). *Nonverbal communication.* Chicago: Aldene-Atherton.

Mehrabian, A., & Ferris, S. R. (1976). Influence of attitudes from nonverbal communication in two channels. *Journal of Consulting Psychology, 31,* 248–252.

Mejia, D. (1983). The development of Mexican-American children. In G. J. Powell, J. Yamamoto, A. Romero, A. Morales (Eds.). *The psychosocial development of minority group children* (pp. 77–114). New York: Brunner/Mazel.

Mejia, D. (1985). The development of Mexican-American children. In G. J. Powell, J. Yamamoto, A. Romero, A. Morales (Eds.), *The psychosocial development of minority group children* (pp. 26–38). New York: Burnner/Mazel.

Meketon, M. J. (1983). Indian mental health: An orientation. *American Journal of Orthopsychiatry, 53,* 110–115.

Menacker, J. (1971). *Urban poor students and guidance.* Boston: Houghton Mifflin.

Mercer, J. R. (1971). Institutionalized anglocentrism. In P. Orleans, & W. Russel (Eds.), *Race, change, and urban society.* Los Angeles: Sage.

Meredith, G. M. (1966). Amae and acculturation among Japanese-American college students in Hawaii. *Journal of Social Psychology, 70,* 171–180.

Merluzzi, T. V., Banikiotes, P. G., & Missbach, J. W. (1978). Perceptions of counselor characteristics: Contributions of counselor sex, experience, and disclosure level. *Journal of Counseling Psychology, 25,* 479–482.

Merluzzi, T. V., Merluzzi, B. H., & Kaul, T. J. (1977). Counselor race and power base: Effects on attitudes and behavior. *Journal of Counseling Psychology, 24,* 430–436.

Miller, D. (1980). The Native American family: The urban way. In E. Corfman (Ed.), *Families today* (pp. 441–484). Washington DC: U.S. Government Printing Office.

Minuchin, S. (1974). *Families and family therapy.* Cambridge, MA: Harvard University Press.

Mirels, H. (1970). Dimensions of internal versus external control. *Journal of Consulting and Clinical Psychology, 34,* 226–228.

Mizio, E. (1983). The impact of macro systems on Puerto Rican families. In G. J. Powell, J. Yamamoto, A. Romero, & A. Morales (Eds.), *The psychosocial development of minority group children* (pp. 216–236). New York: Brunner/Mazel.

Montijo, J. A. (1985). Therapeutic relationships with the poor: A Puerto Rican perspective. *Psychotherapy, 22,* 436–440.

Moynihan, D. P. (1965). Employment, income and the ordeal of the Negro family. *Daedalus,* 745–770.

Munoz, J. A. (1982). The Spanish-speaking consumer and the community mental health center. In E. E. Jones and S. J. Korchin (Eds.). *Minority mental health* (pp. 362–398). New York: Praeger Publishers.

Munoz, R. F. (1982). The Spanish-speaking consumer and the community mental health center. In E. E. Jones and S. J. Korchin (Eds.), *Minority mental health* (pp. 362–398). New York: Praeger.

Murphy, K. C., & Strong, S. R. (1972). Some effects of similarity self-disclosures. *Journal of Counseling Psychology, 19,* 121–124.

Myers, H. F., & King, L. M. (1983). Mental health issues of the development of the Black American child. In G. J. Powell, J. Yamamoto, A. Romero, & A. Morales (Eds.), *The Psychosocial development of Minority group children* (pp. 275–306). New York: Brunner/Mazel.

National Commission on the Causes and Prevention of Violence. (1969). *To establish justice, to insure domestic tranquility.* New York: Award Books.

Neighbors, H. W. (1984). Professional help use among Black Americans: Implications for unmet need. *American Journal of Community Psychology, 12,* 551–565.

Newton, B. J., & Arciniega, M. (1983). Counseling minority families: An Adlerian perspective. *Counseling and Human Development, 16,* 1–12.

Nguyen, L. T., & Henkin, L. B. (1983). Change among Indochinese refugees. In R. J. Samada & S. C. Woods (Eds.), *Perspectives in immigrant and minority education.* New York: University Press of America.

Nguyen, S. D. (1985). Mental health services for refugees and immigrants in Canada. In T. C. Owan (Ed.). *Southeast Asian mental health: Treatment, prevention, services, training, and research* (pp. 261–282). Washington, D.C., NIMH.

Nidorf, J. F. (1985). Mental health and refugee youths: A model for diagnostic training. In T. C. Owan (Ed.), *Southeast Asian mental health treatment, prevention, services, training, and research.* Washington, DC: National Institute of Mental Health.

Nisio, K., & Bilmer, M. (1987). Psychotherapy with southeast Asian American clients. *Professional Psychology: Research and Practice, 18,* 342–346.

Nobles, W. W. (1976). Black people in white insanity: An issue for Black community mental health. *The Journal of Afro-American Issues, 4,* 21–27.

Norton, D. G. (1983). Black family life patterns, the development of self and cognitive development of Black children. In G. J. Powell, J. Yamamoto, A. Romero, & A. Morales (Eds.), *The Psychosocial development of Minority group children* (pp. 181–193). New York: Brunner/Mazel.

Nwachuku, U. T., & Ivey, A. E. (Paper submitted for publication). Teaching culture-specific counseling using microtraining technology.

O'dell, J. W., & Bahmer, A. J. (1981). Rogers, Lazarus, and Shostrom in content analysis. *Journal of Clinical Psychology, 37,* 507–510.

Odin, P. (1987a). Community colleges: Higher education's leading melting pot. *Black Issues in Higher Education, 4,* 1, 6

Odin, P. (1987b). Hispanics help shape the educational landscape. *Black Issues in Higher Education, 4,* pp. 1, 7, 11.

Office of Refugee Resettlement, Social Security Administration. *Report to Congress: Refugee resettlement program.* Washington, DC: U. S. Government Printing Office.

O'Guinn, T. C., Imperia, G., & MacAdams, E. A. (1987). Acculturation and perceived family decision-making input among Mexican-American wives. *Journal of Cross-Cultural Psychology, 18,* 78–92.

Oler, C. H. (1989). Psychotherapy with Black clients' racial identity and locus of control. *Psychotherapy, 26,* 233–241.

Ornstein, R. E. (1972). *The Psychology of consciousness*. San Francisco: Freeman.

Owan, L. C. (1985). Southeast Asian mental health: Transition from treatment services to prevention—A new direction. In T. C. Owan (Ed.), *Southeast Asian mental health treatment, prevention services, training, and research*. Washington, DC: National Institute of Mental Health.

Padilla, A. M., & DeSnyder, N. S. (1985). Counseling Hispanics: Strategies for effective intervention. In P. B. Pedersen (Ed.), *Handbook of cross-cultural counseling and therapy* (pp. 157–164). Westport, CT: Greenwood Press.

Padilla, A. M., Ruiz, R. A., & Alvarez, R. (1975). Community mental health services for the Spanish-speaking/surnamed population. *American Psychologist, 30,* 892–905.

Parham, T. A. (1989). Cycles of psychological nigrescense. *The Counseling Psychologist, 17,* 187–226.

Parham, T. A., & Helms, J. E. (1981). Influence of a Black student's racial identity attitudes on preference for counselor race. *Journal of Counseling Psychology, 28,* 250–257.

Parham, T. A. & Helms, J. E. (1985). Relation of racial identity attitudes to self-actualization and affective status of Black students. *Journal of Counseling Psychology, 32,* 431–440.

Parham, T. A., & McDavis, R. J. (1987). Black men and endangered species: Who's really pulling the trigger? *Journal of Counseling and Development, 66,* 24–27.

Parker, W. M., & McDavis, R. J. (1983). Attitudes of Blacks toward mental health agencies and counselors. *Journal of Non-White Concerns, 11,* 89–98.

Paster, V. S. (1985). Adapting psychotherapy for the depressed, unacculturated, acting-out, Black male adolescent. *Psychotherapy, 22,* 408–417.

Patterson, C. H. (1972). Psychology and social responsibility. *Professional Psychology, 3,* 3–10.

Patterson, C. H. (1980). *Theories of counseling and psychotherapy* (3rd ed.). New York: Harper & Row.

Pavkov, T. W., Lewis, D. A. & Lyons, J. S. (1989). Psychiatric diagnosis and racial bias: An empirical investigation. *Professional Psychology: Research & Practice, 20,* 364–368.

Pearson, J. C. (1985). *Gender and communication*. Dubuque, IA: W. C. Brown.

Pearson, R. E. (1985). The recognition and use of natural support systems in cross-cultural counseling. In P. B. Pedersen (Ed.), *Handbook of cross-cultural counseling and therapy*. Westport, CT: Greenwood Press.

Pedersen, P. (1988). *Handbook for developing multicultural awareness*. Alexandria, VA: AACD Press.

Pedersen, P. B. (1987). Ten frequent assumptions of cultural bias in counseling. *Journal of Multicultural Counseling and Development, 15,* 16–24.

Pedersen, P. B. (1988). *A handbook for developing multicultural awareness*. Alexandria, Virginia: American Association for Counseling and Development.

Pedersen, P. B., Draguns, J. G., Lonner, W. J., & Trimble, J. E. (Eds.). (1981). *Counseling across cultures*. Honolulu: University of Hawaii Press.

Peoples, V. Y., & Dell, D. M. (1975). Black and white student preferences for counselor roles. *Journal of Counseling Psychology, 22,* 529–534.

Pinderhughes, C. A. (1973). Racism in psychotherapy. In C. Willie, B. Kramer & B. Brown (Eds.). *Racism and mental health* (pp. 61–121). Pittsburgh: University of Pittsburgh Press.

Pine, G. J. (1972). Counseling minority groups: A review of the literature. *Counseling and Values, 17,* 35–44.

Pomales, J., Claiborn, C. D., & LaFromboise, T. D. (1986). Effects of Black students' racial identity on perceptions of white counselors varying in cultural sensitivity. *Journal of Counseling Psychology, 34,* 123–131.

Ponterotto, J., & Sabnani, H. (1989). Classics in multicultural counseling: A systematic five-year content analysis, *Journal of Multicultural Counseling and Development, 17,* pp. 23–37.

Ponterotto, J. G. (1987). Counseling Mexican-Americans: A multimodal approach. *Journal of Counseling and Development, 65,* 308–312.

Ponterotto, J. G. (1988). Racial consciousness development among white counselors' trainees: A stage model. *Journal of Multicultural Counseling and Development, 16,* 146–156.

Ponterotto, J. G., & Benesch, K. F. (1988). An organizational framework for understanding the role of culture in counseling. *Journal of Counseling and Development, 66,* 237–245.

Ponterotto, J. G., & Casas, J. M. (1987). In search of multicultural competence within counselor education programs. *Journal of Counseling and Development, 65,* 430–434.

Ponterotto, J. G., & Casas, J. M. (in progress). *Handbook of racial/ethnic minority counseling research.*

Ponterotto, J. G., Lew, D. E., & Bullington, R. (1990). *Affirmative action in student affairs.* San Francisco: Jossey-Bass.

Ponterotto, J. G., & Wise, S. L. (1987). Construct validity study of the Racial Identity Attitude Scale. *Journal of Counseling Psychology, 34,* 123–131.

Powell, G., & Powell, R. (1983). Poverty: The greatest and severest handicapping condition in childhood. In G. Powell (Ed.), *The psychosocial development of minority group children.* New York: Brunner/Mazel.

Powell, G. J. (1983). Coping with adversity: The psychosocial development of Afro-American children. In G. J. Powell, J. Yamamoto, A. Romero, & A. Morales (Eds.), *The Psychosocial development of minority group children* (pp. 49–76). New York: Brunner/Mazel.

President's Commission on Mental Health. (1978). *Report from the President's Commission on Mental Health.* Washington, DC: U.S. Government Printing Office.

Proctor, E. K. & Rosen, A. (1981). Expectations and preferences for counselor race and their relation to immediate treatment outcomes. *Journal of Counseling Psychology, 28,* 40–46.

Rabaya, V. (1971). Filipino immigration: The creation of a new social order. In A. Tachiki, E. Wong, F. Odo, & B. Wong (Eds.), *Roots: An Asian American reader.* Los Angeles: UCLA.

Rabkin, J. G., & Struening, E. L. (1976). Ethnicity, social class and mental illness, Working Paper Series No. 17. New York: Institute on Pluralism and Group Identity.

Racial incidents continue. (1989, October 12). *Black Issues in Higher Education, 6,* 23–25.

Ramsey, S., & Birk, J. (1983). Preparation of North Americans for interaction with Japanese: Considerations of language and communication style. In D. Landis & R. W. Buslin (Eds.), *Handbook of Intercultural training: Volume III.* New York: Pergamon.

Red Horse, J. (1983). Indian family values and experiences. In G. J. Powell, J. Yamamoto, A. Romero, & A. Morales (Eds.), *The psychosocial development of minority group children* (pp. 258–272). New York: Brunner/Mazel.

Red Horse, J. G., Lewis, R., Feit, M., & Decker, J. (1981). In R. H. Dana (Ed.), *Human Services for cultural minorities*. Baltimore: University Park Press.

Red Horse, Y. (1982). A cultural network model: Perspectives for adolescent services and paraprofessional training. In S. M. Manson (Ed.), *New directions in prevention among American Indian and Alaska Native Communities* (pp. 173–184). Portland, OR: Oregon Health Sciences University.

Rhoades, E. R., Marshall, M., Attneave, D., Echohawk, M., Bjork, J., & Beiser, M. (1980). Mental health problems of American Indians seen in outpatient facilities of the Indian Health Services, 1975. *Public Health Reports, 96*, 329–335.

Richardson, E. H. (1981). Cultural and historical perspectives in counseling American Indians. In D. W. Sue (Ed.), *Counseling the culturally different: Theory & practice* (pp. 216–255). New York: John Wiley.

Ridley, C. R. (1984). Clinical treatment of the nondisclosing Black client. *American Psychologist, 39*, 1234–1244.

Riessman, F. (1962). *The culturally deprived child*. New York: Harper & Row.

Rivera, A. N. (1984). *Toward a psychotherapy for Puerto Ricans*. Rio Piederis, Puerto Rico: CEDEPP.

Rogers, C. (1980). *A way of being*. Boston: Houghton Mifflin.

Rogers, C. R. (1961). *On becoming a person*. Boston: Houghton Mifflin.

Rogler, L. H., Malgady, R. G., Constantino, G. & Blumenthal, R. (1987). What do culturally sensitive mental health services mean? The case of Hispanics. *American Psychologist, 42*, 565–570.

Romero, D. (1985). Cross-cultural counseling: Brief reactions for the practitioner. *The Counseling Psychologist, 13*, 665–671.

Root, M. P. P. (1985). Guidelines for facilitating therapy with Asian American clients. *Psychotherapy, 22*, 349–356.

Rosenthal, R., & Jacobson, L. (1968). *Pygmalion in the classroom*. New York: Holt, Rinehart, & Winston.

Rotter, J. (1966). Generalized expectancies for internal versus external control of reinforcement. *Psychological Monographs, 80*, 1–28.

Rotter, J. (1975). Some problems and misconceptions related to the construct of internal versus external control of reinforcement. *Journal of Consulting and Clinical Psychology, 43*, 56–67.

Ruiz, A. (1981). Cultural and historical perspectives in counseling Hispanics. In D. W. Sue (Ed.), *Counseling the culturally different: Theory & practice* (pp. 186–215). New York: John Wiley.

Ruiz, A. S. (1990). Ethnic identity: Crisis and resolution. *Journal of Multicultural Counseling and Development, 18*, 29–40.

Ruiz, P., & Ruiz, P. P. (1983). Treatment compliance among Hispanics. *Journal of Operational Psychiatry, 14*, 112–114.

Ruiz, R. A., & Casas, J. M. (1981). Culturally relevant and behavioristic counseling for Chicano college students. In P. B. Pedersen, J. G. Draguns, W. J. Lonner, & J. E. Timble (Eds.), *Counseling across cultures*. Honolulu: University of Hawaii Press.

Ruiz, R. A., & Padilla, A. M. (1977). Counseling Latinos. *Personnel Journal, 55*, 401–408.

Rumbaut, R. B. (1985). Research concerns associated with the study of southeast Asian refugees. In T. C. Owan (Ed.), *Southeast Asian mental health treatment, prevention, services, training, and research*. Washington, DC: National Institute of Mental Health.

Ryan, D. W., & Gaier, E. L. (1968). Student socioeconomic status and counselor contact in junior high school. *Personnel and Guidance Journal, 46,* 466–452.

Ryan, W. (1971). *Blaming the victim.* New York: Pantheon.

Sabnani, H. B., Ponterotto, J. G., & Borodovsky, L. G. (in press). White racial identity development and cross-cultural counselor training: A stage model. *The Counseling Psychologist.*

Sanchez, A. R., & Atkinson, D. R. (1983). Mexican-American cultural commitment, preference for counselor ethnicity, and willingness to use counseling. *Journal of Counseling Psychology, 30,* 215–220.

Sanger, S. P., & Alker, H. A. (1972). Dimensions of internal-external locus of control and the women's liberation movement. *Journal of Social Issues, 28,* 15–129.

Satir, V. (1967). *Conjoint family therapy.* Palo Alto: Science & Behavior Books.

Schindler-Rainman, E. (1965). The poor and the PTA. *PTA Magazine, 61*(8), 4–5.

Schinke, S. P., Schilling II, R. F., Gilchrist, L. D., Barth, R. P., Bobo, J. K., Trimble, J. E., & Cvetkovich, G. T. (1985). Preventing substance abuse with American Indian youth. *Social Casework, 66,* 213–217.

Schmidt, L. D., & Strong, S. R. (1971). Attractiveness and influence in counseling. *Journal of Counseling Psychology, 18,* 348–351.

Schofield, W. (1964). *Psychotherapy: The purchase of friendship.* Englewood Cliffs, NJ: Prentice-Hall.

Seattle Public Schools (1986). *Disproportionality task force preliminary report.* Seattle: Seattle Public Schools.

Seligman, M. E. P. (1982). *Helplessness: On depression, development and death.* San Francisco: Freeman.

Shin, L. (1971). Koreans in America: 1903–1945. In A. Tachiki, E. Wong, F. Odo, & B. Wong (Eds.), *Roots: An Asian American reader.* Los Angeles: UCLA.

Shockley, W. (1972). *Journal of Criminal Law and Criminology, 7,* 530–543.

Shore, J. H. Introduction (1988). *American Indian and Alaskan Native Mental Health Research, Vol. 1,* pp. 3–4.

Shostrom, E. L. (Producer). (1966). *Three approaches to psychotherapy: I* [Film]. Santa Ana, CA: Psychological Films.

Shostrom, E. L. (Producer). (1977). *Three approaches to psychotherapy: II.* [Film]. Santa Ana, CA: Psychological Films.

Shostrom, E. L., Knapp, L., & Knapp, R. (1976). Actualizing a therapy: Foundations for a scientific ethic. San Diego: Edits.

Shuey, A. (1966). *The testing of Negro intelligence.* New York: Social Science Press.

Smalley, W. A. (1984). Adoptive language strategies of the Hmong: From Asian mountains to American ghettos. *Language Science, 1,* 241–269.

Smith, E. J. (1973). *Counseling the culturally different Black youth.* Columbus, OH: Charles E. Merrill.

Smith, E. J. (1977a). Counseling Black individuals: Some stereotypes. *Personnel and Guidance Journal, 55,* 390–396.

Smith, E. J. (1977b). Counseling Black women. In P. B. Pedersen (Ed.), *Handbook of cross-cultural counseling and therapy* (pp. 213–237). Westport, CT: Greenwood Press.

Smith, E. J. (1981). Cultural and historical perspectives in counseling Blacks. In D. W. Sue (Ed.), *Counseling the culturally different: Theory and practice.* New York: John Wiley.

Smith, E. J. (1982). Counseling psychology in the marketplace: The status of ethnic minorities. *The Counseling Psychologist, 10,* 61–67.

Smith, E. M. J. (1985). Ethnic minorities: Life stress, social support, and mental health issues. *The Counseling Psychologist, 13,* 537–579.

Smith, M. E. (1957). Progress in the use of English after twenty-two years by children of Chinese ancestry in Honolulu. *Journal of Genetic Psychology, 90,* 255–258.

Smith, M. E., & Kasdon, L. M. (1961). Progress in the use of English after twenty years by children of Filipino and Japanese ancestry in Hawaii. *Journal of Genetic Psychology, 99,* 129–138.

Snowden, L. R. & Cheung, F. K. (1990). Use of inpatient mental health services by members of ethnic minority groups. *American Psychologist, 45,* 347–355.

Sommers, V. S. (1960). Identity conflict and acculturation problems in Oriental-Americans. *American Journal of Orthopsychiatry, 30,* 637–644.

Special Populations Task Force of the President's Commission on Mental Health. (1978). *Task panel reports submitted to the President's Commission on Mental Health,* Vol. 3. Washington, DC: U.S. Government Printing Office.

Spence, J. T. (1985). Achievement American Style. *American Psychologist, 40,* 1285–1295.

Spiegel, J., & Papajohn, J. (1983). Final report: Training program on ethnicity and mental health. Waltham, MA: The Florence Heller School, Branders University.

Spiegel, S. B. (1976). Expertness, similarity, and perceived counselor competence. *Journal of Counseling Psychology, 23,* 436–441.

Sprafkin, R. P. (1970). Communicator expertness and changes in word meaning in psychological treatment. *Journal of Counseling Psychology, 17,* 191–196.

Stanback, M. H., & Pearce, W. B. (1985). Talking to "the man": Some communication strategies used by members of "subordinate" social groups. In L. A. Samovar & R. E. Porter (Eds.), *Intercultural communication: A reader.* Belmont, CA: Wadsworth.

Staples, R., & Mirande, A. (1980). Racial and cultural variations among American families: A decennial review of the literature on minority families. *Journal of Marriage and the Family, 42,* 887–903.

Steiner, C. (Ed.) (1975). Readings in radical psychiatry. New York: Grove Press.

Stewart, E. C. (1971). *American cultural patterns: A cross-cultural perspective.* Pittsburgh: Regional Council for International Understanding.

Stewart, E. C., Danielian, J., & Festes, R. J. (1969, May). *Stimulating intercultural communication through role playing* (Hum RRo Tech. Rep. 69–67). Alexandria, VA: Human Resources Research Organization.

Stonequist, E. (1977, September). The problem of the marginal man. *American Journal of Counseling Psychology, 24,* 420–429.

Stonequist, E. V. (1937). *The marginal man.* New York: Charles Scribner's Sons.

Stumphauzer, J. S., & Davis, L. C. (1983). Training community-based Asian-American mental health personnel in behavior modification. *Journal of Community Psychology, 11,* 253–258.

Strickland, B. (1971). Aspiration responses among Negro and white adolescents. *Journal of Personality and Social Psychology, 19,* 315–320.

Strickland, B. (1973). Delay of gratification and internal locus of control in children. *Journal of Consulting and Clinical Psychology, 40,* 338.

Strong, S. R. (1969). Counseling: An interpersonal influence process. *Journal of Counseling Psychology, 15,* 215–224.

Strong, S. R., & Schmidt, L. D. (1970). Expertness and influence in counseling. *Journal of Counseling Psychology, 15,* 31–35.

Success story of one minority group in the U. S. (1966, December). *U. S. News & World Report.*

Success story: Outwhiting the whites. (1971, June). *Newsweek.*

Sudarkasa, N. (1988). Interpreting the African heritage in Afro-American family organization. In H. P. McAdoo (Ed.), *Black families.* Newbury Park, CA: Sage.

Sue, D., Bernier, J., Durran, A., Feinberg, L., Pedersen, P., Smith, E., & Vasquez-Nuttal, E. (1982). Position paper: Cross-cultural counseling competencies. *The Counseling Psychologist, 10,* 45–52. In P. B. Pedersen (Ed.), *Handbook of cross-cultural counseling and therapy.* Westport, CT: Greenwood Press.

Sue, D., Sue, D. W., & Sue, S. (1990). *Understanding abnormal behavior.* Boston: Houghton Mifflin.

Sue, D. W. (1973). Ethnic identity: The impact of two cultures on the psychological development of Asians in America. In S. Sue & N. Wagner (Eds.), *Asian Americans: Psychological perspectives.* Palo Alto: Science & Behavior Books.

Sue, D. W. (1975). Asian Americans: Social-psychological forces affecting their life styles. In S. Picou & R. Campbell (Eds.), *Career behavior of special groups.* Columbus, OH: Charles E. Merrill.

Sue, D. W. (1977a). Barriers to effective cross-cultural counseling. *Journal of Counseling Psychology, 24,* 420–429.

Sue, D. W. (1977b). Counseling the culturally different: A conceptual analysis. *Personnel and Guidance Journal, 55,* 422–424.

Sue, D. W. (1978). Eliminating cultural oppression in counseling: Toward a general theory. *Journal of Counseling Psychology, 25,* 419–428.

Sue, D. W. (1981). Evaluating process variables in cross-cultural counseling and psychotherapy. In A. J. Marsell & P. B. Pedersen (Eds.), *Cross-cultural counseling and psychotherapy.* New York: Pergamon.

Sue, D. W. (1989, December). *Culture specific techniques in counseling: A conceptual framework.* Paper presented at the Asian Pacific Symposium on Guidance and Counseling. Taiwan, Taipei.

Sue, D. W., & Frank, A. C. (1973). A topological approach to the study of Chinese- and Japanese-American college males. *Journal of Social Issues, 29,* 129–148.

Sue, D. W., & Kirk, B. A. (1972). Psychological characteristics of Chinese-American college students. *Journal of Counseling Psychology, 6,* 471–478.

Sue, D. W., & Kirk, B. A. (1973). Differential characteristics of Japanese-American and Chinese-American college students. *Journal of Counseling Psychology, 20,* 142–148.

Sue, D. W., & Kirk, B. A. (1975). Asian Americans: Use of counseling and psychiatric services on a college campus. *Journal of Counseling Psychology, 22,* 84–86.

Sue, D. W., & Sue, D. (1972). Ethnic minorities: Resistance to being researched. *Professional Psychology, 2,* 11–17.

Sue, D. W., & Sue, D. (1973). Understanding Asian Americans: The neglected minority. *Personnel and Guidance Journal, 51,* 386–389.

Sue, D. W., & Sue, D. (1977a). Barriers to effective cross-cultural counseling. *Journal of Counseling Psychology, 24,* 420–429.

Sue, D. W., & Sue, D. (1977b). Ethnic minorities: Failures and responsibilities of the social sciences. *Journal of Non-White Concerns in Personnel and Guidance, 5,* 99–106.

Sue, D. W., & Sue, S. (1972a). Counseling Chinese-Americans. *Personnel & Guidance Journal, 50,* 637–644.

Sue, D. W., & Sue, S. (1972b). Ethnic minorities: Resistance to being researched. *Professional Psychology, 2,* 11–17.

Sue, S. (1977). Community mental health services to minority groups: Some optimism, some pessimism. *American Psychologist, 32*, 616–624.

Sue, S., Akutsu, P. D., & Higashi, C. (1985). Training issues in conducting therapy with ethnic minority-group clients. In P. B. Pedersen (Ed.), *Handbook on cross-cultural counseling and therapy* (pp. 275–280). Westport, CT: Greenwood Press.

Sue, S., Allen, D., & Conaway, L. (1975). The responsiveness and equality of mental health care to Chicanos and Native Americans. *American Journal of Community Psychology, 45*, 111–118.

Sue, S., Ito, J., & Bradshaw, C. (1982). Ethnic minority research: Trends & directions. In E. E. Jones & S. J. Korchin (Eds.), *Minority mental health.* New York: Praeger.

Sue, S., & Kitano, H. H. L. (1973). Stereotypes as a measure of success. *Journal of Social Issues, 29*, 83–98.

Sue, S., & McKinney, H. (1974). Delivery of community health services to black and white clients. *Journal of Consulting and Clinical Psychology, 42*, 794–801.

Sue, S., & McKinney, H. (1975). Asian Americans in the community mental health care system. *American Journal of Orthopsychiatry, 45*, 111–118.

Sue, S., McKinney, H., Allen, D., & Hall, J. (1974). Delivery of community health services to black & white clients. *Journal of Consulting Psychology, 42*, 794–801.

Sue, S., & Morishima, J. K. (1982). *The mental health of Asian Americans.* San Francisco: Jossey-Bass.

Sue, S., & Sue, D. W. (1971a). Chinese-American personality and mental health. *Amerasia Journal, 1*, 36–49.

Sue, S. & Sue, D. W. (1972). Chinese American personality and mental health: A reply to Tong's criticisms. *Amerasia Journal, 1*, 60–65.

Sue, S., & Sue, D. W. (1971b). *The reflection of culture conflicts in the psychological problems of Chinese and Japanese students.* Paper presented at the American Psychological Association Convention, Honolulu, HI.

Sue, S., & Sue, D. W. (1974). MMPI comparison between Asian-American and non-Asian students utilizing a student health psychiatric clinic. *Journal of Counseling Psychology, 21*, 423–427.

Sue, S., Sue, D. W., & Sue, D. (1975). Asian Americans as a minority group. *American Psychologist, 31*, 906–910.

Sue, S., & Zane, N. (1987). The role of culture and cultural techniques in psychotherapy: A reformation. *American Psychologist, 42*, 37–45.

Sue, S., & Zane, N. W. S. (1985). Academic achievement and socioemotional among Chinese university students. *Journal of Counseling Psychology, 2*, 570–579.

Sumada, R. J. (1975). From ethnocentrism to a multicultural perspective in educational testing. *Journal of Afro-American Issues, 3*, 4–18.

Sundberg, N. D. (1981). Cross-cultural counseling and psychotherapy: A research overview. In A. J. Mansella & P. B. Pedersen (Eds.), *Cross-cultural counseling and psychotherapy.* New York: Pergamon.

Sung, B. L. (1967). *Mountains of gold.* New York: Macmillan.

Susman, N. M., & Rosenfeld, H. M. (1982). Influence of culture, language and sex on conversation distance. *Journal of Personality and Social Psychology, 42*, 66–74.

Sutherland, J. E., Lavant, R. F., Franz III, W. B., Monzon, C. M., & Stark, N. M. (1983). Indochinese refugee health assessment and treatment. *Journal of Family Practice, 16*, 61–67.

Szapocznik, J., Santisteban, D., Kurtines, W. M., Hervis, O. E., & Spencer, F. (1982). Life enhancements counseling: A psychosocial model of services for Cuban elders. In E. E. Jones & S. J. Korchin (Eds.), *Minority mental health* (pp. 296–329). New York: Praeger.

Szapocznik, J., Scopetta, M. A., Kurtines, W., & Aranalde, M. A. (1978). Theory and measurement of acculturation. *International Journal of Psychology, 12,* 113–130.

Szasz, T. S. (1970). The crime of commitment. In *Readings in Clinical Psychology Today* (pp. 167–169). Del Mar, CA: CRM Books.

Szasz, T. S. (1971). *The myth of mental illness.* New York: Hoeber.

Takayama, G. (1971, Winter). Analysis of data on Asian students at U. C. Berkeley. Project Report, AS 150, Asian Studies Division, University of California, Berkeley.

Tedeschi, J. T., & O'Donovan, D. (1971). Social power and the psychologist. *Professional Psychology, 2,* 59–64.

Tefft, S. K. (1967). Anomie, values, and cultural change among teen-age Indians: An exploration. *Sociology of Education,* 145–157.

Thomas, A., & Sillen, S. (1972). *Racism and psychiatry.* New York: Brunner/Mazel.

Thomas, C. W. (1969). Black-white campus and the functions of counseling. *Counseling Psychologist, 1,* 70–73.

Thomas, C. W. (1970). Different strokes for different folks. *Psychology Today, 4,* 49–53, 80.

Thomas, C. W. (1971). *Boys no more.* Beverly Hills, CA: Glencoe Press.

Thomas, M. B., & Dansby, P. G. (1985). Black clients: Family structures, therapeutic issues, and strengths. *Psychotherapy, 22,* 398–407.

Tinker, J. N. (1973). Intermarriage and ethnic boundaries: The Japanese American case. *Journal of Social Issues, 29,* 49–66.

Trimble, J. E. (1981). Value differentials and their importance in counseling American Indians. In P. B. Pedersen, J. G. Draguns, W. J. Lonner, & J. E. Trimble (Eds.), *Counseling across cultures.* Honolulu: University of Hawaii Press.

Trimble, J. E., & LaFromboise, T. (1985). American Indians and the counseling process: Culture, adaptation, and style. In P. B. Pedersen (Ed.), *Handbook of cross-cultural counseling and therapy* (pp. 127–134). Westport, CT: Greenwood Press.

Trimble, J. E. & Fleming, C. M. (1989). Providing counseling services for Native American Indians: Client, counselor, and community characteristics. In P. B. Pedersen, J. G. Draguns, W. J. Lonner, & J. E. Trimble (Eds.), *Counseling across cultures,* 3d edition (pp. 177–204). Honolulu: University of Hawaii Press.

Tsui, P., & Schultz, G. L. (1985). Failure of rapport: When psychotherapeutic engagement fails in the treatment of Asian clients. *American Journal of Orthopsychiatry, 55,* 561–569.

Tulkin, S. (1968). Race, class, family and school achievement. *Journal of Personality and Social Psychology, 9,* 31–37.

Tung, T. M. (1985). Psychiatric care for southeast Asian: How different is different? In T. C. Owan (Ed.), *Southeast Asian mental health, treatment, prevention services, training, and research.* Washington, DC: National Institute of Mental Health.

Turner, C. B., & Wilson, W. J. (1976). Dimension of racial ideology: A study of urban Black attitudes. *Journal of Social Issues, 32,* 193–252.

Uhlemann, M., Lee, D. Y., & Hett, G. G. (1984). Perception of theoretically derived counseling approaches as a function of preference for counseling orientation. *Journal of Clinical Psychology, 40,* 1111–1116.

Urban Associates. (1974). A study of selected socioeconomic characteristics based on the 1970 census. *Asian Americans,* vol. 2. Washington, DC: U.S. Government Printing Office.

U.S. Bureau of the Census (1980). *Census population totals for racial and Spanish origin groups in U.S. Washington, D.C.: U.S. Government Printing Office.*

U.S. Bureau of the Census (1980). *Census of the population: Supplemental report. Race of the population by states.* Washington, D.C.: U.S. Government Printing Office.

U.S. Bureau of the Census. (1982). Household and family characteristics: March 1982. Current Population Reports Series P. 20, No. 380.

U.S. Bureau of the Census (1983). Statistical abstract of the United States. Washington, DC: U.S. Government Printing Office.

U.S. Department of Education (1987). Percent of minority enrollment in U.S. colleges and universities, Fall 1968–1984. State Task Force on Minority Student Achievement.

U.S. Department of Health, Education, and Welfare (1980). *Health status of minorities and low-income groups.* Washington, DC: U.S. Government Printing Office.

Vega, W. A., Hough, R. L., & Romero, A. (1985). Family life patterns of Mexican-Americans. In G. J. Powell, J. Yamamoto, A. Romero, & A. Morales (Eds.), *The psychosocial development of minority group children* (pp. 194–215). New York: Brunner/Mazel.

Ventura, S. J., & Heuser, R. (1981). Births of Hispanic parentage. *Monthly Vital Statistic Report, 29,* 12.

Vernon, P. E. (1982). *The abilities and achievements of Orientals in North America.* New York: Academic Press.

Vontress, C. (1981). Racial and ethnic barriers in counseling. In P. Pedersen, J. G. Draguns, W. J. Lonner, & J. E. Trimble (Eds.), *Counseling across cultures.* Honolulu: University of Hawaii Press.

Vontress, C. E. (1971). Racial differences: Impediments to rapport. *Journal of Counseling Psychology, 18,* 7–13.

Watanabe, C. (1973). Self-expression and the Asian-American experience. *Personnel and Guidance Journal, 51,* 390–396.

Weber, S. N. (1985). The need to be: The socio-cultural significance of Black language. In L. A. Samovar & R. E. Porter (Eds.), *Intercultural communication: A reader.* Belmont, CA: Wadsworth.

Weinrach, S. G. (1986). Ellis and Gloria: Positive or negative model? *Psychotherapy, 23,* 642–647.

Weinrach, S. G. [in press (a)]. Rogers and Gloria: Positive or negative model? *Psychotherapy.*

Weinrach, S. G. [in press (b)]. Rogers and Gloria: The controversial film and the enduring relationship. *Psychotherapy.*

Weiss, M. S. (1970). Selective acculturation and the dating process: The patterning of Chinese-Caucasian interracial dating. *Journal of Marriage and the Family, 32,* 273–282.

Westermeyer, J. J. (1972). Options regarding alcohol use among the Chippewa. *American Journal of Orthopsychiatry, 42,* 398–403.

White, G. M. (1982). The role of cultural explanations in "somatization" and "psychologization." *Social Science and Medicine, 16,* 1519–1530.

White, J. L. & Parham, T. A. (1990). *The psychology of Blacks.* Englewood Cliffs, NJ: Prentice Hall.

White, R. W. (1963). Ego and reality in psychoanalytic theory: A proposal regarding independent ego energies. *Psychological Issues, 3,* 1–210.

Williams, R. L. (1974). The death of white research in the Black community. *Journal of Non-White Concerns in Personnel and Guidance, 2,* 116–132.

Willie, C. V. (1981). *A new look at black families*. Bayside, NY: General Hall.

Willie, C. V., Kramer, B. M., & Brown, B. S. (1973). *Racism and mental health*. Pittsburgh: University of Pittsburgh Press.

Wise, F., & Miller, N. B. (1983). The mental health of American Indian children. In G. J. Powell, J. Yamamoto, A. Romero, & A. Morales (Eds.), *The psychosocial development of minority group children* (pp. 344–361). New York: Brunner/Mazel.

Wolfgang, A. (1973). Cross-cultural comparison of locus of control, optimism towards the future, and time horizon among Italian, Italo-Canadian, and new Canadian youth. *Proceedings of the 81st Annual Convention of the American Psychological Association, 8*, 229–330.

Wolfgang, A. (1985). The function and importance of nonverbal behavior in intercultural counseling. In P. B. Pedersen (Ed.), *Handbook of cross-cultural counseling and therapy*. Westport, CT: Greenwood Press.

Wolinsky, J. (1982, October). Black jobless suffer despair, self-blame. *APA Monitor*, 21.

Wong, H. Z. (1981). Community mental health services for Asian and Pacific Americans. In L. Snowden (Ed.), *Annual Reviews of Community Mental Health*. Los Angeles: Sage.

Wong, H. Z. (1985). Training for mental health service providers to Southeast Asian refugees: Models, strategies, and curricula. In T. C. Owan (Ed.), *Southeast Asian mental health treatment, prevention, services, training, and research* (pp. 345–390). Washington, DC: National Institute of Mental Health.

Wood, P. S. & Mallincrodt, B. (1990). Culturally sensitive assertiveness training for ethnic minority clients. *Professional Psychology: Research & Practice, 21*, 5–11.

Wrenn, C. G. (1962). The culturally-encapsulated counselor. *Harvard Educational Review, 32*, 444–449.

Wrenn, C. G. (1985). Afterward: The culturally-encapsulated counselor revisited. In P. B. Pedersen (Ed.), *Handbook of cross-cultural counseling and therapy*. Westport, CT: Greenwood Press.

Wright, B. R. (1964). Social aspects of change in the Chinese family pattern in Hong Kong. *Journal of Social Psychology, 63*, 31–39.

Yamamoto, J., & Acosta, F. X. (1982). Treatment of Asian-American and Hispanic-Americans: Similarities and differences. *Journal of the Academy of Psychoanalysis, 10*, 585–607.

Yamamoto, J., James, J. C., & Palley, N. (1969). Cultural problems in psychiatric therapy. *Archives of General Psychiatry, 19*, 45–59.

Yamamoto, J., James, Q. C., & Palley, N. (1968). Cultural problems in psychiatric therapy. *Archives of General Psychiatry, 19*, 45–59.

Yamamoto, J., & Kubota, M. (1983). The Japanese American family. In J. Yamamoto, A. Romero, & A. Morales (Eds.), *The psychosocial development of minority group children*. New York: Brunner/Mazel.

Yao, T., Sue, D., & Hayden, D. (in progress). Untitled research.

Yoshioka, R. B., Tashima, N., Chew, M. & Murase, K. (1981). *Mental health services for Pacific/Asian Americans*. San Francisco: Pacific American Mental Health Project.

Yuen, K. W., & Tinsley, H. (1981). International and American student's expectations about counseling. *Journal of Counseling Psychology, 28*, 66–69.

Zitzow, D., & Estes, G. (1981). The heritage consistency continuum in counseling Native American children. In spring conference on Contemporary American Issues (Ed.), *American Indian issues in higher education* (pp. 133–139).

INDEXES

SUBJECT INDEX

Abnormality, 9–11
Active-resistance stage, of Black identity development, 95
Active systems intervention, 72
Activity dimension, and family counseling, 131–32
Ambiguity, counseling situations and, 42
American Indians:
  alcohol/substance abuse, 182–84; children/adolescents, 178, 185–86 counseling, 175–88; education, 184–85; family characteristics, 177–78; tribe, 176–77; values, 178–82
Asian Americans:
  and adjustment difficulties, 202–8; communication styles, 54–56; communities, 191–92; counseling, 189–208; divorce rates, 190; education, 191; emotional problems, 192; forces shaping identity of, 193–96; high-low context communication, 59; historical experience in America, 193–96; immigrants/refugees, 196–97; juvenile delinquency, 190–92; myths/stereotypes about, 192–93; physical complaints as sign of emotional stress, 199; restraint of feelings, 54, 69; social distance between Whites and, reduction of, 190; success of, 190–93; treatment strategies, 199–201; U.S.-born Asian Americans, special problems of, 201–2
Authority set of clients, 86

Behavioral expressiveness, and culture-bound values, 36–38
Behavior-expertness, 88
Biculturalism, 123–24

Black Americans:
  average family income, 209; behavior patterns toward Whites, 78; children/adolescents, 213–15; communication styles, 46–47, 54–56, 64–66, 80; consultation, 223–24; counseling, 209–26; as counselors to Black clients, 70; education, 210–11; family characteristics, 211–12; family therapy, 212–13; group counseling, 222–23; high-low context communication, 58–59; juvenile delinquency rates, 209; paranoid label, 9–10; values, 215–17
Black identity development models:
  conformity stage, 96–101; dissonance stage, 101–2; integrative awareness stage, 106–7; introspection stage, 104–6; resistance and immersion stage, 103–4
Black Rage (Grier/Cobbs), 10
Body language, See Kinesics
Burt, Cyril, 19

Cause/effect orientation, 33, 40–41
Children/adolescents:
  American Indians, 178, 185–86; Black Americans, 213–15; Hispanic Americans, 240–41;
Class-bound values, 34, 43–46
  biased quality of treatment, 44–45; poverty, effect of, 43–44;
Clients, psychological sets of, 83–87
Colville Indian Reservation Study, 22
Communication, 170–71
  patterns of, 42–43; styles, 51–74; See also Nonverbal communication
Communications approach, to family counseling, 123

Conflicting value systems, 123
Conformity stage:
   of Black identity development, 96–101;
   counseling implications, 108–9; of
   White identity development, 114
Consistency set of clients, 84–85
Consultant role, family counselors, 135
Control ideology, 142–43
Counseling:
   American Indians, 175–88; Asian Americans, 189–208; Black Americans,
   209–26; as communication style,
   66–74; generic characteristics, 30–34;
   Hispanic Americans, 227–42; as interpersonal influence, 82–83; and mental
   health literature, 16–21; minorities' expectations of, 6, 45–46; politics of,
   3–26; and self-disclosure, 39–40;
   sources of conflict/misinterpretation in,
   34–47; style-shift counseling, 72–73;
   See also Cross-cultural counseling; Family counseling
Counseling profession, 24–26
Counseling styles, 49–74
Counselors:
   credibility, 87–92; education and training
   programs, 7–16; perceptions of, 80;
   self-disclosure by, 71
Critical incident cases:
   Assert Yourself case, 258–59, 277–78;
   Burning Out case, 267–68, 284–85;
   Can Culture Justify the Practices? case,
   252–54, 274–75; case list, 251; case vi-
   gnettes, 246–47; Culture Conflict case,
   259, 278–79; critical incident analysis
   (form), 248; cross-cultural counseling
   critical incident, creation of, 249–50;
   Dormitory Living case, 268–69, 286;
   Equality of Relationships case, 256–58,
   276–77; Express Your Thoughts and
   Feelings case, 270–71, 287; Fair Grad-
   ing case, 261–62, 280–81; Fitting In
   case, 260–61, 279–89; Helping These
   People case, 265–67, 284; I'm Not a
   Racist case, 254–56, 275–76; Language
   "Problem," The, case, 252, 274; similarities of cases, 245; Stereotypes or
   Truths? case, 263–64, 282–83;
   usefulness/benefits of, 245–46; What
   They Want Is Not What They Need!
   case, 272–73, 288–89; Who Am I:
   Asian or White? case, 269–70, 286;
   Who Is the Victim? case, 271–72,
   287–88; Who's to Blame? case, 264–65,
   283–84; Winning Isn't Everything—It's
   the Only Thing case, 262–63, 281–82
Cross-cultural counseling:
   barriers to, 27–48; communication/
   counseling styles, 49–74; counseling
   practice, 71–73; credibility/
   attractiveness in, 81–92; differential
   skills in, 69–70; family counseling,
   118–36; microcounseling, 70;
   processes/goals, 160–65; inappropriate
   process, appropriate goals, 163–65; inappropriate process, inappropriate
   goals, 165; sociopolitical considerations

of mistrust in, 75–92; training and re-
   search, implications for, 73–74; See also
   Counseling; Family counseling
Cultural assumptions and values, American
   patterns of, 146–47
Cultural encapsulation, 8–9, 15
Culturally deficient model, 20
Culturally different, world view of, 5
Culturally diverse or different model, 21
Culturally skilled counselor:
   characteristics of, 165–66; self-awareness,
   166–68
Culture-bound values, 34
   ambiguity, 42; cause/effect orientation,
   40–41; individual-centered therapy,
   35–36; mental and physical functioning, distinctions between, 41–42; patterns of communication, 42–43; self-
   disclosure (openness and intimacy),
   39–40; self-exploration, 38–39; verbal/
   emotional/behavioral expressiveness,
   36–38;
Culturocentrism, 104–5

Demographics:
   Asian Americans, 191–92; Hispanic
   Americans, 228–29
Discriminatory attitudes/beliefs, in conformity stage, 100–101
Dissonance stage:
   of Black identity development, 101–2;
   counseling implications, 109; of White
   identity development, 114–15

EC-ER philosophy, See External locus of
   control (EC)-external locus of responsibility (ER)
EC-IR philosophy, See External locus of
   control (EC)-internal locus of responsi-
   bility (IR)
Economic set of clients, 86
Education:
   American Indians, 184–85; Asian Ameri-
   cans, 191; Black Americans, 210–11;
   Hispanic Americans, 229–30;
Education and training programs:
   curriculum and training deficiencies,
   13–16; mental health, definitions of,
   8–13;
Ellis, Albert, 66–69, 73
Emotional expressiveness, and culture-
   bound values, 36–38
Encounter stage, of minority identity trans-
   formation, 94–95
Ethnic differences, 124
Ethnicity, 124
Ethnic minority reality, 122–23
Expertness, counselors, 87–89, 91
External locus of control (EC)-external lo-
   cus of responsibility (ER), 150–52
External locus of control (EC)-internal locus
   of responsibility (IR), 149–50, 156–57
Eye contact, 53–56

Facial expressions, as nonverbal communication, 54

Facilitator of indigenous support systems
    role, family counselors, 135–36
Family characteristics:
    American Indians, 177–78; Black Ameri-
    cans, 211–12; Hispanic Americans,
    230–33
Family counseling:
    communications approach, 123; concep-
    tual model, 124–33; cross-cultural
    counseling, 118–36; goal of, 121; is-
    sues, 122–24; practical implications,
    133–36; structural approach, 122
Family therapy, Black Americans, 212–13

Generalizations, 47–48
Generic characteristics, counseling, 30–34
Genetically deficient model, 18–20
Gestures, 54
Goals, cross-cultural counseling, 160–65
Group-appreciating attitude/beliefs, 101,
    102, 103–4, 105, 106–7
Group counseling, Black Americans,
    222–23
Group-depreciating attitudes/beliefs, 100,
    102, 104, 106

Handshaking, 54
Head movements, 54
High-low context communication, 58–59
Hispanic Americans:
    acculturation, 235–37; children/
    adolescents, 240–41; client problems,
    237–38; communication styles, 54–56;
    counseling, 227–42; demographics,
    228–29; education, 229–30; family
    structure, 232–33; family and values,
    230–32; high-low context communica-
    tion, 58; physical characteristics,
    227–28; sex-role conflicts, 233–35
Historical/current oppression, effects of,
    77–81

IC-ER philosophy, See Internal locus of
    control (IC)-external locus of responsi-
    bility (ER)
IC/IR philosophy, See Internal locus of con-
    trol (IC)-internal locus of responsibility
    (IR)
Ideal mental health, as criterion of normal-
    ity, 10–11
Identity set of clients, 85
Immersion-emersion stage, of minority
    identity transformation, 94–95
Individual-centered therapy, 35–36
Institutional racism, 78
Integrative awareness stage:
    of Black identity development, 106–7;
    counseling implications, 112; of White
    identity development, 116
Internal-external (I-E) dimension, 140–43
Internalization stage of minority identity
    transformation, 94–95
Internal locus of control (IC)-external locus
    of responsibility (ER), 152–55, 157
Internal locus of control (IC)-internal locus
    of responsibility (IR), 146–49, 156
Intervention strategies/techniques, 170–71

Intimacy, See Self-disclosure
Introspection stage:
    of Black identity development, 104–6;
    counseling implications, 111
Introspective stage, of White identity devel-
    opment, 115–16
IQ scores, normality and, 9

Juvenile delinquency:
    among American Indians, 178, 185–86;
    among Asian Americans, 190–92;
    among Black Americans, 209; among
    Hispanic Americans, 240–41

Kinesics, 54–56

Labels, differential treatment and, 13
Language, and ethnicity, 124
Language barriers, 34, 46–47
Locus of control, 140–43
Locus of responsibility, 143–45
Low context (LC) communication, 58–59

Maslow, Abraham, 10
Media-based training packages, use of, 15
Mental health, definitions of, 8–13
Microcounseling, 70
Militancy, 153–54
Minorities:
    as clients, 28–29, 44, 61–62, 168–69; ex-
    pectations of counseling, 6, 45–46; and
    pathology, 17–21; psychological costs
    of racism on, 99
Minority experience, in U.S., result of, 79
Minority identity transformation, stages of,
    94–95
Monolingual orientation, 33, 46
Motivation, 147

Nature of people dimension, 132–33, 139
Nonverbal communication:
    high-low context communication, 58–59;
    kinesics, 54–56; paralanguage, 56–57;
    power of, 61; proxemics, 53–54; as re-
    flections of bias, 60–63; sociopolitical
    facets of, 60–66; as triggers to biases/
    fears, 63–66

"Objective" psychological inventories, as
    indicators of maladjustment, 12
Ombudsman role, family counselors, 135
Openness, See Self-disclosure
Outreach role, family counselors, 135

Paralanguage, 56–57
Paranorm, 10, 12
Passive-acceptance stage, of Black identity
    development, 95
People-nature relationship, and family
    counseling, 125–27
Perls, Fritz, 66, 73
Person-centered orientation, 143–45
"Playing the dozens," 65–66
Powerlessness, 142
Preencounter stage, of minority identity
    transformation, 94
Problem-solving set of clients, 83–84

Proxemics, 53–54
Psychological sets of clients:
  authority set, 86; consistency set, 84–85;
  economic set, 86; identity set, 85;
  problem-solving set, 83–84

QUOID people, 33

Racial/cultural identity development:
  Black identity development models,
  94–107; cautions/limitations in formulation of, 116–17; chart, 97; counseling
  implications, 107–12; White identity
  development, 112–16
Racial pride and identity, 152–64
Racism:
  institutional racism, 78; psychological
  costs on minorities, 99; rise in, 4–5;
  scientific racism, 17–18; in U.S., 4
R/CID model, See Racial/cultural identity
  development
Redirection stage, of Black identity development, 95
Relational dimension, 138–39
  family counseling, 129–31
Research:
  ethics of, 23; motives of researcher,
  21–22; published data, 24;
Resistance and immersion stage:
  of Black identity development, 103–4;
  counseling implications, 109–11; of
  White identity development, 115
Rogers, Carl, 10, 21–22, 66–69

Scientific racism, 17–18
Selective appreciation, 107
Self-appreciating attitudes/beliefs, 102, 103,
  105, 106
Self-depreciating attitudes/beliefs, 100, 102
Self-disclosure:
  by counselors, 71; and counseling, 39–40;
  definition, 40; as a measure of mental
  health, 10
Self-exploration, 38–39
Sex-role conflicts, Hispanic Americans,
  233–35
Smiling, as nonverbal communication, 54
Social class, and ethnicity, 124
Squatting, as nonverbal communication, 54
Stereotypes, 47–48, 102
  about Asian Americans, 192–93

Structural approach, to family counseling,
  122
Style-shift counseling, 72–73
Systematic eclecticism, 73

Testing:
  bias of, 12–13; challenge testing by minorities, 61–62
Therapy:
  family, 212–13; individual-centered,
  35–36
Time dimension, family counseling, 127–29
Training packages, media-based, 15
Training programs, See Education and
  training programs
Treatment:
  alcohol/substance abuse in American Indians, 183–84; Asian Americans,
  199–201; class-bound values, biased
  quality of, 44–45; and labels, 13
Trustworthiness, counselors, 89–92
Tuskegee experiment, 22

"Uncle Tom syndrome," 79, 80
U.S.-born Asian Americans, special problems of, 201–2

Value orientation model, of world views,
  138–40
Values:
  American Indians, 178–82; Black Americans, 215–17; class-bound values, 34,
  43–46; culture-bound values, 34,
  35–43; Hispanic Americans, 230–32
Verbal/emotional/behavioral expressiveness,
  36–38

White identity development (WID):
  conformity stage, 114; dissonance stage,
  114–15; integrative awareness stage,
  116; introspective stage, 115–16; resistance and immersion stage, 115
"Woofing," 65–66
World views, 137–58
  formation of, 145–55; internal locus of
  control (IC)- internal locus of responsibility (IR), 146–49; locus of control,
  140–43; locus of responsibility, 143–45;
  value orientation model of, 138–40

YAVIS syndrome, 33

AUTHOR INDEX

Abad, V., 45
Abbott, E., 190
Abbott, K., 190, 193
Abeles, R. P., 140, 154
ACMH, 196
Acosta, F. S., 209, 211, 218, 231
Acosta, F. X., 231, 233, 239, 241
Adams, H. J., 5
Adler, D. A., 189, 199
Akutsu, P. D., 7
Alker, H. A., 140
Allen, D., 7, 28
Allport, G. W., 10
Alpert, M., 46
Alvarez, R., 41, 46
Anderson, M. J., 177, 179, 183
Aranalde, M. A., 236
Arciniega, M., 228
Argyle, M., 61
Arkoff, A., 201
Arrendondo-Dowd, 8, 14, 291
Arrendondo, P., 14, 25, 29
Arrendondo, P. M., 7
Atkinson, D. R., 5, 10, 17, 28, 30, 69, 80, 83, 84, 93, 95, 99, 135, 155, 160, 191, 196, 198, 216, 236
Attneave, C., 46, 176
Attneave, D., 182
Aubrey, R. F., 5
Authier, J., 11, 15, 161, 164
Austin Conference, 15, 159
Avila, A. L., 227
Avila, D. L., 227
Avis, J. P., 11, 140, 144
Axelson, J. A., 156

Baldwin, J., 99
Banikiotes, P. G., 68–69
Banks, W., 11
Barak, A., 83, 87
Baratz, J., 20, 21
Baratz, S., 20, 21
Bardo, J., 8, 10
Baron, J., 23, 163
Baron, R. M., 53
Barth, R. P., 183
Bass, B. A., 209, 211
Battle, E., 141
Baum, M. C., 218
Beattie, M., 140, 142, 145
Beiser, M., 182
Belkins, G. S., 81
Benesch, K. F., 166, 172
Ben, R., 191
Berlin, I. N., 182, 185
Berman, J., 10, 70, 72, 155, 160, 220
Bernal, M. E., 7, 159, 166
Bernier, J., 7, 14, 15, 20,

26, 30, 35, 73, 159, 166
Bernstein, B., 58
Berry, B., 95
Billingsley, A., 17, 25
Bilmer, M., 198
Birk, J., 52, 53
Bjork, J., 182
Black Issues in Higher Education, 4
Blanchard, E. L., 175, 177
Blau, T., 26
Bliatout, B. T., 191
Bliatout, H. Y., 191
Bloom, J., 184, 185
Blumenthal, R., 81, 239
Bobo, J. K., 183
Bogardus, E., 190
Borodovsky, L. G., 15, 60, 113, 115, 117
Boulette, R. R., 239
Boyce, E., 45
Boyd-Franklin, N., 130
Boyd, N., 123, 211, 212, 213
Bradshaw, C., 21, 26
Brammer, L. M., 5, 8, 73
Brecher, E., 22
Brecher, R., 22
Brody, E. B., 99
Brower, I. C., 165
Brown, B. S., 78, 80
Brown, T. R., 192
Bryde, J. F., 142, 187
Bryson, S., 8, 10, 163
Bulhan, H. A., 30
Buss, A. H., 9

Calia, V. F., 47, 162
Canino, G., 240
Canino, I., 240
Caplan, N., 11, 140, 144, 145, 153, 154
Carillo, C., 123, 228, 230, 233
Carkhuff, R. R., 15, 30
Carney, C. G., 14, 73, 159, 166
Carskaddon, G., 83
Carter, R. T., 93, 142, 154
Casas, J. M., 7, 14, 25, 159, 239, 240
Charnofsky, S., 191
Chavez, N., 77, 233, 235, 238, 239
Cheek (1987), 21
Cheung, F., 195
Cheung, L.-R. L., 195, 196
Chew, M., 189
Chien, C. P., 204
Christensen, E. W., 17
Church, G. J., 228, 229, 234
Claiborn, C. D., 216, 217
Clarey (1989), 112
Clark, K. B., 20, 99

Clark, M. K., 99
Cobbs, P. , 9, 10, 40, 78, 79
Cody, J. J., 163
Coleman, H. L. K., 166
Coleman, L. K., 166
Collins, B. E., 83, 84
Conaway, L., 7, 28
Condon, J. C., 52, 127
Cordes, C., 218
Cordova, F., 193
Corsini, R. J., 81
Cortmell, B., 17, 40, 163, 178, 179
Corvin, S., 14, 15, 73, 112, 159
Constantine, G., 81, 240
Crandall, V., 141
Cross, W. E., 94, 155
Cross, W. E. Jr., 94, 96, 102, 216
Cuellar, I., 236
Cummins, J., 229
Cummins, M., 26
Cvetkovich, G. T., 183

Danielian, J., 146
Daniels, R., 191, 193, 194
Danish, S., 74
Dansby, P. G., 123, 130, 135, 211, 212
Darwin, C., 18
Dauphinais, L., 10, 69, 160
Dauphinais, R., 10, 69, 160
Decker, J., 123
de Gobineau, A., 18
De La Cancela, V., 237, 239, 240
Dell, D. M., 69, 83, 87, 88
Deloria, V., 11
Derbyshire, R. L., 99
DeSnyder, N. S., 8, 227, 230, 239, 240, 241
DeVos, G., 193
Diaz-Guerrero, R., 149
Dinges, N. G., 182
Dixon, D. N., 87
Doerner, W. R., 189
Dolliver, R. H., 295
Dominguez-Ybarra, A., 236, 238
Dorfman, D. D., 19
Douglis, R., 52, 53
Downey, N. E., 94
Draguns, J. G., 8, 69, 74
Dublin, F., 56
Dulles Conference Task Force, 15, 159
Durran, A., 7, 14, 15, 20, 26, 30, 35, 73, 159, 166

Eakins, B. W., 54
Eakins, R. G., 54
Ebert, B., 122
Echohawk, M., 182

Egan, G., 15
Ellison, R., 99
Ellis, R. H., 177, 179, 183
Espin, O. M., 234, 235, 236, 238
Estes, G., 180, 181, 186, 188
Evans, D. A., 80
Evans, L. A., 209, 211, 218, 231, 232, 239
Everett, F., 17, 40, 163, 178

Feinberg, L., 7, 14, 15, 20, 26, 30, 35, 73, 159, 166
Feit, M., 123
Ferris, S. R., 56
Festes, R. J., 146
Festinger, L., 84
Fleming, C. M., 176
Fogelson, R. M., 153
Folensbee, R., 74
Foley, V. D., 121
Fong, S. L. M., 201
Forward, J. R., 140, 145, 154
Frank, A. C., 46, 191
Franklin, A. J., 214
Franklin, J. H., 130
Freedle, R., 94, 155
Freire, P., 99, 149, 150
Freud, S., 10
Fujimoto, I., 194

Gaier, E. L., 45
Galton, F., 18
Garcia, D., 141
Garfield, J. C., 44
Garrison, J., 236, 238
Gary, L. E., 218
Gaw, A., 297
Gibbs, J. T., 123, 215, 216, 223
Giddings, M. G., 20
Gilchrist, L. D., 183
Gillie, D., 19
Giorgis, T. W., 145, 158
Gluckstern, N. B., 15
Goering, J. M., 26
Goldman, L., 24
Goldman, M., 53
Gomez, E. A., 17, 40
Gonzales, J., 8, 14
Gonzalez, A., 8, 14, 127
Goodgame, D., 228, 229, 234
Goodtracks, J. G., 164
Gore, P. M., 140, 145, 154
Gossett, T. F., 18
Gray, B. A., 209
Greene, B. A., 77, 78, 164, 219
Green, J. M., 77, 233, 234
Grevious, C., 212, 220
Grier, W. H., 9, 10, 40, 78, 79
Grosgebauer, C., 209
Grover, K. P., 160

Gurin, G., 140, 142, 145
Gurin, P., 140, 142, 145
Gutierrez, J. M., 7, 14, 159
Gwyn, F., 212

Habemann, L., 44
Haley, A., 100
Haley, J., 121
Halleck, S. L., 12, 35
Hall, E. T., 53, 56, 58, 62, 80, 127
Hall, W. S., 28, 94, 155
Hansen, J. C., 5, 61
Hardiman, R., 113, 114
Harris, D. E., 192
Harris, L. C., 236
Harrison, D. K., 78
Harrison, R. P., 52
Hayden, D., 72
Helms, J. E., 15, 60, 85, 93, 107, 112, 113, 114, 115, 117, 145, 154, 158, 159, 172, 216
Henkin, L. B., 191, 197
Henkin, W. A., 43
Hernandez, A., 166
Herrnstein, R., 18
Hersch, P., 141
Hersbo, M., 45
Hervis, O. E., 94, 160, 237
Herzog, E., 26
Hett, G. G., 69
Heuser, R., 234
Higashi, C., 7
Hill, C. E., 68
Hines, P., 130
Holland, D., 160
Hollingshead, A. R., 45
Ho, M. K., 122, 124, 125, 127, 128, 131, 132, 134
Hough, R. L., 233, 236
Hsieh, T., 141
Huang, K., 192
Hurk, W. M., 191
Hurwicz, M. L., 218

Ibrahim, F. A., 7, 137, 139
Imperia, G., 236
Inclan, J., 127, 128, 130, 131, 133, 138, 140, 143, 231, 232, 236
Indian Health Service, 182
Ishisaka, H. A., 197, 199
Ito, J., 21, 26
Ivey, A., 11, 15, 114, 159, 161
Ivey, A. E., 15, 30, 68, 70, 71, 72, 74, 137, 157, 160
Ivey, M. B., 30, 68, 81, 137, 157

Jackson, A. M., 215
Jackson, B., 94, 95, 96, 99, 113, 155
Jacobson, L., 13, 100
Jacobs, P., 192
James, J. C., 11, 44, 190

Jasso, R., 236
Jenkins, A. H., 58, 62, 65
Jenkins, Y. M., 53, 54, 211, 220
Jensen, A., 18
Jensen, J. V., 56, 57
Jepson, D. A., 43, 93, 204
Johnson, M., 160
Jones, A. C., 5, 9, 79, 80, 215, 217, 226
Jones, B. E., 209
Jones, E. E., 9, 78, 143, 220
Jones, J. M., 99, 149
Josephy, A. M., 175, 184
Journard, S. M., 10, 40
Juarez, R., 236, 239
Jung, C. G., 10

Kagan, N., 15
Kagiwada, G., 194
Kahn, K. B., 14, 73, 159, 166
Kain, C. D., 160
Kamin, L., 19
Kanel, K., 160
Kaneshige, E., 204
Kanouse, D., 143
Kardiner, A., 99
Kasdon, L. M., 46
Katkovsky, W., 141
Katz, J., 5, 7, 11, 20, 23, 24, 30, 35, 40, 60, 80, 81, 114, 127, 128, 129, 131, 137, 140, 147, 148, 159
Katz, P., 185
Kaul, T. J., 83
Kelley, H. H., 143
Kikumura, A., 190
Kim, K. C., 123
Kimmel, K., 56
Kimmich, R. A., 190, 192
Kim, S. C., 93, 126, 191
Kimura, A., 126
King, L. M., 209
Kinzie, D., 304
Kinzie, J. D., 198
Kirk, B. A., 46, 123, 190, 192
Kirkpatrick, A., 212
Kitano, H. H., 190
Kitano, H. H. L., 17, 126, 190, 191, 192, 193, 194, 201
Klein, D. C., 26
Kleinfeld, J., 184, 185
Kluckhohn, F. R., 125, 127, 134, 138, 146
Knapp, M. L., 53
Kochman, T., 56, 64, 65, 66, 78, 79, 80
Korchin, S. J., 300
Korman, M., 15
Kramer, B., 78, 80
Kubota, M., 54, 123, 125, 129
Kupers, T., 219
Kurtines, W., 94, 160, 236
Kurtines, W. M., 237

LaBarre, W., 53, 54
Labov, W., 66
La Crosse, M. B., 83, 87
LaFromboise, T., 142, 187, 216, 217
LaFromboise, T. D., 87, 166
Laing, R. D., 11
Lamb, D. H., 218
Lambert, M. J., 200
Lambert, R. G., 200
Landau, S., 192
Lao, R., 140, 142, 145
Lass, N. J., 56
Latting, J. E., 145, 158
Lau, S., 54
Laval, R. A., 17, 40
Leavitt, R., 228, 229, 234
Lee, D. T. T., 191
Lee, D. Y., 69
Lefcourt, H., 140, 141
Leong, F. T., 69, 142, 192
Lerner, B., 44
Levenson, H., 141
LeVine, E. S., 228, 237, 238
Lewis, D. A., 12, 44, 80
Lewis, R., 128, 131
Lewis, R. G., 123
Lin, K.-M., 200
Lin, W. T., 195
Lockard, J. O., 210
London, P., 10, 12, 81
Lonner, W. J., 12, 69
Lopez, J., 228, 229, 234
Lopez, S. R., 160
Lorenzo, M. K., 189, 199
Lorion, R. P., 44, 45, 162
Lotsof, E., 141
Lowe, C. M., 10
Lowrey, L., 180, 184
Lum, R. G., 39
Lyons, J. S., 12, 44, 80

MacAdams, E. A., 236
McCurdy, P. C., 234
McDavis, R. J., 209, 210, 213, 218
McFadden, J., 14
McKinney, H., 7, 28, 190, 192
Mackler, B., 20
McLeod, B., 189
McNamara, K., 94
McRoy, R. G., 222, 223
Majors, R., 220
Malgady, R. G., 81, 240
Manson, S. M., 182
Marcos, L., 46
Marcos, L. R., 238, 239
Margolis, R. L., 172
Marshall, M., 182
Marten, K., 11
Maruyama, M., 10, 69, 93, 155, 160, 204
Marx, G. T., 145, 154
Maslow, A. H., 10
Masuda, M. I., 200

Matsui, S., 10, 69, 93, 155, 160, 204
Mau, W. C., 43, 93, 204
Maykovich, M. H., 94
Mays, V. M., 9, 20, 36, 77, 79, 164
Meara, N. M., 73
Medicine, B., 182, 183
Mehrabian, A., 56, 58, 61
Mejia, D., 233, 234
Mellins, C. A., 160
Menacker, J., 44, 45
Mercer, J. R., 21
Merluzzi, B. H., 83
Merluzzi, T. V., 68, 69, 83
Mertz, P. J., 56
Miller, D., 177
Miller, N. B., 176, 178, 179, 180, 187
Minuchin, S., 122
Mirande, A., 177
Mirels, H., 142
Missbach, J. W., 68–69
Mizio, E., 123, 131, 229, 233, 234
Montijo, J. A., 239
Moreland (1981), 14
Morishima, J. K., 17, 35, 93, 125, 190, 192, 204
Morten, G., 5, 17, 28, 80, 93, 95, 99, 135, 155, 160, 191, 216
Moynihan, D. P., 20
Munoz, J. A., 227, 237, 241
Munoz, R. F., 227, 237, 241
Murase, K., 189
Murphy, K. C., 69
Myers, H. F., 209

National Commission on the Causes and Prevention of Violence, 153
National Conference on Graduate Education in Psychology, 159
Needel, S. P., 53
Neighbors, H. W., 209
Nelson, S. D., 11, 144
Newsweek, 190
Newton, B. J., 228
Nguyen, L. T., 191, 199
Nguyen, Q. T., 197, 199
Nguyen, S. D., 198, 199
Nidorf, J. F., 199, 201
Nikelly, A., 220
Nisbett, R. E., 143
Nisio, K., 198
Nobles, W. W., 36, 215
Norton, D. G., 123, 209, 211
Nwachuku, U. T., 72, 74

Odin, P., 228, 229
O'Donovan, D., 16
Office of Refugee Resettlement, 195
Oglesby, Z., 222, 223
O'Guinn, T. C., 236

Okimoto, J. T., 197, 199
Oler, C. H., 93, 145, 158
Ornstein, R. E., 33, 41
Ovesey, L., 99
Owan, L. C., 198

Padilla, A. M., 7, 8, 11, 30, 40, 46, 159, 166, 227, 228, 230, 237, 238, 240, 241, 292
Paige, J. M., 153, 154
Palley, N., 11, 44, 190
Papajohn, J., 127
Parker (1989), 112
Parham, T. A., 8, 10, 14, 78, 85, 93, 116, 154, 155, 209, 210, 213, 216, 218
Paster, V. S., 214
Patterson, C. H., 23, 82
Pavkov, T. W., 12, 44, 80
Pearce, W. B., 58, 64, 78, 80
Pearson, J. C., 8, 52, 54, 62
Pearson, R. E., 53
Pedersen, P., 7, 14, 15, 20, 26, 30, 35, 40, 73, 140, 146, 159, 166
Pedersen, P. B., 5, 69
Pell, E., 192
Peoples, V. Y., 69, 88
Pepinsky, H. B., 73
Pierce, R., 30
Pinderhughes, C. A., 78
Pine, G. J., 5
Plotkin, L., 20
Pollock, E. A., 44
Pomales, J., 216, 217
Ponterotto, J. G., 7, 14, 15, 25, 60, 73, 93, 112, 113, 114, 115, 117, 159, 160, 166, 172, 196, 228, 236, 238, 239
Powell, G., 44
Powell, G. J., 211
Powell, R., 44
President's Commission on Mental Health, 7, 159
Proctor, N., 17, 40, 163, 178, 179

Rabaya, V., 195
Ramos, J., 45
Ramsey, S., 52, 53
Rardin, D. K., 68
Redlich, F. C., 45
Red Horse, J., 123
Red Horse, J. G., 123, 128, 129
Red Horse, Y., 177, 178, 182, 184, 186
Rhoades, E. R., 182
Rhoner, M. C., 160
Richardson, E. H., 17, 131, 140, 175
Rickard, K. M., 94
Ridley, C. R., 160, 166, 220, 221
Riessman, F., 20

Rivera, A. N., 238
Rogers, C., 68
Rogers, C. R., 10
Rogler, L. H. , 81, 240
Romero, A., 233, 236
Romero, D., 46, 124
Root, M. P. P., 93
Rosenthal, R., 13, 100
Rotter, J., 140, 141, 145, 154
Rotter, J. B., 140, 141, 145, 154
Roush, K. L., 94
Rowe, W., 10, 69, 160
Ruiz, A., 17, 234, 237
Ruiz, A. S., 94
Ruiz, P., 17, 40, 69
Ruiz, P. P., 69
Ruiz, R. A., 11, 30, 41, 46, 234, 239, 240
Rumbaut, R. B., 196, 197
Rungta, S. A., 172
Ryan, D. W., 45
Ryan, W., 11, 45

Sabnani, H. B., 15, 113, 115, 117
Sanchez, A. R., 196, 236
Sanger, S. P., 141
Santisteban, D., 94, 160, 237
Satir, V., 121
Scheibe, K., 141
Schien, S., 85, 93
Schilling II, R. F., 183
Schindler-Rainman, E., 45
Schinke, S. P., 183
Schmidt, L. D., 83, 87
Schockley W., 18
Schofield, W., 33
Schultz, G. L., 197, 199
Scopetta, M. A., 236
Seagull, A. A., 5, 9
Seattle Public Schools, 210
Seligman, M. E. P., 151
Shannon, J. W., 73
Shin, L., 195
Shore, J. H., 178, 182
Shostrom, E. L., 66, 73
Shuey, A., 18
Shybut, J., 141
Sillen, S., 17, 18, 80
Simek-Downing, L., 30, 68, 81, 137, 157
Smalley, W. A., 195
Smith, E., 7, 14, 15, 20, 26, 30, 35, 73, 159, 166
Smith, E. J., 7, 14, 20, 46, 55, 56, 58, 64, 79, 151, 211
Smith, E. M. J., 11, 209
Smith, M. E., 46
Spence, J. T., 129
Spencer, F., 94, 160, 237

Spiegel, J., 83, 127
Spiegel, S. B., 87
Sprafkin, R. P., 87
Stanback, M. H., 58, 64, 78, 80
Staples, R., 177
Steiner, C., 163
Stein, K. M., 192
Stevic, R. R., 5, 61
Stewart, E. C., 146
Stewart, L. H., 11, 140, 144
Stonequist, E. V., 35, 95, 149
Strickland, B., 141
Strodtbeck, F. L., 125, 127, 134, 138, 146
Strong, S. R., 69, 82, 83, 87
Sudarkasa, N., 130
Sue, D. , 7, 9, 10, 12, 56, 72, 93, 159, 166, 190
Sue, D. W., 5, 8, 9, 10, 11, 12, 14, 15, 16, 17, 20, 21, 25, 26, 30, 33, 35, 46, 56, 69, 73, 79, 80, 84, 86, 93, 94, 95, 99, 123, 135, 137, 145, 146, 150, 155, 157, 159, 160, 161, 166, 172, 190, 191, 192, 193, 201, 204, 205, 207, 216
Sue, S., 7, 9, 12, 17, 21, 26, 28, 33, 35, 79, 93, 94, 125, 159, 172, 190, 192, 201, 204, 205, 207, 218
Sumada, R. J., 20
Sundberg, N. D., 12, 33
Susmer (1982), 53
Szapocznik, J., 94, 160, 236, 237
Szasz, T. S., 11, 12, 35

Tashima, N., 189
Tatum, E., 182
Tazuma, L., 200
Tedeschi, J. T., 16
Tefft, S. K., 176
Thames, T. B., 68
Thiry, S., 44
Thomas, A., 17, 18, 80
Thomas, C. W., 22, 78, 94
Thomas, M. B. , 123, 130, 135, 211, 212
Tinker, J. N., 190
Tinsley, H., 204
Trankina, F. J., 77, 233, 234, 235, 238, 239
Trimble, J. E. , 8, 30, 69, 131, 142, 176, 178, 183, 185, 187
Tsui, P., 197, 199
Tulkin, S., 141
Tung, T. M., 199
Turner, C. B., 140, 154

Uhlemann, M. R., 69
Urban Associates, 190, 191
U.S. Bureau of the Census, 123, 209, 211, 228
U.S. Department of Health, Education and Welfare, 177, 210
U.S. Department of Commerce, 228
U.S. New & World Report, 190

Vail Conference, 15, 159
Valins, S., 143
Vasquez-Nuttal, E., 7, 14, 15, 20, 26, 30, 35, 73, 159, 166
Vega, W. A., 233, 236
Ventura, S. J., 234
Vontress, C., 30, 40, 69
Vontress, C. E., 30, 47, 80

Warner, R. W., 5, 61
Watanabe, C., 191
Weber, S. N., 58, 62, 64, 65, 66, 80
Weiner, B., 143
Weiss, M. S., 202
Weiss, S. L., 49
Westermeyer, J. J., 182
White, G. M., 46
White, R. W., 10
Wiggins, F., 14, 15, 73, 112, 159
Williams, J. R., 140, 145, 154
Williams, R. L., 22
Willie, C. V., 78, 80, 130
Wilson, T., 14
Wilson, W. J., 140, 154
Winder, A. E., 45
Wise, F., 176, 178, 179, 180, 187
Wise, S. L., 93
Wolfgang, A., 52, 53, 61, 141
Wolinsky, J., 209
Wong, H. Z., 133, 189, 197
Wrenn, C. G., 7, 8, 159

Yamamoto, J., 11, 44, 54, 123, 125, 129, 190, 204, 218, 231, 239, 241
Yao, T., 72
Yoshioka, R. B., 189
Yousef, F., 52, 127
Yuen, K. W., 204

Zane, N. W. S., 81, 172
Zimbardo, P. G., 127
Zitzow, D., 180, 181, 186, 188